The Political Economy of Rent-Seeking

Topics in Regulatory Economics and Policy

Series Editor:

Michael Crew

The Political Economy of Rent-Seeking

Edited and with contributions by
Charles K. Rowley
Robert D. Tollison
Gordon Tullock

Center for Study of Public Choice
George Mason University

Kluwer Academic Publishers
Boston / Dordrecht / Lancaster

Distributors

for the United States and Canada: Kluwer Academic Publishers, 101 Philip Drive, Assinippi Park, Norwell, MA 02061, USA

for the UK and Ireland: Kluwer Academic Publishers, MTP Press Limited, Falcon House, Queen Square, Lancaster LA1 1RN, UK

for all other countries: Kluwer Academic Publishers Group, Distribution Centre, P.O. Box 322, 3300 AH Dordrecht, The Netherlands

Library of Congress Cataloging-in-Publication Data

The Political economy of rent seeking.
Bibliography: p.
Includes index.
1. Rent (Economic theory) 2. Social choice.
I. Rowley, Charles Kershaw. II. Tollison, Robert D.
III. Tullock, Gordon.
HB401.P64 1987 333′.012 87-16887
ISBN 0-89838-241-6

Printed in the United States.

This book is dedicated to all those entrepreneurs whose profit-seeking contributions have outperformed rent-seeking waste and have thus provided ongoing net contributions to the wealth of nations.

Contents

List of Contributors

Gary M. Anderson, Department of Economics, California State University, Northridge, California 91330.

Terry L. Anderson, Department of Economics, Montana State University, Bozeman, Montana 59717.

Michael A. Brooks, Department of Economics, University of Tasmania, 252C, GPO Hobart, Tasmania 7001, Australia.

Roger Congleton, Clarkson College, Potsdam, New York 13676.

William J. Corcoran, Department of Economics, University of Nebraska, Omaha, Nebraska 68182.

W. Mark Crain, Center for Study of Public Choice, George Mason University, 4400 University Drive, Fairfax, Virginia 22030.

Michael A. Crew, School of Management, Rutgers, The State University of New Jersey, Newark, New Jersey 07102.

Robert Elgin, The Legal Services Corporation, 400 Virginia Avenue, S.W., Washington, D.C. 20024.

Roger L. Faith, Department of Economics, 252C, GPO Hobart, Tasmania 7001, Australia.

Ben J. Heijdra, Department of Economics, 252C, GPO Hobart, Tasmania 7001, Australia.

Richard S. Higgins, The Federal Trade Commission, Pennsylvania Avenue & 6th Street, N.W., Washington, D.C. 20580.

Peter J. Hill, Department of Economics, Montana State University, Bozeman, Montana 59717.

Arye L. Hillman, Department of Economics, Bar-Ilan University, Ramat-Gan, Israel.

Gordon V. Karels, Department of Economics, University of Nebraska, Omaha, Nebraska 68182.

Eliakim Katz, Department of Economics, Bar-Ilan University, Ramat-Gan, Israel.

Dwight R. Lee, Department of Economics, University of Georgia, Athens, Georgia 30602.

Fred S. McChesney, School of Law, University of Chicago, 5801 S. Ellis Avenue, Chicago, Illinois 60637.

William P. Rogerson, Department of Economics, Stanford University, Stanford, California 94305.

Charles K. Rowley, Center for Study of Public Choice, George Mason University, 4400 University Drive, Fairfax, Virginia 22030.

William F. Shughart, II, Center for Study of Public Choice, George Mason University, 4400 University Drive, Fairfax, Virginia 22030.

Robert D. Tollison, Center for Study of Public Choice, George Mason University, 4400 University Drive, Fairfax, Virginia 22030.

Gordon Tullock, Department of Economics, University of Arizona, Tucson, Arizona 85721

Richard E. Wagner, Department of Economics, Florida State University, Tallahassee, Florida 32306.

Preface

It is now twenty years since the concept of rent-seeking was first devised by Gordon Tullock, though he was not responsible for coining the phrase itself. His initial insight has burgeoned over two decades into a major research program which has had an impact not only on public choice, but also on the related disciplines of economics, political science, and law and economics. The reach of the insight has proved to be universal, with relevance not just for the democracies, but also, and arguably more important, for all forms of autocracy, irrespective of ideological complexion. It is not surprising, therefore, that this volume is the third edited publication dedicated specifically to scholarship into rent-seeking behavior.

The theory of rent-seeking bridges normative and positive analyses of state action. In its normative dimension, rent-seeking scholarship has expanded, enlivened, in some respects turned on its head, the traditional welfare analyses of such features of modern economics as monopoly, externalities, public goods, and trade protection devices. In its positive dimension, rent-seeking contributions have provided an important analytical perspective from which to understand and to predict the behavior of politicians, interest groups and bureaucrats, the media and the academy within the political market place. This bridge between normative and positive elements of analysis is invaluable in facilitating an understanding of and evaluating the costs of state activity within a consistent paradigm.

This volume draws together a collection of the most recently published articles on rent-seeking and adds to this collection an almost equal number of original articles specially commissioned to address evident lacunae in the rent-seeking literature. One such contribution contrasts the rent-seeking literature with the rival approach now designated as DUP (directly unproductive profit seeking). Others extend the reach of the rent-seeking insight beyond the narrow arena of legislative politics into the wider domain of constitutional political economy. Throughout, the volume strives to maintain an even balance between articles devoted to the theory of rent-seeking and those offering an empirical and institutional insight. Tullock himself provides original contributions on both facets of this literature.

The editors wish to acknowledge the financial support from the Center for Study of Public Choice and from the Graduate School at George Mason University which facilitated the completion of this volume. The excellent secretarial support, especially of Ellen Ladow, Elizabeth Masaitis, and Carol Robert, is gratefully acknowledged as is the helpful editorial advice of Michael Crew and the patient support of Zachary Rolnik, our publisher. We are indebted to Marjorie and Amanda Rowley for proofreading.

Rent-seeking offers a breath of invigorating fresh air into the smoke-filled anterooms of conventional political economy. It shifts the emphasis of political economy away from the naïve notion that scholars have only to signal the right path for government to follow. Instead, it recognizes once again the classical nostrum of David Hume that "mean sensual man is here to stay" and attempts to center attention on those avenues of institutional reform that will channel self-seeking behavior into wealth-enhancing forms.

If our readers leave this volume with a clearer view as to why government is not a free lunch, and with a better methodology for estimating the tab for government activities, our effort will have been well worthwhile.

Charles K. Rowley
Robert D. Tollison
Gordon Tullock

Acknowledgments

We are grateful to the following for their permissions to reprint previously published papers in this volume: The American Economic Review, The Bell Journal of Economics and Management Science, Economic Inquiry, The Economic Journal, The Journal of Institutional and Theoretical Economics, The Journal of Legal Studies, The Journal of Public Economics, Public Choice, The Southern Economic Journal, The Swiss Journal of International Relations.

Prologue

Ode to a Rent Seeker
Charles K. Rowley

> Mr. Iacocca is best on the frustrations he encountered in Washington before it was agreed, against considerable opposition,... to grant Chrysler a federal loan guarantee. That experience seems to have made Mr. Iacocca...deeply suspicious of free enterprise ideologues.... The book ends with the appropriately titled section "Straight Talk."...On the deficit, one of his solutions is interesting: a tax on domestic petrol prices. (Chrysler is long in small cars–Ed.) While from Japan he sees the threat of colonization of America's industrial and technological base—or, as he more colorfully puts it, *veni*, *vidi*, *vici* economics. But the most enduring message is the need to respect and live by basic American values. Mr. Iacocca knows how to make a buck and values the country that has allowed him to do it so successfully. (*The Economist*, 16–22 February 1985, p. 87)

I aim to seek out every rent
be it honest or be it bent

I seek out rent on every margin
let fools engage in wealth enlarging

Some may shirk whilst others toil
I spend my time on fertile soil

Government transfers I endorse
as a highly fruitful income source

Receipts in excess of gains foregone
mean others lose what I have won

With outlays less than Tullock cost
no one can argue that I have lost

Stigler and Peltzman tell the truth
I make more than Babe(y) Ruth

Rectangles win, trapezoids lose
No wonder Harberger sings the blues

I spend upfront with great delight
to seize a durable monopoly right

Give me monarchs, divine right kings
for then the monopoly market sings

Congress I accept, even Tip O'Neill
though there rent margins tend to reel

Wealth is still transferred for all to see
but at a much greater cost to G.N.P.

God protect me from the final blow
when all the margins of rent are low

Let the margins be many and always high
so that I shall thrive 'til the day I die.

I PERSPECTIVES

1 INTRODUCTION

Charles K. Rowley and Gordon Tullock

Research into rent-seeking is now so extensive that it is difficult fully to appreciate that the insight itself was absent as late as 1966 (Tullock, 1967) and that the phrase itself was not coined until 1974 (Krueger). Within the short span of twenty years, scholarship employing the rent-seeking concept has developed into a major research program, achieved an almost dominant role in public choice, and attained a significant foothold in the literature of economics, political science and law and economics. At the time of this writing, the concept is poised to penetrate more popular thinking. Although it is not yet the standard fare of congressional speeches or of *Wall Street Journal* editorials, the time for such invasions is excitingly close.

It is the purpose of this book to consolidate the rent-seeking research program, to disseminate its major contributions throughout the academy of social sciences, to excite a new generation of students to join in the promulgation of the program, and to popularize the insight, to the extent possible, among the informed lay public. The book should make a timely contribution in guiding the energies of a burgeoning research program into a stable pattern of growth in which the rent-seeking insight becomes a conventional component of ongoing social science research.

To this end, the book collects together, in one accessible volume, the most relevant and useful articles currently scattered across the journals of economics and public choice. To these it adds an almost equal number of original articles specifically commissioned to treat apparent lacunae in the extant literature. In our view, the outcome is a whole which is significantly more important than the sum of its parts, encompassing and interrelating the normative and positive aspects of rent-seeking research, both at the level of legislative politics and at the level of constitutional political economy. For the novice, the text will serve as an indispensible guide through a complex literature. For the expert, the book is a repository of recent findings and a compendium of future research possibilities.

Readers will discover that rent-seeking as analysed in this book is almost, though not quite, exclusively confined to economic behavior in the political, bureaucratic and regulatory marketplace. Rent-seeking behavior in private markets receives a much less central treatment. This emphasis is not to be viewed as the consequence of conservative methodology, though none of the editors is notable for socialist leanings. Nor should it be inferred that rent-seeking is exclusively a facet of public rather than of private choice. Private monopolies were analysed in early papers on rent-seeking as prime examples of social welfare loss. The balance of this book simply reflects the relative predominance in contemporary economics of rent-seeking in the public marketplace.

Had the rent-seeking insight found its way earlier into social science scholarship, and had this book been written in the 1890s, undoubtedly the U.S. trusts, epitomized by the cartelization activities of rent-seeker J.P. Morgan, would have found themselves center stage. Instead, written as it is in the 1980s, this work recognizes that the regulatory and trade protection activities in political markets, epitomized by rent-seeker Lee Iacocca, demand priority attention. The thrust of this text simply reflects the major preoccupations of the times, together with a growing awareness that even private monopolies are dependent on governments for sustained durability.

Readers should not draw the inference from the particular emphasis of this book that determined rent-seekers can maneuver governments at will. As Stigler (1971) and Peltzman (1974) have emphasized, regulatory market solutions reflect an equilibrium which balances a diversity of rent-seeking and rent-protection outlays. As public choice also warns, political actions may be influenced additionally by constraints on spatial mobility imposed by ideology and/or by considerations of a wider public image. As Olson (1971) has advised, not all interest groups are equally effective in their lobbying of governments. As Niskanen (1971) has warned, bureaucracies often have discretionary power of their own which will be utilized, predictably, for self-serving ends. Contributions in this text reflect recent scholarship on these important issues.

The book deals with matters of substantial public policy significance. Most (though perhaps not all) scholars would concur that, *ceteris paribus*, rent-seeking behavior should be minimized as imposing waste upon society. Concurrence on this judgment would appear to be independent of methodology, be it that of Chicago, New England, Cambridge, England, or even, it would seem, the Kremlin. For those Americans concerned with advancing the nation's wealth, the elimination of rent-seeking/rent-protection outlays must be on a par (almost) with support of the flag, motherhood, and apple pie.

Finally, in these preliminary remarks, it is important to clarify the relationship between rent-seeking and wealth and income transfers in favor of the poor. Confusion concerning this relationship has led to unjustified reluctance among certain scholars to embrace the rent-seeking insight. Most individuals are willing to a limited extent to make sacrifices in order to help the poor. "Tullock's Law" suggests that such altruism motivates five percent of the individual calculus. Insofar as government is utilized as a vehicle for such redistribution, for example to overcome public good problems, there is no rent-seeking or rent-protection waste involved. Given the very limited redistribution to the poor evident via the political process (indeed, some would say, its negative characteristic), inferences of effective rent-seeking by the poor simply cannot be sustained.

Rent-seeking in the redistribution process (Tullock 1983 and 1985) takes a quite different form. Middle income groups in the democracies appear to rent-seek effectively into the property rights both of the poor and the rich, rerouting the offerings of charity to their own pockets and coercing transfers via a pluralist system of government. In the autocracies, wealth and income transfers occur at a yet more significant social cost via the instruments of violence, threatened or pursued, as well as in response to rent-seeking outlays. Welfare redistribution to the poor undoubtedly is highly desirable in many, perhaps in most, societies. The literature of rent-seeking merely raises some hard public choice questions concerning the effective implementation of desirable redistribution policy and points up some avenues of potentially fruitful institutional reform.

We now turn to the most important role of this introductory essay, namely the provision of a brief overview, designed to outline the specific insights of the separate chapters. It is our intention in this exercise primarily to introduce the reader to an extensive literature and to whet appetites for a comprehensive reading. We shall not attempt to reiterate the detailed arguments of each paper or to present our own appraisal of the chosen contributions.

Although the initial rent-seeking insight was due to Tullock (1967), the phrase itself was coined by Krueger (1974), ironically writing from a scholarly perspective quite distinct from that of public choice. Krueger's approach has proved to be extremely popular among scholars of international economics, most notably Bhagwati. Bhagwati (1984) has redesignated this approach as DUP (directly unproductive profit-seeking), thus distinguishing it from the rent-seeking approach of public choice. In chapter 2, Rowley compares and contrasts these two approaches, noting that DUP is much more closely related to the new welfare economics than to public choice and criticizing it for its failure to encompass fully the selection of trade protection instruments as a central feature of the rent-seeking/rent-protection equilibrium. Rowley also defends the rent-seeking methodology in this chapter against forceful criticisms that have been levelled against it both in its normative and in its positive dimensions.

Chapter 3, by Brooks and Heijdra, also centers attention on differing emphases in the rent-seeking/DUP literature while mounting a somewhat more critical evaluation of aspects of both literatures. DUP is criticized for its tautologous assumption that DUP activities represent waste because individuals undertake expenditure on non-productive activities. By defining the rent-seeking rectangle as social loss, DUP begs the fundamental issue as to why it should be so evaluated. This questioning is reflective of a similar debate in the *x*-inefficiency literature some 15 years ago (Ng, 1973). The rent-seeking literature is absolved from this charge of unjustified tautology, especially in its general equilibrium form, which Brooks and Heijdra vigorously manipulate. However, the authors conclude that static resource allocation models do not capture the rent-seeking phenomenon adequately, and they hint that the entire rent-seeking argument, as it is conventionally applied, may be conceptually flawed. They urge the mounting of future research into the Tullock insight from a dynamic rather than a static perspective.

Chapter 4, by Tullock, carefully distinguishes between "good rents" and "bad rent-seeking" and demonstrates that the latter activity is more injurious to society in dynamic than in static settings. By adding back as rent-seeking waste not only the Harberger and Tullock costs associated with monopoly creation, but also the sacrificed present value of future surpluses that might have been anticipated from investment opportunities foregone, Tullock paints a picture of the rent-seeking society more pessimistic than any previously provided. Tullock's contribution is replete with new insights, not least for the general theory of economic growth and for theories concerning property rights and institutional reform.

Chapters 5 to 13 shift the emphasis of the text to the pure theory of rent-seeking, offering a range of insights into the complex problem of valuing the social loss due to rent-seeking under a variety of model situations. All such contributions confirm the initial insight that the cost of market restrictions, at least in the dynamic context, significantly exceed the Harberger deadweight loss. The exact measure of rent-seeking costs, however, turns out to be elusive, even at the level of pure theory.

Chapter 5, by Rogerson, relaxes the assumption that rent-seeking firms are homogeneous to allow for input heterogeneity in the rent-seeking competition. Inframarginal firms, in such circumstances, earn profit which is not transformed into social waste. Rogerson suggests that inframarginal advantages of this kind may arise as a consequence of the presence of fixed organization costs or incumbency advantages. He does not explore the dynamics of this insight for the process of investing in efficient rent-seeking.

Chapter 6, by Hillman and Katz, introduces risk-aversion into the rent-seeking model, and demonstrates again that such a circumstance will result in a significantly less-than-full dissipation of available rents in social waste, especially when the available rents are large. Their model does not allow for organizational adjustment, in the form of diversification or of the hiring of risk-neutral senior management, to reduce the behavioral impact of risk-aversion. Equally, however, it does not add on the psychic costs of risk-bearing experienced by those who are risk-averse, as a social cost of engaging in rent-seeking competitions.

Chapter 7, by Tullock, reintroduces an unresolved mathematical problem concerning efficient rent-seeking initially posed by Tullock in 1980. By presenting the rent-seeking competition as a formal lottery, with information evenly disseminated among all potential competitors, Tullock demonstrates that there may not be a bidding equilibrium, and that even where an equilibrium exists it may exhibit peculiar characteristics, not least of which is the presence of the paradox of the liar problem. This paper stimulated a flurry of responses, the more important of which are published as chapters 8 to 11. Chapter 12, by Tullock, firmly pushes all would-be resolutions back into the swamp and encourages further attempts to attain the terra firma of effective mathematical resolution.

Chapter 13, by Higgins and Tollison, draws the pure theory of rent-seeking to a close by pointing up yet another apparent paradox. The presence of high rates of rent dissipation in a particular society may result in few monopolies, since the returns to rent-seeking definitionally are low. By contrast, where the rate of rent dissipation is low, monopolies may abound. It is not clear that the former society, with high Tullock costs per monopoly but few monopolies, would suffer more social waste than the latter, despite low Tullock costs, since Harberger deadweight losses abound in the latter scenario. The authors further demonstrate, in contradiction to earlier intuitions by Posner (1974), that distribution effects from rent-seeking cannot be ignored. Finally, they note that rent protection costs are not captured in the normal social cost accounting of triangles and trapezoids.

With chapter 14, by Crew and Rowley, the emphasis of the book shifts, applying rent-seeking theory to important issues in the political economy of public choice. The authors evaluate the notion, due to McCormick, Shughart, and Tollison (1984), that disinterest in deregulation is a consequence not of the logic of collective action, but of the absence of any Tullock cost-saving benefits from deregulation. Crew and Rowley develop a taxonomy of regulation models in which there can exist a normative case for deregulation of a substantial nature. They employ positive public choice to demonstrate the essential vulnerability of all regulatory equilibria, whether or not based on upfront rent-seeking outlays, in societies where "rights" are not constitutionally protected. What political markets give, so they can take away, without any necessary concern for economic efficiency, compensation, or the integrity of rights.

Chapter 15, by McChesney, focuses attention on the role of politicians in the economic theory of regulation, not as brokers in the sense of Peltzman (1974), but as independent actors in the regulation market. He develops a model which demonstrates how politicians benefit, first by threatening and then by forbearing from extracting private rents already in existence. Such private rents, unlike politically created rents, represent returns to entrepreneurship and to firm-specific private investments. McChesney's model of rent extraction supplements rather than undermines the basic rent-seeking approach, recognizing alternative sources of political gain. He concludes that there is no such thing as a free market.

Chapter 16, by Anderson and Tollison, provides a radical reinterpretation of one of the most famous episodes in the history of political economy: the repeal of the corn laws in England. They present evidence that disputes the popular conception of the anti-corn law league as the public interest embodiment of the writings of classical liberal economists. Rather, the league was a special interest group, manipulated by cotton textile manufacturers more concerned to repeal the import duty on raw cotton and to ameliorate the impact of the Factory Acts than to repeal the import duty on grain. The league was successful with respect to cotton imports, but unsuccessful in its attempt to return England to the sweatshop. It disbanded once its special interest objectives were expended. This rent-seeking hypothesis, controversial as it is, has not yet provoked substantive criticism from the conventional literature.

Chapter 17, by Rowley and Tollison, applies the public choice rent-seeking insight to the issue of trade protection. The authors carefully distinguish their own approach from that of DUP, as developed by Bhagwati and other scholars specialized in the pure theory of international trade. Unlike DUP, they evaluate the implications of rent-seeking/rent-protection outlays for the choice of protective instrument as well as for the magnitude of social welfare loss. They predict the dominance of quota over tariff protection instruments in the regulation market and offer a convincing explanation of the recent increase in voluntary export agreements and in other bilateral quantitative restrictions. They conclude that efforts to reinforce free trade on a multilateral basis are most effectively targeted at high rather than low levels of decision-making and should be conducted with maximum possible transparency.

Chapter 18, by Crain, Shughart and Tollison, utilizes the rent-seeking insight in an attempt to resolve the paradox of voting. The authors eschew the "all-or-nothing" view of the benefits attached to voting, which denies any viable motivation other than consumption utility as relevant in inducing voter turnout in large elections. Instead, they adopt the "continuous spectrum" approach of Stigler (1972), whereby the effective mandate of an elected government is seen to be an increasing function of its vote plurality. Unlike Stigler, however, they associate this spectrum with interest groups rather than with individuals, emphasizing the investment function of interest groups in marshalling blocks of marginal vote suppliers to the polls. They determine, in support of this hypothesis, that the legislative output of the U.S. Congress, over the period 1824 to 1976, was significantly influenced by the magnitude of the President's popular vote majority. Sceptics like ourselves, who see free-riding as a problem for interest groups themselves, still must cling a little more tentatively than was the case prior to this contribution to our belief in the consumption utility hypothesis.

Chapter 19, by Congleton, provides an ingenious illustration that rent-seeking may be less when awards decisions are the responsibility of committees than when they are made by an individual administrator. His argument, which is based upon plausible assumptions, offers an economic efficiency justification for an organization form which has attracted almost universal abuse. Although Congleton's analysis is based upon a Cournot-type model of committee member interactions, which has limited appeal in the well-informed, extensive interaction environment, history does provide support for his viewpoint. Committees abound in all societies, and they tend to grow in size. Even the authors of this Introduction, who would both staunchly defend the notion that the optimum committee size is one, have opted for a size of two as a basis for surveying the contents of this book.

Chapter 20, by Rowley and Elgin, surveys recent contributions to the theory of bureaucracy within the bilateral monopoly bargaining framework established by Niskanen (1971). This approach is contrasted with the contractarian, exchange-oriented approach favored by Breton and Wintrobe, and with the principal-agent approach that has emerged from the property rights approach to the theory of the firm. Rowley and Elgin favor the principal-agent approach and develop a nexus of contracts theory of the interrelationships between bureaus, politicians, voters, and interest groups. The discretionary power provided to bureaus by the residual principal-agent problem, endemic in the contracts nexus, leaves scope for rent-seeking/rent-protection behavior directed at the bureaus rather than the polity. This paper suggests a rich agenda of future research opportunities which should act as a magnet for the ambitious young scholar.

Chapter 21, by Tullock, proselytizes the application of the demand revealing approach (Tideman and Tullock, 1975) to the problem of rent-seeking into the wealth transfer mechanism. A characteristic of the Clarke tax, which is generally a source of unease, is that it tends to be very high when the interests of the parties are strictly opposed. Since it is this characteristic of transfers that gives rise to rent-seeking, the size of the Clarke tax becomes beneficial as a basis for preventing transfers that would end up anyway as social waste. Tullock extends this notion further to indicate the superiority of demand revealing over majority voting on transfer issues even when wealth redistribution is desired by practically the whole of society.

Chapter 22, also by Tullock, and incidentally the most ancient of the articles republished in this text, views governments as rent seekers, vying with each other for aid via the wasteful outlay of resources. Directed at the competitive behavior of lower-level government confronted with rents available from the higher-levels, Tullock's insight is especially relevant to the U.S. federal system. His article points up a telling example of how even well-intentioned government programs can go badly wrong. It suggests yet more serious outcomes when the higher-level programs are actually pork-barreled in response to initial rent-seeking outlays.

Chapter 23, by Faith, Higgins, and Tollison, investigates the nature of rents and the opportunities for rent-seeking within the internal organization of the Coasian firm. Utilizing the principal-agent model, they demonstrate the opportunities for rent appropriation by management afforded by the lower-level discretion that equity interests must accept as the price of any hierarchical structure. Unlike Fama (1980) they view the relevant defense against rent-seeking as arising not from the outside labor market opportunity cost wage as such but from the active outside recruitment of management as an explicit device for eliminating rent-seeking conspiracies among a well-established management collective. Certainly, such a theory explains the tendency of large corporations to shift management from location to location, presumably at some cost in plant-specific human capital. The authors model the Coasian (contracts nexus) firm with explicit emphasis upon outside recruitment as a defense against the principal-agent problem, deriving predictions that diverge from internal labor market theories advanced by Williamson et al. (1975) Their test does not invalidate their theory.

Chapter 24, by Lee and Tollison, attacks optimal taxation theory from the rent-seeking insight perspective, challenging the connection conventionally advanced between the optimal pattern of excise taxes and demand elasticities of the taxed commodities. They show that rent-seeking increases the marginal social cost of excise taxation across commodities in such a manner as to confound the conventional result, and they make a case for taxing commodities more vigorously when demand elasticity is high than when it is low.

Chapter 25, by Lee, pursues a similar attack on optimal tax theory, this time directed at the tax-price solution to problems of Pareto-relevant environmental externalities. He demonstrates that when evaluating tax-price outcomes, account should be taken not only of the immediate impact upon resource allocation, but also of the rent-seeking waste encouraged by tax revenue rents thus generated. This insight should stimulate important reconsiderations of existing research findings on the taxation/direct control alternatives for dealing with environmental negative externalities.

Chapter 26, by Anderson and Hill, uses the rent-seeking insight to demonstrate that efficiency gains potentially available from property rights (privatizing the commons) may be wasted entirely in the process of rights definition and rights enforcement. The "tragedy of the commons" may be no worse, in efficiency terms, than the rent dissipation implicit in the process of private property establishment. Anderson and Hill theorize that the rules for defining and enforcing rights are much more likely to promote rent dissipation when the rule makers are not potential residual claimants. They support this theory by reference to the relative absence of rent-seeking on the American frontier by comparison with the evident rent dissipation promoted by the Homestead Act which followed. The role of ingenious government officials in the promotion of rent-seeking waste is seen to predominate wherever property rights are exogenously determined.

Chapter 27, by Shughart and Tollison, applies the rent-seeking insight to the process of legal innovation, arguing that its relevance in that field parallels its relevance for economic innovation. They utilize, as an example, late nineteenth and early twentieth century developments in the deregulation by U.S. states of corporate charters, epitomized by the replacement of special chartering by incorporation under general laws. Evidence presented in their paper suggests that the spread of deregulation reflected a pattern explained by the comparative benefits and costs of using the political machinery of the state. There is no support for the alternative hypothesis that legal innovation was the result of public-spirited government in enlightened states.

Chapter 28, by Tullock, reexamines the source of the industrial revolution within a rent-seeking perspective, and hypothesizes that it was an unanticipated outcome of changes generated by the English Civil War, rather than a response to classical liberal writings as epitomized by Adam Smith's *Wealth of Nations* (1776). Specifically, the abolition of the Star Chamber, motivated primarily by the desire to avoid ship money tax impositions on the part of the victorious parlimentary forces, left the English legal system almost entirely under the influence of the common law. Juries could not be depended upon, as Star Courts surely could, to imprison or otherwise penalize those who violated monopoly privileges purchased by successful rent seekers. In such circumstances, rent-seeking was unattractive, and the avenues for profit-enhancing innovations were widely available.

Chapter 29, by Wagner, elevates the rent-seeking insight to the higher level of constitutional design. His starting point is that of classical liberalism, as enshrined in the U.S. Constitution, that rights of person and of property are logically prior to the existence of government itself. He acknowledges that this constitutional vision has been betrayed by rent-seeking invasion and that representative government, as envisaged by Madison in the U.S. and by Wicksell in Sweden, has failed. Wagner employs the principal-agent model as a mechanism for understanding the failure of the U.S. Constitution to deliver on the promises of the Founding Fathers. He concludes with pertinent suggestions for constitutional reform designed to reestablish the benificent invisible hand of Adam Smith and to consign to oblivion the destructive visible boot of the rent-seeking society.

Chapter 30, by Rowley, further relates the rent-seeking concept to central issues in constitutional political economy. He questions the validity of the trade-off diagram in *The Calculus of Consent* (1962), which is a central pivot of the contractarian model. He also challenges the well-established view that vote trading is a welfare-enhancing process. His paper indicates that the time is now ripe for a fundamental reconsideration of *The Calculus of Consent*, a challenge that will be joined by Tullock (appropriately, in the bicentennial of the U.S. Constitution and the twenty-fifth anniversary of "the Calculus" itself).

Chapter 31, by Tullock, draws the book to its conclusion with an appropriate discussion of the opportunities for further research into rent-seeking issues. The study of rent-seeking is yet in its infancy, and should be pursued with vigor. Tullock presents a rich research agenda for the dying years of the twentieth century.

Readers should be aware—and will be once they have read this book—of the gravity of the research agenda that is here proferred. Civilizations may be ravaged internally by disease, as the present AIDS pandemic threatens, or they may be savaged from without, as envious barbarians threaten to impose a new Dark Age. For the most part, however, they self-destruct from within, as the forces of redistribution overwhelm those of entrepreneurial zeal. This book is offered as a small but relevant contribution to the retention of wealth-enhancing opportunities and to the hindrance of the forces that lead to wealth destruction.

2 RENT-SEEKING VERSUS DIRECTLY UNPRODUCTIVE PROFIT-SEEKING ACTIVITIES

Charles K. Rowley

Introduction

The rent-seeking literature and the literature on directly unproductive profit-seeking (DUP) activities both focus attention upon individual or group economic behavior of a rational, solipsist nature which nevertheless destroys rather than enhances the resources available to society. As such, both contributions have radically changed our understanding of the positive behavior of political and bureaucratic markets and have shifted many of our views on normative politcal economy. Yet the two approaches differ significantly in important respects, not least in terms of their coherence within the broader framework of public choice.

This paper briefly traces the separate histories of rent-seeking and DUP, distinguishing those areas of essential agreement from those of fundamental divergence, and justifies the alleged preeminence of the rent-seeking over the DUP approach. The paper concludes by addressing criticisms levelled at the rent-seeking literature by scholars working on transaction costs within the framework of the new institutional economics. It is suggested that, given careful treatment, the rent-seeking insight is the most important contribution to public choice since the publication of *The Calculus of Consent* in 1962.

The *X*-Inefficiency Contribution

Early post-Second World War estimates of the welfare loss from monopoly, by Harberger and others, had suggested that the monopoly problem was one of trivial importance. Loss measures suggested that monopoly accounted for something between 0.1 and 1 percent of U.S. gross national product. Even writers broadly sympathetic to neoclassical economics (such as Robert Mundell) were concerned by the apparent mismatch between the resources devoted to monopoly analysis and the magnitude of the problem in terms of welfare loss:

> Unless there is a thorough theoretical examination of the validity of the tools upon which these studies (of losses from monopoly) are founded. . .someone will inevitably draw the conclusion that economics has ceased to be important. (Mundell, 1962)

In 1966, Harvey Leibenstein responded to this fundamental challenge by introducing into economics the concept of *x*-inefficiency and applying it in justification of the public concern over monopoly welfare losses. Leibenstein suggested that, in imperfectly competitive situations, production costs, in practice, would tend to be higher than the minimum level which efficient production could achieve.

> Firms and economies do not operate on an outer-bound production possibility surface consistent with their resources. Rather they actually work on a production surface that is well within that outer bound. This means that for a variety of reasons people and organizations normally work neither as hard nor as effectively as they could. (Leibenstein, 1966)

In large part, this outcome was seen to be the consequence of management and workers substituting their own objectives, including a desire for the quiet life, for those of the equity interests. By viewing such behavior either as causing deadweight loss (Crew, Jones-Lee, and Rowley, 1971) or as offering transfers that were excluded from the social welfare function as reflecting contract breach (Rowley, 1973), the full rectangle of producers' surplus, as well as the Harberger triangle, was seen to be at risk in markets characterized by monopoly power. For management and labor to be able to dispropriate stockholders or to dissipate surplus, strong assumptions were required concerning stock market inefficiency.

During a period when the efficient capital market hypothesis was riding high, this was seen to be a mortal weakness for *x*-inefficiency. In addition, the concept was subjected to a Chicagoan counter-blast which derided the notion that transfers might be excluded from the social welfare calculus (Stigler, 1976), as well as to an earlier counterattack that such transfers actually should be given an enhanced rather than a diminished or even zero welfare ranking (No, 1972). By 1976, the *x*-inefficiency justification for antitrust economics simply had run out of steam.

The Rent-Seeking Insight

In the meantime, the rent-seeking insight had been made and slowly had gathered momentum as an alternative, more convincing explanation of the public preoccupation with monopoly power.

Prior to the rent-seeking insight, and with the notable exception of Austrian economics, the new welfare economics had concentrated attention on private monopoly power, regarding government as a corrective agent rather than as an active participant in the process of monopoly creation and monopoly protection. With only limited exceptions, such was the case with the entire *x*-inefficiency contribution (but see Rowley and Peacock, 1975). Not so Gordon Tullock, who hammered at the monopoly paradox in 1967 from the perspective of the Virginia political economy program.

Tullock's target was government. His weapon was public choice. His battlefield was tariffs, considered by the new welfare economics to impose trivial welfare losses upon society. However, the monopoly power under Tullock's surveillance was the creature not of private but of public markets, and this was to prove of momentous long-term significance. Tullock's insight was that the welfare loss from tariffs, monopoly, and theft was much larger than that conventionally measured. It included not only the Harberger triangle, but also the entire amount of the tariff revenue, the monopoly surplus or the theft transfer. His reasoning was as follows: individuals would compete for the rents or lobby for the revenues; assuming competition in rent-seeking, each rent seeker would outlay the full expected value of perceived rents or revenues in their pursuit; in combination, such individuals would compete away the total value of the perceived rents or revenues.

The initial 1967 contribution directed attention away from private toward public monopoly, as one would expect given Tullock's specialization in public choice. In one pregnant sentence, Tullock also hinted at the public choice implications of his insight, noting that governments usually do not introduce tariffs in the absence of interest group lobbying in favor of such a protective instrument. In retrospect, somewhat surprisingly, he failed to develop this implication as a central feature of his paper, thus delaying the public choice insight for some four years. It should also be noted that Tullock did not coin the term *rent-seeking*, which was the subsequent contribution of Anne Kreuger, writing in 1974 within the DUP tradition.

The public choice thrust came in 1971 with Tullock's important paper on the cost of transfers. For most neoclassical economists, transfers were viewed as costless, even wealth enhancing, engineering movements from one point to another on the outer-bound production frontier, and possibly shifting the economy to Pareto-preferred positions as a consequence of interdependent utility functions. Not so Tullock, who applied the rent-seeking insight to demonstrate that the mere possibility of transfers imposed costs on society. The opportunity to effect wealth transfers, through the machinery of government, on at least a partially coercive basis, encourages lobbying and counter-lobbying of a negative sum nature as individuals and groups invest resources in attempting to obtain a transfer or to resist a transfer away from themselves.

The crucial public choice aspect of this insight was the notion that the mere possibility of transfers would attract rent-seeking and rent protection, and that a suitable analysis therefore requires a detailed understanding of public choice. DUP, in contrast, would analyse the nature of competition over predetermined transfers, with the government either essentially exogenous to the competition or only shadowly endogenized. It is to this latter approach that we now must turn, before comparing in terms of a detailed example the differing methodologies of the two approaches.

The DUP Alternative

The first DUP contribution (which ironically introduced the rent-seeking concept) was that by Anne Krueger in 1974. Noting that government restrictions upon economic activity in many market-oriented economies are pervasive facts of life, and that such restrictions, which she treated as exogenous, gave rise to rents, Krueger evaluated the economics of the rent-seeking society. She developed a formal rent-seeking model which she applied to the restriction of international trade by quotas, thereby deriving the first complete empirical estimates of the welfare loss implicit in this form of trade protection. She argued that individuals compete for the rights to import in order to win the monopoly rents associated with such rights. She recognized that such activities imposed a loss upon society. Despite Tullock's earlier analysis both of tariffs and of transfers, Krueger appears to have been unaware of his contributions.

Krueger's 1974 contribution was to generate a lively literature dedicated to the application of DUP analysis to the economics of international trade. Foremost among contributors in this field is Jagdish Bhagwati and his co-author T.N. Srinivasan, neither of whom by either methodology or ideology would claim membership of the Virginia School. The methodology of DUP analysis is markedly more formal and less intuitive than that of public choice, essentially bereft of institutional detail, as is typical of scholarship in the pure theory of international trade. The approach is general equilibrium, and the institutions through which it operates are for the most part treated as given, at least with respect to form, even when the revenue magnitudes that they generate are themselves endogenized. Section 5 of this paper will highlight this emphasis.

Ideologically, also, the two approaches differ, although this difference is relevant only in normative analysis. Two central ideas run through most of the public choice literature, and almost all of that of the Virginia School: first, that rent-seeking occurs primarily through the political process; and second, that the best way to limit rent-seeking is to limit government (Colander, 1984). In the views certainly of Buchanan (1980), Rowley (this volume), and Wagner (1987), constitutional rather than legislative constraints are emphasized as the effective route to reform. There is no such ideology discernible in the DUP approach, and certainly no reference to constitutional economics as a framework for institutional reform.

Rather, the normative thrust of DUP analytics is that of the new welfare economics of early 1950s vintage. Even the term DUP itself suggests that profit-seeking may be *indirectly productive* in some convoluted environment of second-best. Tariffs are compared with quotas, for the most part, by reference to standard welfare economics adjusted to take account of profit-seeking losses. The implications of profit-seeking for the choice of a trade protection instrument essentially is disregarded in the DUP literature. Instead, attention centers upon a single instrument, deemed to have an independent existence from the rent-seeking market.

Diversity of approach not infrequently is beneficial, accelerating the pace of scientific advance. Competition in ideas, no less than in other product markets, is a forcing agent that societies are foolish to destroy. In the rent-seeking/DUP approaches, strengths and weaknesses are apparent that offer enticing prospects of gains-from-trade (Magee, 1984). Specifically, if the public choice, rent-seeking literature would incorporate a little more of the formal modelling of DUP, while DUP would pay more attention to the institutional perspective of public choice, the overall quality of rent-seeking contributions should rise. Whether this quality improvement would be bought at too high a price in terms of public choice originality, however, is the unresolvable problem.

Trade Protection in a Rent-Seeking and in a DUP Perspective

An interesting example of the divergent perspectives of rent-seeking and DUP is to be found in their applications to trade protection (see Rowley and Tollison, this volume). In 1965, Bhagwati had introduced a welfare economics equivalence theorem for a tariff and its quota counterpart, based on the provision by each of identical levels of protection for some predesignated domestic industry. This theorem directed the attention of international trade theorists to the issue of trade protection levels rather than to the nature of trade protection instruments.

In 1974 contribution to rent-seeking into quota protection by Anne Krueger disturbed Bhagwati's equivalence theorem, rendering quotas inferior to tariffs in terms of welfare cost by reason of the perceived profit-seeking losses associated with the former instrument of protection. It also suggested that overall real equilibrium of the economy would differ under Bhagwati's protection equivalence. The 1980 reaction by Bhagwati and Srinivasan to this insight offers an excellent example of DUP analytics. They countered Krueger's argument by (rightly) asserting that tariff revenues also give rise to rent-seeking. On this basis, they claimed protection equivalence for the tariff and quota in post-profit-seeking welfare cost terms, recognizing only that overall equilibrium in the two outcomes might differ as a consequence of differing capital/labor ratios in the alternative profit-seeking industries.

This DUP debate avoids completely the issue central to the public choice, rent-seeking insight into trade protection: will differential rent-seeking into the alternative trade protection instruments systematically distort the regulation market in favor of or against the tariff or the quota? To resolve this latter issue, a detailed institutional knowledge is necessary concerning all actors in the regulation market, their goals and reward cost-structures, and the information environment within which they operate. Such an exercise, which is currently in process within the Virginia School political economy program, has no real counterpart in the DUP literature.

That is not to say that DUP always treats the instruments of trade protection as entirely exogenous. As Bhagwati clearly stated (1984), "the endogenization of policy *via* DUP activity is also subversive of traditional institutions." He recognized that, once policy is endogenized, economic agents attempt to influence policy in their favor, and that there is a noneconomic marketplace in which economic agents can simultaneously conduct their profit-making activities. Thus, there are two components of the overall model: the orthodox economic specification, and the political specification. Then, significantly, Bhagwati draws back with the following decisive judgment: "Profit motivation may equally extend to both, but the economic returns accrue through induced-policy changes influencing economic returns in the traditionally economic sphere of the model."

The rent-seeking literature would never thus dichotomize. Once a political market is invaded, there can be no distinction between economic and political activity. That is precisely why public choice is alternatively designated "the economics of politics."

Rent-Seeking, Rights and Transaction Costs—Science or Ideology?

In a pungent critique of rent-seeking theory, Samuels and Mercuro (1984) raise a number of important, perceived ideological biases that they argue renders rent-seeking suspect by comparison with DUP analysis. Their conclusion challenges the claim of rent-seeking theory to be a positive science, and does so in the most uncompromizing of terms:

> The theory of rent-seeking subtly, and with much irony, affirms the moral propriety of the competition for the control of the state. The state is a principal vehicle for achieving values and interests, no less through and within a market system than any other. There is, then, an inevitability to efforts to redesign and redirect state activity. And that is precisely what the theorists of rent-seeking are seeking to do while analytically castigating and normatively trying to eliminate rent-seeking. They are rent-seeking with regard to their ideological position, using the theory as a Schumpeterian handle, as it were, to change the structure of social power. They are participating in the processes through which are determined who will use government to change rights by law. It is but another chapter in a long-and honorable-quest for building blocks with which to erect a conservative intellectual fortress. (Samuels and Mercuro, 1984)

In almost equally pungent terms, North (1986) castigates rent-seeking theory for its ignoring of transaction cost considerations in its positive analysis of political markets:

> They take a rent-seeking view of government; that is, they view government as nothing but an extortionist activity. The dilemma comes out of a traditional public choice school that continues to view government as nothing but a mechanism for redistributing income and that implicitly uses a zero transactions cost model to measure the amount of rent-seeking. Certainly this approach is in direct conflict with the property rights literature, which recognizes that

> government specification and enforcement of property rights is the basic underpinning of efficient property rights and consequently of economic growth. (North, 1986)

These are forceful criticisms and, if correct, shake the intellectual foundations of the public choice approach to the rent-seeking insight. As such, they merit serious consideration in this debate between rent-seeking and DUP, not least because of the domination of rent-seeking contributions in this volume as a whole.

Mercuro and Samuels are highly attuned to the close association between efficiency and distribution and have since argued elsewhere (Mercuro and Samuels, 1986) against studies that center attention upon efficiency without paying close attention to the impact on rights of specific policy initiatives. From a general equilibrium perspective on welfare economics their logic carries considerable force. If those who engage in rent-seeking (or, for that matter, in rent protection) gain utility either from the battle over rights itself, or from the employment of specific rent-seeking/rent protection agents, then such utilities should count as social positives, even if the activities themselves are destructive of material wealth. Malevolence and envy may well give rise to utility-enhancing wealth destruction, as Brennan demonstrated in 1974. Brennan, however, is a member of the Virginia School.

In such an environment, narrow definitions of waste and productiveness, derived from partial equilibrium geometry, can be misleading in normative analysis. In essence this same criticism was mounted against the x-inefficiency concept much earlier by Ng and by Stigler (see above). Too rigid an adherence to the triangles and trapezoids of partial equilibrium theory, in such circumstances, may well result in an exaggerated defense of the status quo, and in an excessive denigration of attempts to change the structure of rights via the political process. This is a compelling reason why scholarly welfare economists predicate their policy conclusions upon a clearly outlined set of value assumptions.

It is unfair, however, to single out the public choice, rent-seeking approach for especial criticism on this score. For this school has been among the most meticulous in setting out the value assumptions of conventional welfare economics and of critiquing them (Rowley and Peacock, 1975). Moreover, Paretian welfare economics, which is espoused by the majority of the rent-seeking school, is not conservative, once the potential compensation test is embraced, as it is more frequently than not. It overrides rights in favor of efficiency without a second thought. The libertarian strand of Virginia political economy, represented by this author, is the substantive defender of rights. However, there is a chasm of difference between the libertarian and the conservative, at least as these are conventionally defined. Samuels and Mercuro recognized this distinction in their 1986 critique of Posner's efficiency of the law hypothesis.

No doubt some rent-seeking analysts are less scrupulous than others in their normative evaluations of interest group behavior. Given free entry into the research arena, outrageous abuse will not find its way unchallenged into the developing conventional wisdom. For this reason alone, Mercuro and Samuels protest too much about the long-term significance of any failure by public choice to take the general equilibrium road. In my view, the transaction cost critique of North, because of its significance for the positive as well as the normative branch of rent-seeking theory, is worthy of the more serious consideration.

North approaches the analysis of institutional adjustment from a perspective which differs radically from that of the public choice, rent-seeking school. He defines institutional arrangements as contractual agreements among principals or between principals and agents entered into for wealth maximization purposes. His approach thus harkens back to that of *The Calculus of Consent* (1962), and is based upon a gains-from-trade motivation which ignores the rent-seeking insight, but which does center attention on the costs entailed in capturing gains-from-trade.

This framework of analysis rests on three fundamental assumptions: (1) that individuals behave in their own, rather than in the collective, interest; (2) that specifying and enforcing the rules that underlie contracts is costly; and (3) that ideology modifies maximizing behavior. In such a framework, the role of ideology becomes critical. If there is ideological conformity in society, formal institutional rules will be minimal and enforcement procedures unimportant. But to the degree that society has diverse ideologies, resources increasingly will be devoted to rules-definition and to rules-enforcement.

North envisions a monopoly state which is concerned to provide a set of property rights designed to maximize its rents, but which is also designed to reduce transaction costs in order to foster its tax base. He recognizes inconsistency in these objectives (at least in the short run), and views such inconsistency as an explanation for inefficient property right regimes as conventionally evaluated. He sees the process of growth in such a model as inherently destabilizing.

This approach to political market analysis, in addition to constraining maximization over all margins via ideology, centers attention on the cost of transactions as a central determinant of the structure of rights. As noted earlier, North castigates the rent-seeking approach for its neglect of such transaction costs. There is some force to this criticism, though transaction cost analysis is more treacherous than North would like to believe.

For North, as for others working in the new institutional economics, transaction costs are directly measurable, in more or less objective terms, as a mechanism for delineating efficient from inefficient institutions. This approach is fundamentally flawed. If, following Buchanan, cost is recognized as a subjective concept, with choice-influencing cost an ephemeral, *ex ante* visitor to the mind of the decision-maker at the moment of choice alone, how can outside investigators possibly put numbers on them? The *ex post* numbers that they employ are measures not of the determinants but of the consequences of choice. Such costs are irrelevant to the issue of contract efficiency or to the comparative efficiency of institutions.

Of course, transaction-costs are important, not least for discriminating between the new institutions approach of North and the rent-seeking approach of public choice. Sooner or later, someone is going to have to dirty their hands and find some numbers. But let us not delude ourselves as to the likely success of such an exercise or as to the confidence that should be placed upon *ex post* outcomes as a guide to *ex ante* behavior.

References

Bhagwati, J.N. "On the Equivalence of Tariffs and Quotas." In: R.E. Caves; P. Kenen; and H.G. Johnson, (eds.), *Trade, Growth and the Balance of Payments*. Chicago: Rand McNally, 1965.

Bhagwati, J.N., and Srinivasan, T.N. "Revenue Seeking: A Generalization of the Theory of Tariffs." *Journal of Political Economy* no. 61, 88 (1980): 1069–87.

Bhagwati, J.N.; Brecher, R.A.; and Srinivansan, T.N. "DUP Activities and *Economic Theory*." In: D.C. Colander (ed.), *Neoclassical Political Economy*. Cambridge, Mass.: Ballinger, 1984.

Brennan, H.G. "Pareto Desirable Redistribution: The case of Malice and Envy." *Journal of Public Economics*, no. 2 (April, 1973): 173–84.

Buchanan, J.M., and Tullock, G. *The Calculus of Consent*. Ann Arbor: The University of Michigan Press, 1962.

Buchanan, J.M. *Cost and Choice*. Markham, 1969.

Buchanan, J.M. "Reform in the Rent-Seeking Society." In: J.M. Buchanan, R.D. Tollison; and G. Tullock (eds.), *Toward a Theory of the Rent-Seeking Society*. College Station: Texas A & M University Press, 1980.

Crew, M.A.; Jones-Lee, M.; and Rowley, C.K. "*X*-Theory Versus Management Discretion Theory." *Southern Economic Journal*, no. 2, 38 (October, 1971): 173–84.

Colander, D.C. "Introduction" to D.C. Colander (ed.), *Neoclassical Political*

Economy. Cambridge, Mass.: Ballinger, 1984.

Krueger, A.O. "The Political Economy of the Rent-Seeking Society." *American Economic Review* 64, (June, 1974): 291–303.

Leibenstein, H. "Allocative Efficiency vs. *X*-Efficiency." *American Economic Review* (June, 1966).

Magee, S.P. "Endogenous Tariff Theory: A Survey." In: D.C. Colander (ed.), *Neoclassical Political Economy*. Cambridge, Mass.: Ballinger, 1984.

Mundell, R. "Review of Jannsen, Free Trade, Protection and Customs Union." *American Economic Review*, no. 52 (June, 1962): 622.

Ng, P. "The Social Loss to *X*-Inefficiency." *Economica* (1972).

North, D.C. "*Three Approaches to the Study of Institutions*." In D.C. Colander (ed.) *Neoclassical Political Economy*. Cambridge, Mass.: Ballinger, 1984.

North, D.C. "The New Institutional Economics." *Journal of Institutional and Theoretical Economics*, no. 1, 142 (March, 1986).

Rowley, C.K. *Antritrust and Economic Efficiency* New York: Macmillan, 1973.

Rowley, C.K., and Tollison, R.D. "*Rent-Seeking and Trade Protection*." (This volume).

Rowley, C.K., and Peacock, A.T. *Welfare Economics: A Liberal Restatement*. Martin Robertson, 1975.

Rowley, C.K. "Rent Seeking in Constitutional Perspective." (This volume).

Rowley, C.K. "The Law of Property in a Virginia School Perspective." *Washington Law Quarterly Journal*, forthcoming (1987).

Samuels W.J., and Mercuro, N. "Posner and the Efficiency of the Common Law." *International Review of Law and Economics*, no. 1, 6 (1986).

Samuels, W.J., and Mercuro, N. "A Critique of Rent-Seeking Theory." In: D.C. Colander (ed.), *Neoclassical Political Economy*. Cambridge, Mass.: Ballinger, 1984.

Stigler, G.J. "The *x*-istence of *x*-Efficiency." *American Economic Review* (1976).

Tullock, G. Welfare Costs of Tariffs, Monopolies and Theft." *Western Economic Journal* 5 (June, 1967): 224–32.

Tullock, G. "The Cost of Transers." *Kyklos* 4 (December, 1971): 629–43.

Wagner, R.E. "Parchment, Guns and the Maintenance of Constitutional Contract." In C.K. Rowley (ed.). *Democracy and Public Choice*. Basil Blackwell, 1987.

3 IN SEARCH OF RENT-SEEKING

Michael A. Brooks and Ben J. Heijdra

Introduction

Over the last five or so years a good deal has been written on the topic of rent-seeking.[1] It is hard, however, to feel satisfied with the existing state of the literature: terminological and paradigmatic differences abound; there does not appear to be any consensus on an analytical core, and few of the existing results are accepted widely. Basically there is little agreement between the school of thought which labels these activities as rent-seeking and the other which places them under the general rubric of directly unproductive expenditure (hereafter DUPE). The aim of this paper is to critically analyze some of the existing themes in the literature and clarify the direction in which this area of research should turn. We begin by inquiring whether the rent-seeking process as envisaged by the DUPE school offers a satisfactory explanation of why certain forms of competition should be considered as wasteful. We then argue that the rent-seeking school has offered a fundamentally different explanation of why competition can be wasteful. We couch our discussion in terms of a general equilibrium model of the rent-seeking process. We discuss different waste measures to be derived from our model. In light of these discussions, we explore the idea that the central insight of the rent-seeking literature has been emasculated by the use of static equilibrium models. Finally, we present the main conclusions to be drawn from the paper. Some tangential issues are dealt with in an appendix. It should be mentioned at the outset that no attempt is made here to exhaustively survey all of the literature on rent-seeking. The object is to explore what we see as some of the major weaknesses and problems in this field, and to suggest a fundamental reorientation of the literature.

Modeling DUPE Activity

The earliest approach to modeling the effects of rent-seeking by Tullock (1967) made use of a simple partial equilibrium framework. He showed that the so-called Harberger triangle can severely underestimate the welfare cost of a monopoly. In figure 3–1 the traditional measure of the welfare cost of transforming a competitive industry into a monopoly is BAD. Tullock aruges that if resources are expended in the attempt to create a monopoly, then this measure will underestimate the measure of

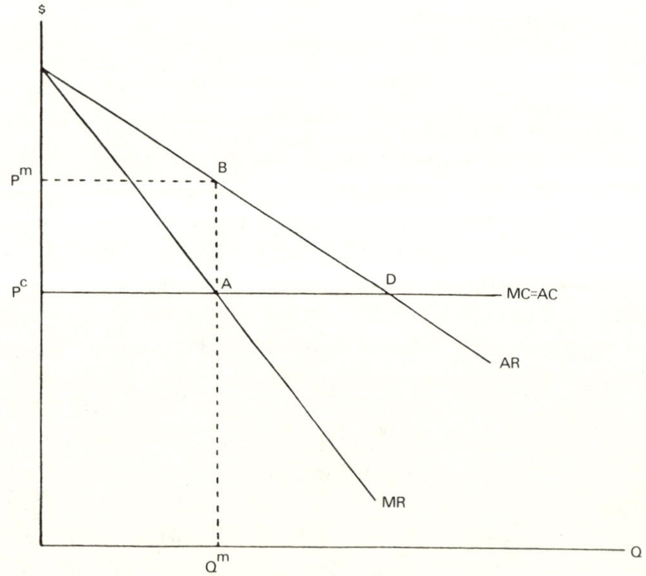

Figure 3–1

waste by P_mBAP_c.[2] There are two explanations of why such expenditure will lead to social waste. One falls under the general rubric of rent-seeking which is defined as "...behavior in institutional settings where individual efforts to maximize value generate social waste rather than social surplus." (Buchanan, 1980a)[3] The other falls under the heading of directly unproductive expenditure. To the DUPE theorists the activity represents waste because individuals undertake expenditure on non-productive activities. A central question raised by these two definitions is whether or not they represent competing descriptions of wasteful competition. The DUPE theory appears to provide the more simplistic account of why competition may result in waste, so we turn to that explanation first. After having done so, we focus on the rent-seeking theory. The relationships, if any, between the two theories are explored once the two accounts have been set out.

In the DUPE literature, waste arises from the fact that individuals in their pursuit of monopoly rents, or wealth in general, undertake expenditure on activities which are only valued for the role they serve in securing a change in property rights. The expenditure is on activities which do not have any intrinsic worth, i.e., on unproductive activities. Bhagwati and Srinivasan define such activities as those which while profitable do not contribute

> ... directly or indirectly into output that enters the utility function. In short, these activities are tantamount to a contraction of the availability set of the economy, defined on goods and services entering the utility function. (Bhagwati and Srinivasan, 1983)

Given this definition it is obvious why the expenditure on the attempt to secure the monopoly right will lead to social waste: it is wasteful *by definition*. It is worth exploring the basic logic of the DUPE school in further detail, for the significance of their results stands or falls on whether this is a satisfactory explanation of waste.

Consider expenditure undertaken on an activity of a new commodity used solely for the purpose of lobbying, x_3. This "commodity" could be, for example, information distributed by lawyers' lobbyists designed to persuade the politicians of the industry's case. The amount of resources therefore left over for the so-called productive activities, x_1 and x_2, in this three-good world will have decreased. For example, if the amount of x_3 produced in figure 3–2 is x_3', then the maximum amount of x_1 and x_2 which can still be produced is given by the curve $x_1''x_2''$ on the production surface $x_1^0x_2^0x_3^0$. When this curve is projected onto the (x_1, x_2) plane, then it appears that the production possibilities frontier for productive activities has

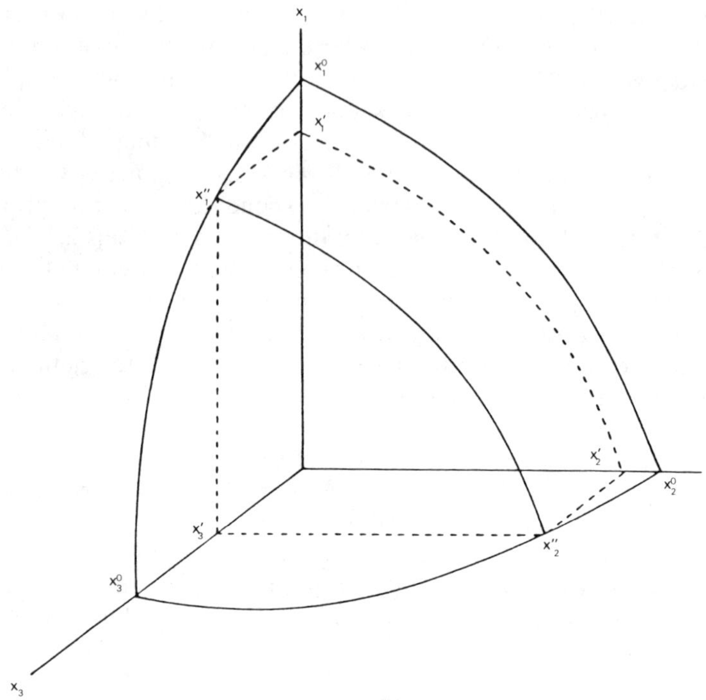

Figure 3–2

shifted inwards. The welfare significance of this is clear. Given the inward shift of the production possibilities curve, the grand utility possibilities curve will also shift inwards. In a first-best setting DUPE activity must decrease the satisfaction of at least one of the individuals. On the other hand, in a second-best setting, DUPE theorists such as Bhagwati and Srinivasan (1982) have pointed out that expenditure of a rent-seeking kind may be welfare improving. Rent-seeking theorists have cast doubt on how much significance ought to be placed on such findings.[4] We do not wish to comment on that debate here, however. To our mind there are much more deep-seated flaws pervading the entire DUPE literature.

As indicated above the basic *deus ex machina* which lies behind all of the DUPE results is that individuals in the pursuit of wealth switch from productive to unproductive activities. Recall that they are unproductive because they do not enter either directly or indirectly into the utility function of any individual. A moment's reflection indicates that such an assumption is unsatisfactory for two reasons. First, the assumption is made at the outset that activities like lobbying are wasteful or unproductive; DUPE theorists simply posit that the expenditure is wasteful. Yet, as Samuels and Mercuro (1984) note, no acceptable criterion is provided by which one could discern whether or not something is unproductive. How would we know whether or not some activity should be left out of a utility function? Second, this definition of waste does not provide us with any idea of why wealth seekers would want to undertake such activities in the first place. If DUPE theorists are taken at face value when they argue that such activities do not enter either directly or indirectly into the utility function of any agent, then it is difficult to understand why the expenditure would be undertaken at all. If the politician/bureaucrat is not made better off, for example, in the lobbying process, then there is no reason why he would respond to the pressure at all. In order to rectify the apparent lack of any rationale for government action it would appear that the DUPE literature must be saying one of two things.

First, they could argue that the politician/bureaucrat is made better off, which would of course explain why the bureaucrat would be in favor of the regulation. this would mean, however, that the rent-seeking activity will be one of the indirect arguments in the politicians/bureaucrats' utility function which clearly contradicts the DUPE theorists' claim that the activity does not enter any agent's utility function either directly or indirectly. One interpretation of the DUPE theorists' position on this score might be that while these activities do enter an individual's utility function they should not enter the social utility function. Although this interpretation may save the DUPE theorists from some embarrassment for failing to provide any explanation of purposeful behavior on the part of bureaucrats, it is not an acceptable position. As noted previously this literature provides no criterion to indicate which activities should be left out of the social utility function.

Second, the DUPE theorists might be arguing instead that the lobbying changes the politicians' tastes; the politicians are persuaded of the "propriety" of the lobbyist's cause. But this is even more problematic. To the extent that the subject of concern is the welfare significance of the DUPE activity, and accepting that in such calculations the regulator's welfare ought to be taken into account, then the problem is that there is no generally accepted way of evaluating the welfare significance of expenditure which results in a new set of preferences. The DUPE definition of such activity therefore leads to two equally problematic courses of action. DUPE theorists can continue to evaluate the welfare significance of government regulation for which they cannot provide any clue as to why it might exist, or they can explain that government action arises from persuasive lobbying but then cannot carry out an acceptable evaluation of the welfare significance of the wealth-seeking activity.

Modeling Rent-Seeking

In our view the literature on rent-seeking is not necessarily marred by such problems, and it is to that approach we now turn. This theory is often associated with Buchanan, Tollison and Tullock. The basic explanation of why wealth-seeking behavior here generates waste is that individuals withdraw resources from some sector of the economy, and spend these resources on rent-seeking activities without at the same time expanding the output of the sector they wish to enter. Our objective here is twofold: first, to demonstrate that this approach provides a conceptually distinct theory of wealth destruction; second, to indicate that the rent-seeking approach is not marred by the problems which plague the DUPE literature.

In order to structure our argument, we use an example which has figured prominently in a number of explanations of the wastefulness of rent-seeking activity. We believe that this example reflects the central features of the current rent-seeking school.[5] Entrepreneurs or courtiers learn of the fact that one of them could be granted the right to be the single seller of playing cards. The potential rents encourage the individuals to court the monarch to shift the monopoly right in their direction. Buchanan concludes that

> . . . [r]ent seeking on the part of potential entrants in a setting where entry is blocked or can at best reflect one-for-one substitution must generate social waste. Resources devoted to efforts to curry the queen's favor might be used to produce valued goods and services elsewhere in the economy, whereas nothing of net value is produced by rent-seeking. (Buchanan, 1980a)

It is still not clear why this activity necessarily leads to social waste. Is the expansion of output in rent-seeking activities such as banquets for the queen's ministers not counted as valued output? If this were the case, then there would appear to be no difference between this explanation and that provided by the DUPE theorists, i.e., rent-seeking is wasteful by *assumption* rather than by the outcome of a sustained argument. The central point of Buchanan's argument strikes us as being that waste is the *outcome* of the rent-seeking process, and not an assumption built into the analysis. (Buchanan, 1980a)

It is worth noting from the outset that the rent-seeking explanation implies that a strict partial equilibrium framework cannot be used to examine the effects of rent-seeking; waste arises from the fact that resources which could be employed creating social value in some sector of the economy are used instead to procure wealth transfers. Even though the geometrical analysis has often been cast in partial equilibrium terms, the basic thrust of the rent-seeking literature relies on general equilibrium notions. Thus before we turn to the welfare implications of rent-seeking activity, we must first reinterpret the card-playing example in simple general equilibrium terms.[6]

Assume that the economy consists of n individuals, of which n_1 are regulators/bureaucrats, and n_2 are common people. The two types of agents differ only in the sense that regulators can instigate regulations, whereas common people cannot. For simplicity assume that all individuals have the following utility function:

$$U = (x_1^{1/2} + x_2^{1/2})^2 \tag{3.1}$$

where x_1 denotes the consumption of goods produced in industry 1, and U is the utility level attained by each individual. Agents maximize utility subject to their budget constraint:

$$I = P_1x_1 + P_2x_2 \tag{3.2}$$

where P_1 is the price charged in industry 1, and I is the income level of each individual. All individuals have identical endowments of labor equal to unity, supplied perfectly inelastically. There are no other sources of income apart from labor income. The nominal wage rate is denoted by W. Hence:

$$I = W \tag{3.3}$$

Maximization of (3.1) subject to (3.2) yields the demand functions for the two goods of each individual:

$$x_1 = (P_1[1 + (P_1/P_2)])^{-1}I \tag{3.4}$$

$$x_2 = (P_2[1 + (P_2/P_2)])^{-1}I \tag{3.5}$$

Producers in both industries are assumed to produce under identical constant returns to scale technologies, with labor as the only variable input:

$$Q_1 = L_1 \tag{3.6}$$

$$Q_2 = L_2 \tag{3.7}$$

Profit maximization in both industries yields the demand for labor and supply of goods in both industries.[7] These are perfectly elastic at $W/P_1 =$

$W/P_2 = 1$, where we have chosen labor as the numeraire ($W = 1$). The model is closed by postulating equilibrium in the labor and goods markets. By Walras' Law we can delete one market clearing condition. Hence:

$$x_1 = nx_1 = Q_1 \tag{3.8}$$

$$n = L_1 + L_2 \tag{3.9}$$

Equation (3.8) implies that aggregate demand for good 1 equals aggregate supply. Equation (3.9) is the labor market equilibrium condition. This simple model can now be used to describe the following two cases.

Competitive Equilibrium

The first case that we can analyze with the help of this simple model is that in which there is perfect competition in both industries. This implies that the bureaucrats/regulators have not imposed any regulations, and so serves as a benchmark for the discussion of the welfare effects of rent-seeking. It is straightforward to show that the competitive equilibrium implies the following levels of output and employment in the two sectors:

$$x_1^c = L_1 = n/2 \tag{3.10}$$

$$x_2^c = L_2 = n/2 \tag{3.11}$$

And, of course, we have the result that $P_1^c = P_2^c = 1$. The central features of this simple model are depicted geometrically in figure 3–3. The competitive equilibrium involves production of x_1^c and x_2^c units of commodities 1 and 2. The initial demand curves for the two goods, as obtained by aggregating equations (3.4) and (3.5) over all n individuals, are depicted as $D_1(P_1; P_2 = P_2^c)$ and $D_2(P_2; P_1 = P_1^c)$, respectively.

Nature of the Rent-Seeking Equilibrium

Now suppose that the courtiers or entrepreneurs who are presently involved in the production of industry 1, say competitively produced playing cards, attempt to establish a monopoly by lobbying the monarch, through the bureaucrats/regulators, i.e., ministers of the crown. Assume that they use x_2 in their lobbying effort, and that the potential rent is exactly dissipated. In this parable commodity x_2 represents, for example, foodstuffs. The lobbying effort consists of an amount of x_2, say x_2^R, that is distributed, free of charge, to a significant portion of the bureaucrats.

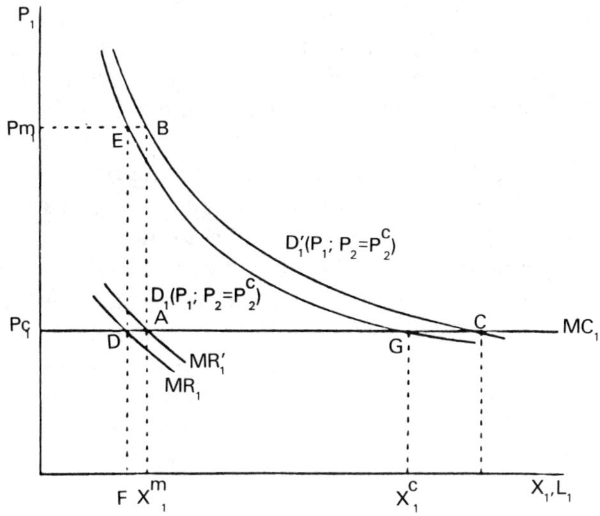
P_1
P^m_1
E
B
$D'_1(P_1;\ P_2=P^c_2)$
$D_1(P_1;\ P_2=P^c_2)$
A
P^c_1
D
MR'_1
MR_1
G
C
MC_1
F
X^m_1
X^c_1
X_1, L_1

(a)

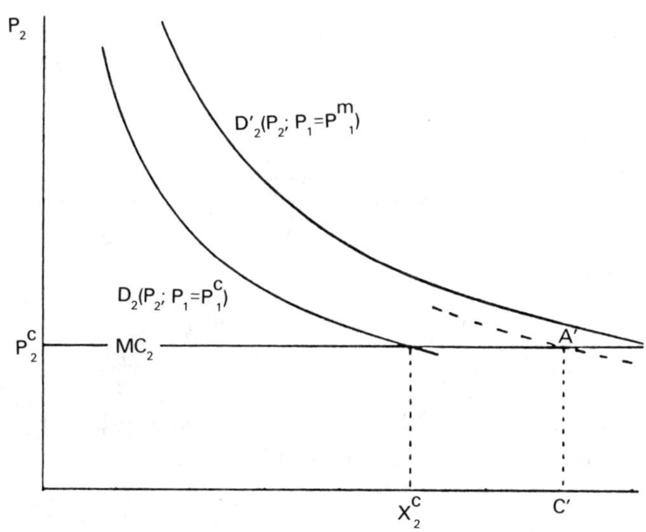
P_2
$D'_2(P_2;\ P_1=P^m_1)$
$D_2(P_2;\ P_1=P^c_1)$
P^c_2
MC_2
A′
X^c_2
C′

(b)

Figure 3–3

Assume that, in order for the lobbying effort to be successful, at least a^* percent of the bureaucrats must be lobbied adequately (in the sense explained below). The parable is thus as follows. There are n_1 bureaucrats that are called to a special audience with the monarch. The bureaucrats do not communicate with each other. One of the items on the agenda is the proposed monopolization of industry 1. The voting rule is supposed to be of the following simple kind. If a* percent (or more) of the bureaucrats vote in favour of the regulation, then the monopoly privilege will be granted, for the monarch heeds the advice of this majority. Assume that bureaucrats' votes can be "bought" by supplying them with an adequate amount of x_2, say x_2^R. This amount must be such that lobbied bureaucrats are better off in utility terms after the regulation is passed. Since, as is shown below, unlobbied bureaucrats are made worse off by the monopolization, they will vote against the proposal. We can define therefore the actual fraction of votes in favor of the regulation as follows:

$$a = x_2^R/(n_1 x_2^R) \tag{3.12}$$

A successful lobbying effort implies that the following constraint must be met:

$$a \geq a^* \tag{3.13}$$

A bureaucrat that has been lobbied successfully receives in effect a transfer in kind equal to $P_2 x_2^R$. Hence, his budget constraint is now:

$$P_1 x_1 + P_2 x_2 = 1 + P_2 x_2^R = I_L \tag{3.14}$$

where I_L is the lobbied bureaucrat's new income level. All unlobbied individuals (subscripted by U) have the old income level equal to unity. By aggregating over the two types of individuals the total demands for the two commodities are obtained:

$$x_1 = (P_1[1 + (P_1/P_2)])^{-1}(n + P_2 x_2^R) \tag{3.15}$$

$$x_2 = (P_2[1 + (P_2/P_1)])^{-1}(n + P_2 x_2^R) \tag{3.16}$$

Given the demand curve, the profit maximizing price (P_1^m) that the intending monopolist wishes to set in industry 1 is:

$$P_1^m = 1 + [1 + P_2]^{1/2} \tag{3.17}$$

This implies that total rents in industry 1 are equal to:

$$R = (P_1^m - 1)x_1 = [1 + P_2]^{1/2} x_1 \tag{3.18}$$

This area is depicted as $P_1^m BAP_1^c$ in figure 3–3. As the rents (R) are exactly dissipated by expenditure on x_2, this implies the following derived demand for x_2 used in rent-seeking (x_2^R):

$$x_2^R = R/P_2 \tag{3.19}$$

The model is closed by postulating equilibrium in the labor and goods markets:

$$n = L_1 + L_2 \tag{3.20}$$

$$L_1 = x_1 = Q_1 \tag{3.21}$$

$$x_2 = Q_2 \tag{3.22}$$

Since the marginal cost curves in the two industries do not shift (they remain at W = 1), it is obvious that P_2 continues to be unity. In terms of figure 3–3, the demand curve in industry 1 shifts out to D_1' as a result of the income effect borne by the lobbied bureaucrats. The demand curve in industry 2 shifts out to D_2' for two reasons. The introduction of the monopoly price in industry 1 leads to a substitution away from the consumption of x_1 to x_2. And the provision of free lunches to the lobbied bureaucrats results in a positive income effect and shifts the demand curve to the right. The demand curve for x_2, inclusive of the income and substitution effects, is $D_2'(P_2; P_1 = P_1^m)$. The dashed curve through A′ is the demand for x_2, exclusive of the income effect. Since all rent income is spent, we have that $A'B'x_2^{rc}C' + EBX_1^m F = P_1^m BX_1^m F$. In the rent-seeking equilibrium, output in industry 1 has fallen to x_1^m, while the price has risen to P_1^m. Total output in industry 2 is equal to x_2^{rc}. The solution values are:[8]

$$P_1^m = 2.4142 \tag{3.23}$$

$$P_2 = 1.0 \tag{3.24}$$

$$x_1^m = 0.1464n = L_1 \tag{3.25}$$

$$R = 0.2070n = x_2^R \tag{3.26}$$

$$x_2 = 0.8536n = Q_2 = L_2 \tag{3.27}$$

Feasibility Conditions

Before the welfare implications of rent-seeking are discussed, it must be established that this rent-seeking equilibrium is feasible in the sense that the available rent is adequate to buy the necessary votes as given in (3.13).

As indicated in (3.26) the potential rent from monopolizing industry 1 is equal to 0.2070n. If a^*n_1 bureaucrats are lobbied, then each lobbied bureaucrat will receive:

$$x_2^R = x_2^R/(a^*n_1) = 0.2070/(a^*b) \qquad (3.28)$$

where b is the relative size of the bureaucracy in the economy ($b = n_1/n$), which is exogenous in the model. This amount has to be such that the lobbied bureaucrat is better off after the regulation is passed. The indirect utility function defined by equations (3.1) and (3.2) is equal to:

$$V = [P_1^{-1} + P_2^{-1}]I \qquad (3.29)$$

Hence, the utility level in the competitive equilibrium is equal to 2. The utility level of a lobbied bureaucrat (V_L) can be seen to be equal to:

$$V_L = [(P_1^m)^{-1} + P_2^{-1}]\,[1 + 0.2071/a^*b] \qquad (3.30)$$

This implies a critical level for a^*b, denoted by $(a^*b)^c$ such that the following holds:

$$V_L \gtreqless 2 \text{ iff } (a^*b) \lesseqgtr (a^*b)^c = 0.5 \qquad (3.31)$$

It may be helpful to put a geometrical interpretation on part of this argument. In figure 3–4 the horizontal axis reflects the fraction of

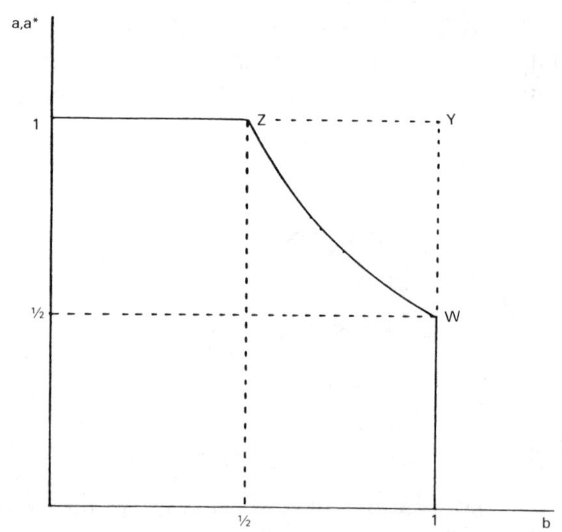

Figure 3–4

bureaucrats in the economy which is, of course, between zero and one. The vertical axis measures the fraction of lobbied bureaucrats (a), as well as the fraction of bureaucrats' support required for a bill to be passed (a^*). This axis is also scaled from zero to unity because the maximum percentage of bureaucrats which can be lobbied is 100 percent and the most restrictive voting rule is unanimity. The line labelled lZWl is the boundary of the feasible set defined by $0 < a \leq 1$, $0 < b \leq 1$, and $a^*b \leq 0.5$. For example, suppose the economy is completely composed of bureaucrats and the monarch requires all of his ministers to be in favor of a proposal before he will place his seal on the document. Point Y is consistent with these two conditions. This point is not however feasible. As indicated in equation (3.31), the potential rent from monopolizing commodity 1 is only large enough to successively lobby 50 percent of the bureaucrats. This is consistent with point W on the lobby-feasibility locus; there are insufficient rents available to lobby successively in this economy. On the other hand, if the fraction of bureaucrats in the economy was 50 percent, then there would be just enough rents to lobby each and every bureaucrat successfully. This is consistent with point Z on the frontier. In fact the lobbying would have been rewarding if the voting rule had been less restrictive. The scenario outlined here is, of course, one among many. For example, if the monarch only required 50 percent of his ministers to approve of a proposal, then the fraction of bureaucrats which would have to be effectively on side of the industry would be 50 percent also. This would appear to raise the possibility that the potential rent may not be fully dissipated; for after all there was enough potential rent to lobby all of the bureaucrats at point Z. But as indicated previously, the scope of inquiry here is one of competitive rent-seeking which implies that the rent is fully dissipated. The way to accommodate this in our analysis is to increase the size of the free lunch which is received by each lobbied bureaucrat. In technical terms this implies that although for a given (a^*, b) all values of a in the interval $[a^*, 1]$ are feasible, we will assume a boundary solution $(a = a^*)$ for simplicity.

Welfare Implications

Given that the rent-seeking equilibrium is feasible, attention now turns to the level of waste associated with the solution. It is readily apparent that our explanation of wasteful competition differs from that put forward in the DUPE literature. No assumption has been made here that the resources used in rent-seeking do not enter the utility function of any economic agent. Commodity x_2 enters positively the utility function of all the agents who continue to treat it as final consumption. Since it is not possible to easily identify the losses and gains in terms of figure 3–3, we use the underlying expenditure functions to analyze the welfare implications of rent-seeking. (See, for example, Varian, 1984, and Hausman, 1981.) The expenditure function corresponding to the CES utility function given in equation (1) is:

$$E^*(P_1, P_2; U) = [P_1^{-1} + P_2^{-1}]^{-1} \cdot U \tag{3.32}$$

In order to calculate the effects of rent-seeking we need only distinguish between lobbied bureaucrats (subscript L) and all other individuals (subscript U). Each lobbied bureaucrat receives free lunches equal to $0.2070/(a^*b)$, which is treated as an income payment. In view of (3.30) the utility level attained by the lobbied bureaucrat is equal to $V_L = 1.4142 + (0.2927/a^*b)$. In view of (3.23), (3.24), and (3.32) the expenditure level associated with V_L is equal to:

$$E_L^*(P_1^m, P_2; V_L) = 1 + 0.2070/a^*b \tag{3.33}$$

The net gain per lobbied bureaucrat can be measured as follows:

$$E_L^*(P_1^m, P_2; V_L) - E_L^*(P_1^m, P_2; 2) = 1 + 0.2070/a^*b - 1.4142 \tag{3.34}$$

where the second term on the LHS(3.34) measures the expenditure level which would return the lobbied bureaucrat to the original pre-rent-seeking utility level. Since there are a^*bn lobbied bureaucrats, their total gains (G) are equal to:

$$G = a^*bn\ [1 + 0.2070/a^*b - 1.4142] \tag{3.35}$$

Similarly the loss to any unlobbied individual is equal to:

$$E_U^*(P_1^m, P_2; 2) - E_U^*(P_1^m, P_2; V_U) = 1.4142 - 1 \tag{3.36}$$

where V_U is the maximum attainable utility level of unlobbied individuals at the new prices. This can be calculated by using (3.29) and noting that their income is equal to 1. Since $(1 - a^*b)n$ individuals remain unlobbied, the total losses (L) are equal to:

$$L = (1 - a^*b)n\ [1.4142 - 1] \tag{3.37}$$

Inspection of (3.35) and (3.37) reveals that the winners cannot compensate the losers and the net loss to society of the monopoly is equal to:

$$L - G = 0.2072n > 0 \tag{3.38}$$

A possible criticism against our waste calculation might be that the preferences of regulators/politicians should not be counted in discussions of the collectivity's welfare. After all, if these representatives were completely immune from the sort of political pressure under consideration here, then society would bear little in the way of costs due to rent-seeking and therefore these unmeritorious preferences should not be included. Strict adherence to methodological individualism requires, however, that the bureaucrats' preferences ought to be taken into account, except when there has been some constitutional decision to ignore them when in-period welfare comparisons are made. Besides, if the general implication was accepted that preferences ought not be taken into account when other individuals are made worse off, then almost the entire fields of social choice and welfare economics would fall by the wayside. We guess few economists would be willing to accept this extreme position.

On seemingly more acceptable ground it might be argued, as it has been by Posner, "...that expenditures on monopolizing [which] yield such by-products will be ignored in the development of the model, and its principal relevance, therefore, is to methods of monopolizing that have little or *no* social value." (1975) (italics added) This will not do, for precisely the same reasons which were advanced in our criticism of the DUPE literature. A possible defence of the Posner type position might be that politicians/bureaucrats *themselves* will waste resources in their attempt to be elected or promoted to a senior position in which they will receive these free benefits of office. If electoral candidates, for example, spend up to G dollars (where G is given in equation (3.35) worth of resources in the attempt to become the successful candidate, then it would appear that the traditional measure would be acceptable. But even this will not do. As long as the politicians-to-be provide some benefits to other agents in the economy then the traditional measure will continue to overestimate the welfare costs of rent-seeking.[9]

It is straightforward to show that the loss calculated by us is less than that put forward in the rent-seeking literature. Due to the general equilibrium nature of our model, there are several ways in which the level of waste can be calculated. By showing these different methods the inherent dangers of using partial equilibrium analysis on a general equilibrium phenomenon like rent-seeking and waste are exposed. The first way in which the waste due to the monopoly with rent-seeking might be measured is to simply calculate the area $P_1^m P_1^c CB$ in figure 3–3—the traditionally proposed measure. The first measure is equal to:[10]

$$W_1 = \int_{P_1^c}^{P_1^m} \frac{1.207n}{P_1(1 + P_1)} \, dP_1 = 0.4183n \qquad (3.39)$$

This measure, aside from failing to measure the change in consumer surplus with reference to the compensated demand curve, is deficient for the following reason. It is based upon the demand for x_1 alone when all rents are paid as income to the consumers, and therefore fails to take account of the benefits which accrue to the bureaucrats as consumers in other markets. It will overestimate the cost of the monopoly substantially.

Another possible measure of waste could be the area $P_1^m EGP_1^c$ in figure 3–3. This measure is based upon demand for x_1 *net* of the rent income, and is equal to:

$$W_2 = \int_{P_1^c}^{P_1^m} \frac{n}{P_1(1 + P_1)} dP_1 = 0.3466n \qquad (3.40)$$

This measure is also deficient, although this only becomes clear in a general equilibrium context. What this approach implies is that whereas rent is generated from the monopolization of x_1, no agent within the model receives it. It is clear that such a treatment of rent-seeking is highly unsatisfactory since it introduces a fundamental inconsistency into the model. Put simply, resources can not vanish into thin air.

A third measure of waste removes this inconsistency by distributing the rent equally over all agents. This implies that each agent receives a total income of 1.207, and the total level of waste is equal to:

$$W_3 = n[E^*(P_1^m, P_2; 2) - E^*(P_1^m, P_2; V_0)] = 0.2072n \qquad (3.41)$$

where V_0 is the maximum level of utility attained when income is 1.207. This measure is identical to the one proposed in (3.38).[11] An inspection of the waste measures as calculated in (3.38) and (3.41) leads to a startling conclusion. The rent-seeking school has been at pains to point out that the welfare cost of a monopoly is larger when rent-seeking effects are taken into account. We have now demonstrated that if rent-seeking takes place by distributing lunches or theater tickets, for example, then the welfare cost of the monopolization is no different from that proposed by Harberger more than three decades ago. The simple intuition behind this surprising result (at least from the perspective of the rent-seeking literature) is that expenditures of this kind involve a *redistribution* of income. And, as is widely known, there is no welfare cost associated with pure redistribution.

The Dynamics of Rent-Seeking

The final result of the previous section is of course problematic. The general equilibrium model developed there was designed to capture the central features of Buchanan's example of wasteful competition. As we argued in section 3 above, this example centers on the proposition that rent-seeking results in waste when entrepreneurs withdraw resources from some other sector of the economy, without at the same time expanding the output of the sector they wish to enter. Apart from the fact that in our model the resources are withdrawn from the monopolized sector itself, our argument follows the logic of Buchanan's position. Despite this, we were not able to generate any waste other than the Harberger cost of the monopoly. This leads us to believe that either the whole rent-seeking argument is conceptually flawed, or else static resource allocation models are unable to capture the rent-seeking phenomenon adequately.[12] We believe that there is no need to adopt the first position. A careful reading of the literature on rent-seeking reveals that the secondary literature has lost sight of the essential feature of the rent-seeking process. The first paper on rent-seeking, by Tullock (1967), draws attention to the fact that the issue of wasteful competition should be examined in a dynamic setting. Although he did not put it quite this way, rent-seeking results in waste because resources are withdrawn from productive activities such as the production of new investment goods or human capital. This in turn decreases the productive capacity of the economy. This interpretation of Tullock is more clearly exemplified in a later paper, where he discusses the social waste of the examination system for the Chinese civil service. There Tullock makes the following point:

> [t]he education given to the students preparing for the exam was of little or no use in any walk of life other than government. Further, most of the people who passed the examination and received minor government jobs would make only modest use of their highly intensive and expensive educational backgrounds. (Tullock, 1980)

Clearly the story here is not one of static resource allocation effects, but rather a dynamic one of unproductive human capital formation.

Some care needs to be exercised in interpreting Tullock's point. Education must not be seen as unproductive *a priori*, since that would bring us back to the troubled DUPE world. Rather, following Buchanan's lead, the education must be judged in terms of its unintended consequences: the effect on the dynamic path of the economy. It may be helpful to explain this argument by means of figure 3–5. Assume that Y_U describes the initial steady state growth path of an economy. Suppose that at time t education requirements are imposed on aspiring civil servants. The initial effect of the education is to lower the output produced by the economy since resources are used for an activity which is unproductive at time t. Suppose, however, that over time the education produces unintended

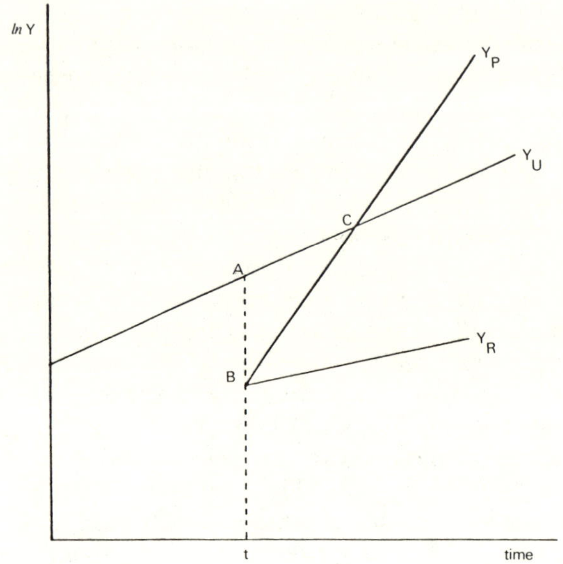

Figure 3–5

externalities, and that the economy follows the growth path Y_P. Then, as long as the present value of the gains outweighs the present value of the losses (ABC), the competition has to be judged as desirable. To use Buchanan's term, this would be an example of profit seeking. If, on the other hand, the economy ends up on a growth path such as Y_R, then the activity at time *t* must be seen as wasteful competition, i.e., rent-seeking. We have found almost nothing in the secondary literature which acknowledges that rent-seeking is a dynamic process. The literature has somehow forgotten to take account of Tullock's essential insight that rent-seeking is an intertemporal phenomenon. It is our contention that unless the literature is fundamentally reoriented to take account of time, it will continue to define waste *a priori*, rather than as the outcome of a process.

Conclusions

The paper has attempted to model rent-seeking processes in a simple general equilibrium context. On this basis we have analysed what we believe to be some of the major flaws in the DUPE and rent-seeking schools of thought.

The DUPE literature simply asserts rather than explores why lobbying is wasteful. Therein lies its major flaw. The DUPE school cannot offer any explanation why the government would enact the policy in the first place. It has to simply assert that regulatory policies exist. Moreover, in their evaluaton of such policies the DUPE school overestimates the welfare cost of monopoly, since they have assumed away the possibility that some groups, particularly the bureaucracy, might benefit from the competitive process.

The rent-seeking literature is flawed too, but for fundamentally different reasons. This school has attempted to exemplify its general equilibrium explanations of why competition can be wasteful with partial equilibrium techniques. Therein lies one of its flaws. The partial equilibrium techniques provide a reasonable, though not entirely accurate, depiction of what is going on in the market which is the subject of the regulation. These techniques do not, however, provide a clear idea of what is happening in the other sectors of the economy. If these other sectors are explicitly taken into account, then the welfare cost of a monopoly in a rent-seeking environment turns out to be no different from the traditional Harberger measure.

The rent-seeking literature is superior to the DUPE literature in the sense that it does not define waste from the outset. Indeed, the rent-seeking literature has consistently maintained that waste must be judged as the possible result of a competitive process. Unfortunately, the bulk of this literature is couched in static terms. As our model shows, there is very little mileage in this approach. We believe that the direction of future research in this area must return to Tullock's crucial insight that rent-seeking is a dynamic phenomenon.

Appendix

Rent-Seeking and the Production Possibilities Frontier

It is instructive to return to a theme of section 1 in the text by asking what are the implications, if any, of our view of rent-seeking for the commonly held claim that wasteful competition leads to a contraction of the production possibilities frontier (ppf). In figure 3–6, *nn* is the initial ppf and point E describes the competitive levels of production and consumption. Following the logic of the DUPE position, it would appear to be the case that the ppf ought to be shifted in by $R = 0.207n$ units of x_2, which is the level of output in terms of x_2 devoted to rent-seeking as indicated in

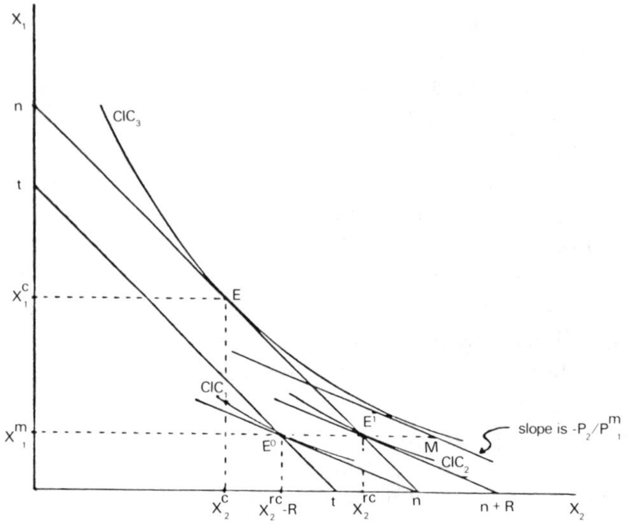

Figure 3–6

equation (3.26). This means that the ppf shifts from *nn* to *tt*. Point E^0 would presumably describe the level of outputs which enter into the utility function of the various agents.

It is relatively easy to see, however, that there can be no such universally held claim in the rent-seeking literature; contraction of the ppf is not a necessary feature of the rent-seeking process. As indicated in the above discussion the level of output of x_2 which is used for rent-seeking purposes does enter the utility function of the politician/bureaucrats. Point E^1, as indicated in equations (3.25) and (3.27), reflects therefore the level of outputs under the rent-seeking equilibrium which do in fact contribute in some way to utility. Clearly there has been no contraction of the ppf. There is no reason to believe that this result can be generalized to all cases of wasteful competition. But equally clearly it demonstrates that a contraction in the production possibility curve is not a necessary outcome of rent-seeking. Analyses which start off with a contraction in the ppf as the indispensable effect of rent-seeking are presenting a misleading approach to the process.

While we are aware of the conceptual problems associated with the idea of community indifference curves (CICs), this technique is used in order to exemplify the basic differences between our position and that of the DUPE literature, which has made heavy use of the technique. In figure 3–6 the CIC passing through the rent-seeking equilibrium E^1 is CIC_2. The loss in social welfare from CIC_3 to CIC_2 evaluated in terms of x_2 is given by E^1M. (In our example E^1M is equal to $0.2072n$). The DUPE theorists, however, would have us evaluate the movement from CIC_3 to CIC_1, which evaluated in terms of x_2 is E^0M. This is certainly larger than the correct measure E^1M. (In our example E^0M is equal to $0.207n + 0.2072n = 0.4142n$). Hence, by erroneously shifting the production possibilities frontier, the DUPE literature dramatically overestimates the welfare cost associated with rent-seeking.

For completeness' sake it must be pointed out that it is possible to generate an inward shift of the ppf in our model as well. Suppose, for example, that the lobbied bureaucrats, their stomachs swollen from the bribes, decide to withdraw their labor supply. This would have a number of implications. First, the feasibility region would shrink since the bribes to bureaucrats must now also be sufficiently high to compensate for the lost labor income ($a^*b \leq 0.1277$). Second, the total supply of labor will fall by a^*n_1 units. Hence, the ppf will shift in a parallel fashion by a^*n_1 units of x_2 as well. Defining the post-regulation labor supply as $n' = (1 - a^*)n_1 + n_2$, it is straightforward to calculate that $x_1 = 0.1464n'$, $x_2 = 0.8536n'$, $R = 0.2070n'$. The welfare cost, using the method of (3.35), (3.37), and (3.38) can in this case be calculated as: $L - G = 0.2072n + 1.207a^*bn$. This is clearly greater than the Harberger cost, but also less than the sum of Harberger and Tullock costs (the maximum feasible value of which is 0.3613).

This case is rather less interesting since it may not be sustainable over time. If the monopoly privilege is permanent, then there is no reason for the free lunches to continue after the vote has been won. If it is not permanent, as is implicitly assumed in our model, then there would be an incentive to the working bureaucrats to sell their votes for less than what the leisurely bureaucrat is currently receiving. Hence, over time, the latter would have to go back to work. This problem does not exist in our model because each and every period the meeting is reconvened and only a fraction of the bureaucrats is given a free lunch. The bureaucrats do not know in advance whether they are going to receive a free lunch or not, so that it is rather like a lottery: having received a free lunch in one meeting does not imply that one receives a free lunch in the next period.

Notes

1. The books are Buchanan et al (1980), and Colander (1984). Some recent articles are Benson (1984), Anderson and Hill (1983), Bhagwati (1980, 1982a, 1983), and Posner (1975). A good survey article is Tollison (1982).

2. Recent work by Tullock (1980) and others suggests that the cost of rent-seeking may be greater or less than the area of monopoly profits.

3. Rent-seeking is sometimes defined as "...the expenditure of scarce resources to capture an artificially created transfer" (Tollison, 1982) which has been created by some governmental process. But, as Tollison goes on to admit, this definition is too narrow; rent-seeking does occur also in private settings.

4. See the debate between Bhagwati (1980, 1982b), Tollison (1982), and Tullock (1981).

5. It was used, for example, by Buchanan (1980a) and Tollison (1982). In their discussion, rent-seeking takes place over a monopoly right which had been granted previously by the King. We have modified the story so that the rent-seeking takes place over the initial creation of the monopoly for reasons of expositional simplicity.

6. The only other explicit general equilibrium model with rent-seeking that we are aware of is that by Varian (1983). In that paper, he examines the implications of "lobbying" for a per-unit subsidy on a commodity which proceeds by way of expenditure on some other commodity. Varian assumes away substitution possibilities between the two commodities and does not model the lobbying process. In that sense, our model is more general than his.

7. This constant returns to scale case enables us to ignore profit redistribution issues (since profits are zero) and focus on the rent-seeking effects per se. As is shown in the text, it also obviates the restrictive assumption of non-substitution in consumption that Varian (1983) makes.

8. These values have been rounded to the nearest four decimal places.

9. The point that rent-seekers may confer benefits on other economic agents is not new. Buchanan (1980b) indicates, in passing, that the bureaucrats/politicians may be made better off by the reassignment of property rights and that as a result the welfare cost of rent-seeking should be suitably modified.

10. The integral can be written as the sum of two simple integrals:

$$\int P_1^{-1}(1 + P_1)^{-1}dP_1 = \int P_1^{-1}dP_1 - \int (1 + P_1)^{-1}dP_1 = \log |P_1| - \log |1 + P_1|$$

11. Of course, a direct consequence of equations (3.35), (3.37), and (3.38) is that the manner in which the rents are distributed does not matter in the calculation of total waste. Distribution effects *do* matter in the feasibility calculations, however.

12. In the appendix we show one possible way in which our model could generate additional waste. As is indicated there, we do not believe this case to be very interesting, since it is not sustainable over time.

References

Anderson, T.L., and Hill, P.J. "Privatizing the commons: an improvement?" *Southern Economic Journal* 50 (1983): 438–50.

Bhagwati, J.N. "Lobbying and welfare." *Journal of Public Economics* 14 (1980): 355–63.

Bhagwati, J.N. "Directly Unproductive, Profit Seeking (DUP) Activities." *Journal of Political Economy* 90 (1982a): 998–1002.

Bhagwati, J.N. "Lobbying, DUP Activities and Welfare: a response to Tullock." *Journal of Public Economics* 19 (1982b): 395–401.

Bhagwati, J.N. "DUP Activities and Rent-seeking." *Kyklos* 36 (1983): 634–637.

Bhagwati, J.N.; Brecher, R.A.; and Srinivasan, T.N. "DUP activities and economic theory." In D.C. Colander (ed.), *Neoclassical Political Economy: the Analysis of Rent-seeking and DUP Activities*. Cambridge, MA: Ballinger, 1984.

Bhagwati, J.N., and Srinivasan, T.N. "Revenue Seeking: a Generalization of the Theory of Tariffs." *Journal of Political Economy* 88 (1980): 1069–97.

Bhagwati, J.N., and Srinivasan, T.N. "Revenue Seeking: a Generalization of the Theory of Tariffs: a Correction." *Journal of Political of Economy* 90 (1982): 188–90.

Bhagwati, J.N., and Srinivasan, T.N. *Lectures on international trade*. Cambridge, MA: MIT Press, 1983.

Benson, Bruce L. "Rent Seeking from a Property Rights Perspective." *Southern Economic Journal* 51 (1984): 388–400.

Buchanan, J.M. "Rent Seeking and Profit Seeking." In: J.M. Buchanan, R.D. Tollison, and G. Tullock (eds.), *Toward a Theory of the Rent-seeking Society*. College Station: Texas A&M University Press, 1980a.

Buchanan, J.M. "Rent-seeking under External Diseconomies." In: J.M. Buchanan, R.D. Tollison, and G. Tullock (eds.), *Toward a Theory of the Rent-seeking Society*. College Station: Texas A&M University Press, 1980b.

Buchanan, J.M.; Tollison, R.D.; and Tullock, G. (eds.) *Toward a Theory of the Rent-seeking Society*. College Station: Texas A&M University Press, 1980.

Colander, D.C. (ed.) *Neoclassical Political Economy: the Analysis of Rent-seeking and DUP Activities*. Cambridge, MA: Ballinger, 1984.

Hausman, J.A. "Exact Consumer's Surplus and Deadweight Loss." *American Economic Review* 71: 662–676.

Posner, R.A. "The Social Costs of Monopoly and Regulation." *Journal of Political Economy* 83 (1975): 807–27. (Reprinted in Buchanan et. al, 1980: 71–94).

Samuels, W., and Mercuro, N. "A Critique of Rent-seeking Theory". In: D.C. Colander (ed.), *Neoclassical Political Economy: the Analysis of Rent-seeking and DUP Activities*. Cambridge, MA: Ballinger, 1984.

Tollison, R.D. "Rent-seeking: a Survey." *Kyklos* 35 (1982): 575–602.

Tullock, G. "The Welfare Costs of Tariffs, Monopolies, and Theft." *Western Economic Journal* 5 (1967): 224–32. (Reprinted in Buchanan et. al, 1980: 39–50).

Tullock, G. "Rent-seeking as a Negative-sum Game." In: J.M. Buchanan, R.D. Tollison, and G. Tullock (eds.), *Toward a Theory of the Rent-seeking Society*. College Station: Texas A&M University Press: 16–36.

Tullock, G. "Lobbying and Welfare: a Comment." *Journal of Public Economics* 16 (1981): 391–94.

Varian, H. "Models of Rent-seeking." Discussion paper no. 40 (1983), Centre of Policy Studies, Monash University.

Varian, H. *Microeconomic Analysis*, second ed. New York: W.W. Norton.

4 RENTS AND RENT-SEEKING

Gordon Tullock

Rents are a perfectly good economic category and there is absolutely nothing in general against seeking them. If I were to invent and patent a cure for cancer and then became extremely wealthy by claiming rents on the patent, most people would regard me as a public benefactor. Nevertheless, "rent-seeking" is regarded as an unadulterated evil. The reason of course is the type of rent. The rents that attract rent-seeking waste resources in static models. In dynamic settings, their injury to society is even greater. The purpose of this essay is to clearly distinguish between what we may call "good rents" and "bad rent-seeking".

But before we turn to this issue, let us look more carefully into the traditional theory of rents. For this purpose we will adopt the simplifying assumptions that there are no transactions costs and that everybody has the kind of perfect information which is customary in economics articles. Figure 4–1 shows Ricardo's pure land rent. There is a demand for wheat, shown by DD, and six tracts of land of varying fertility. The opportunity cost of producing wheat on each of them (assuming that appropriate technical decisions are made on all other factors) is shown by the line CC. The equilibrium price is P, and there is further land of even worse quality to the right of Q. It is, of course, not farmed. In each case the rent is the

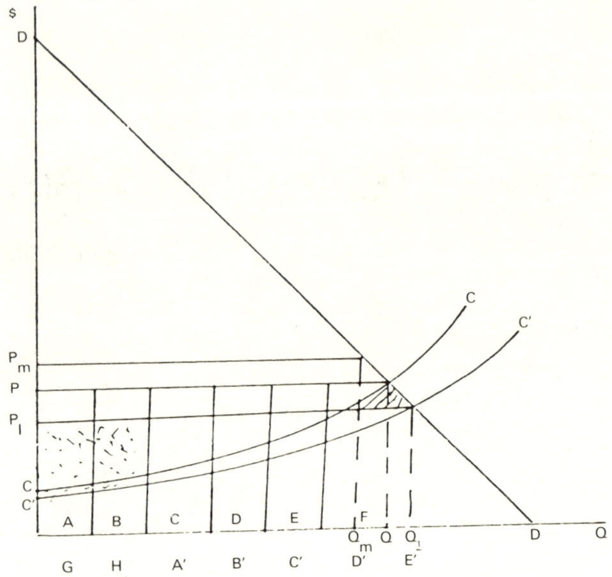

Figure 4–1

area above CC and below P and the six owners, A, B, C, D, E, and F, are collecting that rent.

Suppose now that technical innovators G and H appear and produce new land, possibly by draining the sea, or discovering America. Their land is somewhat superior to the existing land, although not very much. As a result, we rearrange our diagram so that G's and H's land is to the left, and the land of Mr. A, now rechristened A′, moves over two spaces to the right. He is still going to produce at the same cost as before, as are Mr. B, C, and D, who also have been rechristend B′, C′, and D′. F will go out of production and E, now E′, will be able to use only half of his land. The new cost curve is C′C′ which is identical to CC on the original plots of land which have been moved to the right. The new plots, G and H, have been added at the left, and have a lower cost than A and B.

With this new land in production, the new equilibrium is at the point where line C′C′ intersects the demand curve and the price is P′. Consumers have gained from the fall of the price from P to P′. All of the previous farmers have lost since the value of their land has gone down. Perhaps they will organize to restrict G and H, but we will leave that for later.

But do G and H net the rent shown by the dotted area? Probably not. The production of this new land, whether it involved draining the sea or getting into a boat and running the danger of falling off the edge of the world, was costly. People would on the average invest the present discounted value of the rent to be derived, i.e., the dotted area. Resources were invested in the search for rent and we would anticipate that these resources would in the average case approximate the present discounted value of the rent to be derived.

Resources have been invested up to the value of the rent, on plots G and H, and the net social gain from all of this is only the small shaded area on the right. This includes both the traditional welfare triangle and some costs previously incurred in producing wheat at higher than the new price on Mr. F's land. The most important effect of this technical innovation is a sizeable transfer from the owners of the previous farm land to the consumers.

But suppose, guided by Professor Coase, we had insisted on full compensation. With no transactions cost such compensation would, of course, be possible. It is obvious that transactions costs would be extremely high in the real world. Different consumers would be charged different amounts and the landholders would also have to be differentially compensated. It is, to say the least, dubious that the transactions costs could be overcome in any realistic setting.

In the real world any compensation for the owners of the former farm land would almost of necessity have to come out of the profits of the redeveloped land. It is clear that if such compensation were attempted the total resources to be invested in actually creating the new land would be very small indeed. This matter will be taken up later in connection with conflict between different lobbying groups.

The usual solution to this problem, one held by most economists, although rarely clearly expressed, is that the innovators be permitted to drive the owners of pre-existing capital out of business and that the owners of pre-existing capital not be compensated. The Western Sizzling Steak House opened in Blacksburg and drove Rustlers into bankruptcy. No one suggested that the very prosperous franchisee of the Western Sizzling Steak House should compensate the bankrupt franchisee of the Rustler.

In essence, we have a system in which any investment is to some extent risky because of the possibility that innovations, new inventions, change in social climate, etc., will make it worthless or sharply reduce its value. This of course means that the return on any capital investment includes an implicit risk premium. Note that this would be true of the capital invested for production of the new land as well as the capital already invested in the old land. In both cases, there would be an implicit risk premium with the result that the total market rate of return on capital invested in either of these activities would be somewhat higher than that on a riskless investment.

Traditionally this risk premium was visible in the difference in the dividends on common stock and the interest on government bonds. Today the prospect of inflation makes a government bond far from riskless, and the income tax makes capital gains more attractive than dividends. Thus we have no simple market measure of this implicit risk premium.

In figure 4–2 we have taken the same land and assumed the organization of a monopoly by the original landholders. This leads to the price P_m and quantity Q_m. Until the discovery of rent-seeking, the loss here would have been measured by the small triangle above line P, below P_m, and to the right of Q_m. The contribution of the rent-seeking literature from the time of "The Welfare Effects of Monopolies, Tariffs and Theft", has been that the actual cost should include the dotted rectangle which represents the resources invested in obtaining the monopoly. The traditional literature tended to ignore the possibility of true Ricardian rents in production and hence did not consider the loss of rents on land which is taken out of production as a result of the creation of the monopoly. We

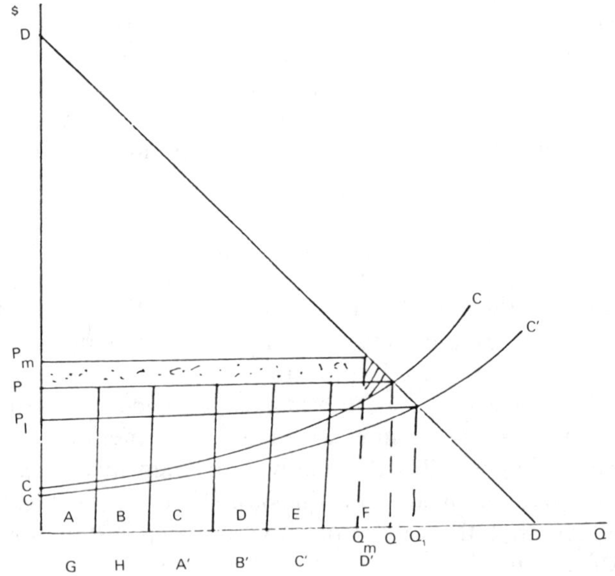

Figure 4–2

have shown this by extending the shaded triangle below P down to the line of the cost. Thus, part of the cost of organizing the monopoly from the standpoint of society as a whole is the removal of part of F's land from production. The same effect would be felt from the loss of quasi-rents on fixed factors of production in almost any newly organized monopoly.

Even in the traditional, pre-rent-seeking vein, however, both the shaded triangles in figures 4–1 and 4–2 should be counted as the social cost of creating the monopoly as opposed to the new land. This alone would be about four times as great as the Harberger triangle.

Earlier we remarked that there is an implicit risk premium in capital values. Although it will be analyzed with some care later, let us for the moment ignore it. Looked at from the standpoint of an entrepreneur who contemplated either of these investments, the monopolizing one or the creation of the new land, the situation is more or less even. In both cases, he invests the same resources, and receives only a normal return on them. In the first case, the efficiency improvement case, the largest effect is a massive transfer from the old landholders to the consumers.

If, on the other hand, he invests his resources in obtaining the monopoly, once again he obtains a normal return on his investment, but that return comes straight out of the pockets of the consumers. There is also the traditional welfare loss shown by the shaded triangle to the right of figure 4–2. If we compare the two situations it is obvious that both of these shaded areas should be included as being in the advantage for society of the innovation over the monopoly, and the usual rent-seeking arguments for including the dotted area as cost are real also. What we have done so far is to slightly increase the welfare costs given in the traditional rent-seeking literature.

The inventor or the producer of any new efficiency improvement and the lobbyist receive the fair market value of their efforts, but the value to society of their activities is radically different. In one case, they produce an externality which benefits the consumers as well as improving pure efficiency enough to cover all their costs. In the other case, they reduce efficiency while extracting their entire cost from the consumers.

We have by no means finished our analysis here. In at least one way of looking at the matter, the landholders who suffered a reduction in their rent did not actually bear a cost. I earlier mentioned that any return on investment in the modern society carries with it an implicit risk premium because the investment itself may be made obsolete by further development Schumpeter referred to this as the "perpetual gale" and Von Mises also was fond of that phrase. It is surely true in the modern world that unexpected improvements in some other person's enterprise or in some other part of the economy can make your investment much less valuable. Presumably investors take this into account.

If this is so, then what happened when the value of this land fell sharply was that the landholders in essence were forced to absorb the value of the additional payments they had previously been receiving on their investment because it was risky. They made choices between saving and expenditure in full knowledge that there was a risk on the savings. They might not get their money back, and the risk has now eventuated. There is no reason to regard this as any worse from their standpoint than the requirement on the insurance company to pay out when one of its customer's houses burns down. In both cases, no doubt, the landholder and the insurance company would rather not make the payment, but it is part of their business.

Note that the same kind of risk argument can be made with respect to the monopoly. Indeed, if we look at the real world, monopolies are probably among the least secure types of investment. Monopolies which are created by simple entrepreneurial activity in the market almost always are eliminated in time by market forces. Monopolies provided by obtaining government action, strenuous lobbying, etc., normally also are eroded over time, partly by political forces and partly by market forces. If looked at in this way, the fall in price stimulated by the technical innovation is actually a net benefit to society with no real cost. The land owners were in essence insurers of themselves, in that they were taking a larger return as a sort of premium on the prospects that their capital would fall in value.

Note that consumers here probably have the same general anticipations as the producers; i.e., they anticipate that there will be technical developments which will make them better off. It is for them, however, almost a pure gift. They do nothing to achieve this benefit. Indeed, economic growth to a very, very large extent consists of just this. The actual product rises by an amount which is must larger than the return on capital invested and we as consumers all benefit.

It is, by the way, possible that this phenomenon means that we will save more money. This is not because the return on investments are higher, but because the general rate of progress means that a dollar next year will purchase somewhat more than a dollar this year. It will be possible to buy new products or the same products at lower prices.

Although we have now a good measure of the well-being of society, particularly the consumers, being obtained from these two different kinds of investments, it is not necessarily a good measure of the well-being of individuals with resources to invest. From their standpoint, investment in attempting to obtain rents through manipulating the government or creating monopolies (or, for that matter, burning down their competitors' factory) has about the same potential return as the productive activities.

We mentioned earlier that the existing landholders who are going to have their rents reduced by the introduction of the new land might attempt to organize to prevent it from being brought into production. There is no reason that this could not be, from their standpoint, a wise investment of resources, regardless of what we think of it from the social standpoint.

Let us assume therefore that the landholders do indeed organize. In this particular case we will assume that the organization takes the form of hiring lobbyists to pressure the government to get the new land banned. Clearly, this to some extent reduces the likelihood that the new land will be brought into production. It could mean that the entrepreneurs who were bringing the new land into production (G and H in our case) would be well advised to hire their own lobbyist.

The first thing to be said about this is that if the innvoators know that there is a realistic possibility that they will have to hire a lobbyist in order to protect themselves against possible restrictions, then the innovation itself becomes somewhat less desirable. Suppose, for example, that the income to be expected from the new land (discounted to the present) was $1 million. The estimated cost of bringing the new land into production, including normal profit, is one dollar less than $1 million. On the other hand, the cost of the lobbyist will be $100,000. For simplicity we temporarily assume that if the lobbyist is sent there will be no restrictions.

Under these circumstances the innovation would not be attempted because its total cost would be $1,100,000 and its value $1 million. Only those innovations which could be made for $900,000 (including normal profit) and which would bring in $1 million would be attempted, with the result that society would be worse off.

However, the above assumption contains the unrealistic statement that the entrepreneurs know for certain that their lobbyist will be successful. In fact, all they could have would be some kind of probability distribution. As a result, innovations would only be attempted if the cost of obtaining one worth $1 million was, say, $450,000.

In practice the effect is apt to be considerably stronger. The landholders and the potential innovators would have to invest resources in lobbying in Washington to the point where the present discounted value of each, including the risks of success or failure, was equivalent to their net return. Since from the standpoint of the holders of existing land the cost of the innovation is very great, they are obviously motivated to invest in lobbying if there is any significant chance of success. Further, it should be pointed out that the existence of an organization of professional lobbyists in

Washington designed to defend the existing landholders would be a warning to potential entrants that they would have to not only produce the new land, but also run a fairly large lobbying cost and have a fairly large risk of not getting any return on their investment. Under the circumstances, the net effect of an institution which permits this kind of lobbying would be a very sharp retardation in investment in improved production methods.

So far, we have developed an argument that the cost of rent-seeking is actually twice as large as even the rent-seeking literature has normally counted it. Of course this argument could easily be extended to quality improvements or a new product rather than cost saving. There is, however, a technical difficulty having to do with the implicit risk premium on any investment. Clearly, this involves some cost to society. People do find themselves facing risks and presumably even wide diversification can not totally eliminate it.

It is not obvious whether this kind of risk would increase or decrease the total amount of savings in society. People buy insurance for which they pay more than the present discounted value of the income they will receive because they want to guarantee at least some return. This might well be true here. If the risk here did not reduce the total investment, then there would be no cost to society other than a certain amount of nervous tension.

On the other hand, the social gains from institutions which permit people simply to wipe out other persons' investment by being more efficient are obviously very great. Note that this is not truthfully a Paretian argument. Strictly speaking, persons who are injured should be compensated for their injury. It is clear that our existing landholders would think they had been injured and demand a compensation. This has been avoided in traditional literature by referring to the problem as "merely a pecuniary externality." I think that this phrase can be taken as implying an externality which we will not count or at least not require compensation for. Clearly that is my attitude toward it.

So far, we have only mentioned briefly rent-seeking aimed not at creating a monopoly but simply at protecting existing rents. It is a fairly obvious characteristic of our political process that protecting what you have is somewhat easier than acquiring a new income source or wealth. That some business will be driven out of existence if the Japanese are permitted to import something or other is far more likely to be accepted by Congress as an argument for protection than the converse, which is that the business can expand if it is protected from competition.

This being so, we do have the possibility that the existing landholders would organize to prevent the introduction of the new invention. Unfortunately, this might well lead to organization of a general cartel. It is therefore sensible before we begin talking about the conflict between the existing landholders and the potential entrant to talk about the monopolistic side of the matter. Suppose then that a monopoly has been already organized and is charging the price P_m for quantity Q_m, making a nice profit on the existing land. It is suggested that this monopoly invest resources in order to search for new plots of land which will be owned by the monopolists. Would they be interested in investing the same amount of resources as our original example, in which new land is brought in by outsiders? Unfortunately, it all depends on the details of the case.

There is a good deal of literature which indicates that monopolies always select the lowest-cost method of production, the best product, etc., but there is little on how much research they should do on producing new devices or cutting costs.

It is clear in our case that there will be very considerable gains to the monopoly by pushing the cost curve down from CC to C′C′. It is also clear that if they did push the cost curve down, the monopoly optimizing price would be somewhat lower than it is with the CC cost curve. Once again, the consumers would gain a sort of externality from technical progress. Both the monopolists and the consumers would gain, but would the monopolist be motivated to put as much resources into the search for new land as G and H in our previous example? The answer to this question unfortunately is that it all depends on the specific parameters of the problem. It is fairly easy to produce a set of cost prices and cost savings, in which the monopolist makes sizable investments. Unfortunately it is just as easy to produce a set in which the monopolist will invest much less than competitive entrepreneurs.

Still, there does not seem to be any strong argument that monopoly would be particularly slow in innovating. It might be slower than the competitive market, or it might be faster. What we can say for certain is that the price would be higher and the quantity sold lower than in a competitive market, but the rate of change in those two quantities might be as high in a monopoly as in the competitive market.

Let us return to the potential conflict between current landowners. The mere existence of the potential for conflict means that innovation almost automatically has to have a higher payoff per unit of invested capital (other than that invested in fighting your way through the regulations) than otherwise. Further, the existing well-organized groups always have an advantage.

Let us take a very brief history of the cable television industry as an example. At the very beginning of television Dumont attempted a fee-for-viewing television using a combination of over the air broadcast and the telephone lines. This failed, but, almost immediately thereafter, people began talking about connecting television by cables which would of course permit at least some direct fee collection from the viewers.

The well-organized television companies who, in the early days, frequently had congressmen on their board of directors, were able to fight off this menace. They had no particular objection to cables being laid out in areas with very poor visibility, i.e., in marginal reception areas. Thus a number of small companies developed in these marginal areas. The big television companies confined their lobbying activity to compelling these stations to carry signals of the nearest regular television stations. In essence the cable people thus raised the advertising revenue of the regular stations slightly.

With time, the number of such cable television systems increased. They formed an association and began lobbying in Washington and gradually were able to force back the restrictions which were imposed on them by the over-the-air T.V. people. This led to the present situation in which a very large part of the country is wired for cable and organizations like HBO directly transmit to the receivers. There is no doubt, however, that the development of cable was immensely impeded for a long time not by technical considerations, but by the lobbying power of the entrenched special interest.

There is, however, another aspect of this story which is even more interesting. As part of the payment for their political privileges, both the over-the-air television and the cable networks are forced to carry a good deal of material that nobody wants to watch. For example, in the cable business, there is the "rent-a-citizen" part of the expenditures of the average cable network. They characteristically devote a contractually agreed upon portion (usually fifteen percent) of their total capacity to carrying programs of local political or cultural interests. It is likely that the only people watching these programs are the families of those who happen to be featured.

They are, in essence, entertainment, and very expensive entertainment, though valuable for the people who are appearing on them. It is likely that this particular element of waste is larger in total cost to society than all the direct lobbying. This is by no means exceptional. In almost all cases in which we see active lobbying, the lobbyists not only put pressure on Congress, etc., but Congress etc., puts pressure on them and through them on their principals. The product has changed in various ways to make it more politically acceptable. "Rent-a-citizen" programs are merely a particularly clean example of this phenomenon.

The regular over-the-air television faces a very large number of regulatory restraints on its programming. Defense industries place their factories in the district of influential members of the Armed Services Committee. They may even redesign their aircraft in order to purchase components from the district of an influential congressman.

But all of this is simply a statement of how the competition goes on, not a statement about the competition between lobbying groups themselves. The diversion of resources into lobbying is, as pointed out in the early rent-seeking literature, a cost. The cost of the other improvements in our society that we do not recieve as a result of this malinvestment is also real. Turning to figures 4–1 and 4–2, the customers in figure 4–2 are worse off, not solely by the rent-seeking cost and the welfare triangles, but also by the cost of the innovation forgone. If the resources put into a new innovation must in part take the form of rent protection, this latter gain will be smaller.

Suppose, for example, that although there was no possibility of talking the government into giving the current producers a formal monopoly, it would be fairly easy to talk the government into preventing G and H from coming in and depriving them of a large part of their rent. Under these circumstances, the traditional rent-seeking losses would not occur, but the gains from the innovation would also vanish. Indeed, we might go further. It might be that the current owners are compelled to maintain a significant lobbying organization simply to protect themselves. In this case, there would be a direct wasteful outlay as well as the cost of no innovation. The cost of this protective lobbying then would not only be preventing the innovation, but also its own direct cost.

If we are to become wealthier than we are now, we must have continuous innovations. Whether these innovations take the form of new inventions or simply the opening of a Western Sizzling Steak House is unimportant from this standpoint. In both cases we need a property law in which the innovator is not hampered in introducing his innovation by the fact that his competitors will be injured. A situation in which the government may restrict innovations because they damage competitors is highly undesirable.

We also want a property system in which there is little to be gained from going to the government and lobbying for special privileges of any sort. Note the emphasis on little to be gained. The government will no doubt behave more efficiently if the people concerned with various measures inform it of their concerns. After all, it has to have some information about cost and benefit. We would like this information cost to be modest and in fact simply improve the structure of government.

When investments, in influencing the government, are capable of doing more than simply improving the efficiency of the government, then those resources will be invested. The cost will not be merely the Harberger Welfare Triangle, plus the additional welfare triangle we have added on here, plus the total cost of the resources invested in influencing the government, but also the cost of the benefit which we would have received if those resources had been invested elsewhere. It is important that the govenment provide us with a secure property system, but it is equally important that it only be secure in certain ways. The legal system of Mr. Gladstone's England, or of the United States in most of the 19th century, met this test. We are still better off in this respect than most of the world, but that is weak praise.

Further, although the property system of much of the 19th century and of the English-speaking world did tend to meet the test given above, it surely could be improved upon. Whether such improvements are in fact possible, granted the nature of the political process, is an open question. The rent-seeking literature points to problems in the market process, but these problems are very largely the product of problems in the political process. A cure must proceed in both areas simultaneously.

II THEORETICAL DEVELOPMENTS

5 THE SOCIAL COSTS OF MONOPOLY AND REGULATION: A GAME-THEORETIC ANALYSIS

William P. Rogerson

Introduction

Suppose that a regulatory board meets every period and assigns the monopoly franchise for an industry to one of a competing number of entrants; the successful firm then earns π dollars in monopoly profits for that period. The theory of rent-seeking suggests that firms will in the aggregate spend some fraction of π dollars competing for the franchise by hiring lawyers, making presentations, etc. To the extent that these resources are misallocated, they represent a social cost of monopoly in addition to the normal deadweight loss.

Posner (1975, p. 812) asserts that firms' expenditures will tend to be equal to π:

> If ten firms are vying for a monopoly having a present value of $1 million, and each of them has an equal chance of obtaining it and is risk neutral, each will spend $100,000 (assuming constant costs) on trying to obtain the monopoly. Only one will succeed and *his* costs will be much smaller than the monopoly profits, but the total costs of obtaining the monopoly—counting losers' expenditures as well as winners'—will be the same as under certainty.

The major purpose of this article is to show that this is a more sweeping statement than is warranted. It establishes the accounting identity that the firms' expected aggregate profits from the regulatory game are equal to the untransformed rents. Therefore, asking whether some rents are not transformed is equivalent to asking whether profits are earned in the regulatory game. This article shows that there are at least two respects in which firms can be inframarginal and thus earn profits.

First, different firms may face different fixed organization costs in forming an organization and acquiring the necessary information to participate in the rent-seeking process. For example, a firm which has participated in other regulatory hearings concerning related technologies might experience almost no start-up costs. The extreme case of differential start-up costs is the case where n firms have no fixed costs and all other firms have infinite fixed costs. For this case that firms' expectations are less than π and approach π as n goes to ∞. And, more generally, that to the extent there are differential fixed costs, firms' expenditures will be less than π. Firms with low fixed costs possess a scarce resource and these inframarginal firms earn rents.

Second, firms may be inframarginal with respect to incumbency. Last year's franchise holder may well possess an advantage in this year's hearings because it has been able to establish a relationship with its regulators or to obtain extra information. Because potential entrants would perceive their chances of success as smaller, such an incumbency advantage might be expected to reduce entrants' expenditures in vying for the monopoly and thus reduce the social costs of monopoly. Posner (1975) correctly pointed out that an incumbency advantage would also make the prize worth more and thus encourage expenditures.[1] The accounting identity of Section 2 sheds light on the net effect of these two factors by shifting the focus from expenditures to profits. Section 3 shows that the incumbent in such a game could well earn positive discounted profits, even if an infinite number of potential entrants with identical fixed costs exist. To the extent that this occurs, rents remain untransformed.

One response to these two factors would be to push Posner's arguments one stage further back. The existence of an incumbent and/or differential fixed costs is exogenously given in this model. If firms competed to gain an initial incumbency advantage or firms spent money to lower their fixed costs in anticipation of the regulatory game, we might observe untransformed rents being competed away at this earlier stage. Two points should be noted. First, many regulatory agencies are created to regulate firms already in existence. Second, the rent transformation argument requires that firms anticipate the size of rents being competed for. Williamson (1977) was the first to make this point. He argues that "whether the full-transformation or incomplete-transformation scenario is the more accurate, one depends in the final analysis on the computational powers of economic agents in relation to the degree of complexity and uncertainty with which they are expected to contend." (p. 721) Pushing the competition further and further back in time increases the uncertainty with which agents can estimate rents and thus makes them less likely to be competed away.

Finally, it is shown that a unique degree of incumbency advantage maximizes firms' expenditures and furthermore that the maximizing degree of advantage varies in predictable ways with other observable characteristics of the game. This knowledge is not particularly interesting for the regulatory game where the degree of advantage is not necessarily changeable and goals such as obtaining information may be as important as minimizing expenditures. However, it is argued that the model can be interpreted as an R&D game where the successful innovator in one period has an advantage in the pursuit of subsequent innovations. The degree of this advantage can be affected by the government through changes in trade secrets legislation and disclosure requirements on government-sponsored research. The results of this section suggest a manner in which government might want to offer differing degrees of incumbency advantage across differing industries, depending on the value of certain observable characteristics of the industries.

The General Case

We wish to model the idealized situation where n firms compete for the right to operate a monopoly franchise which generates profits. At the start of each period, a government agency assigns rights to the franchise for that period. Firms spend money attempting to influence this decision.

Formally, we construct an n-person infinite period game. There are n states; let state j be the state where firm j is currently the monopolist. Let x_{ij} be the amount of money spent by firm i when state j occurs. The state space and firms' strategies are stationary. They are not dependent on t. A firm's probability of obtaining the franchise will clearly depend upon its and others' lobbying expenditures. It may also depend upon the state of the world. For example, a firm's chances of success may be greater if it is the monopolist, because it now has greater knowledge and expertise or because it has established a relationship with its regulators. Let f_{ij} be the probability of firm i's succeeding in state j; f_{ij} is a function of $(x_{1j}, \ldots, x_{nj})$. It must be true for every $(x_{1j}, \ldots, x_{nj})$ that

$$\sum_{i=1}^{n} f_{ij} = 1 \text{ for all } j \tag{5.1}$$

$$f_{ij} \geq 0 \text{ for all } i, j. \tag{5.2}$$

Let π be the profits that the successful firm earns in a period by operating the franchise.

Firm i selects the strategy vector $(x_{i1}^*, \ldots, x_{in}^*)$. That is, firm i spends x_{ij}^* if state j occurs. Let θ_{ij} be firm i's probability of success in state j with the given strategies:

$$\theta_{ij} = f_{ij}(x_{1j}^*, x_{2j}^*, \ldots, x_{nj}^*). \tag{5.3}$$

Let θ be the matrix with (i, j) entry of θ_{ij}:

$$\theta = [\theta_{ij}]. \tag{5.4}$$

By (5.1) and (5.2) θ is a stochastic matrix. The associated stochastic process is the one that determines which firm will be the monopolist for each period.

Such a matrix always has a steady-state solution—a vector $\gamma = [\gamma_1, \ldots, \gamma_n]$ such that

$$\text{(i) } \gamma_i \geq 0 \text{ for all } i \tag{5.5}$$

$$\text{(ii) } \sum_{i=0}^{n} \gamma_i = 1 \tag{5.6}$$

$$\text{(iii) } \gamma = \theta\gamma. \tag{5.7}$$

The steady state may not be unique; as well, the stochastic process may actually converge to some sort of cycle. However, at a minimum, the average of the cycle which the stochastic process converges to equals one of the steady states. Therefore, one of the steady states describes the long-run average probability distribution which the stochastic process will exhibit. (Which steady state does this depends on the initial point.) Long-run expected values for this process are therefore calculated by using one of the steady-state distributions. See Gantmacher (1960) for a complete discussion of these points.

Before stating and proving the main theorem of this section, more notation needs to be introduced. Let θ_{ij}^t be the probability of firm i's becoming the monopolist in period t, given that firm j is currently the monopolist. That is, θ_{ij}^t is the (i, j) entry of θ^t. Let R_{ij}^t be the expected profit to firm i in period t, given that the world is currently in state j. These returns can be defined recursively as follows:

$$R_{ij}^1 = \theta_{ij}\pi - x_{ij}^* \tag{5.8}$$

$$R_{ij}^t = \sum_{k=1}^{n} \theta_{kj}^{t-1} R_{ik}^1, \qquad t = 2, 3, \ldots. \tag{5.9}$$

Assume that all firms calculate the value of the game by summing discounted expected profits with firm i using the discount rate c_i. Let V_{ij} be the value of the game to firm i in state j:

$$V_{ij} = \sum_{t=1}^{\infty} c_i^{t-1} R_{ij}^t. \tag{5.10}$$

Finally, let S_j be the surplus of π over total firm expenditures which occurs in state j:

$$S_j = \pi - \sum_{i=1}^{n} x_{ij}^*. \tag{5.11}$$

We can now prove the accounting identity for this game. The long-run expected surplus that this game generates is a nonnegative weighted sum of the values $\{V_{ij}\}$.

Theorem 1. Let γ be a steady-state solution to θ. Then

$$\sum_{j=1}^{n} \gamma_j S_j = \sum_{i=1}^{n} \sum_{j=1}^{n} \gamma_j (1 - c_i) V_{ij}. \tag{5.12}$$

Proof. The value functions must all satisfy

$$V_{ij} = R_{ij}^1 + c_i \sum_{k=1}^{n} \theta_{kj} V_{ik}. \tag{5.13}$$

Sum this over indices as required, using (5.7). *Q.E.D.*

The value of the game to every player must always be nonnegative if we assume that the strategy of doing nothing at zero cost is available to each player. Therefore, the right-hand side of (5.12) is nonnegative and so is the left-hand side. As a result, the long-run expected surplus of π over total expenditures is nonnegative.

Note that V_{ij} is the present discounted value to player i from being in state j. Therefore, $(1 - c_i)V_{ij}$ is the "annual value" of this multiyear value and $\sum_{i=1}^{n} (1 - c_i)V_{ij}$ represents the aggregate annual profits for the firms in state j. Equation (5.12) therefore states that the long-run expected surplus (left-hand side) equals the long-run expected annual aggregate profits (right-hand side). That is, expenditures fall short of π to the extent that firms make positive expected profits.

A Special Case: No Fixed Costs

The remainder of the article deals with a special case where the f_{ij} functions are given a particular functional form. This section makes the additional assumption that fixed costs of entry into the game are zero for $n + 1$ firms and infinite for all others. Let f_{ij} be given by

$$f_{ij}(0, \ldots, 0) = 0 \tag{5.14}$$

and by

$$f_{ij}(x_{1j}, \ldots, x_{n+1,j}) = \begin{cases} \dfrac{\beta x_{ij}}{\beta x_{ij} + \sum_{k \neq j} x_{kj}}, & i = j \\ \dfrac{x_{ij}}{\beta x_{ij} + \sum_{k \neq j} x_{kj}}, & i \neq j \end{cases} \tag{5.15}$$

for every $(x_{1j}, \ldots, x_{n+1,j}) \neq 0$, where β is some real number greater than or equal to 1. Each firm's chance of obtaining the franchise is simply the proportion of total lobbying expenditures that it accounts for weighted by 1 if it is not currently the monopolist and by β if it is the current monopolist. For any fixed vector of expenditures $(x_{ij}, \ldots, x_{n+1,j})$ it is easy to see that f_{ij} decreases in β for $i \neq j$ and increases in β for $i = j$. Therefore, to the extent that β is greater than 1, the current monopolist has an advantage in regulatory hearings to determine the next franchise holder. All potential entrants receive equal treatment. Each firm faces the same return function if it becomes the monopolist. This is, therefore, in some sense the simplest specification of a case where the monopolist has an advantage.[2] As well, assume that each firm uses the same discount rate, c.

We shall use the Nash equilibrium concept.

Definition. The strategy vectors $\{x_1^*, \ldots, x_{n+1}^*\}$ are equilibrium strategies if for every i and j, x_i^* satisfies

$$V_{ij}(x_i^*, \ldots, x_i^*, \ldots, x_{n+1}^*) = \sup_{x_i \in R_+^{n+1}} V_{ij}(x_1^*, \ldots, x_i, \ldots, x_{n+1}^*). \tag{5.16}$$

That is, x_i^* must maximize $(V_{i1}, \ldots, V_{i,n+1})$ given others' behavior. Note that the domain of x_i is R_+^{n+1} (where $R_+ = [0, \infty)$). In particular, the firm always has the option of doing nothing at zero cost and zero return.

A possible criticism of this definition is that it does not allow firms to consider nonstationary strategies. A nonstationary strategy for firm i would be an infinite vector of n-tuples $(x_i^1, x_i^2, \ldots)$, where x_i^t is the n-tuple representing firm i's strategy at time t. Fortunately, an equilibrium in the game where firms are restricted to stationary strategies is also an equilibrium in the game where firms are allowed to choose nonstationary strategy. If firm i observes all the other firms' choosing a stationary strategy, it finds itself facing a stationary dynamic program and can do no better by using a nonstationary strategy than a stationary one. (See Denardo (1967) for proof of this.) Therefore, the equilibrium defined above is more robust than the formal definition indicates.

Recall from (5.13) that the return functions are particularly simple—a firm's probability of winning is not affected by which of the others is the monopolist so long as they all spend the same. Therefore, we might hope for a particularly simple sort of equilibrium to occur; each firm's strategy is one number, x_e, if it is an entrant and another number, x_m, if it is the monopolist. We shall call this a symmetric equilibrium.

Definition. An equilibrium $\{x_i^*\}_{i=1}^{n+1}$ is a symmetric equilibrium if there exist two numbers x_e and x_m such that for every i and j

$$x_{ij}^* = \begin{cases} x_e, & i \neq j \\ x_m, & i = j \end{cases}. \tag{5.17}$$

The major result of this section is the constructive proof of the existence and uniqueness of such a symmetric equilibrium. Since each player has the same strategy and it only varies as he is the entrant or monopolist, it will be seen that all of the variables indexed by (i, j) will only assume two values. We shall employ the notational convenience of indexing them by "e" or "m" for the state of being the entrant or the monopolist, respectively.

Theorem 2. The unique[3] symmetric equilibrium for $n \in \{1, 2, 3 \ldots\}$ is:

$$x_e = \frac{\beta n \pi}{an^2 + 2bn + 1} \tag{5.18}$$

$$x_m = \left(n - \frac{n-1}{\beta}\right) x_e, \tag{5.19}$$

where

$$a = c(2\beta - 1) + (1 - c)\beta^2 \tag{5.20}$$

$$b = c + (1 - c)\beta. \tag{5.21}$$

other variables assume the following values (uniquely):

$$\theta_e = \frac{1}{\beta n + 1} \tag{5.22}$$

$$\theta_m = \frac{\beta_n + 1 - n}{\beta n + 1} \tag{5.23}$$

$$V_e = \frac{\pi}{(1 - c)(an^2 + 2bn + 1)} \tag{5.24}$$

$$V_m = [(1 - c)(\beta^2 - (2\beta - 1))n^2 + 2(1 - c)(\beta - 1)n + 1]V_e. \tag{5.25}$$

Proof: See the Appendix.

The untransformed rents are equal to

$$\pi - nx_e - x_m. \tag{5.26}$$

It is easy to show that $nx_e + x_m$ increases with the number of firms, n. As n goes to infinity, aggregate expenditures are

$$\frac{2\beta - 1}{\beta^2 - c(\beta - 1)^2}\pi. \tag{5.27}$$

This number equals π when β is 1, equals 0 when β goes to ∞, and decreases for values of β in $[1, \infty]$. Therefore, untransformed rents are always positive. They are smaller if there are more potential entrants. If the incumbent has no advantage, untransformed rents go to zero as n increases. However to the extent that there is an incumbency advantage, a progressively higher floor is created for the size of untransformed rents which bounds them strictly away from zero.

The duality between untransformed rents and firms' profits provides the intuition for these results. The accounting identity proven in Theorem 1 for this particular example is

$$\pi - nx_e - x_m = (1 - c)(nV_e + V_m). \tag{5.28}$$

That is, untransformed rents equal the annualized expected present discounted value of the n entrants and one incumbent from playing the game. As n increases, competition drives the aggregate values of the entrants, nV_e, to zero. However, to the extent the incumbent has an advantage, even an infinite number of potential entrants cannot reduce his discounted expected profits to zero.

A Special Case with Fixed Costs

The sources of incomplete rent transformation. This subsection uses the same functional form for the f_{ij} functions as Section 5–3, but relaxes the particular assumption about fixed costs made in that section. A firm with positive fixed start-up costs will participate in the hearings if and only if V_e exceeds its costs. Firms with progressively larger fixed costs will join the game and thereby reduce V_e until entry is no longer profitable. Formally, assume that there are N possible participants in the game, where N can be ∞. Index members of the set by i in such a way that firms with lower fixed costs have lower index numbers. Let $F(i)$ be firm i's fixed costs. Then n^* is an equilibrium number of nonincumbent firms (for a total of $n^* + 1$ firms) if two conditions are satisfied. First, every firm must make nonnegative profits as a nonincumbent (or there must be no nonincumbent players):

$$n^* = 0 \qquad \text{or} \qquad F(n^* + 1) \leq V_e(n^*). \tag{5.29}$$

Second, any other firm which contemplated entering the game would make negative profits (or all N − 1 firms are nonincumbent players):

$$n^* = N - 1 \qquad \text{or} \qquad F(n^* + 2) > V_e(n^* + 1). \tag{5.30}$$

Since V_e is decreasing in n, continuous, and zero in the limit and since F is nondecreasing, it is easy to see that an equilibrium number of nonincumbent players always exists and is unique.

With nonzero fixed costs, annualized fixed costs now need to be included in the rent transformation equation. If there are n nonincumbent firms, the surplus of π over expenditures is

$$\pi - nx_e(n) - x_n(n) - (1 - c) \sum_{i=1}^{n+1} F(i), \tag{5.31}$$

which, by the accounting identity of (5.26) is equal to

$$(1 - c)\left[nV_e(n) + V_m(n) - \sum_{i=1}^{n-1} F(i) \right]. \tag{5.32}$$

Expression (5.32) can be divided into two terms as follows:

$$(1 - c)[\sum_{i=1}^{n+1} (V_e(n) - F(i))] + (1 - c)[V_m(n) - V_e(n)]. \tag{5.33}$$

The first term of (5.33) represents annualized rents accruing to firms which are inframarginal with respect to fixed costs. As in any situation generating inframarginal rents, smaller numbers of firms with low fixed costs will increase the amount of inframarginal rent earned by them.

The second term of (5.33) represents the annualized rents accruing to the incumbent because of his incumbency advantage. From Section 5–3, $V_m(n) - V_e(n)$ is always greater than or equal to $\lim_{n \to \infty} V_m(n)$[4] which is positive. In fact, $\lim_{n \to \infty} V_m(n)$ can be made arbitrarily close to $\pi/(1 - c)$ by increasing β.

Comparative statics of fixed cost. In this subsection the effect of an increase in all firms' fixed costs is considered. Since the equilibrium number of players is a nonincreasing function of the level of fixed costs, the results of Section 5–3 imply that the surplus of π over $nx_e + x_m$ is a nondecreasing function of the level of fixed costs. As fixed costs rise, the smaller number of players results in less rent transformation into annual expenditures.

Although lowering fixed costs increases the amount of π eaten up by annual expenditures, this does not fully describe the transformation process. Fixed expenditures should also be considered as rent transformation, if they are actually made. When fixed organizational costs suddenly drop for an existing regulatory process, existing firms which joined the regulatory game previously cannot retroactively reduce their fixed expenditures. The only effect will be to induce marginal firms to enter the game. Therefore, aggregate expenditures on fixed costs will rise along with expenditures on annual costs, and the surplus of π over total expenditures will fall. When fixed organizational costs suddenly rise for an existing regulatory process, existing firms will not have to pay more fixed costs or be induced to leave the game. Obviously no new firms will be induced to enter, and, as a consequence, expenditures on fixed costs will not change. Therefore, the surplus of π over total expenditures will rise.

Finally, we need to compare two regulatory processes which have always had different fixed costs of entry but are similar in other respects. In this case, the decrease in fixed costs and increase in annual expenditures work in opposite directions, and no unambiguous prediction concerning the effects on the amount of rent transformation is possible. Two examples illustrate this. First, consider a case where $n + 1$ firms have zero fixed costs, and the remainder of the firms have infinite fixed costs. Lowering fixed costs corresponds to making n larger. In this case firms' profits are $nV_e(n) + V_m(n)$. This sum decreases in n. Therefore, as fixed costs drop (rise) the amount of rent transformation increases (decreases). Second, consider a case where fixed costs fall only for inframarginal firms, but remain unchanged for the marginal firm and extramarginal firms. It is clear that the equilibrium number of firms, V_e, and V_m are not affected. Therefore, total profits of all firms rise, and the amount of rent transformation increases.

In summary, when comparing two existing regulatory processes with different fixed costs, the process with lower fixed costs will have more players and higher annual expenditures. However, if costs are calculated by including annualized fixed costs, either process might exhibit larger expenditures and thus more rent transformation.

Comparative Statics of β5

Corollary 1 summarizes the effects of β on aggregate expenditures.

Corollary 1. There exists a function,

$$\gamma\colon \{1, 2, 3, \ldots, N-1\} \times [0, 1] \to [1, \infty],$$

such that

$$\text{(i)}\ \beta < \gamma(n, c) \Rightarrow \frac{\partial}{\partial\beta}(nx_e + x_m) > 0$$

$$\beta = \gamma(n, c) \Rightarrow \frac{\partial}{\partial\beta}(nx_e + x_m) = 0 \qquad (5.34)$$

$$\beta > \gamma(n, c) \Rightarrow \frac{\partial}{\partial\beta}(nx_e + x_m) < 0$$

$$\text{(ii)}\ \frac{\partial\gamma}{\partial n} < 0 \qquad (5.35)$$

$$\text{(iii)}\ \frac{\partial\gamma}{\partial c} > 0. \qquad (5.36)$$

Proof. From Theorem 2 we can write

$$\frac{\partial}{\partial\beta}(nx_e + x_m) = \frac{-2n^4(1-c)\beta^2 + 2n^3(1-c)\beta + 2n^3 + cn^2}{(an^2 + 2bn + 1)^2} \qquad (5.37)$$

From this, it follows that if we define

$$\delta(\beta, n) = \frac{\beta n^2(\beta - 1) + \beta n - n}{\beta n^2(\beta - 1) + \beta n + 1}, \qquad (5.38)$$

then

$$\text{(i)}\ c \lesseqqgtr \delta \quad \text{according as} \quad \frac{\partial(nx_e + x_m)}{\partial\beta} \lesseqqgtr 0, \qquad (5.39)$$

$$\text{(ii) for every } (\beta, n) \in (1, \infty) \times \{1, 2, 3 \ldots\},\ 0 \le \delta(\beta, n) < 1, \qquad (5.40)$$

$$\text{(iii)}\ \frac{\partial\delta}{\partial\beta} > 0, \qquad \frac{\partial\delta}{\partial n} > 0. \qquad (5.41)$$

Define γ implicitly by

$$c = \delta(\gamma(c, n), n). \; Q.E.D. \tag{5.41}$$

The effect of β on aggregate expenditures can be conceptually separated into a short-run and long-run effect. In the short run increasing the incumbent's advantage increases the incumbent's chances of winning and reduces the attractiveness of expenditures for everyone. However, in the longer run the prize of winning is more attractive, because the incumbent finds it easier to maintain his position; this should increase firms' expenditures. Result (i) is that the long-run effect dominates for small values of β, but eventually aggregate expenditures begin to fall with β.

Result (ii) says that increasing the number of players in the game reduces the relative influence of the long-run effect. The reasons for this are not clear. *A priori* reasoning suggests any result could be possible. Result (iii) is more intuitive; as all firms discount the future more heavily, the influence of the short-run effect becomes larger.

Applications

A theory of regulation which assumes that no rents are transformed would suggest that the regulator be careful to set π as low as possible to minimize deadweight loss in the regulated market. A theory which takes rent transformation into account, but which assumes that all of the firms' expenditures have no social value, simply adds another reason for setting π close to zero. However, at least some of the expenditures by firms may be socially useful. For example, firms may spend money on designing better products or generating useful information for the regulatory agency in the process of competing with one another. This view provides a rationale for choosing π to be positive. The regulator is essentially funding firms' expenditures from participating in the regulatory process through choosing π to be greater than zero.

In this model, the regulator views its choice of π and its choices of rules and procedures which affect β and the level of fixed costs as one coordinated plan to maximize social surplus.[6] The aggregate level of expenditures can be directly affected by choosing π. Therefore, the goals of the regulator in choosing β and the level of fixed costs should be to (i) increase the fraction of rents transformed and (ii) alter the patterns of expenditures in ways which increase their social usefulness. The rationale for the first goal is that, for a given level of aggregate expenditures, increases in the fraction of π transformed allow π to be chosen smaller and thus deadweight loss in the regulated market to be reduced.

The first goal suggests that a regulatory process should be designed so that the assignment procedure is as competitive as possible; as many potential entrants as possible should be encouraged to participate and, especially if there are many entrants, the incumbency advantage should be as low as possible. The second goal, however, may conflict with the first. For example, if there are increasing returns to scale in preparing a well-planned service or a well-designed product, increasing the fixed costs of at least some potential entrants (possibly by simply arbitrarily excluding all but a small number) could alter the pattern of expenditures in a desirable manner. Although aggregate expenses would fall, average expenses per firm would rise.

This article can also be interpreted as modeling certain aspects of the R&D process. At the beginning of each period, firms each decide how much money to spend on R&D for that period. A firm's probability of discovering a profitable new product increases as its expenditures increase and decreases as its competitor's expenditures increase. The expected revenues of the firm therefore depend on the expenditures of that firm relative to all other firms. Furthermore, success in the past period gives a firm a head start in this period's R&D. The size of β measures the size of this advantage.

Government has some control over the size of β in an industry. Trade secrets legislation and disclosure rules for government-funded research clearly affect β. By having more stringently enforced trade secrets legislation or by not requiring firms operating under government contracts to make their research public, the government grants the winning firm an increased advantage relative to its opponents in the next round. Note that the role of trade secrets legislation is distinct from any role the government may play relating to the appropriability of an invention. (Firms cannot copy an invention if some aspect of it is secret.) In the model, this second effect simply amounts to ensuring that the winning firm actually receives π. The first effect of increasing β is separate.

Corollary 1 shows that a unique level of β exists which maximizes R&D expenditures. Furthermore, it increases with the discount rate and decreases with the number of firms. Therefore, if the government wanted to use trade secrets legislation as a spur to innovative activity,[7] it might choose different levels of enforcement in different types of industries. For example, trade secrets legislation may be more important in smaller industries as an incentrive for innovative activity. As regards the discount rate, if we hold the time discount rate over continuous time constant and increase the rate of innovative activity, we shorten the length of each period and thus increase the discount rate in our discrete model. Therefore, this model suggests that industries characterized by rapid innovative activity need stricter trade secrets legislation and fewer disclosure requirements on government-sponsored research to induce greater R&D effort than industries characterized by a slower pace of innovative activity.

Appendix

Proof of theorem 2

Only an outline of the proof is given here. A complete proof appears in Rogerson (1981).

The standard approach for calculating a symmetric Nash equilibrium is followed. First we characterized firm *i*'s optimal strategy, given fixed strategies of the other firms. Then we solve for a strategy vector of the required form such that firm *i* will choose it, given that other firms have chosen it.

The functional equation of dynamic programming (Denardo, 1967) is used to characterize firm *i*'s optimal choice. Let the other firms' choices be given by $\{x_j^*\}_{j \neq i}$. Suppose that firm *i* chooses x_{ij} in state *j* and that y_j is the present discounted value to firm *i*, given it is in state *j*. Firm *i*'s choice of strategy determines the transition probabilities. We shall write $\theta_{ij}(x_{ij})$ to show this dependence. The immediate expected payoff to firm *i* is the expected return from winning minus its expenditure:

$$\theta_{ij}(x_{ij})\pi - x_{ij}. \tag{A.5.1}$$

As well, firm *i* will find itself in state *k* with probability $\theta_{ij}(x_{ij})$ next period. The expected present discounted value of this is

$$(1 - c) \sum_{k=1}^{n+1} \theta_{kj}(x_{ij})y_k. \tag{A.5.2}$$

Let $g_{ij}(x_{ij}, y_1, \ldots, y_{n+1})$ denote the total present discounted value of state *j* to firm *i*, which is the sum of these two terms. The functional equation of dynamic programming says that x_i^* is an optimal strategy for firm *i* with associated values $(y_i^*, \ldots, y_n^*)$ if and only if for every $j = 1, \ldots, n + 1$,

(i) x_{ij}^* maximizes $g_{ij}(x_{ij}, y_1^*, \ldots, y_{n+1}^*)$ over $x_{ij}^* \in [0, \infty]$

and

(ii) $y_j^* = g_{ij}(x_{ij}^*, y_1^*, \ldots, y_{n+1}^*)$.

Part (i) states that x_{ij}^* must maximize g_{ij}, since g_{ij} determines the value of state j to firm i. However, y_j^*, is supposed to be this value. Therefore, (ii) must also hold.

It is now straightforward (at least conceptually, if not algebraically) to write out explicitly the g_{ij}'s and solve for a symmetric equilibrium.

Notes

1. See Section III.7. For example, on p. 824 Posner states: "Consider, for example, a market that is a natural monopoly.... [Social] costs can be reduced, however, by a rule limiting entry.... But the rule is not very satisfactory.... [T]he more efficient the rule at keeping out new entrants at low cost to the monopolist, the greater will be the expected value of having a natural monopoly—and, hence, the greater will be the resources that firms expend on trying to become the first to occupy a natural monopoly market."

2. It is possible to solve the game explicitly when each x_{ij} is weighted by some constant β_{ij}. However, it is not clear how to interpret this more general specification so the simpler model is presented.

3. For the case $c = 0$ (when the world ends after the first period) the symmetric equilibrium is in fact the unique equilibrium. Therefore, although it has not been shown that the symmetric equilibrium is the unique equilibrium for the case of $c \geq 1$, the solution is a generalization of the unique solution for the one-period case.

4. To see this it is sufficient to show that $(\partial/\partial n)[(V_m(n) - V_e(n))] \leq 0$. From Theorem 2.

$$\frac{\partial}{\partial n}(V_m(n) - V_e(n)) = \frac{-\beta n^2 + (\beta - 1)n + 1}{(an^2 + 2bn + 1)^2}\pi,$$

which can be shown to be negative.

5. For simplicity of presentation, the case where $n + 1$ firms have zero fixed costs and all others have infinite fixed costs is formally considered. To the extent that reducing β induces entry, reducing β might be generally more desirable. The qualitative propositions of this analysis, however, are unchanged.

6. Of course, various equity considerations are also likely to be important.

7. Of course, government would not necessarily desire to stimulate R&D effort in all industries. To evaluate whether increased R&D expenditures would be welfare improving and then to determine an optimal value for β would require explicit modeling of the R&D production function so that such factors as potential duplication of effort and economies of scale could be taken into account. See Scherer (1980) for a discussion of market structure and R&D and for references to other sources. This article simply identifies how government might use trade secrets legislation as a spur to innovative activity.

References

Denardo, E.V. "Contraction Mappings in the Theory Underlying Dynamic Programming." *SIAM Review* 9 (1967): 165–77.

Gantmacher, F. R. *The Theory of Matrices*, Vol. II. New York: Chelsea Publishing Company, 1960.

Krueger, A. O. "The Political Economy of the Rent-Seeking Society." *American Economic Review* 64 (1974): 291–303.

Marris, R. and Mueller, D. C. "The Corporation, Competition, and the Invisible Hand." *Journal of Economic Literature* (March 1980): 32–63.

Posner, R. "The Social Costs of Monopoly and Regulation." *Journal of Political Economy* 83 1975: 807–27.

Scherer, F. M. *Industrial Market Structure and Economic Performance*. Chicago: Rand McNally College Publishing Company, 1980.

Tullock, G. "The Welfare Costs of Tariffs, Monopolies, and Theft." *Western Economic Journal* 5 (1967): 224–32.

Williamson, O. E. "Economies as an Antitrust Defense Revisited." *University of Pennsylvania Law Review* 125 (1977): 699–736.

6 RISK-AVERSE RENT SEEKERS AND THE SOCIAL COST OF MONOPOLY POWER

Arye L. Hillman and Eliakim Katz

There is now quite general recognition that the social cost of monopoly power encompasses the resources expended by individuals seeking to become the beneficiaries of monopoly rents. However, since the activity of rent seeking is generally not observable, direct estimates of resources expended in quests to acquire monopoly power are usually impossible to come by.[1] As a consequence, the indirect approach of taking the observed value of monopoly rents as indicative of the unobserved value of the resources expended in rent seeking is quite generally adopted in approaches to evaluation of the social cost of such activity.

When a particular rent is biddable and the resources used in rent-seeking have positive shadow prices, competitive rent-seeking by risk-neutral rent seekers results in complete rent dissipation and the full amount of rent reflects a social loss. In some instances rents are not biddable but are preassigned, as for example where the premium-carrying import licences and revenues analysed by Krueger (1974) and Bhagwati and Srinivasan (1980) are preallocated. Then the incentive to expend resources in rent-seeking is clearly absent. Also, the general theory of directly unproductive profit-seeking activities as expounded by Bhagwati (1982) makes clear that because of intrinsic second-best considerations resources used in rent-seeking may not have positive shadow prices, implying that individuals' quests to secure biddable rents need not always entail socially wasteful activity. When neither of these qualifications are pertinent, so that biddable rents are sought using positively-valued resources, rent dissipation will still nevertheless be less than complete if rent-seeking is not perfectly competitive: Tullock (1980) has shown how, in small-numbers cases, substantial portions of biddable rents may remain undissipated as a consequence of game-theoretic considerations.

Suppose that perfectly competitive rent-seeking takes place in quest of a biddable rent, with socially positively valued resources being expended. Then there remains the question of the effect of attitudes to risk on rent dissipation. Uncertainty is intrinsic in a competitive quest to attain a biddable monopoly rent, since the rent by its nature accrues indivisibly to the one rent seeker who is to be ultimate monopolist. In face of this uncertainty rent seekers may quite reasonably be risk averse, and, if this is so, individual rent seekers will allocate less to a particular rent-seeking quest than the expected value of the gain from the activity.

However, although individual allocations to rent-seeking are reduced as a consequence of risk aversion, in a competitive environment a large number of individuals is nevertheless each allocating some resources (perhaps ε) in the quest to obtain a biddable rent. So to what extent, then, will a biddable rent be dissipated by competitive rent-seeking when rent seekers are risk averse? Should competitive rent dissipation be revealed to remain more or less complete notwithstanding risk aversion on the part of rent seekers, then the procedure of equating the observed value of monopoly profits to the value of the resources expended in the quest for monopoly power would be provided with some justification. But the procedure of taking observed monopoly profits as a guide to the social cost of monopoly power due to rent-seeking would be called into question if as a consequence of risk aversion rent dissipation were to be substantially reduced.

To address this issue of the effect of risk aversion on the appropriateness of taking the value of a particular rent as indicative of the value of the resources expended in seeking that rent, we derived earlier a limiting expression describing competitive rent dissipation when rent seekers are risk averse and proceed to show how rent dissipation is sensitive to both the degree of risk aversion and to initial wealth. The limiting expression is valid only for small rents. By introducing a particular form for rent seekers' utility functions (logarithmic utility), we were able via direct computation to provide illustrative values for rent dissipation when monopoly rents are large. A brief concluding summary will be then presented later.

The focus of our analysis will be on competitive rent-seeking. However, an appendix demonstrates how risk aversion can be introduced into the strategic rent-seeking settings investigated by Tullock.

Competition for Small Rents

We shall consider a market which is monopolised and which yields, as a result of monopolistic profit maximisation, a monopoly profit of value X.[2] The right to monopoly power which allows this monopoly rent to be secured is taken to be biddable, and we suppose that any of n firms might potentially secure the rent. Of the n firms, only one can be the ultimately successful monopolist. No firm is assured of success, and hence any firm seeking to acquire the monopoly power in question confronts uncertainty. Given this uncertainty, let each firm's behaviour be as described by the Von Neumann-Morgenstern axioms,[3] with firms having a common utility function U(.) and common initial wealth A.

The sole means available to any firm of increasing the likelihood of its success in the quest for the monopoly rent is an increase in its allocation to rent-seeking activity relative to its rivals. There is no favoritism in the rent-seeking quest; an increase in the allocation to rent-seeking by any particular firm increases its likelihood of success to the same extent as does a corresponding increase in the allocation to rent-seeking by any other firm. Denoting by Π_j the probability that firm j will be the ultimate monopolist and by P_i the value of the resources allocated to rent-seeking activity by firm i, we posit

$$\Pi_j = f_j(P_1, P_2, \ldots, P_j, \ldots, P_n), \tag{6.1}$$

where $f_j(.)$ is concave, differentiable, and $\partial f_j/\partial P_j > 0$, $\partial f_j/\partial P_i < 0$ $(i \neq j)$.

With $f_j(.)$ identical for all firms, in equilibrium each firm allocates the same sum in the quest to attain the monopoly rent. If rent-seeking is a competitive activity, then, regardless of the particular form which the function $f_j(.)$ might have, the value of the resources expended by each firm in rent-seeking is implicitly given by $P = P_j (j = 1, \ldots, n)$ in

$$E(U) = [(n - 1)/n]\, U(A - P) + (1/n)\, U(A - P + X) = U(A). \tag{6.2}$$

This is the basic rent-seeking equilibrium condition, and it states that the expected utility of the marginal firm entering rent-seeking activity is equal to the utility to be derived by that firm's maintaining its initial wealth with certainty by refraining from rent seeking.

Now, taking a Taylor Expansion (with a remainder), we obtain the expressions

$$U(A - P) = U(\tilde{A}) - PU'(A) + \frac{P^2}{2} U''(\tilde{A}) - \frac{P^3}{6} U'''(\tilde{A}), \quad (6.3)$$

and

$$U[A + (X - P)] = U(\hat{A}) + (X - P)U'(\hat{A}) + \frac{(X - P)^2}{2} U''(\hat{A}) + \frac{(X - P)^3}{6} U'''(\hat{A}) \quad (6.4)$$

where $\tilde{A} = (A - \alpha P)$ and $\hat{A} = [A + \beta(X - P)]$, with $0 < \alpha < 1$ and $0 < \beta < 1$. Substituting (6.3) and (6.4) into (6.2) yields

$$(X - P)U' + \frac{(X - P)^2}{2} U'' + \frac{(X - P)^3}{6} U'''(\hat{A}) - (n - 1)PU' + \frac{(n - 1)P^2}{2} U'' - \frac{(n - 1)P^3}{6} U'''(\tilde{A}) = 0 \quad (6.5)$$

where U′ and U″ in (6.5) are defined at A.From (6.5) one can then readily establish that

$$\lim_{n \to \infty} P = 0. \quad (6.6)$$

That is, as the number of firms becomes very large, the amount which an individual firm is prepared to expend in the quest for the rent approaches zero.[4] However, although the small likelihood of any particular firm's success means that rent dissipation by any one firm is small, this cannot be taken to imply that overall the total rent dissipated with also necessarily be small.

Denote by S the *total* rent dissipated by all rent seekers (i.e. S = *n*P). Then, using (6.5) and (6.6) we have

$$\lim_{n \to \infty} \frac{S}{X} = 1 + \frac{XU''(A)}{2U'(A)} + \frac{X^2U'''(\hat{A})}{6U'(A)}. \quad (6.7)$$

Hence, if X is relatively small, we obtain the limiting expression for rent dissipation,

$$\lim_{n \to \infty} \frac{S}{X} = 1 - \frac{kR}{2}. \quad (6.8)$$

where R is the coefficient of relative risk aversion and k = X/A. Not surprisingly, rent dissipation declines as risk aversion increases. However, rent dissipation also decreases as the value of the rent declines relative to initial wealth.

Suppose for example that rent seekers exhibited unitary relative risk aversion.[5] Then, if the monopoly rent as a percentage of initial wealth were 1%, (6.8) indicates the limiting percentage of monopoly rent dissipated to be 99.5%. On the other hand, if X/A = 5%, 97.5% of the rent is dissipated; when X/A = 10%, 95% is dissipated; when X/A = 20%, 90% is dissipated.

These outcomes suggest that, at least for relatively small rents, the value of a rent observed to accrue as a consequence of monopoly power approximates the value of the resources expended in the course of competitive rent-seeking in quest of that rent.

Competition for Large Rents

The limiting expression (6.8) is restricted in its application to instances where rents are small. When rents are large, the evaluation of rent dissipation requires solving the equilibrium rent-seeking condition (6.2) directly for a particular specification of rent seekers' utilities.

Let us assume that utility is logarithmic. The coefficient of relative risk aversion is accordingly unity, and is equal then to that in the small-rent examples based on (6.8). Resource dissipation outcomes for logarithmic utility are indicated in Table 6.1 for rents ranging from 10% to ten times initial wealth,[6] and with the number of rent seekers ranging from 2 to 1,000. We observe that in the small-rent cases where the rent is 10–20% of initial wealth, rent dissipation as indicated by the limiting approximation (6.8) is approached by competition among 50 rent seekers. Since increasing the number of rent seekers beyond 50 does not affect rent dissipation in other cases, this number of rent seekers also appears to suffice to approximate the competitive limit for larger rents with respect to which direct comparisons with (6.8) cannot be made.

Table 6–1 points to a revealing relationship between the size of the rent sought and the extent to which a rent is dissipated: as the size of the rent increases, smaller proportions of the rent are dissipated. For example, rent dissipation is around 70% when the rent is equal to initial wealth, but dissipation falls to just over a third at five times initial wealth; and at ten times initial wealth only a quarter of the rent is dissipated.

This falling away in rent dissipation as the size of the rent increases is not to be attributed to limits imposed by the nonavailability of resources

Table 6–1. Competitive rent dissipation, logarithmic utility, A = 100

	n						
X/A	*2*	*3*	*5*	*10*	*50*	*100*	*1,000*
0.10	98	97	96	96	95	95	95
0.20	95	94	93	92	91	91	91
0.50	88	85	83	82	81	81	81
1.00	76	74	72	70	70	69	69
5.00	32	34	35	36	36	36	36
10.00	18	21	22	23	24	24	24

to be dissipated in rent seeking. In particular, in the competitive limit, there are infinitely many individuals each with strictly positive initial wealth which can in part be allocated to rent-seeking activity.

Summary

Evaluations of the social cost of monopoly which encompass the resources expended by individuals seeking to acquire monopoly power yield measures of social loss which are high relative to outcomes when rent seeking is not accounted for. Indeed, Littlechild (1981) has suggested that the Cowling and Mueller (1978) measures of the social cost of monopoly power which make allowance for the role of rent seeking are inordinately high.[7] A central question relating to the indicated high social cost of monopoly power concerns the extent to which it is appropriate to take observed monopoly profits to reflect the value of resources expended in seeking to acquire monopoly power. Presupposing that resources expended in rent seeking have positive marginal social value, competition among rent seekers for a biddable rent dissipates that rent in its entirety *if rent seekers are risk neutral*; but one cannot presuppose that, when confronted with the intrinsic uncertainty associated with competing to acquire monopoly power, rent seekers will be risk-neutral. Acknowledging that rent seekers may be risk averse, we find that competition among risk-averse rent seekers appears to result in substantial rent dissipation for small rents; but, on the other hand, when rents are large, competitive rent dissipation by risk averse rent seekers may be far from complete. Accordingly, for small rents, risk aversion does not appear to compromise the presumption that the observed value of a monopoly rent can be taken as an approximate guide to the unobserved value of the resources expended by individuals seeking to become the beneficiary of the rent; but not so for large rents, where the value of the resources expended in competitive rent seeking may deviate substantially from the value of the rent to be obtained by the rent seeker who is ultimately successful in securing the rights to monopoly power.

Appendix

When rent-seeking is not competitive, dissipation of a biddable rent is incomplete even if rent seekers are risk neutral. The non-competitive or small-numbers case has been analysed by Tullock (1980) under the assumption of risk neutrality. In this appendix we provide some illustrative values of the extent of rent dissipation which might be expected to occur when in small-numbers cases rent seekers are risk averse. Following Tullock, we assume non-cooperative behaviour with rent-seeking outcomes established by Cournot-Nash equilibria.

To consider non-competitive or strategic rent-seeking when rent seekers are risk averse, denote the probability that firm j will be the ultimate monopolist by

$$\Pi_j = P_j / \sum_{\substack{i=1 \\ i \neq j}}^{n} P_i = P_j / [(n-1)\,Q + P_j], \tag{A.6.1}$$

where Q is the average outlay by firm j's rivals in rent-seeking activity. If firms adopt Cournot conjectural variations with respect to rivals' behaviour, then each firm chooses its allocation to rent-seeking P_j to solve

$$\max_{P_j} \; [\Pi_j U_j(A + X - P_j) + (1 - \Pi_j) U_j(A - P_j)], \tag{A.6.2}$$

where Π_j is given by (A.6.1). In the subsequent Nash-Cournot equilibrium, assuming an interior solution (and dropping the subscript j)

$$\frac{P}{(n-1)Q+P}[U'(A-P) - U'(A+X-P)] - U'(A-P) + \frac{(n-1)Q}{[(n-1)Q+P]^2}[U(A+X-P) - U(A-P)] = 0. \tag{A.6.3}$$

Because of symmetry between firms, in equilibrium P = Q, so

$$\frac{1}{n}[U'(A-P) - U'(A+X-P)] - U'(A-P) + \frac{n-1}{n^2 P}[U(A+X-P)] = 0. \tag{A.6.4}$$

Table 6.2. Strategic rent dissipation, logarithmic utility, A = 100

	n						
X/A	*2*	*3*	*5*	*10*	*50*	*100*	*1,000*
0.10	50	66	78	87	94	94	95
0.20	50	64	75	83	90	90	91
0.50	48	60	69	75	80	81	81
1.00	45	53	60	65	68	69	69
5.00	21	25	29	32	35	35	36
10.00	12	15	18	21	23	24	24

Noting that, as $n \rightarrow \infty$, $P \rightarrow 0$ and letting $n\text{P} = \text{S}$ we then obtain

$$\lim_{n \to \infty} \frac{\text{U}(\text{A} + \text{X}) - \text{U}(\text{A})}{\text{S}} - \text{U}'(\text{A}) = 0. \tag{A.6.5}$$

Now expanding $\text{U}(\text{A} + \text{X})$ and substituting in (6.13) yields

$$\lim_{n \to \infty} \frac{\text{S}}{\text{X}} = 1 + \frac{\text{XU}''(\text{A})}{2\text{U}'(\text{A})} + \frac{\text{X}^2\text{U}'''(\text{A})}{6\text{U}'(\text{A})}. \tag{A.6.6}$$

Hence, if X is relatively small,

$$\lim_{n \to \infty} \frac{\text{S}}{\text{X}} = 1 - \frac{k\text{R}}{2}. \tag{A.6.7}$$

(A.6.7) is equivalent to (6.8), so confirming that in the limit strategic and competitive rent dissipation under risk aversion coincide. Since (A.6.6) is equivalent to (6.7), this coincidence is not restricted to small rents.

A logarithmic utility function yields the strategic rent dissipation results in *Table 6.2*. For large numbers of rent seekers ($n \geqq 50$), which we previously indicated to approximate competitive outcomes, there is no substantial difference between rent dissipated in the strategic and competitive cases. However, for small numbers of rent seekers (n = 2, 3, 5, 10), more rent is revealed to be dissipated by competitive than strategic rent-seeking, where of course in these latter small-numbers cases the strategic outcomes are the pertinent ones.*

* We thank Jagdish Bhagwati, Peter Neary, and Gordon Tullock for helpful comments.

Notes

1. As Tullock (1967) pointed out: "The problem of identifying and measuring these resources is a difficult one, partly because the activity of monopolizing is illegal." (p. 49, in Buchanan et al. 1980).

2. This rent, given as the outcome of monopolistic optimisation, is assumed to be independent in size of the resources expended in seeking to acquire monopoly power. It should be noted that this does not imply that the ultimate monopolist will not attempt to increase profits by rent-seeking activity after monopoly power is attained. What is implied is that the value of the monopoly profit X already encompasses the anticipated results of such further rent-seeking activities.

3. For a description of these axioms, see for example Hey (1979), chapter 4.

4. Divide through 6.5 by n and then take the limit as n approaches infinity. Of the roots of the resulting equation in P, the relevant solution is $P = 0$.

5. A choice of unity for the coefficient of relative risk aversion is not entirely arbitrary. Arrow suggested (1970, p. 98) that one would expect relative risk aversion "to hover around" unity.

6. Since equation (6.2) is homogeneous of degree zero in A, P, and X when the utility function is logarithmic, what matters is not the absolute sizes of A and X but only the ratio X/A.

7. See also Cowling and Mueller's reply (1981) to Littlechild.

References

Arrow, K.H. *Essays in the Theory of Risk-Bearing*. Amsterdam: North Holland, 1970.

Bhagwati, J.N. "Directly Unproductive, Profit-seeking (DUP) Activities." *Journal of Political Economy* 90 (August, 1982): 988–1002.

Bhagwati, J.N. and Srinivasan, T.N. "Revenue Seeking: a Generalization of the Theory of Tariffs." *Journal of Political Economy* 88 (December, 1980): 1069–87.

Buchanan, J.M., Tollison, R.D.; and Tullock, G. (eds.) *Toward a Theory of the Rent-Seeking Society*. College Station: Texas A & M Press, 1980.

Cowling, K. and Mueller, D.C. "The Social Cost of Monopoloy Power." *Economic Journal* 88 (December, 1978): 727–48. Reprinted in Buchanan et al. (1980): 125–52.

Cowling, K. and Mueller, D.C. "The Social Costs of Monopoly Power Revisited." *Economic Journal* 91 (September, 1981): 721–25.

Hey, J.D. *Uncertainty in Microeconomics*. New York: New York University Press, 1979.

Krueger, A.O. "The Political Economy of the Rent-Seeking Society." *American Economic Review* 64 (June, 1974): 291–303. Reprinted in Buchanan et al. (1980):51–70.

Littlechild, S.C. "Misleading Calculations of the Social Cost of Monopoly Power." *Economic Journal* 91 (June, 1981): 348–63.

Posner, R. A. "The Social Costs of Monopoly and Regulation." *Journal of Political Economy* 83 (August, 1975): 807–27. Reprinted in Buchanan et al. (1980): 71–94.

Tullock, G. "The Welfare Costs of Tariffs, Monopolies and Theft." *Western Economic Journal* 5 (June, 1967): 224–32. Reprinted in Buchanan et al. (1980): 39–50.

Tullock, G. "Efficient Rent-Seeking." Reprinted in Buchanan et al. (1980): 97–112.

7 EFFICIENT RENT-SEEKING REVISITED

Gordon Tullock

In, *Toward a Theory of the Rent-Seeking Society*, there is an article entitled "Efficient Rent-Seeking", which among other things presents a rather difficult mathematical problem. The next 5 articles in this collection are devoted to the essentially mathematical discussions set off by this problem. In order not to keep the reader in suspense, I should say that it is still a problem and, indeed, one of the points of publishing this exchange is the hope that it will inspire mathematically inclined readers to solve the matter.

In my initial paper, "The Welfare Effects of Tariffs, Monopolies, and Theft," I said rent-seeking had aspects of a lottery. For example, if a number of people made efforts to obtain tariff protection, only some of them will succeed. This is of course realistic, but a little hard to deal with in its full institutional complexity. In "Efficient Rent-Seeking" I formalized the problem into a true lottery. Specifically, it is a special form of lottery intended to closely approximate the nature of rent-seeking activity under conditions of risk and/or uncertainty. Assume that some number of rent seekers are permitted to buy tickets in the lottery. Each of the rent seekers is permitted to buy as many tickets as he or she wants, and write his or her name on each one. They are then put in a hat. One of them is drawn out and the person whose name is on it gets the rent. For the purpose of this illustration, let us assume that the rent is a prize of $100.

What is the appropriate number of tickets to purchase? If there is a correct answer to this question, then any individual rent seeker would have to assume that not only he but other players would figure it out. He does not have a monopoly on information. This means, more or less, that each individual should assume that if there is a correct strategy, others will also follow it. The mathematical problem is that there may or may not be an equilibrium in this case, and where there is an equilibrium it is sometimes most peculiar.

There is one further complication. We do not know the production function for influence in lobbying. There could be economies of scale or diseconomies of scale. It is even possible that there are neither.[1] In table 7–1, we have indicated increasing or decreasing returns to scale by the exponent. In other words, it is assumed that when you put in a given amount of money on the first line, you get the cube root of that number of tickets. This is rising marginal cost with a vengeance. On the second line the rent seeker gets a number of tickets equal to the square root of his investment, and on the third he gets one ticket for each dollar. On the fourth line we show economies of scale by giving him the square of the amount he invested. Even greater economies of scale are shown by the lower rows.

For simplicity of exposition, the table shows the "equilibrium" investment for specific numbers of rent seekers, but general equations which can be found both in the original article and in the following chapter permit solutions with any number of potential rent seekers. Table 7–2 shows the

Table 7–1. Individual investments (N-person, no bias, with exponent)

	Number of players				
Exponent	*2*	*4*	*10*		*15*
1/3	8.33	6.25	3.00		2.07
1/2	12.50	9.37	4.50	I	3.11
1	25.00	18.75	9.00		6.22
2	50.00	37.50	18.00		12.44
3	75.00	56.25	27.00		18.67
5	125.00	93.75	45.00	II	31.11
8	200.00	150.00	72.00		49.78
12	300.00	225.00	108.00		74.67
		III			

Table 7–2. Sum of investments (N-person, no bias, with exponent)

	Number of players					
Exponent	*2*	*4*	*10*	*15*		*Limit*
1/3	16.66	25.00	30.00	31.05		33.30
1/2	25.00	37.40	45.00	46.65	I	50.00
1	50.00	75.00	90.00	93.30		100.00
2	100.00	150.00	80.00	186.60		200.00
3	150.00	225.00	270.00	280.05		300.00
5	250.00	375.00	450.00	465.65	II	500.00
8	400.00	600.00	720.00	746.70		800.00
12	600.00	900.00	1,080.00	1,120.05		1,200.00
			III			

sum of all of the investments made by the rent seekers with varying combinations of rising or falling marginal costs and numbers of rent seekers.

The problem is that except for an infinite number of players and constant marginal costs, the market does not clear. With two players and constant marginal costs, for example, each will invest $25 for a 50-50 chance of $100. This seems absurd, but if the reader will experiment with his pocket calculator he will quickly discover that if he invests more, he increases the likelihood that he will win but with the winnings less than the value of the investment.

To take a converse case, the exponent of three row shows pronounced economies of scale. In this case, the two parties in "equilibrium" would each put in $75 for a 50-50 chance on $100. Once again it seems absurd, but your trusty pocket calculator will show that this is the only point where neither player can gain by changing his investment. Dropping out of the game might be better than playing, but this guarantees a profit for the other player.

The reader will note that the tables are divided into three regions, I, II, and III. Region I is the area where the total amount invested in the "equilibrium" condition is equal to or less than the prize. In other words it is sensible to play such games. In region II the sum of all of the investments is greater than the prize. In region III the individual investments are greater than the prize. In most of region I the total investment is sharply lower than the prize. In other words, the market does not really clear. Regions II and III would appear to be games that no one would play, but they have the interesting characteristic that if no one else is playing you should play. In other words, the paradox of the liar is involved. For the mathematically inclined, it perhaps should be pointed out that there is no Nash equilibrium in this game because there is a pronounced discontinuity at zero.

This then is the puzzle to which the following five articles are devoted. They do not reach a solution, although I think they clarify the problem. It is our hope that one of our readers can find the solution. Good hunting!

Note

1. The reader who finds this discussion too compressed is advised to turn to the original article in *Toward A Theory of the Rent-Seeking Society*.

8 LONG-RUN EQUILIBRIUM AND TOTAL EXPENDITURES IN RENT-SEEKING

William J. Corcoran*

Introduction

How important rent-seeking is as a part of the total monopolistic waste hinges on the size of the total expenditures induced by a given level of excess profits.[1] Posner (1975) and Becker (1968) assert that total expenditures in the rent-seeking process will just equal the value of the rents to be gained although neither is specific about how this result would occur. This hypothesis has been adopted by those writing about rent-seeking and, more recently, it appears to have attained the status of an axiom (Foster, 1981). If rent-seeking could fit within the perfectly competitive model one would expect—in the long run—the equality of total expenditures and total revenues. The analogy with perfect competition, however, is not accurate. One difference is that the expenditures in rent-seeking are made to influence the probability of winning, not to cover the cost of production. Another is that in the case of one payoff only one

* Thanks are due to Gordon Karels and several anonymous referees for valuable comments leading to substantial improvements in this paper.

competitor wins and obtains a positive return on his investment, the rest lose everything. Tullock (1980) shows that in a simple two-player lottery each player will maximize his expected value by investing one-quarter of the payoff at stake, not one-half, where total expenditures would equal the payoff. He goes on to show that the total expenditures can be greater, equal, or less than the payoff; the result depends upon the number of players and the marginal cost of influencing the probability of winning. Thus, it cannot be assumed, as first thought, that a given rental payoff will give rise to wasteful expenditures of equal value.

Upon further consideration, however, it can be seen that Tullock's model, as portrayed, pertains to the short-run. Each solution for total expenditures is for a given number of players which is analogous to the short-run solution in perfect competition for a given number of firms. Presumably, the assertion that total expenditures equals the payoff is made with a long-run perspective in mind, since it is in the long-run that the perfectly competitive model has this property.

This paper will incorporate long-run considerations into Tullock's model of the competitive process with the object of reconsidering the total expenditures attracted by a given payoff. First the shortrun results will be reviewed.

Short Run

In the model used by Tullock competitors attempt to maximize their expected net present value, V, which is given by:

$$V_A = \frac{a^r}{a^r + b^r} Pe^{-\varrho t} - a \tag{8.1}$$

where a and b are expenditures by players A and B; P, the payoff at time t; ϱ the player's discount rate and $a^r/(a^r + b^r)$ is a generalized probability function where r reflects the ease of affecting the probability of winning. As r increases the marginal cost decreases. The probability function is considered within a lottery framework, where a and b can, for example, be the number of one dollar tickets being purchased to obtain the payoff. In the simplest case where r equals one, the probability of winning by player A is equal to the ratio of the number of tickets he purchased to the total number of tickets purchased, i.e., $(a/a + b)$. If the number of players involved were increased, c, d, etc., would be added to the denominator, as appropriate.

To determine the expenditure by each player a Cournot reaction process is employed, whereby equation (8.1) is differentiated and the derivative set equal to zero. This results in a Cournot-Nash equilibrium solution whereby each of n competitors spends

$$a = \frac{(n\text{-}1)r}{n^2} Pe^{-\varrho t} \tag{8.2}$$

It is clear that since each player spends an equal amount, the solution is symmetric, the probability of their winning is the same, i.e., l/n. Multiplying (8.2) by n gives the total expenditure in rent-seeking by all players

$$T = \frac{(n\text{-}1)r}{n} Pe^{-\varrho t} \tag{8.3}$$

This last equation provides the basis for Tullock's short-run policy recommendations for minimizing total expenditures or total waste in rent-seeking. First, it is desirable to minimize the number of players involved in rent-seeking activity. This results in a lower value for the term $(n\text{-}1)/n$. Total expenditures would be zero where the number of players is held to one.[2] In this regard Tullock remarks that "nepotism is a good thing." Second, the marginal cost of affecting the probability of winning should be steeply rising. Total expenditures vary directly with the value of r, that is, inversely with marginal cost. It can be added for the short-run, that total expenditures also vary inversely with the opportunity cost rate of discount, ϱ. Thus policies which increase the opportunity cost (for instance, delay receipt of the payoff) will reduce total expenditures.

Long Run

The crucial consideration for determining the long-run solution is the possibility of entry and exit in the rent-seeking process. Players considering entry or exit will take into account the alternative uses of their funds. This opportunity cost will be measured by the rate of return which incorporates a separation in time between expenditures and receipts. If the rate of return obtainable on other projects is less than that offered by the rent-seeking option then players will enter; if greater, players will exit.

The expected rate of return, π, to each competitor in the lottery is a function of the ratio of the expected payoff and individual expenditures; thus

$$e^{\pi t} = \frac{P/n}{(n\text{-}1)rPe^{-\varrho t}/n^2} \tag{8.4}$$

or

$$\pi = \varrho + \frac{1}{t}\ln\frac{n}{(n\text{-}1)r} \tag{8.5}$$

Players will enter until $\pi = \varrho$ which occurs when

$$\ln\frac{n}{(n\text{-}1)r} = 0 \tag{8.6}$$

or

$$n = \frac{r}{r\text{-}1} \tag{8.7}$$

An alternative approach to long-run equilibrium must be taken where the payoff is received as soon as expenditures are made, i.e., $t = 0$ in equations (8.2) and (8.3). In this case, rather than focusing on the profit rate which will be infinite, a decision to enter will consider the existence of positive profits as given by

$$\mathrm{P}/n - a = \mathrm{P}\frac{n + r - nr}{n^2}. \tag{8.8}$$

Entry will occur until this falls to 0 which happens when

$$n = \frac{r}{r\text{-}1} \tag{8.9}$$

the same result as (8.7). If $r \leq 1$, entry is unbounded; this is akin to the results expected in industries with persisting decreasing returns to scale.[3]

Substituting (8.7) into the equation for total expenditures (8.3) we obtain

$$\mathrm{T} = \mathrm{P}e^{-\varrho t} \tag{8.10}$$

which indicates that in long-run equilibrium the total expenditures by all competitors in the rent-seeking process will equal the payoff discounted by the opportunity cost rate of return.

The results of (8.10) show that if long-run equilibrium can be attained, the r-value, a measure of the marginal cost of influencing the chances of success, falls out of consideration. Consequently, it would be incorrect to conclude that an increase in the marginal costs will lower total expenditures in rent-seeking (Tullock, 1980). As r decreases (as marginal costs increase) we can see from equation (8.2) that individual expenditures decrease. We can also see from equation (8.5), however, that the expected rate of return to each competitor increases, or from equation (8.8) that profits increase which induces entry.[4] The resulting increase in the number of competitors exactly offsets the decline in individual expenditures so the total expenditure remains constant. Therefore, as equation (8.10) indicates, T is invariant with respect to r.

An obvious question concerns the length of time to achieve long-run equilibrium. It includes both the time for information of a rent-seeking opportunity to become available,[5] and the time necessary to make the appropriate expenditures. The latter is usually the sole consideration in perfect competition where the long-run is determined by the length of time it takes to vary all inputs. In some situations, as in the case of a lottery, these expenditures could be made within a relatively brief period and the time for information to transpire would then be of central importance. There will certainly be sufficient time for both to take place where similar rent-seeking opportunities occur at regular intervals. The long-run can also exist, however, for a one-time never-to-be-repeated payoff when prior knowledge is widespread and expenditures can be made with little delay.

Implications and Summary

The objective of this paper is to investigate the assertion that a given rent payoff gives rise to an equal value of total expenditure. An analogy with perfect competition suggests a long-run perspective, which would allow the number of players to vary. Accordingly, a game theoretic model of the competitive process where competitors anticipate rival reactions and expend resources to increase their probability of winning is extended to include entry. Long-run equilibrium occurs when the incentive for entry is dissipated, i.e., expected profits equal 0 or the expected rate of return equals the opportunity cost discount rate. When this occurs total expenditure in rent-seeking is found to equal the payoff as in the standard competitive case.

How does this result affect Tullock's policy recommendations? His first finding that total expenditures in rent-seeking can be minimized by holding the number of players down remains intact. Essentially, this requirement restricts entry and as a result maintains the short-run conditions indicated by equations (8.2) and (8.3) for a given number of firms. His second recommendation, that of increasing the marginal cost of improving a player's probability of winning must, however, be qualified. If the long-run equilibrium is attained total expenditures will equal the payoff regardless of the marginal cost. If the marginal cost is such that the long-run equilibrium is unbounded, there exists a continuous incentive for new entry. It is possible that total expenditures will increase as entry mounts, but this cannot be determined. A policy of increasing the marginal cost will work, however, if carried out in conjunction with a restriction on entry. In this case the short-run results still apply. Finally, an additional policy recommendation can be deduced. From equation (8.10) total rent-seeking expenditures will be reduced if the opportunity cost discount rate of return is increased. This may be achieved by such actions as increasing the lag between rent-seeking expenditures and the associated payoff, or unfettering alternative productive investments (reduced taxes, deregulation, etc.). Both result in a larger discount of the payoff.

The results support the concern with rent-seeking behavior. It indicates that in the long-run each opportunity for rent—a transfer of wealth—displaces an opportunity for the creation of value which will be equal to or greater than the rent payoff. It will be greater, of course, where the investment alternative cannot capture the full social gain.[6]

Notes

1. Competition as used here refers to rivalrous behavior which implies that a degree of influence can be exerted by each participant in determining the outcome; this is markedly different from perfect competition, where each is powerless to affect the price (see McNulty, 1968).

2. When n equals 1, n-1 equals zero; at the other extreme, as n becomes very large the $\lim_{n \to \infty} \frac{n-1}{n} = 1$.

3. See, for example, Varian (1978: 60).

4. The variation of profits with r can be determined by taking the derivative, d/dr $(P(n + r - nr)/n^2)$. This result in $P(1-n)/n^2$, which indicates a negative relationship between profits and r, the marginal cost, for $n > 1$.

5. More exactly, it involves the time for the number of players necessary to obtain equilibrium to be informed.

6. This would occur where an innovator could not capture the total consumer's surplus of a newly introduced product.

References

Becker, G.S. "Crime and punishment: An economic approach." *Journal of Political Economy* 76 (March–April, 1968): 169–217.

Foster, E. "The Treatment of Rents in Cost-benefit Analysis." *American Economic Review* 71 (March, 1981): 171–78.

McNulty, D.J. "Economic Theory and the Meaning of Competition." *QJE* 82 (November, 1968): 639–56.

Posner, R. A. "The Social Cost of Monopoly and Regulation." *Journal of Political Economy* 83 (1975): 807–827.
Tullock, G. "The Welfare Cost of Tariffs, Monopolies, and Theft." *Western Economic Journal* 5 (June, 1967): 224–232.
Tullock, G. "Efficient Rent-seeking." In: J.M. Buchanan, R.D. Tollison, and G. Tullock (eds.), *Towards a Theory of Rent-seeking Society*. College Station: Texas A&M University Press, 1980.
Varian, H.R. *Microeconomic Analysis*. New York: Norton, 1978.

9 LONG-RUN EQUILIBRIUM AND TOTAL EXPENDITURES IN RENT-SEEKING: A COMMENT

Gordon Tullock

Although Corcoran is mathematically correct, I believe his comment is not very helpful. In order to discuss the matter in some detail, the reader should consult table 7–1 from my original "Efficient Rent-Seeking" reproduced on page 92.[1] This shows the equilibrium investment of each individual, different numbers of individuals playing the game (n), and differing values of r. Table 7–2, also reproduced on page 93, shows the total investment.

Corcoran assumes that in a dynamic process the profits would be exhausted, i.e., that people would enter or leave until such time as there was no profit in doing so. In his equation 8.7, he calculates the number of entrants necessary to meet this condition. I have no complaints about his algebra, but as I shall point out below, equation 8.7 is not very helpful.

In terms of tables 7–1 and 7–2, if individuals are able to enter, they have an incentive to enter as long as the value in Table 7–1, for the appropate values of n and r, is less than $\frac{1}{n}$. For any given value of r, the total return to rent-seeking with equilibrium entry, is 1 (the "prize") minus the total investment (the value in table 7–2 at the given value of r and the last value of n for which total investment is ≤ 1.) It may be noted that the total return to rent-seeking is not generally zero. Consider first situations in which r is less than 1. Corcoran says: "If $r \leq 1$ entry is unbounded." (The solution to equation 8.7 is a negative number of people.) In this case it is clear that the profits are not exhausted, as can be seen from my table 7–2. If r is one-third, then even if an infinite number of people choose to play, only one-third of the profits will be exhausted.

Turn next to the case where r is between 1 and 2. It is in this case that I think Corcoran makes what contribution his article does make. If, for example, r is 1.5 then n is 3, and it does seem to me quite likely that entry would proceed until such time as three people had entered, at which point profits would be exhausted. Suppose, however, that r is 1.6. Then n is 2⅔. But the number of entrants must be an integer.

If only two people have entered there are profits for that collectivity of two, whereas a third entrant will guarantee for himself and his predecessors net losses. It is also not possible for two people to enter in full, and the third person to put in only two-thirds as much as they have because it would be a losing bet for the third person.

When $r > 2$, all solutions lie with some number between 1 and 2 playing the game. Thus, entry would cease with one entrant, who would have positive profits.

For the benefit of those who have not read my original article, it will be noted that there are lines in table 7–2 dividing the parameter space into categories I, II, and III. Categories II and III raise the problem that it does not seem sensible to play these games but, on the other hand, refraining from playing them guarantees very large profits to the one person who does play. Thus there is another game in the precommitment stage, in which the parties attempt to make the first commitment so that no one else will enter. This other game must be investigated, and it seems to me that the major value of Corcoran's paper is in laying out some of the framework in which this precommitment game would be played.

It should be kept in mind that although an economist is annoyed to discover opportunities for true profit in a competitive economy, that is merely an intellectual problem. The real problem of rent-seeking is the waste of resources. We do not want the rent-seeking cost to work out to the same as the benefit. We would much prefer that the benefit come at zero rent-seeking cost, and if that is not possible that the cost at least be low.

So much for Corcoran. I should like to take this opportunity to clear up some loose ends on the original article on which he comments. Turning back to tables 7–1 and 7–2, I said that, in zones II and III as shown on the figure, "There is no stable solution (page 92). I was more correct than I realized. I had made only a partial check of the second order conditions and it turns out that for the bulk of the numbers in zones 2 and 3, specifically those where $r < \frac{n}{n-2}$, the second-order conditions for mutual maximization are not met. Thus we really should have had zones 2, 3, and 4, but what I have said about zones 2 and 3 would remain true in respect to 2, 3, and 4.

Although it makes no practical difference in the outcome, it may be of some interest to explain how I came to make this mistake. Because of the way in which our research proceeded, I began by establishing that all of the two-person equilibria were stable. There were a few tests of individual outcomes in other areas, but unfortunately I chose, in order to simplify my work, those in which the exponent was 1. Thus the area of instability was missed.

With respect to tables 7–1 and 7–2, in the original while having to do with two persons, biased processes, there are corrections of two sorts that must be mentioned. First, due to an error in the calculation procedure, the numbers are correct only if the column headings are reinterpreted as b_r, rather than b. For the second-order conditions to be satisfied the bias factor must be between $\frac{r-1}{r+1}$ and its reciprocal. Thus, bias has an even greater impact in reducing rent-seeking than I suggested.

But although in this case the failure to check the second order conditions thoroughly turned out to be irrelevant, I certainly do not believe we could always count on that. To repeat the advice which you hear so often but which is unfortunately frequently disregarded, always check the second-order conditions.

Note

1. "Efficient Rent-Seeking," in *Toward a Theory of the Rent-Seeking Society*, edited by James M. Buchanan, Robert D. Tollison, and Gordon Tullock, 1980, pp. 97–112. College Station: Texas A&M University Press.

10 RENT-SEEKING BEHAVIOR IN THE LONG RUN

William J. Corcoran
Gordon V. Karels*

Introduction

The original work on rent-seeking conjectured that rent-seeking expenditures would completely dissipate the rent sought. Tullock (1980) using a game-theoretic approach with a Cournot-Nash (C-N) response function showed that total expenditures can be greater than, equal to, or less than the rent payoff depending on the number of players and the marginal cost of influencing the probability of winning. Corcoran (1983) extended Tullock's model to a long-run setting, i.e., free entry, and found that under these conditions rents will be dissipated. Tullock (1983) agreed in part, but still maintained that where marginal costs were rapidly falling or rising throughout, Corcoran's long-run solution does not pertain.

The models employed by Corcoran and Tullock assume the probability of winning with an expenditure of a is given by:[1]

$$Pr(a) = \frac{a^r}{a^r + b^r} \tag{10.1}$$

* The usual disclaimer applies. The authors are grateful to Gordon Tullock for helpful comments and suggestions.

where b is the expenditure of the other player and r reflects the marginal cost of influencing the probability of winning. The expected profit with an expenditure of a is then given by:

$$E[\pi(a)] = \frac{a^r}{a^r + b^r}X - a \tag{10.2}$$

where X is the value of rents.[2]

The C-N equilibrium solution to the maximization of expected profits yields:

$$a = \frac{n - 1}{n^2} rX \tag{10.3}$$

where n is the number of players.

Since each player is assumed identical this solution holds for all players. The amount of money expended to capture the rents will simply be the number of players times the value of a from equation (10.3). this was the basic equation used by Tullock when he noted that whether or not rents were dissipated depended upon the values of n and r.

Corcoran, building on Tullock's work, assumed entry would continue until profits are reduced to zero for each firm. He then proceeded to solve for the long-run equilibrium number of players by setting equation (10.2) equal to zero and substituting equation (10.3). This yields:

$$n = \frac{r}{r - 1} \tag{10.4}$$

From this equation we can see the difficulties that Tullock raises with Corcoran's result. He points out that when $r \leq 1$, the equilibrium number of players would be negative and that rents are not exhausted even with an infinite number of players. Corcoran noted that in this case entry was unbounded with the situation analogous to production under strictly decreasing returns in a competitive industry. In that case each firm ends up producing an infinitesimal output level with a profit positive level and an infinite number of firms in the industry.

A second difficulty is the equilibrium number of players is not necessarily integer valued when r is greater than one. For example, when r is equal to 1.6, the solution value for n is 2.6. By solving equation (10.4) for r we can find the values of r that are consistent with an integer number of players. That is:

$$r = \frac{n}{n - 1}. \tag{10.5}$$

A third problem pointed out by Tullock is that if the solution is not integer valued, one firm could make positive profits but a potential entrant would be dissuaded by anticipated losses upon entry. For example, if $r = 3$, then $n = 1.5$ and one player alone would make expected profits but the two together would have expected losses under the C-N solution. Tullock suggested that the rent-seeking game for such a case would shift to a "precommitment stage" in which parties anticipate other entrants and possibly make a commitment whereby no one else is willing to enter.

A fourth problem arises in terms of the validity of the C-N solution for certain values of r greater than one. If for instance, $r = 3$ and $n = 2$ then each player would bet \$75 according to equation (10.2). Total expenditures would be \$150 in a game where the payoff is only \$100. Each player has an expected loss of \$25 with such a bet.

Tullock (1980) addresses this problem by stating that in such cases no Nash equilibrium exists and there is no stable solution to the game. For example, if both players were to bet \$50 (with $r = 3$) then it would be profitable for one to increase his bet to \$51. Tullock then points out that it then becomes marginally profitable for the other player to also increase his bet to \$51. The betting would increase in this manner to \$75.

From a long-run standpoint a player must consider alternative earnings possibilities of the rent-seeking expenditures. Thus, in the case just cited where it is marginally profitable (expected losses fall by more than \$1) to match the \$51 bet, it is also a strategy that yields negative expected profits as a whole. The question is whether or not a player will choose a strategy which guarantees expected losses. If we require all players to consider the alternative of a zero loss with a zero bet then it must be the case that the value of expenditures in rent-seeking by all participants can never exceed the prize.

One obvious implication of the assumption of no strategies that yield expected losses is, as stated, the fact that expenditures could never exceed the value of rents. This result appears counterintuitive because of the competitive nature of rent-seeking activity. A similar result exists, however, in the competitive sealed bid auction for prizes of uncertain value. Wilson (1977) showed that the winning bid for such an item (all other bids returned) approaches the true value of the item from below. This implies that no over-bidding occurs even when the true value is not known, because each participant plays a strategy of avoiding the "winners' curse" problem of only winning those tracts where values have been overestimated. One implication of these models as pointed out by Capen, Clapp and Campbell (1971) is that the optimal bid of a firm should decrease, not increase, in the face of increased competition.

Having set out some of the basic problems with the long-run solution to rent-seeking behavior, the remainder of the paper addresses possible solutions. In the next section we look at the game where $r \leq 1$. We then explore the more complex case where $r > 1$ and look at several definitions of long-run competition. The last section summarizes our findings. We point out at this stage that all numerical examples utilized in the paper assume a payoff of \$100.

Values of *r* Less Than or Equal to One

When r takes on a value of one or less the C-N solution has several interesting characteristics. First, no matter how many competitors there are, no firm ever incurs an expected loss. This is important in the long run, as entry would always be invited with such an incentive.

Second, it will always pay for each player to split its bets, assuming the other firm maintains its current bet. Both of these statements are illustrated in table 10–1. First, assume $r = .5$ and $n = 2$. Then the optimal bet for each player is \$12.50 with expected profits of \$37.50 each. Suppose one of the players decides to submit two bets with total profits being the combined value of the individual profits. This is equivalent to having $n = 3$, with an optimal bet of \$11.11. The resulting expected profit per bet is \$22.22. Since one of the players owns two of the bets, his overall expected profit is \$44.44, which exceeds his profit when there were just two bets. Notice also that the player making just one bet now has an incentive to split his bet. The optimal bet of each is now \$9.375 with profits of \$31.25 by splitting the bet versus the \$22.22 without. Table 10–1 also presents two other r values which yield the same result.

As can be seen from the above example, each firm, in the long run, has an incentive to keep splitting bets. The number of bets submitted (n) must eventually go to infinity and the optimal bet approaches zero. Note from table 10–1 that the expected profit on each bet is still positive even when n is very large (1000). This is analagous to the output-plant size decision of the competitive price-taking firm under strictly decreasing returns. Long-run adjustment always results in a smaller plant size.

The reason for this result has to do with the behavior of the probability of winning function specified in equation (10.1). It can be shown that when $r \leq 1$, the function is strictly concave which implies that the probability of winning increases at a decreasing rate as the bet "a" increases.[3] Therefore, the biggest incremental change in the probability of winning occurs close to $a = 0$ and, hence, each player is driven to bet near that level.

Table 10–1. Optimal bets and associated expected profits for selected values of r and n

r	n	*Optimal bet*	*Expected profit*
.5	2	12.50	37.50
.5	3	11.11	22.22
.5	4	9.375	15.625
.5	10	4.50	5.50
.5	50	.98	1.02
.5	100	.495	.505
.5	1000	.0004995	.0995005
.75	2	18.75	31.25
.75	3	16.67	16.67
.75	4	14.0675	10.9375
.75	10	6.75	3.25
.75	50	1.47	.53
.75	100	.7425	.2575
.75	1000	.074925	.0025075
1	2	25	25
1	3	22.22	11.11
1	4	18.75	6.25
1	10	9.00	1.00
1	50	1.96	.04
1	100	.99	.01
1	1000	.0999	.0001

As an example of splitting one's bets, consider the efforts of a lobbyist in attempting to persuade a senator to vote a given way on a bill. The effort could involve meeting with the senator once and spending an hour of time explaining the issue or the alternative strategy of meeting several times and reminding the senator of the critical issues involved. If the marginal impact of the meeting is greatest for the initial minutes of contact ($r \leq 1$) then the strategy of meeting several times will yield the highest overall probability of influencing the senator. It is in this general sense we refer to the concept of splitting the bet.

Tullock has pointed out that in the cases where $r < 1$ the value of expenditures by all participants is less than the payoff and, hence, not all rents are dissipated in the long run. While this is not disputed, note that the game itself is not very meaningful, as the bet is infinitesimally small and the number of players is infinite.

One possible solution to this degeneration of the game is to impose a minimum bet on all participants. For each player the problem is to maximize expected profits as before but now subject to a minimum value on an individual bet.[4]

The solution to this problem is as follows:

1. If the value from the C-N solution is greater than, or equal to, the minimum bet, the C-N solution is the optimal bet.
2. If the value from the C-N solution is less than, or equal to, the minimum bet, the minimum bet is the optimal value.

Such a restriction on the game is illustrated in table 10–2 for several values of r and n. In the first example where $r = .5$ and the minimum bet is $1, each player must bet the minimum when there are 50 or more players (actually 49 or more players forces a minimum bid). With fifty players each bidding one dollar, each player still expects to make $1 of profit. Thus, to an outside player there are positive expected profits to be made through entry.[5] These profits exist until 100 players are in the game. At that point all rent is dissipated and no entry is invited.

Table 10–2. Optimal bets and associated expected profits for selected values of *r* and *n* with a minimum bid constraint

r	*n*	*Cournot-Nash solution*	*Minimum bet*	*Optimal bid*	*Expected profit*
.5	2	12.50	$1	12.50	37.50
.5	10	4.50	1	4.50	5.50
.5	25	1.92	1	1.92	2.08
.5	50	.98	1	1	1
.5	75	.657	1	1	.33
.5	100	.495	1	1	0
.5	110	.492	1	1	−.09
1	2	25	1	25	25
1	10	9	1	9	1.00
1	25	3.84	1	3.84	.16
1	50	1.96	1	1.96	.04
1	75	1.315	1	1.315	.0178
1	100	.99	1	1.00	0
.5	2	12.50	.99	12.50	37.50
.5	10	4.50	.99	4.50	5.50
.5	25	1.92	.99	1.92	2.08
.5	50	.98	.99	.99	1.01
.5	100	.495	.99	.99	.01
.5	101	.4902	.99	.99	.000099
.5	102	.4852	.99	.99	−.0096

For the case where $r = 1$ with a minimum bet again of \$1 we get the long-run equilibrium solution of 100 players each submitting the minimum bet. By examining table 10–2 it should become apparent that all the rent will be dissipated if the size of the payoff is integer divisible by the minimum bet. The final example in table 10–2, where $r = .5$ and a minimum bet of \$0.99 yields positive expected profits with 101 players and negative profits with 102 players. That last player would not enter as there is no bet that will give positive expected profits to all players.[6]

Generally most rent-seeking activities do not have minimum bet requirements.[7] A part of rent-seeking activity which closely parallels that of the minimum bet requirement, however, is transactions costs. An example occurs in the mail-in sweepstakes lottery. In such a case, instead of a minimum bet requirement there is a fixed entry fee—the cost of postage, stationary and the entrant's time cost. Before mailing in the entry, assuming profit maximization, the probability of winning times the payoff would have to exceed the cost of entry. An interesting article by Selby and Beranek (1981) provides an analysis with regards to sweepstakes contests. Their estimate of the transactions costs of entry into a sweepstakes lottery (direct and indirect) amounted to \$.20, which was little more than the price of a postage stamp at that time.

If we assume utility maximization instead of profit maximization then we would need to include in the payoff the pleasure received from the gamble. Under such a model individuals may play even if the expected payoff is less than the entry fee because of the utility generated by the game itself.

Values of *r* Greater Than One

This section of the paper addresses Tullock's main concern with Corcoran's original article, i.e., the behavior of players in a dynamic lottery where the r value is greater than one. His concern focuses on the point where existing players would make profits but an entrant will cause expected losses for all. This suggests a precommitment stage where existing players consider their bets with the intent of deterring further entry.

The long run is understood to mean a game that could be replayed continually under the postulated conditions. With a given number of players already in the game, they would want to bet in a manner which guarantees non-negative expected profits for themselves (existing players are referred to as incumbents henceforth) and insuring only negative profits to a potential entrant. We define such a bet as a "preemptory" bet.

It can be shown that a range of preemptory bets exists for different values of r and n. Assuming that all incumbents place equal bets (follow the same strategy) the range of preemptory bets is determined as follows: First, because each incumbent must receive non-negative expected profits, the upper end of the range is determined by dividing the payoff by the number of incumbents. Thus, with two incumbents the maximum preemptory bet, independent of the value of r, is \$50; with three incumbents \$33.33; etc. Second, the low end of these bets is determined by the point below which positive profits can be made by an entrant. Within the range it is also the point of maximum expected profit for the incumbents. Although, the low end declines as the number of incumbents increases, it does so at a slower rate than the upper end.[8] At some point it becomes impossible for the incumbents to eliminate positive profit opportunities for a potential entrant while ensuring positive expected profits for themselves, i.e., the upper end and the lower end are equal. This suggests an equilibrium number of incumbents.

To illustrate this, consider the range of preemptory bets for an r-value of 1.4 in Table 10.3. With two incumbents this range is \$33.51 to \$50. With eight incumbents it narrows to \$12.45 to \$12.50. At nine a bet of \$11.11 by each player dissipates total rents—the maximum bet—but \$11.44 is the minimum necessary to insure negative profits for a potential entrant. Thus, to keep out potential entrants each player would have to be willing to accept an expected loss or suffer expected losses due to their entry. This choice is not viable in the long run, and players will exit.

A similar result occurs where incumbents settle at the C-N solution. For example at $r = 1.4$ in table 10–3 the C-N solution for four players is \$26.25 which is larger than the maximum preemptory bet. The resulting negative expected profits implies that the number of players must be less than four in the long run.

It can also be seen in table 10–3 that the maximum number of incumbents for a positive range of preemptory bets declines as the r-value increases. For example, at $r = 1.4$ the maximum number is eight and declines to two when $r = 3.0$. Note also that the minimum preemptory bet first declines as the r-value increases, and then increases. For one player the minimum is 50.00 at an r-value of 2.0.

Hit-and-Run Competition

We are interested in determining the long-run equilibrium solution. Consider first where players will enter as long as positive expected profits

Number of players

Exponent (r-value)	1	2	3	4	5	6	7	8	9	10	11	12	13	14	15	28	29
1.1	100.00– 73.74	50.00– 39.27 (27.50)	33.33– 27.07 (24.44)	25.00– 20.92 (20.63)	20.00– 17.08 (17.60)	16.67– 14.47 (15.28)	14.29– 12.58 (13.47)	12.50– 11.14 (12.03)	11.11 10.01 (10.86)	10.00 9.10 (9.90)	9.09 8.34 (9.09)	8.33– 7.70 (8.40)	7.69– 7.17	7.14– 6.70	6.67– 6.29	3.571– 3.565	3.448– 3.453
1.2	100.00– 67.73	50.00– 35.77 (30.00)	33.33– 25.52 (26.67)	25.00– 20.08 (22.50)	20.00– 16.67 (19.20)	16.67– 14.32 (16.67)	14.29– 12.60 (14.69)	12.50– 11.27	11.11– 10.22	10.00– 9.35	9.09– 8.64	8.33– 8.04	7.69– 7.52	7.14– 7.07	6.67– 6.68		
1.3	100.00– 58.27	50.00– 34.19 (32.50)	33.33– 25.03 (28.89)	25.00– 20.06 (24.38)	20.00– 16.90 (20.80)	16.67– 14.69	14.29– 13.05	12.50– 11.77	11.11– 10.75	10.00– 9.92	9.09– 9.22						
1.4	100.00– 54.98	50.00– 33.51 (35.00)	33.33– 25.09 (31.11)	25.00– 20.43 (26.25)	20.00– 17.42	16.67– 15.29	14.29– 13.70	12.50– 12.45	11.11– 11.44								
1.5	100.00– 52.92	50.00– 33.34 (37.50)	33.33– 25.44 (33.33)	25.00– 21.00	20.00– 18.10	16.67– 16.03	14.29– 14.46										
1.6	100.00– 51.61	50.00– 33.47 (40.00)	33.33– 25.98 (35.55)	25.00– 21.70	20.00– 18.88	16.67– 16.85											
1.8	100.00– 50.32	50.00– 34.24 (45.00)	33.33– 27.33 (40.00)	25.00– 23.30	20.00– 20.58												
2.0	100.00– 50.00	50.00– 35.36 (50.00)	33.33– 28.87 (44.44)	25.00– 25.00	20.00– 22.37												
2.5	100.00– 51.02	50.00– 38.67 (62.50)	33.33– 32.88	25.00– 29.31													
3.0	100.00– 52.92	50.00– 42.00 (75.00)	33.33– 36.69														
4.0	100.00– 56.99	50.00– 47.93 (100.00)	33.33– 43.31														
5.0	100.00– 60.63	50.00– 52.79															
6.0	100.00– 63.73	50.00– 56.78															

exist for placing a bet. We denote this usual profit incentive as "hit-and-run" competition. Incumbents, or those looking at the game in a "precommittal" sense, can thus prevent this hit-and-run competition by bidding in the preemptory range.

Within the preemptory range an infinite number of solutions exists. Two of these were considered. One is the C-N solution given by equation (10.3) which may come about because of internal competition. As indicated the C-N solution will only be admissible if it results in non-negative expected profits, i.e., when it falls within the preemptory range. A given number of players cannot be sustained if the C-N solution is above the upper end of the range, and exiting will occur. There also exists the possibility that the C-N solution can lie below the preemptory range. Where this occurs entry will take place because of positive expected profit opportunities. Eventually, as the number of players increases, the C-N solution for incumbents will move within the preemptory range and eliminate the positive profit incentive for entrants. Thus for $r = 1.1$ in table 10–3, between 5 and 11 players are viable in the long run when they place a C-N bet.

The second long-run solution considers players recognizing their mutual interdependence and colluding to maximize profits. This is the solution to the original Cournot problem suggested by Chamberlin (1962). The collusion solution would be at the lower end of the preemptory range where incumbents can maximize their expected profits while deterring hit-and-run entrants through expected losses. Thus for $r = 1.4$ in table 10–3, 5 incumbents would each bet $17.42, the low end of the preemptory range. It may be possible, however, for the number of incumbents to be too large to exclude potential entrants. This occurs, for example, with nine incumbents when $r = 1.4$. A bid of $11.11 per player yields zero expected profits for the incumbents, while a larger bet of $11.45 is necessary to exclude hit-and-run competition. Exit would have to occur until there were eight players in the game.

Hit-and-run competition allows multiple equilibria in the number of incumbents both when they collude and when they settle at the C-N solution. Total expenditure will vary accordingly. Table 10–4 provides aggregate expenditures for the hit-and-run competition long-run equilibrium where incumbents collude and table 10–5, where incumbents bet at the C-N solution.

In table 10–4 aggregate expenditures range from a minimum of $50 for 1 player at an r-value of 2.0 to a maximum of $100, the value of the payoff. For solutions where at least two incumbents exist, the minimum is $66.68 at the r-value 1.5. It can be seen that the greater the number of players the greater the dissipation of rents. For example, at $r = 1.2$ one player bets

Table 10–4. Sum of individual investments at equilibrium (hit-and-run entry, incumbents collude)

Exponent (r-value)	*Number of players* 1	2	3	4	5	6	7	8	9	10	11	12	13	14	. . . 28
1.1	73.74	78.54	81.51	83.68	85.40	86.82	88.06	89.12	90.09	91.00	91.74	92.40	93.21	93.80	99.82
1.2	63.73	71.54	76.56	80.32	83.35	85.92	88.20	90.16	91.98	93.50	95.04	96.48	97.76	98.98	
1.3	58.27	68.38	75.09	80.24	84.50	88.14	91.35	94.16	96.75	99.20					
1.4	54.98	67.02	75.27	81.72	87.10	91.74	95.90	99.60							
1.5	52.92	66.68	76.32	84.00	90.05	96.18									
1.6	51.61	66.94	77.94	86.80	94.40										
1.8	50.32	68.48	81.99	93.20											
2.0	50.00	70.72	86.61	100.00											
2.5	51.02	77.34	98.94												
3.0	52.92	84.00													
4.0	56.99	95.86													
5.0	60.63														
6.0	63.73														

\$63.73 while 14 players in aggregate bet \$98.18. Finally, for a given number of players aggregate expenditures increase with the r-values although for six or less players they first decline. For three players aggregate expenditures fall from \$81.51 at an r-value of 1.1 to \$75.09 at $r = 1.3$ and thereafter increase to \$98.84 at $r = 2.5$.

In table 10–5 showing aggregate expenditures when players settle at the C-N solution a smaller range of players make up possible equilibria than in the collusion case. This occurs because of the additional constraint that the C-N solution must fall within the preemptory range. Here again, aggregate expenditures increase as the number of players increases and as the r-value increases.[9] At each value of n and r the C-N solution which assumes competitive behavior, dissipates more of the payoff than the collusion solution.

Hardball Competition

Another type of competitive response in a precommittal or long-run sense can be explored. We denote this response as "hardball" competition. In hardball competition it is assumed entry will occur so long as a player can be accommodated (positive expected profit opportunities exist with him in the game) even though it may mean incurring short-run expected losses.

Entry occurs in this hardball case because the potential entrant recognizes that he can impose expected losses on the incumbents through his entry. The incumbents are then forced to revise their bets to insure non-negative expected profits. For the preemptory ranges given in table 10–3 it can be shown that, given that incumbents maintain their existing bets, a potential entrant can impose expected losses on them and himself if he enters.[10] Further, the greater the expected profits of the incumbents the smaller the expected losses of an entrant. Such a situation gives an entrant some bargaining leverage over the incumbents. To forestall such entry completely, the incumbents would have to place a zero-expected profits bet, the maximum of the preemptory range.

If incumbents accommodate the hardball entrant the revised bets could be either the C-N bet or, if it can be arranged, the collusion bet. With either, however, more hardball entry will be invited. The number of players increases until, as in the hit and run case, the minimum bet of the preemptory range yields negative expected profits. Entry of players beyond this point would guarantee expected losses for all, and as a result the numbers cannot be sustained. Thus, an equilibrium number of players exist where the lower end of the preemptory range equals the upper end of

Table 10–5. Sum of individual investments at equilibrium (hit-and-run entry, incumbents at Cournot-Nash solution)

	Number of players										
Exponent (r-value)	*1*	*2*	*3*	*4*	*5*	*6*	*7*	*8*	*9*	*10*	*11*
1.1	73.74[a]				88.00	91.68	94.29	96.24	97.74	99.00	100.00
1.2	63.73[a]		80.01	90.00	96.00	100.00					
1.3	58.27[a]		86.67	97.52							
1.4	54.98[a]	70.00	93.33								
1.5	52.92[a]	75.00	100.00								
1.6	51.61[a]	80.00									
1.8	50.32[a]	90.00									
2.0	50.00[a]	100.00									
2.5	51.02[a]										
3.0	52.92[a]										
4.0	56.99[a]										
5.0	60.63[a]										
6.0	63.73[a]										

[a] Cournot-Nash solution not applicable to one player; minimum investment for maximum expected profit is indicated.

the range. This number can easily be determined for the different r-values in table 10–3. For instance, with $r = 1.1$, the hardball equilibrium would have 28 players; with $r = 1.5$, 6 players; with $r = 2.0$, 4 players; etc. For r-values larger than 4, only one player can be sustained.

The total expenditures by r-value under hit-and-run and hardball competition are given in table 10–6. From this it can be seen that hardball competition tends toward a larger number of competitors and a greater tendency to dissipate the payoff. Aggregate expenditures (where more than one incumbent exists) range from \$75 for two players at the C-N solution and an r-value of 1.5 (from \$84 for two colluding players at an r-value of 3.0) to \$100. Aggregate expenditures for most cases exceed \$90. The C-N solution results in less aggregate expenditure (marginally greater for r-values 1.1 and 1.2) than the collusion solution. This may appear surprising, but is not so when one considers that a given number of players colluding provides more profits at each r-value and thus a greater potential for entry than the C-N solution.

One further consideration is that resources may be expended to participate in the bidding process, i.e., transactions costs. Examples of this include: information gathering, and organizing and maintaining a cartel. The direct effect of these transactions costs is to reduce by an equal amount the expected payoff of the incumbent players and, correspondingly, it will also reduce the maximum—zero expected profits—bid, which is the upper end of the preemptory range. Since long-run equilibrium occurs where the upper and lower ends of the preemptory range are equal, the existence of transactions costs implies that total expenditures in the process of rent-seeking will be reduced by the amount of transactions' costs.

The analysis of the effect of transactions costs suggests a policy recommendation to reduce resource use in rent-seeking. If a lump sum licensing arrangement can be applied to the participants of a rent-seeking process it will displace by an equal amount for each player the resources used in actual rent-seeking. And, therefore, total expenditures in rent-seeking will be less by the total expenditures on the license.

Summary and Implications

We have analyzed long-run behavior in rent-seeking under several conditions and behavioral hypotheses. The question of interest is whether or not the long-run expenditures will exactly equal the value of the rents. Our results depend on the type of competitive response which is assumed

Table 10–6. Sum of individual investments at equilibrium (hardball entry)

Exponent (r-value)	Number of players 1	2	3	4	5	6	7	8	9	10	11	12	13	14	. . .	28
1.1											100.00[a]					98.82[b]
1.2						100.00[a]								98.98[b]		
1.3				97.53[a]						99.2[b]						
1.4			93.33[a]					99.60[b]								
1.5		75.00[a]				96.18[b]										
1.6		80.00[a]			94.40[b]											
1.8		90.00[a]		93.20[b]												
2.0		100.00[a]		100.00[a]												
2.5	51.02[a]		98.64[b]													
3.0	52.92[a]	84.00[b]														
4.0	56.99[a]	95.86[b]														
5.0	60.63[a,b]															
6.0	63.73[a,b]															

[a] Incumbents at Cournot-Nash solution. For one player minimum investment is shown.
[b] Incumbents collude.

to exist in the long run and on the r-value governing the probability of winning.

For the case where the r-value is less than or equal to one, Tullock has pointed out that aggregate expenditures will always be less than the value of the game. The long-run solution, however, results in each firm submitting an infinitesimal bid—not a very realistic solution. We showed that when a minimum bet requirement is imposed, the number of players is determined in the long-run, and all rents will be dissipated if the minimum bet is integer divisible into the payoff. If not, aggregate expenditures depend upon the size of the minimum bet relative to the total payoff; however, the tendency towards complete dissipation of expected profits still exists.

For r-values greater than one we looked at entry under hit-and-run and hardball competition. Under hit-and-run competition entry occurs if the potential entrant can make positive expected profit. In the long run this suggests that incumbents make their bets to preempt potential competition. We found a range of possible preemptory bets. Using this range we considered the Cournot-Nash and the collusion solutions. For both cases the hit-and-run entry assumption allows various numbers of incumbents to be a stable equilibrium. For high r-values, however, only one player can exist. Aggregate expenditures under both kinds of solutions dissipate the greater part but not all of the available rents. As the number of players is increased greater dissipation of the rents results.

Hardball competition was defined as entry occurring so long as accommodation could be forced by imposing expected losses on the incumbents if accommodation and resulting expected profits for the entrant are not obtained. This would require the potential entrant to be willing to absorb a short-run loss. If this type of entry is carried out, the number of players increases to the point where the minimum preemptory bid yields a negative expected profit for the players. The number of players will thus depend upon the r-value. The rents will always be very nearly dissipated in hardball competition whether the incumbents collude or settle at the C-N solution initially.

These results assume the payoff is known with certainty and is treated as if the game is continually replayed. Since all players were assumed identical, the long-run results could also be considered the solution where each possible player has time to consider alternatives and signal "precommittal" behavior.

It is perhaps interesting that the results concerning hardball competition are similar in nature to those obtained in the monopoly analysis of Baumol, Panzar, and Willig (1982) on potential competition. They find that the presence of potential competition dissipates monopoly profits under certainty and non-increasing average costs. This is very similar to our findings that rents are nearly dissipated with the potential for entry if the entrant would be willing to accept short-run losses.

Given the social objective to minimize the expenditure of resources in rent-seeking the following are implied by our results:

1. Disallowing any type of entry and minimizing the number of players will hold down the aggregate expenditure of resources. Further reductions will be obtained if collusion is encouraged allowing players to place the minimum bet to maximize expected profits.
2. If entry cannot be disallowed then regulate against hardball competition whereby entrants incur short-run expected losses to gain accommodation by incumbents. Here again collusion is preferable, not only because it results in minimum expenditures by each incumbent but also because the C-N solution is unstable at low numbers of players for certain r-values and hit-and-run entry will result.
3. If hardball entry cannot be prevented then encouraging competition among the incumbents with a likely C-N solution appears to be marginally preferable to allowing collusion.
4. Application of a lump sum cost as a condition for participating in the rent-seeking process, e.g., a license, will reduce the total expenditure in rent-seeking by an equal amount.

Notes

1. For the sake of simplicity here and throughout the paper, the probability of winning is expressed assuming only two players. This assumption does not change our results and more players can be accommodated by changing the term b^r to $\sum_{i=1}^{n-1} b_1^r$, where $n - 1$ is the number of opponents.

2. Corcoran used the discounted value of rents given by Xe^{-pt} for his long-run analysis. His long-run solution assumed entry as long as the rate of return exceeded the discount rate, p. In the simpler case where the payoff is received immediately upon placing the bet, entry would occur so long as profits are positive. The main results of the analysis are unchanged with the simplifying assumption.

3. The probability of winning with a bet of a is assumed to have the explicit form:

$$F(a) = \frac{a^r}{a^r + \sum_{i=1}^{n-1} b_1^r}$$

$F'' < 0$ is a sufficient condition for F to be strictly concave in a. Performing the differentiation and simplifying yields:

$$F'' < 0 \text{ if}$$

$$a^{-1}(r - 1) < 2[ra^{r-1}(a^r + b^r)^{-1}].$$

Assuming $a, b > 0$ then $r \leq 1$ is a sufficient condition for this. Concavity of F also assures that the second-order condition of the C-N solution is satisfied.

4. Mathematically we can set up this constrained maximization problem with the following Lagrange function

$$L = F(a)X - a + \lambda(Z - a)$$

where X is the value of the payoff
a is the bet
Z is the minimum bet
$F(a)$ is the probability of winning
and λ is the unknown Lagrange multiplier.

With $F(a)$ defined as $a^r/(a^r + b^r)$ with $r \leq 1$ the objective function will be strictly concave and with the associated linear constraint the Kuhn-Tucker sufficient conditions are:

1. $F'(a)X\text{-}1\text{-}\lambda \leq 0,\ a(F'(a)X\text{-}1\text{-}\lambda) = 0,\ a \geq 0$
2. $Z\text{-}a \geq 0,\ \lambda(Z\text{-}a) = 0\lambda \geq 0$

where all expressions are evaluated at the solution value of λ and a. We know that a will always be positive so we have two possible cases.

First, $\lambda = 0$ which means the constraint is not binding. Making use of this information in equation (1) above yields

$$F'(a)X\text{-}1 = 0$$

which is the usual condition for the Cournot-Nash and yields

$$a = \frac{n-1}{n^2} rX.$$

The second case is where $\lambda > 0$ so the constraint is binding. With both a and λ positive equation (2) above gives us:

$$(Z - a) = 0$$

or

$$a = Z.$$

Thus, the optimal bet is the minimum bet when the constraint is binding in the Cournot-Nash equilibrium.

5. There is as illustrated earlier, an incentive for those already in the game to submit another bet and increase expected earnings. In either case the total number of bets rises so long as expected profits are still positive.

6. One could make the argument that players would always be constrained in the betting by the smallest unit of currency. In the U.S., one cent becomes the constraint and since one is divisible into every payoff, all rents would be dissipated.

7. One exception is the sealed bid auctioning of public lands for mineral leases. In these auctions, the government has a reservation price on each tract although the reservation price is not known prior to the submission of bids. If the maximum bid falls short of the reservation price, the tract is retained by the government for auctioning at a later date. In these auctions only the winning firm's bid is retained and thus the effect is somewhat different in that it is to insure that all rents cannot be captured by the bidder.

8. We can solve for the incumbents minimum preemptory bet to maximize profits from equations

$$1.\quad E[(a)] = \frac{a^r}{a^r + \sum_{i=1}^{n-1} b_1^r X - a = 0}$$

and

$$2.\quad E'[(a)] = 0$$

This insures that the entrant's optimal bet can at best attain zero expected profits. The solution for each incumbent's bet is:

$$b = \frac{r-1}{r} x/[n(r-1)]^{1/r}$$

9. This can also be determined by multiplying equation (30) by n.

10. For example, the optimal bet by an entrant (derived from 1) and 2) in note 8) is $(r\text{-}1)X/r$. When entry occurs the expected value of an incumbent betting for maximum expected profits while preventing hit and run entry, is negative.

References

Baumol, W.J.; Panzar, J.C.; and Willig, R.D. *Contestable Markets and the Theory of Industry Structure*. New York: Harcourt Brace Jovanovich, Inc., 1972.

Becker, G.S. "Crime and punishment: An economic approach." *Journal of Political Economy* 76 (1968): 169–217.

Capen, E.C.; Clapp, R.V.; and Campbell, W.M. "Competitive Bidding in High-risk Situations." *Journal of Petroleum Technology*, (June, 1971): 641–651.

Chamberlin, E.H. *The theory of Monopolistic Competition: A Re-orientation of the Theory of Value*, 8th ed. Cambridge, MA: Harvard University Press, 1962.

Corcoran, W.J. "Long-run Equilibrium and Total Expenditures in Rent-seeking." *Public Choice* 43 (1984): 89–94.

Demsetz, H. "Economics as a Guide to Antitrust Regulation." *Journal of Law and Economics* 19 (August, 1976): 371–384.

Foster, E. "The Treatment of Rents in Cost-benefit Analysis. *American Economic Review* 71 (March, 1981): 171–178.

Posner, R.A. "The Social Cost of Monopoly and Regulation." *Journal of Political Economy* 83 (1975): 807–27.

Selby, E.B., Jr., and Beranek, W. "Sweepstakes Contests: Analysis, Strategies, and Survey." *American Economic Review* 71 (March, 1981): 189–95.

Tullock, G. "The Welfare Cost of Tariffs, Monopolies and Theft." *Western Economics Journal* 5 (1967): 224–32.

Tullock, G. "Efficient Rent-seeking." In: J.M. Buchanan, R.D., Tollison, and G. Tullock (eds.). *Towards a Theory of the Rent-seeking Society*. College

Station: Texas A&M University Press, 1980.
Tullock, G. "Long-run Equilibrium and Total Expenditures in Rent-seeking: Comment." *Public Choice* 43 (1984): 95–97.
Wilson, R.B. "A Bidding Model of Perfect Competition." *Review of Economic Studies* (October, 1977): 511–518.

11 FREE ENTRY AND EFFICIENT RENT-SEEKING

Richard S. Higgins, William F. Shughart II, and Robert D. Tollison*

Introduction

This paper concerns rent-seeking and the extent to which rents are dissipated under various circumstances. Gordon Tullock's (1967) insight that expenditures made to capture an artificially created transfer represent a social waste suggested that the cost to the economy of monopoly and regulation is greater than the simple Harberger (1954) deadweight loss. Indeed, under Tullock's original formulation and in the extensions of his work by Krueger (1974) and Posner (1975), rents are exactly dissipated at the social level ($1 is spent to capture $1), so that the total welfare loss from such activities is equal to the Harberger triangle plus the rectangle of monopoly profits.

More recent contributions have identified instances of imperfect rent dissipation. Rogerson (1982) finds that rent dissipation will be incomplete when rent seekers face differential start-up costs or in situations where a monopoly franchise is reassigned periodically in such a way as to give advantage to the incumbent monopolist. Hillman and Katz (1984) obtain

* We have benefitted from comments by James Buchanan, Gerard Butters, Robert Mackay, Gordon Tullock, and two anonymous referees. Remaining errors are our own.

similar results when rent seekers exhibit risk aversion and the value of the transfer is "large." Lastly, using a model in which rent seekers know the correct strategy (if it exists), but where the probability of obtaining a transfer is not a linear function of rent-seeking expenditures, Tullock (1980) finds situations of either underbidding or overbidding. We shall have more to say about Tullock's analysis later.

While the importance of these results to the measurement of the social cost of monopoly and regulation is transparent, there is a curious aspect to most of the models in the literature on rent seeking. Both the value of the transfer and the number of rent seekers are normally fixed. The latter assumption removes from consideration the method by which rents are dissipated where entry is possible. Indeed, since monopoly rights are assigned in these models either by a pure lottery or by award to the highest bidder among a predetermined number of contestants, an important antecedent question is left unanswered: What determines the equilibrium number of rent seekers?

In this paper, we investigate the degree of rent dissipation when the number of active rent seekers is endogenous. Building upon Tullock's (1980) model, we show that in a market where the award is based on "effort," entry fees are nonrefundable, and contestants are risk neutral, there exists a symmetric mixed-strategy zero-profit equilibrium. This result implies that all rents are dissipated (expectationally), and that the expected number of active rent seekers depends on the value of the rents to be appropriated, among other things. Moreover, we are able to demonstrate that under-, over-, or exact dissipation of the monopoly rents is possible depending on the actual number of active rent seekers. On average, however, rents are completely dissipated.

This paper is organized as follows, First, we provide a summary of Tullock's model, introducing along the way the key elements in our analysis. Our model is then presented and contains some concluding remarks.

A Critique of the Tullock Model

Consider the static monopoly depicted in figure 11–1. A competitive industry with constant long-run marginal costs (LMC) equal to P_c is costlessly transformed into monopoly. Output falls from Q_c to Q_m as a result, and market price rises to P_m. In the standard analysis, the welfare loss is represented by the triangle ABC, and the rectangle of monopoly profits, P_mABP_c, is treated as a pure transfer from consumers to the monopolist.

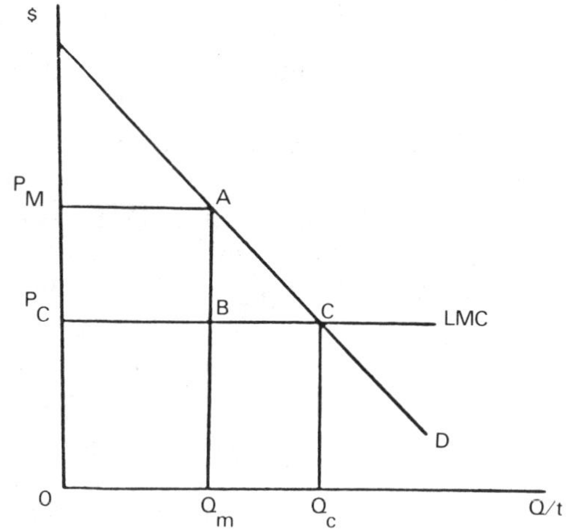

Figure 11–1

Tullock's (1967) insight was that any resources spent to capture P_mABP_c were also part of the social cost of monopoly. Posner's (1975) example is instructive on this point. Suppose that 10 bidders vie for a transfer worth \$100,000. If the bids are nonrefundable and all contestants are risk neutral, each will offer \$10,000 for the right to be the monopolist. At the social level, the monopoly returns are exactly dissipated—\$100,000 is spent to capture \$100,000. The welfare cost of the monopoly is thus equal to the area of the trapezoid, P_mACP_c.

Tullock (1980) subsequently proposed a model in which results other than exact dissipation of rents are possible.[1] In the model, N participants seek a prize, L. The probability of winning is assumed to be

$$p_i = X_i^R / \sum_{j=1}^{N} X_j^R,$$

where X_i is the amount bid by individual i and the value of the exponent, R, denotes possible marginal cost structures confronting the participants. (The higher is R, the easier it is for contestants to raise their probability of winning at the margin.) Tullock assumes further that if a correct individual strategy exists, each participant knows it and plays with the presumption that the other parties can discover the same solution. Given these circumstances, each individual chooses the bid, X_i^*, that maximizes $LP_i - X_i$. The joint solution of these N marginal conditions is

$$X_i^* = R(N - 1)L/N^2$$

Thus, Tullock shows that, depending on N and R, the players will spend in the aggregate more or less than L. Actually, however, the value of R drives the entire result. In the case of two participants, for example, overbidding occurs whenever R exceeds two. Indeed, with two players and $R > 2$, *each* of the bids will be greater than the value of the prize.

We can illuminate the relationship between R and N further by entending Tullock's model to allow entry of participants until there is zero profit from playing the game, that is, until all rents are dissipated. Zero profit occurs when $NX_i^* = L$. Solving this expression for N yields

$$N^* = R/(R - 1).$$

Note, first, that N^* is independent of L. This suggests that for a given R, the same number of people will play the game when the prize is \$1 as will participate when the prize is \$100,000. Second, when $R = 1$, underbidding obtains with any finite N; it requires an infinite number of players to dissipate all rents. Third, as R increases from 1, N falls asymptotically to unity. (These relations are depicted in figure 11–2.) In short, R must lie on the interval (1, 2) for the zero-profit result to make sense. Only if we are willing to assert $1 < R < 2$ is there an optimal N that dissipates all rents.

Extending Tullock's model by allowing for entry, we find that all rents are dissipated, but only under such restrictive conditions that we are led to

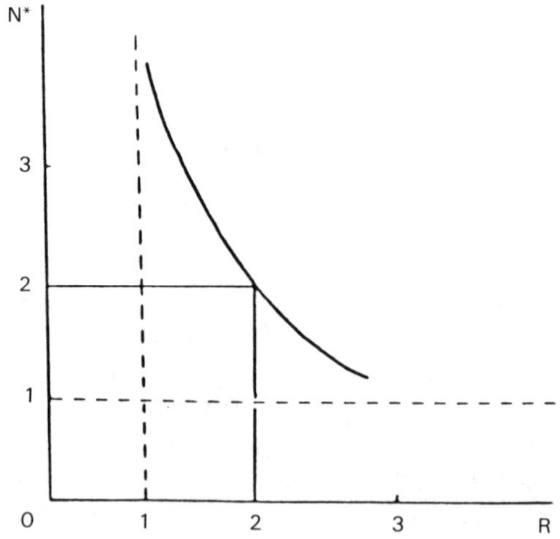

Figure 11–2

ask, why does the probability of winning the game have the particular form assumed by Tullock? Moreover, within that structure, what determines R? In what follows, we offer a more general specification of the competition for rents.

Free Entry and Rent Dissipation

In our model there are N potential rent seekers.[2] Each of them has two decisions to make. Each first decides whether or not to compete for the monopoly right. Each of the $m(\leq N)$ active rent seekers then chooses a level of effort to maximize the expected value of securing rents, given the efforts of other active participants.[3] In contrast to existing models in the literature, we let the expected number of active rent seekers be defined by a zero-profit condition.[4] The *actual* number of active players may under- or overdissipate rents, but *ex ante* and on average, rents are exactly dissipated when the players exhibit risk neutrality. We first describe how the rents are assigned among the active rent seekers, and then we analyze potential rent seekers' decisions concerning whether to participate actively.

It is useful to think of our model of rent assignment in terms of the "comparative hearings" conducted by the Federal Communications Commission (FCC) in granting a radio or television license. We suppose the license to be worth L, and individuals expend effort U_i to qualify for the franchise.[5] They invest in market research, program development, lobbying activities, and so forth. The effort costs $C(U_i)$, assumed to be identical for all contestants. We also suppose, however, that the FCC's decision-making process is subject to error. Perhaps there is some room for (unbiased) discretion, the effort of applicants can be observed only imperfectly, or in the case that several applicants supply equal effort, the winner is chosen at random. Thus, the FCC looks at the vector of efforts $(U_1, U_2, \ldots, U_m)$ and grants the license to the applicant supplying the highest level of effort, subject to the error element. Each contestant's measured effort (relevant effort) is thus $W_i = U_i + E_i$, the true effort plus a random variable. We assume that the E_i are independently distributed with zero mean and constant variance.

First, consider the case of two contestants. The license will be awarded to applicant 1 when $U_1 + E_1 > U_2 + E_2$, or when $U_1 - U_2 + E_1 > E_2$. Thus, the probability of winning for applicant 1 is given by

$$P_w^1(U_1, U_2) \equiv \int_{-\infty}^{\infty} \theta(E_1) \int_{-\infty}^{V_1} \theta^1(E_2)\, dE_2\, dE_1, \tag{11.1}$$

where $V_1 = U_1 - U_2 + E_1$.

We now use the Nash condition to define equilibrium. Applicant 1 chooses the level of effort, U_1, that maximizes

$$LP_w^1(U_1, U_2) - C(U_1)$$

holding U_2 constant, and applicant 2 optimizes over the symmetric problem.

The marginal conditions are

$$L(\partial P_w^1/\partial U_1) - C'(U_1) = 0, \text{ and} \tag{11.2a}$$

$$L(\partial P_w^2/\partial U_2) - C'(U_2) = 0, \tag{11.2b}$$

where the $C'(\cdot)$ represent each contestant's marginal cost of effort. Using the definition in (11.1), the two first-order conditions become

$$L \int_{-\infty}^{\infty} \theta(E_1)\theta(U_1 - U_2 + E_1)dE_1 - C'(U_1) = 0, \text{ and} \tag{11.3a}$$

$$L \int_{-\infty}^{\infty} \theta(E_2)\theta(U_2 - U_1 + E_2)dE_2 - C'(U_2) = 0. \tag{11.3b}$$

These relations give reaction functions that in equilibrim define equal efforts U_1^* and U_2^* described by

$$L \int_{-\infty}^{\infty} \theta^2(E)dE - C'(U^*) = 0. \tag{11.4}$$

Equation (11.4) is obtained by exploiting the symmetry properties of the problem, noting that $\theta(U_1 - U_2 + E_1)$ and $\theta(U_2 - U_1 + E_2)$ are in equilibrium equal to $\theta(E_1)$ and $\theta(E_2)$, respectively, since $U_1^* = U_2^*$.

Equation (11.4) suggests that equilibrium effort depends on the value of the license, L, on the steepness of marginal costs, and on the nature of the error distribution, specifically the "mean density" (see, e.g., Nalebuff and Stiglitz, 1983). In particular, the applicants will each expend a greater level of effort the more valuable the prize and the less rapidly marginal costs rise with effort. (If marginal costs are constant, there is no optimal effort.)

In order to examine the relationship between total rents and total rent-seeking effort, we must specify the functions more completely. Suppose that E follows a uniform distribution on the interval $[-D/2, D/2]$ and that $C(U) = a + (b/2)U^2$. Equation (11.4) is now

$$L(1/D) - bU^* = 0,$$

which implies that $U^* = L/bD$. Total rents are, of course, L, and from the cost function aggregate rent-seeking expenditures are $2[a + (b/2)(L1/bD)^2]$. The net gains are therefore $L - [2a + (L^2/bD^2)]$. Note that the more error there is in the decision-making process, the lower the effort and hence the lower the cost. In the extreme case where effort does not count, the competition reduces to a pure lottery with fixed entry cost, a. Here the net gain is $L - 2a$.

We next generalize to m applicants. In the special case outlined above where each of m applicants incurs costs of $C(U) = a + (b/2)U^2$ and the distribution of decision-making errors is uniform on $[-D/2, D/2]$, the optimal individual effort is $U^* = L/bD$.[6] Effort is, therefore, independent of m when the E_i are uniformly distributed. Although this is clearly a special case, we retain the uniform distribution because it greatly facilitates the analysis of rent seekers' prior decisions whether to be active participants.

For each number of active participants greater than one there is an expected profit given by $L/m - [a + (b/2)(L/bD)^2] \equiv E\pi(m)$. When $m = 0$, profit is zero, and when $m = 1$, there is really no contest so profit is $L - a$. As m varies from 2 to N, $E\pi(m)$ declines at a constant rate equal to $C(U^*)$.[7] Depending on the parameters of the model, $E\pi$ may be negative beyond some particular value of m. And finally, since m assumes only integer values, there may be no value of m for which $E\pi$ is exactly zero. In the latter case there will be some particular value of m, say m^0, at which $E\pi(m^0) > 0$ and $E\pi(m^0 + 1) < 0$.

To model the N potential rent seekers' participation decisions, we make some simplifying assumptions. First, we assume that all rent seekers announce simultaneously their decisions to play or not to play. The fixed cost component, a, is incurred when a rent seeker decides to be active, and a decision to be active is binding. That is, the rent seeker must pay an entry fee equal to a to be an active participant, which would be forfeited if the entrant were to withdraw. The rent seekers do not decide on their optimal levels of effort at the time they commit to active participation. They choose the appropriate levels of effort only after they know how many other active participants there are.[8]

As Tullock (1980: 105–109) has emphasized, because expected profit is in general negative for some number of active participants less than N, there is no symmetric pure strategy equilibrium in our entry game. He refers to this problem as the "paradox of the liar." We resolve the paradox by allowing our rent seekers to choose mixed strategies.

Furthermore, since effort is independent of m in our example based on the uniform error distribution, expected net return over the variable cost of effort may be negative beyond some number of active players. Under these circumstances, players minimize losses by dropping out according to an optimal mixed strategy, forfeiting the fixed entry fee. To avoid complicating the analysis of the initial entry decision we assume that expected profit (net of variable cost) from the contest is nonnegative for all $m \leq N$.[9]

Each of the N rent seekers chooses to participate actively with probability p_i. The expected value of actively seeking rents is found by weighting $E\pi(m)$ by the probability that only $m - 1$ other rent seekers will actively participate, summing these terms, and multiplying by p_i. In the symmetric mixed-strategy equilibrium the expected value of being an active rent seeker must be zero for each rent seeker. And, each player's choice of p_i, given the probabilities of the others, must simultaneously maximize the expected values for each player, which equal zero.

In the present case, there is a straightforward way to find equilibrium p. We know that the individual expected gain must equal the individual expected cost. Expected cost is $p\{C^*[1 - (1 - p)^{N-1}] + a(1 - p)^{N-1}\} = p\{a + (b/2)U^{*2}[1 - (1 - p)^{N-1}]\}$.[10] Expected gain for the individual is $L[1 - (1 - p)^N]/N$. That is, expected gain is total gains, L, times the probability that at least one rent seeker becomes active, all divided by the total number of rent seekers. Thus,

$$L[1 - (1 - p)^N]/N = p\{a + (b/2)U^{*2}[1 - (1 - p)^{N-1}]\}. \quad (11.5)$$

When N is large, (5) is simply $L/N = pC^*$, and $p^* = L/NC^*$, provided L/NC^* is not greater than 1. When $L/NC^* > 1$, the equilibrium strategy is for all N rent seekers to contest actively for the monopoly rents.

When the N rent seekers choose probability p^* so that there is zero expected profit from engaging in rent seeking, rents are fully dissipated *ex ante*. *Ex post*—that is, after a realization from the binomial distribution of active participants—profit from engaging in the contest may be positive or negative depending on the particular realization. On average, the actual number of active contestants equals the expected number, Np^*, and expected return over the cost of effort in the contest will just equal the fixed cost. For other realizations of active contestants, expected net return from the contest may exceed sunk cost (underdissipation of rents) or be less than sunk cost (overdissipation).

We conclude by noting the relationship between the average number of active rent seekers and the other parameters of the model. Specifically,

$$\begin{aligned} Np^* &= N(L/NC^*) \\ &= L/[a + (b/2)(L/bD)^2]. \end{aligned} \quad (11.6)$$

From (11.6) we determine that $\partial Np^*/\partial a < 0$ and $\partial Np^*/\partial D > 0$. Thus, assuming that $p^* < 1$ to begin with (i.e., $L - a > 0$ and $L/m - C^* < 0$ for all m beyond $m^0 \leq N$), there are fewer active rent seekers the higher the entry fee, and more active rent seekers the greater the role of chance in assigning rents. Moreover, we see from (11.6) that the expected number of active rent seekers is independent of the size of the pool of potential rent seekers. Of course, in general when effort varies with the number of active rent seekers, this result is unlikely.

The relationship between the expected number of active rent seekers and the size of the prize is surprisingly ambiguous. A higher prize induces two opposing responses. For a given level of effort, a higher L increases the expected gain from being an active rent seekers. However, since a higher L induces greater effort the cost of active participation is also raised, and the overall effect of increasing L on the probability of actively seeking rents is ambiguous. Specifically, when the variable cost of effort exceeds the fixed entry fee, an increase in the size of the prize induces less active participation. Finally, when the error in the decision-making process is very large, that is, $D \rightarrow \infty$, the "hearing" reduces to a pure lottery, and effort becomes irrelevant. In this case $Np^* = L/a$ (when $L/a < N$), and an increase in the size of the prize unambiguously increases active participation.

Concluding Remarks

In the competition for a monopoly right in which the number of bidders is fixed, Tullock and others have found the value of the resources spent in the aggregate to capture the transfer to be sometimes less than and sometimes greater than the value of the monopoly. We think this approach to be incomplete since it leaves unanswered the question of what determines the number of individuals who will vie for the right to be the monopolist. It is unsatisfactory to imagine, for example, that the franchisor sets the number of contestants. One could then foresee that rent seeking would arise to influence the permissible number of bidders, and this merely moves the rent-seeking dissipation question one step back.

Our approach has been to extend these models in two ways. First, for a given number of active rent seekers, the monopoly right is granted according to the contest model developed by Nalebuff and Stiglitz (1983). This model clearly reveals that overdissipation of monopoly rents generally occurs only when there is some fixed cost of effort—or, what amounts to the same thing, when active participation requires a nonrefundable entry fee. According to the contest model of granting rents, the extent to which rents are dissipated depends positively on the number of active rent seekers.

Second, since expected profit in the contest is generally negative beyond some number of contestants less then the potential number of contestants, we construct an economic model of the entry decision. To avoid Tullock's "paradox of the liar"—the absence of a symmetric pure-strategy equilibrium—our potential rent seekers adopt mixed entry strategies. We show that there is a symmetric mixed-strategy zero-profit equilibrium in which each of N potential rent seekers actively engages in the rent-seeking contest with probability p. Thus, the actual number of active rent seekers is a draw from the binomial distribution with parameters N and p. For the expected number of contestants, Np, rents are exactly and fully dissipated. Over- and underdissipation of monopoly rents are possible, but only *ex post.*

The implications of our analysis are straightforward. First, when there are no restrictions on the number of individuals who may vie for the right to capture an artificially created transfer, entry will occur, and resources will be spent up to the point where the expected net value of the transfer is zero. Such competition leads to exact dissipation of the present value of the flow of rents associated with the transfer, and in static terms, makes the social cost of the monopoly equal to the value of the Tullock trapezoid. Second, even if entry is limited, overbidding for the franchise will in general not occur, the value of the Tullock trapezoid sets an upper limit on the social cost of monopoly.

The result that rents are fully dissipated depends critically on the assumption of risk neutrality. While we have not analyzed the case of risk aversion completely, several predictions about the characteristics of equilibrium appear straightforward. First, if the marginal contestant is risk averse, then setting net expected utility equal to zero implies that in the limit the monetary value of the rents will not be fully dissipated. Moreover, the extent to which rents are dissipated will be less the greater the degree of risk aversion, the smaller the value of the appropriable rents relative to initial wealth, and the higher the fixed cost of entry (see Hillman and Katz, 1984: 107). Second, the extent of rent dissipation will also depend on the assumptions made concerning the supply of rent seekers and their risk aversion distribution. For example, there may be a large enough pool of potential rent seekers with zero risk aversion that the equilibrium number of active rent seekers will all be risk neutral. In this case all rent will be dissipated expectationally. Third, and most importantly, with risk aversion as with risk neutrality, overdissipation will not be observed *ex ante.*

Finally, the theory of rent-seeking, as exposited here and elsewhere, puts considerable pressure on the argument that monopoly promotes a transfer of wealth from consumers to owners of monopoly firms (Comanor and Smiley, 1975). As Posner (1975: 821) observed, rent-seeking implies that monopoly profits are dissipated, not transferred. This argument is correct as far as it goes. Only it does not go far enough, and it would carry us well beyond the scope of this paper to present a careful analysis of the impact of rent-seeking on the level and distribution of wealth. Suffice it to say here that the effect of rent-seeking on the level and distribution of wealth will be a function of the mechanism used to assign rents in a society, attitudes toward risk, comparative advantages in rent-seeking, and so on (Higgins and Tollison, 1984).

Notes

1. In a recent paper, Corcoran (1984) raises several of the same points about Tullock's analysis which we independently noted, and which are set out in the remainder of section 2. He suggests, for example, that bidders will enter until in the long run the expected payoff from playing the game is just equal to the return realizable from alternative investments, and that in equilibrium, the number of contestants depends only upon the value of the parameter, R, which in Tullock's model represents the structure of marginal costs facing the participants. Corcoran goes on to state, correctly, that aggregate rent-seeking expenditures will in the long run be invariant with respect to R. What Corcoran fails to note (and what Tullock, 1984, shows suspicion of, but does not fully demonstrate in his comment) is that for the zero-profit result to make sense, R must be restricted to the interval (1, 2). Where we differ from Corcoran is in our development of a more general approach to the question of rent dissipation under conditions of free entry (see section 3).

2. The number of potential rent seekers is fixed in our model. We do not analyze the decision to be among the pool of potential rent seekers.

3. Thus, our rent-seeking model is analogous to Shubik's (1959) game-theoretic model of oligopoly in which firms in-being are distinguished from active competitors.

4. The major exception is Corcoran (1984); see note 1. One may question whether equilibrium is the appropriate restriction to apply to the problem of rent seeking for a known monopoly right. Consider Frank Knight's example of the California gold rush. Overinvestment occurred in that case because no one entrant could possibly determine how many others would attempt to stake claims. Admittedly, our model requires that all players have this type of information, but we think that the assumption is justifiable on the ground that it permits us to derive testable implications about the determinants of rent-seeking activity.

5. If the license is perfectly durable, L reflects the discounted value of the flow of rents in perpetuity. On the other hand, if there is some positive probability that the rents will be expropriated in the future, this will reduce the present value of the license. The exact nature of the license right in this regard is immaterial to our results.

6. When there are m rent seekers, individual i wins when $W_i > W_j$ for all $j \neq i$, that is, when $U_i - U_j + E_i > E_j$ for all $j \neq i$. If we assume that the errors are distributed independently, the probability that player i wins given E_i is

$$\prod_{j \neq i} \int_{-\infty}^{V_i} g(X_j)\, dX_j, \tag{a}$$

where $V_i = U_i - U_j + E_i$. To get the probability that i is successful, we integrate (a) over E_i and obtain

$$\int_{-\infty}^{\infty} \left[\prod_{j \neq i} \int_{-\infty}^{V_i} g(X_j)\, dX_j \right] g(X_i)\, dX_i \equiv P(U_1, \ldots, U_i, \ldots, U_m). \tag{b}$$

The partial derivative of P(U) with respect to U_i evaluated at the symmetric solution is

$$(m - 1) \int_{-\infty}^{\infty} g^2(X) G^{m-2}(X)\, dX. \tag{c}$$

Thus, the marginal condition in the symmetric case when g is the uniform density over $[-D/2, D/2]$ is

$$L(1/D) - bU^* = 0. \tag{d}$$

7. Obviously, if U^* were not independent of m, $E\pi$ would depend on m in a more complex way.

8. Alternatively, we might have supposed the N rent seekers to make a joint effort and entry decision. We have not worked through the implications of such a model.

9. The drop-out decision would have to be modeled in the same way as the initial decision to enter. The drop-out game would be played repeatedly until the expected return to effort in the contest was nonnegative for the remaining players. Thus, for all m for which expected net return over variable cost would be negative, $E\pi$ will be limited to the loss of fixed cost.

10. Expected cost is not simply pC^* because when there is only one active participant no effort needs to be expended. The probability that a particular individual incurs only cost a is $(1 - p)^{N-1}$. The probability that a particular individual is not the only active rent seeker and thereby incurs cost C^* is $1 - (1 - p)^{N-1}$.

References

Corcoran, W.J. "Long-run Equilibrium and Total Expenditures in Rent-seeking." *Public Choice* 43 (1984): 89–94.

Comanor, W.S., and Smiley, R.H. "Monopoly and the Distribution of Wealth." *Quarterly Journal of Economics* 89 (May, 1975): 177–94.

Harberger, A. "Monopoly and Resource Allocation." *American Economic Review* 44 (May, 1954): 77–87.

Higgins, R.S., and Tollison, R.D. "Notes on the Theory of Rent-seeking." Unpublished manuscript.

Hillman, A.L., and Katz, E. "Risk-averse Rent-seekers and the Social Cost of Monopoly power." *Economic Journal* 94 (March, 1984): 104–10.

Krueger, A.O. The Political Economy of the Rent-seeking Society." *American Economic Review* 64 (June, 1974): 291–303.

Nalebuff, B.J., and Stiglitz, J.E. "Prizes and Incentives: Towards a General

Theory of Compensation and Competition." *Bell Journal of Economics* 14 (Spring, 1974): 21–43.

Posner, R. A. "The Social Costs of Monopoly and Regulation." *Journal of Political Economy* 83 (August, 1974): 807–27.

Rogerson, W.P. "The Social Costs of Monopoly and Regulation: A Game-theoretic Analysis." *Bell Journal of Economics* 13 (Autumn, 1982): 391–401.

Shubik, M. *Strategy and Market Structure: Competition, Oligopoly, and the Theory of Games*. New York: Wiley, 1959.

Tullock, G. "The Welfare Costs of Tariffs, Monopolies, and Theft." *Western Economic Journal* 5 (June, 1967): 224–32.

Tullock, G. "Efficient Rent-seeking." In: J.M. Buchanan, R.D. Tollison, and G. Tullock (eds.), *Toward a Theory of the Rent-Seeking Society*. College Station: Texas A&M University Press, 1980.

Tullock, G. "Long-run Equilibrium and Total Expenditures in Rent-seeking: A Comment." *Public Choice* 43 (1984): 95–97.

12 BACK TO THE BOG

Gordon Tullock

My role in connection with the efficient rent-seeking model (Tullock 1980) is, I think, a rather ill-omened one. I began the discussion by inventing a model with an apparent paradox. The market does not clear even with free entry and competition. There have been a number of efforts to deal with this problem (Corcoran, 1984; I commented on it in the same issue, pp. 95–98). Corcoran and Karels (1985) and Higgins, Shughart, and Tollison (1985) are further efforts to solve the problem.

It is my unfortunate role, having discovered this particular intellectual swamp, to frustrate efforts to get out by pushing people back in. I first invent a difficult problem and then when people try to solve it, I say that their solutions are either wrong or at least incomplete. I should therefore say, that I do think that the work of Corcoran, Karels, Tollison, Shughart, and Higgins, has indeed made progress toward a solution even if they have not finally solved the problem.

Corcoran and Karels come close to solving the original problem provided we keep the framework of efficient rent-seeking rigid and unchanging. The problem is that there is one assumption in that initial framework which I now realize was unduly restrictive.

It is a usual practice among economists, when we observe a number of people engaging in the same kind of competitive activity, to assume that they all behave the same. The reason for this is partly that they face the same problem and we would assume they reach the same conclusion, but I think even more importantly, that an assumption that they do not behave in the same manner means that you have to explain why some of them carry out one policy and some another.[1] In the particular case of efficient rent-seeking, it is in general more profitable to violate this rule. You will make more money if you do not make the same bid as your colleagues.

Before going further, I should frankly confess that I have no solution to this problem. It appears once again to be a case of the paradox of the liar. If one deviates from the pattern, he makes a profit, if all follow his example, they lose. The sensible behavior for an individual is not sensible unless the other people are doing something else. If this gives the reader a headache, I can only recommend Tylenol.

Let me take an obvious example from Corcoran and Karels (1985: 234 f.) Table 3. Suppose that we are in the area of increasing marginal efficiency, specifically the exponent or r value is 1.5. If seven people are playing, he puts the minimum preclusive bid at \$14.29.[2] Suppose that one of the players instead of putting in \$14.29 puts in \$14.39, while the other six stick to the \$14.29. As a result, he acquires an expectancy equivalent to \$14.41. The \$.10 additional investment has paid off with \$.12. Each other player loses \$.02.

The reason that this would occur is I suppose fairly obvious whenever r is greater than 1. This is the area of increasing marginal returns and hence the return on additional marginal units will always be greater. Many equilibria in which all of the people are assumed to make the same investment will be subject to this problem. Indeed, in many cases, a complete outsider entering and making a large bid can gain. For example, consider eight people playing with r 1.3 and each putting in \$12.50. This is of course spending \$12.50 to buy an expectancy of \$12.50. Suppose that a ninth party arrives and puts in \$25.00. His expectancy is \$26.14. The expectancy of the original eight has of course gone down sharply.

I realize the problems that this will generate. Once again, we seem to be in a situation in which there is no rational way of playing the game. If nine players each put in \$25.00, the result is disastrous.

One way of dealing with this problem of course, is for individuals to attempt to put in individually preclusive bets before anyone else enters. The outcome of such preclusive bets is shown in the left column of Table 5, of Corcoran and Karels (p. 239). The problems here are first, the one that I mentioned in my original article (1980) which is that it leads to a previous game to be first. There is however, a second problem here which is that if we look at real-life rent-seeking activity, it is a little hard to see what the equivalent of making that single large initial investment is. A lobbyist can hardly simultaneously provide a Congressman with twenty-two dinners and five blondes. In corrupt societies where cash is used, this problem of course, is less severe.

When we have an exponent less than 1, i.e., when they are declining returns to scale, Corcoran and Karels essentially depend on the fact that there will, in practice, be a least feasible bid. I have no quarrel with this, but I should point out that there is here a problem analogous to the problem we have discussed above which makes calculation at least difficult. Look at their Table 1 (p. 230), and consider the first line. Suppose that one of the two people who are placing a bet instead of placing a bet of $12.50, places one of $12.00. He of course does not have an even chance of winning, so his expected return is not $50.00, but $49.49. His expected profit is $37.49, instead of $37.50. But his percent return on capital is better. If he had put in $12.50, he would have received a profit three times his initial capital. If he puts in $12.00, he receives a profit 3.12 times his original capital. Of course the other player, the one who still put in his $12.50, does better than he would had the first player also put in $12.50. Specifically, he makes an additional expected $.51. This is however, only a return of 3.04 times his capital. The explanation, of course, is that here we are in an area of declining marginal returns.

Naturally I am not claiming that I have solved the problem. What I have done is make it more difficult. Let us now turn to Higgins, Shughart, and Tollison. The first thing to be said is that all of the problems mentioned above apply here also. When playing one of their stochastic strategies, it will normally not be rational to play the same amount as the others are doing.[3] It is also subject to the problem that a single large preclusive bet normally dominates their stochastic procedure. But once again, the high profitability of such a preclusive bet means that there would be a previous game to obtain such preclusion.

The basic point of the Higgins, Shughart, and Tollison paper is to arrange through stochastic methods that all of the players receive a normal return on their capital (as most economic work, this is shown as zero profit) by stochastic means. There are occasional situations in which the number of players for the zero profit condition is an integer. More commonly however, it is not, and their stochastic model is designed to deal with this much more numerous category. Unfortunately, there is a defect. The mathematical expression they use has the ingenious characteristic that the same (zero as usual) profit is made by playing every time, by playing their stochastic procedure, or by transferring one's capital to some other normally profitable activity. If however, one of their players, instead of playing stochastically, chooses to play every time, he will achieve a normal return on his strategy; the other players will suffer losses.

The reason is clear, although a little involved. When I put my bid in, whether I do it because Higgins, Shughart and Tollison's stochastic process tells me I should at this time, or for some other reason, that stochastic process followed by the other players gives me an expectancy of exactly normal profits. If I play continuously, I will get normal profits. But since I am not playing the stochastic model, I am entering more often than I should and am inflicting a negative cost on others. Everytime that I play when by the stochastic model I should not, I lower the profits of the other players.

In general, in this kind of efficient rent-seeking model, an individual player imposes external costs on others. The Higgins, Shughart and Tollison model guarantees that these external costs are evenly distributed and balanced by profits. A single player who deviates by playing more often injures the other players.

Now it should be pointed out that there is no strong motive for a player to do this. It is true he will be able to invest more capital in an activity which gives a normal return, and he might drive some of the other players out, in which event he would begin making positive profits. The latter possibility of course brings us into the extremely complex area of predatory competition and I do not want to go through that very lengthy argument. I do presume my readers are already familiar with it. Suffice it to say that it does not seem as if this would be a long-run way of obtaining profits.

The other problem here is not that once the Higgins, Shughart and Tollison equilibrium stochastic process has reached equilibrium someone may deviate, but that it is very hard to see how you would get there to begin with. Clearly they are not talking about a carefully calculated conspiracy among all the players, because if there is such a conspiracy, there are far more profitable strategies to play. Their equilibrium would have to be obtained by players who simply find out over time that this is the appropriate strategy. Unfortunately, there seems no path by which they can do so.

As an example illustrating the problem, suppose that we have a situation in which seven players, if they all made the same and optimal bid regularly, would make a positive profit, whereas eight players, if they all made the same and equal bid would lose. We start with eight players. All of them are losing, but one of them who has read Higgins, Shughart, and Tollison calculates the efficient stochastic strategy and begins following it.

There will now be two different kinds of games. Firstly, those games in which this player, after consulting his table of random numbers, plays. In those games there will be eight players and all of them will lose. The second set are the ones in which he does not play, there are seven players, and all of them gain or at least lose less. By his behavior, he has benefitted the others for at least some of the games, while in all the games in which he plays he loses as much as before. If a second player began following the same policy once again, the players who were not playing stochastically would do better than those who were.

Note, there's nothing in this which indicates that anybody will actually make a positive profit. It is just that the non-stochastic players will more often have a profit in a particular play than the stochastic players, and these profits will on the average be larger. Thus there is no way for the players by simple experimenting with different stochastic procedures to reach the Higgins, Shughart, and Tollison equilibrium.

As I said before, my role in this controversy is to watch people trying to get out of the swamp and then push them back in. Clearly, my role is not a constructive one. Nevertheless, I feel it is necessary. On the other hand, it seems to me that if the work of Corcoran, Carroll, Higgins, Shughart, and Tollison has not gotten us out of the swamp, it has at least moved us to a place where the mud is less deep. I do not know much more about the geography of the swamp, but the prospect that we can find a bit of dry land somewhere has improved.

Notes

1. The so called Hawk-Dove literature helps to provide an explanation for this kind of behavior under some circumstances. Unfortunately, it is not applicable to the subject of this comment.

2. This involves rounding. There are seven players and 7 × 14.29 is of course slightly more than $100 but the matter is unimportant for the example.

3. I recently saw a propaganda movie about the Chinese communes. It was made several years ago, and would not be premitted in present day China, but I saw it in Philadelphia. In one sequence each of the commune children was encouraged to work faster than the others.

References

Corcoran, W.J. "Long-run Equilibrium and Total Expenditures in Rent-seeking." *Public Choice* 43, 1 (1984): 89–94.

Corcoran, W.J., and Karels, G.V. "Rent-seeking Behavior in the Long-run." *Public Choice* (1985): 227–246.

Higgins, R.S.; Shughart II, W.F.; and Tollison, R.D. "Free Entry and Efficient Rent-seeking." *Public Choice* (1985): 247–258.

Tullock, G. "Efficient Rent-seeking." In: J.M. Buchanan R.D. Tollison, and G. Tullock (eds.), *Toward a Theory of the Rent-seeking Society*. College Station: Texas A&M University Press, 1980: 97–112.

13 LIFE AMONG THE TRIANGLES AND TRAPEZOIDS: NOTES ON THE THEORY OF RENT-SEEKING

Richard S. Higgins and Robert D. Tollison

Introduction

Some government programs and policies reduce wealth through rent creation. In this paper we focus on the theory of rent-seeking, and armed with an analytical model of the rent-seeking process, we make three basic points. First, we explain why perfect dissipation of rents is *not* equivalent to a competitive return to rent-seeking. Second, we demonstrate that the social cost of rent creation may be *smaller* when all rents are dissipated by rent-seeking than when no rents are dissipated. Third, we explain that regardless of whether rents are dissipated in transferring them, there is a *distribution effect* of rent-seeking that has been ignored in the literature.

A Model of Rent-Seeking

Suppose that a monopoly right has been created with value R. The problem is how to transfer R to the private sector. Suppose further that the right is awarded to the rent seeker with the largest "output," q. For each rent seeker,

$$q_i = u_i + \varepsilon_i,$$

where q_i is output, u_i is effort, and ε_i is a rent seeker-specific random variable. The ε_i have identical distributions and are independent. The probability density function is g, and the distribution function is G. Also, each rent seeker has an identical cost of effort function, $C(u_i)$.

For n rent seekers, the probability, P_i, that rent seeker i is awarded R is identical to the probability that $q_i > q_j$ for all $j \neq i$. For given values of the ε_j, $j \neq i$, the probability that i wins is

$$\prod_{j \neq i} \{1 - G[u_j - u_i + \varepsilon_j]\}.$$

Thus,

$$P_i(u_i, \ldots, u_n) = \int \ldots \int \prod_{j \neq i} \{1 - G[u_j - u_i + \varepsilon_j]\} \prod_{j \neq i} g(\varepsilon_j) \prod_{j \neq i} d\varepsilon_j. \tag{13.1}$$

Each rent seeker thus maximizes

$$RP_i(u_l, \ldots, u_n) - C(u_i) \text{ for all } i. \tag{13.2}$$

The marginal conditions evaluated at the symmetric solution, $u_i^* = u_j^*$, for all i, j, are

$$R \int g^2(\varepsilon) G^{n-2}(\varepsilon) d\varepsilon - C' = 0, \text{ for } i = 1, \ldots, n. \tag{13.3}$$

The equations in (13.3) define equilibrium efforts by the rent seekers as a function of R, n, and the parameters of the functions, g and C.

To illustrate, suppose that g is the uniform density function with range $\bar{q}$. In this special case, equation (13.3) becomes[1]

$$\frac{R}{\bar{q}} - C' = 0. \tag{13.4}$$

From (13.4), we see that effort rises with R and the precision of ε.

Now suppose that n is endogenous. Specifically, suppose that there is zero expected profit in rent-seeking.[2] So, in general, $R = nC\{u^*(R, n)\}$, and in our special case

$$R = n^* C\{u^*(R, \bar{q})\}. \tag{13.5}$$

From (13.5), for example, we find that $\partial n^* / \partial \bar{q} > 0$, that is, the greater the chance element, the more rent seekers there are. When there is only chance because $C = C^0$ independent of effort, there is a lottery, and

$$R = n^*C^0. \tag{13.6}$$

Perfect Dissipation Versus Zero Expected Profit

We are now in a position to discuss the dissipation of rents. Most importantly, note that complete dissipation of rents is *not* identical to zero expected profit from rent-seeking. We illustrate this point with an example. Consider the lottery where $n^* = R/C^0$ rent seekers enter the competition for the monopoly right. Expected profit for each entrant is zero. However, the lottery administrator, the State, receives $n^*C^0 = R$. These receipts may accrue to particular individuals in government or to all citizens. Nevertheless, the rents R are not dissipated; they are transferred. Thus, in the case of a lottery for rents R, consumers of the monopolized product lose the Harberger triangle plus R, the winner of the lottery receives R and pays R, and the holders of the lottery receive R. In this case the social cost of monopoly is only the welfare triangle.

Even if real effort is expended to capture the rents, as indicated above by $n^*C(u^*)$, R is not dissipated unless expended effort has no value outside of obtaining the monopoly right. For example, monetary bribes, three-martini lunches, in-kind bribes, and so forth, all accrue as benefits to the administrator of the rent-transfer mechanism. In such cases rents are not dissipated; they are transferred. So the social cost of monopoly includes the rectangle only to the extent no one benefits from the effort expended by rent seekers.

Of course, rent-seeking competition may occur on any margin, and in those cases where the rent-transfer mechanism does not dissipate all rents, there are rewards for controlling the State. Competition at this stage will assure that there will be zero profit from seeking the right to create and to transfer rents. And, again, whether rents not dissipated through assignment are dissipated at this stage depends on the mechanism for controlling the State. For example, if politicians must do something productive to be elected—perhaps demonstrate a potential to manage the wealth-enhancing activities of the State—rents will not be fully dissipated. We return to this theme in section 4.

The basic point here is that the issue of rent dissipation is largely independent of the rent-seeking equilibrium hypothesis. We now illustrate the difference between zero-profit rent-seeking and rent dissipation with three further examples of alternative mechanisms for assigning rights to a monopoly. For simplicity, in each case the value of the monopoly is certain and equal to R.

Auction

Suppose that politicians can assign the right to restrict entry into a market to the highest bidder, and the winning bid is the property of the politicians. In this case rents are not dissipated; they are merely transferred by the politicians, who expropriated them from consumers, to the highest bidder. Although the winning bidder earns a normal rate of return on the investment, no rents are dissipated.[3]

Paperwork Contests

Consider a contest similar to a comparative hearing at a regulatory agency in which applicants for a valuable license individually substantiate that they would be the most worthy owner according to some criteria. An analytical model of this type of contest is presented in Higgins, Shughart, and Tollison (forthcoming). Under conditions of free entry, where applicants have identical costs of displaying a given degree of merit, there will be an equilibrium number of applicants who present identical cases. Thus, in effect, the winner is chosen by flipping an n-sided coin, where to qualify among the n an applicant must have presented a case that cost $C[u^*(n)]$. In such a model there is zero expected profit, that is, $R - nC[u^*(n)] = 0$. Moreover, all rents are dissipated on paperwork. Consumers lose R plus the deadweight loss triangles, neither consumers nor politicians gain anything to compensate for granting the monopoly, the winner gains R, and all entrants together spend R.

In this example rents would not be fully dissipated if among the entrants there were some inframarginal entrants with lower costs than the marginal entrant. In such a case there would be inframarginal rents in rent-seeking, and the social cost of the monopoly would be less than the trapezoid (Rogerson, 1982).[4]

Political Contests

Next, consider a contest similar to the comparative hearing, but suppose that instead of purchasing "analysis" to qualify as entrants, contestants must purchase the favor of politicians/regulators by taking them out to dinner. Here, expected profit will be zero at the margin, and in the absence of Ricardian rents in lobbying, expected profit will be zero inframarginally as well. However, unlike the comparative hearing, politicians will be compensated for granting a monopoly. Monopoly rents are not dissipated in this case except to the extent that income-in-kind is less efficient in exchange than money income.

Further Considerations

The message in these examples is that while each case assumes a competitive marginal return to rent-seeking, to the extent that the method of assigning monopoly rights by politicians resembles exchange, rents are *not* dissipated. Moreover, the value of holding office is, in general, proportional to the efficiency of the assignment mechanism in controlling rent dissipation. Even when the politician does not appropriate rents directly, an efficient mechanism provides rents that can be used to compensate politicians for creating and assigning rents. For example, the paper-pushing comparative hearing fully dissipates all rents except in the case where some consulting and law firms earn Ricardian rents. These savings can be used to cover the costs of future jobs (at wages in excess of marginal products) for ex-politicians who cooperated in creating rents.

At this point we want to address the role of efforts to avoid monopolization. The mechanism for assigning rents does not prohibit those who gain from a competitive market from entering the contest (Baysinger and Tollison, 1980). Consider an auction. Consumers as a group could bid for the monopoly, which, presumably, if they owned, they would forebear from using. Alternatively, if the product in question were an intermediate product and its users had already made an irreversible capital investment counting on a competitive input market, monopolization would impose capital losses on them. These downstream producers would possibly lose so much that they would be the high bidders at the auction. In this case the downstream producers would pay a tad more than R for the monopoly right and not exercise it. Consumers would lose nothing. Rents would be transferred from the downstream producers to politicians. No rents would be dissipated. Of course, we have supposed considerable myopia by the downstream producers. Anticipating their vulnerability to expropriation, they would only acquire a capital stock appropriate for the long-run monopoly price. In such an event the creation of monopoly would redistribute wealth from consumers to politicians. But still, no rents would be dissipated.

There remains, however, a long-run effect we have not captured. Specifically, *ex ante*, consumers can undertake costly actions to avoid monopoly exploitation. For example, consumers might reduce their investment in capital goods that are complementary with a product they expect to be monopolized in the future. By doing so, they raise demand elasticity above what it would be if they could count on a competitive market in the complementary good. Such actions obviously reduce the monopoly rent that can be expropriated, but altering the extent and the form of capital accumulation is costly. These long-run considerations do not alter our assessment of the relative efficiency of alternative mechanisms to assign monopoly rights. However, in assessing the cost of monopoly in society, a calculation that merely totes up welfare triangles and that portion of Tullock rectangles dissipated through rent-seeking will *understate* the social loss.

The Social Cost of Monopoly

We have shown that zero profit in rent-seeking is not identical to complete dissipation of rents. The degree to which government monopoly rents are dissipated depends on the type of government mechanism used to assign monopoly rights. In this section we show that the overall social cost of monopoly cannot be extrapolated from the degree to which rents are dissipated in the typical instance of government monopoly.

We know that in a particular instance of monopoly, the social cost of monopoly varies directly with the degree of rent dissipation. In the extreme, when all rent is dissipated, the social cost of monopoly is the Harberger triangle plus the Tullock rectangle. Thus, for a given average degree of rent dissipation, the overall social cost of monopoly rises as the amount of government monopoly rises in society. Moreover, as the degree of dissipation rises, the social cost of a given amount of monopoly will rise.

The actual overall social loss of monopoly will depend on the extent of monopoly and the average degree of dissipation of monopoly rents. It is possible for a society to be wealthier, *ceteris paribus*, the higher the social cost of a particular instance of monopoly. Although this proposition appears counter-intuitive, it is obvious when one considers that the extent of monopoly depends *inversely* on the degree to which monopoly rents are dissipated.

Consider two societies which are identical in every way except that in one the founding fathers had the foresight to limit the means available to political representatives for assigning monopoly rents. Specifically, suppose that only highly dissipative mechanisms are permitted for transferring monopoly rights. To keep the problem simple, we further suppose that all goods and services are produced at identical constant costs and market demand functions have the same constant elasticity. Finally, we suppose that competitive output across markets is distributed uniformly.

Now, in this world there is a schedule relating the marginal value of monopoly and the amount of monopoly, given the degree of dissipation. In figure 13–1, the curves $V_{D=0}$ and $V_{D=.8}$ depict these schedules for zero dissipation and for 80% dissipation. Specifically, the height of $V_{D=0}$ at m_1 is the Tullock rectangle for the m_1 most valuable monopoly in society. Also, in figure 13–1, we depict the marginal cost of producing monopoly through government. As can be seen, the amount of monopoly produced when D = 0 is m_0, and the amount of monopoly produced when D = .8 is zero.

Now consider figure 13–2 where two social cost schedules are depicted. These schedules relate the sum of the Harberger triangle and that portion of the Tullock rectangle that is dissipated to the extent of monopoly in society, where the value of monopolies is ordered from left to right along the m-axis. For example, $SC_{D=0}$ is merely the Harberger triangle, which is the same in all markets by virtue of the simplifying assumptions, times the number of monopolies. The curve $SC_{D=.8}$ adds 80% of the appropriate Tullock rectangle to $SC_{D=0}$; thus $SC_{D=.8}$ gets less steep as m

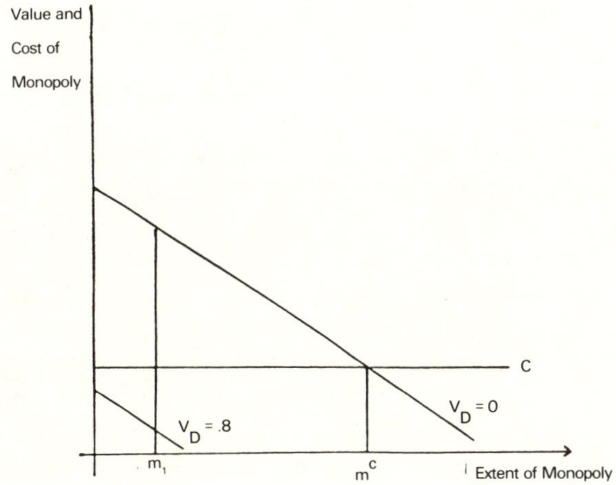

Figure 13–1

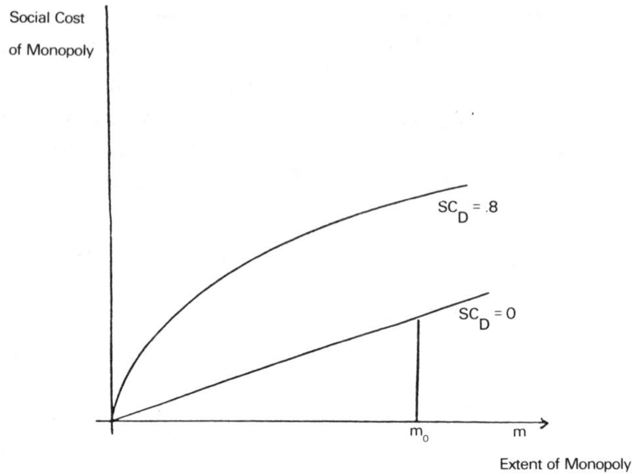

Figure 13–2

increases because by assumption the size of the Tullock rectangles gets smaller at a constant rate as more markets are monopolized.

In our example, one society is constrained by its constitution to transfer monopoly rents in a wasteful manner. This society corresponds to D = .8 in our figures. The other society is not so constrained, and presumably the politicians will design transfer mechanisms that are efficient. We have characterized this society as the zero dissipation society. By now, our point is obvious. The society which dissipates no monopoly rents produces monopoly out to m_0, and the society that dissipates 80% of monopoly rents produces no monopoly.

Matters may be worse yet for the society that produces m_0 monopolies. Figure 13–2 indicates that the overall social cost of m_0 monopolies is $SC_{D=0}(m_0)$. However, though no monopoly rents are dissipated in transferring them, rents may be dissipated in the competition for political office. The value of holding political office is inversely proportional to the degree to which monopoly rent is dissipated.[5] Competition for political office will assure that rates of return are normal at the margin. Just as in the case of rent-seeking described earlier, some mechanisms for securing political office are more wasteful than others. A society that combines an efficient mechanism for assigning rents with an inefficient mechanism for obtaining political office will be unambiguously poorer, all other things the same. Specifically, if the society with D = 0 in the above example also had a completely dissipative means of selecting political representatives, the social cost of monopoly would be $SC_{D=1}(m_0)$, not $SC_{D=0}(m_0)$.

Democracy may represent one of the worst forms of government in this regard. Specifically, if monopoly rights are assigned efficiently through what is in effect an in-kind auction and the returns to holding office are dissipated through expenditures on media campaigns to secure a majority, we have maximal incentives to create monopoly along with maximal dissipation. In this regard the pure entrepreneurial state that gives office holders property rights in the receipts from auctioning monopoly rights and permits the sale of political offices, or rule by the divine right of kingship, fares better than majoritarian democracy.

Rent-Seeking and The Distribution of Income

The distribution of wealth in society may be affected by the mechanism used to assign rents (contrary, for example, to Posner's (1975, p. 821) argument). In all cases, whether it be a lottery or a "comparative hearing" with or without productive effort, $(n^* - 1)$ rent seekers will be poorer by $C(u^*)$ *ex post*, and one individual, the licensee, will be richer by $R - C(u^*)$. There is only one transfer mechanism that leaves the distribution of income unaffected. It is an auction. When monopoly grants are auctioned to the highest bidder, the winning bidder pays R for R, no rents are dissipated, and the social loss of monopoly is limited to the Harberger triangle.

The distributive effect of rent-seeking has been overlooked in the literature. Perhaps, however, the oversight is without consequence. Just as we cautioned above that the social loss per instance of monopoly is not sufficient grounds to weigh the relative social cost of monopoly across societies, a long-run view of the distributive consequences of various transfer mechanisms is appropriate also.

Since rent-seeking is financed by prospects and not realized outcomes, if individuals in society can enter many lotteries, there will be no difference between a society with a lottery and a society with an auction. This neutrality condition depends critically on the assumption of equal rent-seeking abilities, however. More realistically, given society's rent-transfer mechanisms, some individuals will have differential talent for obtaining rents.

Consider again the above lottery, this time with different preferences for risk among participants. If the inframarginal risk-averse participants earn rents, then on average the distribution of wealth in society will reflect the underlying distribution of risk preference in society. In short, the lottery system raises the wealth of less risk-averse individuals relative to the more risk-averse.

Perhaps even more realistically, the assignment mechanism is likely to affect the distribution of wealth by occupation, only affecting the inequality of wealth in society to the extent that Ricardian rents are earned in rent-seeking. Consider the paper-work comparative hearing mechanism described earlier, and suppose that some lawyers or economists earn inframarginal rents in rent-seeking. On average, these individuals will be wealthier than their marginal competitors and wealthier than they would be without a rent-seeking mechanism of the particular type that rewards their skills. The choice of such a transfer mechanism increases the demand for lawyers (and possibly economists) above that which would hold with (say) an auction mechanism. So, first of all, the mechanism will alter the distribution of wealth by occupation. Moreover, if the requisite talents of the favored occupation cannot be reproduced at constant cost, the inequality of wealth in society may be further affected. For example, suppose the qualities of a good businessman/speculator are more fungible among the population than the qualities of a good lawyer. Then inframarginal rents will accrue to the best of the legal profession in comparative hearing cases, whereas with an auction no Ricardian rents would be earned. The distribution of wealth would differ between these two societies as a consequence.

Concluding Remarks

Our basic message is clear, and boils down to three points. First, the theory of rent-seeking must account for the incentive to create monopoly rents. When it does so, the impact of rent-seeking behavior on the wealth of society becomes much less clear than the current literature makes it out to be. A little dissipation may be a good thing. Second, a lot of what is normally called rent-seeking behavior amounts to little more than in-kind transfers to politicians and regulators. Third, there has been little consideration of long-run adjustments in a rent-seeking society. The resources spent on avoidance of monopoly do not show up in the usual analysis of dissipation. This additional shadow cost, in other words, which is positively related to the returns to rent creation, is not captured in the normal accounting of triangles and trapezoids.

Notes

1. Our special case hides an important relationship between u^* and n. In (13.4), u^* is independent of n.

2. All rent seekers are risk neutral. If the marginal rent seekers were risk averse, expected utility would be zero under our free-entry assumption, but expected profit would be positive.

3. In a stochastic environment, where the value of the monopoly is uncertain, the winning bidder will earn zero profit expectationally. Still no rents are dissipated.

4. Even in the case of the lottery, inframarginal rents may accrue to the relatively less risk averse applicants. Specifically, if potential lottery participants differed in their taste for risk, and if the marginal lottery participant were more risk averse than some inframarginal entrants, then the equilibrium number of entrants would be less than the number that makes expected profit equal to zero. On average, inframarginal lottery participants would earn rents, and such rents would limit the extent of rent dissipation.

5. Strictly speaking, this statement is too strong. The value of political office depends also on whether the political process in effect confers property rights to monopoly rents on office holders. For example, if a government limited the creation of market restrictions to the creation of exclusive franchises, required their transfer by auction only, and required that the proceeds go to the Treasury and not the office holders, the value of political office would be insignificant. We have ignored this possibility in our analysis.

References

Baysinger, B., and Tollison, R. D., "Evaluating the Social Costs of Monopoly and Regulation." *Atlantic Economic Journal* 8 (December, 1980): 22–26.

Buchanan, J. M.; Tollison, R. D.; and Tullock, G. (eds.). *Toward a Theory of the Rent-Seeking Society*. College Station: Texas A&M University Press, 1982.

Harberger, A., "Monopoly and Resource Allocation." *American Economic Review* 44 (May, 1954): 77–87.

Higgins, R.; Shughart, W. F.; and Tollison, R. D. "Free Entry and Efficient Rent Seeking." *Public Choice*, forthcoming.

Posner, R. A., "The Social Costs of Monopoly and Regulation." *Journal of Political Economy* 83 (August, 1975): 807–27.

Rogerson, W. P., "The Social Costs of Monopoly and Regulation: A Game-Theoretic Analysis." *Bell Journal of Economics* 13 (Autumn, 1982): 391–401.

Tollison, R. D. "Rent Seeking: A Survey." *Kyklos* 35 (1982): 575–602.

Tullock, G., "The Welfare Costs of Tariffs, Monopolies, and Theft." *Western Economic Journal* 5 (June, 1967): 224–32.

---

* The opinions expressed in this paper are those of the authors and do not necessarily reflect the views of anyone at the Federal Trade Commission.

III APPLICATIONS

A *Regulation*

14 DISPELLING THE DISINTEREST IN DEREGULATION

Michael A. Crew and Charles K. Rowley

Introduction

The penetration of competitive markets by laws and regulations is a highly durable and robust intrusion in the U.S. economy. Despite a not inconsiderable and continuing presence of highly articulate advocates both of *laissez faire* and of liberty, the U.S. economy is arguably as tightly regulated as the more socialistic economies of Western Europe. Even the outbreak of deregulation in specific markets during the early 1980s lost force by the mid-decade as the pro-regulation interest groups began to regain control of relevant markets. The forthcoming re-regulation of U.S. railroads is a predictable outcome of such a regrouping at the present time, as was epitomized by the "change of mind" of Commissioner Andre, a free-market exponent, who voted with the majority of the I.C.C. in late 1986 in favour of railroad re-regulation.

It is against this unpromising history that we attempt, in this article, to evaluate the apparent disinterest in deregulation within the framework of the rent-seeking model of public choice. First, we outline the theory presented in 1984 by McCormick, Shughart, and Tollison that offered an explanation of fairly generalized disinterest in deregulation. Then, internal inconsistencies in this theory are isolated, and the theory is adjusted to present a consistent explanation of disinterest in deregulation. Later, we provide a taxonomy of relevant alternatives, where generalized disinterest in deregulation would not manifest itself, even within the explicit framework adopted by McCormick, Shughart, and Tollison. Finally, we evaluate the total rent dissipation assumption, shifting emphasis from normative to positive analysis, to suggest that the disinterest theory may be a myth and we conclude by drawing out the equilibrium implications of a rent-seeking overview for the market in regulation and deregulation.

The Disinterest in Deregulation

McCormick, Shughart and Tollison (1984) introduced their theory via an explicit rent-seeking model, in which the conversion of a competitive industry into a regulatory monopoly carried with it the dissipation not only of the Harberger consumer surplus triangle, but also of the Tullock rectangle of producers' surplus via wasteful expenditures in search of government-created rents. In searching for an explanation of disinterest in deregulation, however, they pressed the dissipation insight beyond the one-period framework of Tullock to encompass the full present value of all perceived rents available from the regulation.

By assuming, for simplicity, that the monopoly privilege was perfectly durable, the authors were able to infer that rent seekers would dissipate, up front, resources reflecting the full present value of all rents in their scramble for the regulation prize. Since these rent-seeking costs are sunk once the monopoly has been established, abolishing the regulation *ex post* cannot recoup the resources that have been squandered. This would imply that the efficiency argument in favor of deregulation is weak, and, as we shall demonstrate, dependent only on some fraction of the Harberger triangle. The Tullock costs are irreversibly imposed, irrespective of subsequent institutional adjustment. Figure 14–1 attempts to capture the general equilibrium effects of monopolization and deregulation in such circumstances.

In figure 14–1, the production possibilities frontier, P_1, represents the economy in its initial competitive state, both in industry A and in all other sectors of the economy B. In this state, the economy operates at point 1, producing outputs Q_C^A and Q_C^B respectively. In the absence of Tullock costs, the output restriction associated with monopolization of industry A moves the economy along P_1 from 1 to 2, where output elsewhere is augmented by the resources released from A. Point 2 is Pareto inferior

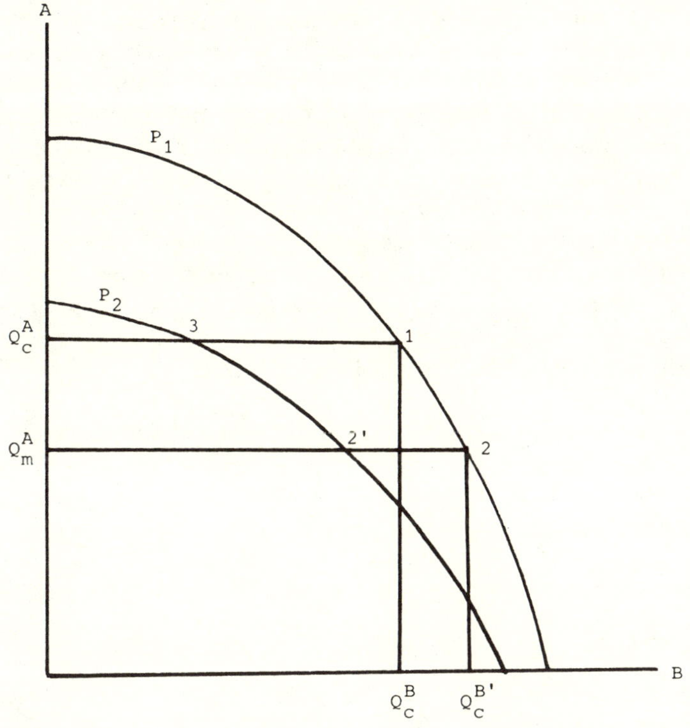

Figure 14–1

to point 1 because of the dead weight Harberger costs incurred by the monopoly. In the standard analysis, deregulation conceivably could return the economy to point 1, the Pareto preferred solution.

Once rent-seeking is accommodated, however, monopolization of industry A shifts the economy from point 1 to point 2′, as the production possibilities frontier shifts inward to P_2, reflecting resources that are wasted forever. Where the resources so wasted are highly specialized to industry A, the inward shift to P_2 is more highly pronounced with respect to A, as figure 14–1 suggests. The shift to P_2, in the case of full upfront rent-seeking waste, implies that any later deregulation of industry A cannot return the economy to point 1. If the economy is returned to the competitive output rate it will be between points 2′ and 3 on the diminished production possibilities curve, P_2 (not at point 3 as indicated by McCormick et al.). The loss of specialized resources in A also implies that it is now more costly in terms of B to produce in industry A.

Figure 14–2, incorporates the corrections of Cherkes et al. The wastage of resources via rent-seeking in industry A is reflected in an upward shift in the long-run marginal cost curve of the once-monopolized industry, from $LRMC_A$ to $LRMC'_A$. Ignoring producers' surplus transfers and losses, there is a deadweight loss of consumers' surplus of BEC in the regulatory monopoly solution. This reflects an output adjustment based on $LRMC'_A$ following monopolization. However, should deregulation occur, the consumers' surplus thus restored amounts only to BGD, a mere fraction of the initial loss experienced by consumers in the initial act of monopolization, since the retrievable competitive position is $P_C^{A'} \cdot Q_C^{A'}$ and not $P_C^A \cdot Q_C^A$ as originally subsisted.

McCormick, Shughart and Tollison utilized this theory to explain

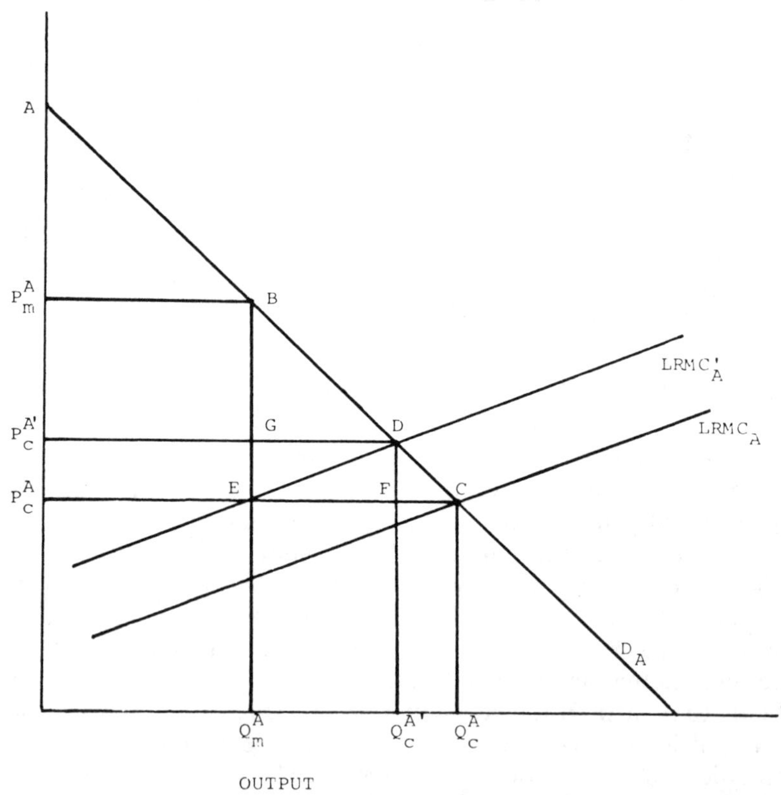

Figure 14–2

disinterest in deregulation. They claimed that disinterest was a function neither of voter ignorance nor of the logic of collective action, but rather was a reflection of the minimal economic return to a deregulatory program. In our view, this judgment confused welfare economics with public choice, intermingling normative with positive propositions, as we shall outline in section 3. Nevertheless, it offered an ingenious and original perspective on the deregulation debate.

A Reformulation of the Disinterest Proposition

Such is the residual grip of the new welfare economics upon the economics profession, that it is difficult even for those immersed in public choice to divest themselves from the discipline of a now badly shaken intellectual structure. Such evidently is the case with McCormick, Shughart, and Tollison. The principal thrust of their paper is that efficiency gains are necessary for a polity to stir itself in favor of deregulation. If the net social return to deregulation is negative, then deregulation will not be manifest. This is a problem with the new welfare economics, as Tollison, subsequently, was to recognize (Rowley and Tollison, 1986).

Only if the monopoly is continuously perceived to be completely durable would a normative efficiency case in favor of continuing regulatory monopoly necessarily coincide with political stability in favor of such an outcome. It cannot reasonably be inferred that all regulatory monopolies always reflect such durability characteristics in political equilibrium, even if initial rent-seeking outlays reflected such an expectation. Even the extreme forms of the rational expectations extravaganza allow for exogenous shocks that stimulate unanticipated performance adjustment.

Political markets, including those which regulate monopoly, are fueled by the desire for transfers—even transfers which involve an overall loss of wealth—as well as by the desire for gains-from-trade which appear to be unavailable in private markets. The market in regulation equilibrates the forces of rent-seeking and rent protection as well as those targeted upon rent destruction. The individual participants do not care whether the transfers that they can obtain come from wealth enhancement or from wealth destruction, or whether they are won at no cost or at substantial cost to others. (In such an environment, however, Becker (1983) has suggested that wealth-enhancing transfers *will* prove more popular.)

This possibly darker side of positive public choice was ignored, with serious consequences, by McCormick, Shughart, and Tollison both in their 1984 address and in their 1986 reply to the comment by Cherkes,

Friedman, and Spivak. We take up these issues in a later section of this paper, while centering attention in this section on the implications for conventional welfare economics of the disinterest in regulation insight.

Let us concentrate, therefore, on the issue of the presence or absence of efficiency gains in deregulating a regulatory monopoly, within the context of the full up-front rent-seeking example. This is an entirely normative exercise, without any evident implictions for positive public choice. It is helpful at this stage to resolve minor errors, inconsistencies and omissions in the McCormick, Shughart, and Tollison presentation, as a means of presenting the full force of their argument.

First, as Cherkes et al. (1986) noted, there is a minor technical error in the 1984 presentation, in that the authors failed to allow for the additional output restriction that a profit-maximizing monopolist would incur when confronted by the rent-seeking augmentation of its long-run marginal cost curve. The only relevant implication of this is that a somewhat larger Harberger consumers' surplus is returnable via deregulation than the 1984 paper allowed. Extremely perverse assumptions are required to reverse the qualitative insight that less than the full original Harberger triangle can be returned to consumers via deregulation.

Second, as we have noted elsewhere, (Crew and Rowley, 1986) the 1984 paper was incorrect in its use of sunk cost in association with the waste, via rent-seeking, of specialized resources. Sunk cost, correctly defined, is a bygone, irrelevant to the calculus of choice. Yet, in their employ, the concept is viewed as impacting on choice-influencing cost by eliminiating irreplaceable resources from the choice set of individuals. The issue does not reach to the heart of their argument, but is rather a problem of semantics. Since the notion that rent-seeking really would irreversibly destroy irreplaceable resources is itself less than plausible, we shall not press the matter further in this paper. In taking this view, we in no sense deny the possibility of up-front rent-seeking waste in the case of durable regulation prospects.

Third, there is evident in the 1984 paper a more serious problem of tautology, which threatens the disinterest insight itself, though fortunately, in our view, not inescapably. In order to drive through the full up-front rent-seeking result, the authors assume "for simplicity that the monopoly privilege is perfectly durable" (p. 1076). In such circumstances, subsequent disinterest in deregulation is self-evident and is unrequiring of an explanation. Evidently, imprecise writing led the authors to the edge of disaster. The solution to this apparent tautology, as so often in the theory of choice, is to be found in re-emphasizing subjective expectations *ex ante* at the moment of choice, rather than deterministic outcomes, as the basis for the initial rent-seeking decision. Since this readjustment of theory lends itself to our own reinterpretation of the myth of disinterest, we will reserve discussion of it.

Fourth, there was an omission in the 1984 paper which cost the authors points in the Cherkes et al. reply. Put simply, the authors failed to specify a social welfare function designed to suppress distribution considerations. Such social welfare functions are commonplace in the literature of the new welfare economics and are designed to augment the policy relevance of that field (Rowley and Peacock, 1975). In our view, Buchanan (1959) notwithstanding, there is nothing wrong in utilizing such a mechanism as a means of focusing attention on the efficiency characteristics of institutions, as illustrated by Crew and Kleindorfer (1986). Fairness is the subject not of economic science but of other disciplines operating on the fringes of moral philosophy.

Alternative Regulatory Rent-Seeking Scenarios

The theory of full up-front rent-seeking developed by McCormick, Shughart, and Tollison is dependent upon an *ex ante* expectation that the monopoly, once granted, will be durable throughout the expected economic lifetime of the activity in the absence of any subsequent rent protection expenditures. To the extent that this is not the perception, either the expected monopoly lifetime must be abated, or later rent protection outlays must be anticipated. In either case, the implications for full up-front rent-seeking outlays are adverse, and the prospects for a subsequent efficiency case for deregulation are enhanced.

In our view, the complete durability case is non-sustainable on grounds of public choice. In such circumstances, the relevant scenarios are (1) that of a slow erosion of the initial monopoly position as a consequence of ongoing competitive rent-seeking from outside the monopoly and/or (2) a progressive expansion of rent protection outlays to neutralize the impact of such competitive rent-seeking or to render it uneconomic on an ongoing basis.

The first scenario, which was advanced by Cherkes et al. (1986) has a somewhat mechanistic joint profit-maximizing cartel flavor, and ignores the central characteristics of regulatory markets in the sense of Stigler (1971) and Peltzman (1976). Cherkes et al. posit a situation in which the monopoly "founders" spend resources to create the monopoly and later contribute to its maintenance, though not to the extent necessary to deter new entrants from joining in the privileges of regulation. Thus their model is that of the cartel rather than of the dominant firm monopoly, as is evident from their example which relates to the licensing of physicians.

In the Cherkes et al. model, both founders and joiners allocate resources for rent-seeking. The representative founder allocates such resources entirely on a profit maximizing calculus, reflecting in its benefit function the eventual appearance of joiners. Because of information asymmetries in favor of founders, the latter are rewarded with a surplus which is available to consumers in the event of subsequent deregulation. Once the joiners arrive, future surpluses are eliminated via ongoing rent-seeking and rent protection. Such activities are not seen to erode the regulatory monopoly itself. Cherkes et al. argue that only the original expenses of the founders constitute sunk cost. This conclusion, which supports an efficiency case in favor of deregulation, is not justified analytically in the 1986 paper, but briefly illustrated by the experience of the American Medical Association from its inception in 1846.

The alternative approach, which we shall emphasize henceforth in this section, is to treat regulation as a market in a monopoly license, subject to varying degrees of contestability and devoid of any initial founder advantages, save those which reflect sunk cost in the sense of Baumol, Panzar, and Willig (1982). In such circumstances, rent-seeking and rent protection will be manifest, among all participants, new or old, to the extent justified by individual expected wealth maximization. The extent to which such expenditures are up-front or ongoing will be a function of complex investment decisions grounded on subjective expectations of the durability of returns in the absence of, or in the presence of, expected future depreciations. In our view, the completely durable, non-depreciating rent-seeking investment is a rarity in real world regulatory markets.

We distinguish here for analytic purposes five important cases of 14–3 regulation monopoly which we illustrate by reference both to figure 14–3 and to simulation results outlined in tables 14–1 and 14–2.

Case 1—Full Up-Front Rent Dissipation By A Single Bidder

In Case 1, the regulatory monopoly is perceived to be completely durable *ex ante*, all expected rents are capitalized up-front and wasted in rent-seeking and no rents manifest themselves subsequently as an inducement to future rent-seeking. Thus, the only gain available from deregulation is the returnable fraction of the Harberger triangle. Welfare economists thus predict only a trivial political interest in deregulation, given the counteractive transaction costs of institutional adjustment. In essence, this is the model posited by McCormick, Shughart, and Tollison in their 1984 paper.

The conditions necessary for such an outcome are more stringent than those usually posited in the rent-seeking literature. Specifically, it is essential that only one risk-neutral firm should expend resources on up-front rent-seeking into the regulatory license, that it should perceive the monopoly, once obtained, to be perfectly durable, and that this perception should subsequently be validated, with respect both to durability and to the extent of the monopoly rent.

Why would a single bidder expend up-front the full present value of future rents, in the full knowledge that no other firms are bidding for the license? There are no easy answers to this important question. It is possible, though implausible, that such complete outlays are perceived to be essential to blot out, *ab initio*, all future bids by potential joiners that might otherwise have necessitated rent protection outlays by the incumbent monopolist. This is the ultimate sunk cost inhibition to contestability. It is also possible that full up-front rent-seeking was forced by countervailing consumer rent protection outlays, though in this case a Stigler/Peltzman market would abate the available monopoly rents. Neither such explanation carries with it a generalized credibility as an explanation of disinterest in deregulation.

Case 2—Full Up-Front Rent Dissipation Via Competitive Bidding

Case 2 explores the implications for disinterest in deregulation of relaxing the single rent seeker assumption of Case 1, while retaining all other assumptions save that of an absence of rents in subsequent time periods. Utilizing an arbitrary model due to Posner (1975), we assume that ten firms bid initially for the regulatory rent, myopically in the belief that success in the rent-seeking competition will secure for the winner a perfectly durable rent, the capitalized present value of which is commonly perceived to be $1 million. Each firm is assumed to be risk neutral and to hold an identical Bayesian a priori probability of success of .1. Thus, each firm expends up-front, on rent-seeking, $100,000 to obtain the rent. Jointly, they waste the full $1 million of perceived present value rent from the regulatory monopoly. The winning firm nets an expected wealth gain of $900,000, while each of the losers experiences a wealth loss of $100,000 unless the bankruptcy constraint intervenes.

In the new situation, the existence of rents in the present value of $900,000 within the given regulatory market raises questions concerning the nature of durability of the incumbent's position. Two alternatives dominate attention. In the first, the initial rent-seeking competition was an equilibrium game, and the secondary rents thus provoke no further rent-seeking and rent protection outlays. Deregulation in such circumstances returns the major portion of the Harberger triangle and simply transforms producers' surplus to consumers. The efficiency interest in deregulation remains low. In the second, the monopolist is vulnerable to secondary rent-seeking as a periodic battle for remaining rents is engaged. In each battle, capitalized residual rents are wasted up-front, although in each case they are discounted for non-durability by the competing rent seekers.

On each occasion, the winner obtains access to the expected value of the residual rents, less its own up-front outlays. The losers suffer capitalized losses in the value of their unsuccessful outlays. Table 14–1 illustrates a process in which the rents accumulate uniformly over thirty years (i.e., a thirty-year annuity) and then cease. They are discounted by all bidders at five percent per annum. By varying the number of rent seekers and the frequency of repeat bids, alternative simulations of rent dissipation are outlined, assuming that each bidder expends the expected value of the residual rent on each occasion of battle.

A number of conclusions follow. The returns to deregulation are always higher the earlier that deregulation occurs. The returns to deregulation are also higher, given the timing, the larger the number of rent seekers involved. For example, in our least favorable scenario, with 30 annual repeat bids by 10 rent seekers, residual rents are virtually emasculated after 29 years. If the perception of durability should decay following repeat bids, the process of rent dissipation would be further retarded. Even in this up-front rent dissipation model, interest in deregulation remains high over a lengthy time period. Moreover, the total rent dissipated over the full cycle is a significant multiple of that initially perceived.

Table 14–1 The Erosion of $1 Million of Initial Rents By Repeated Rent-Seeking

Number of Rent-Seekers	*Number of Repeat Bids*	*Present Value of Rent to Single Successful Rent Seekers*
10	10	$290,810
	20	65,693
	30	2,626
20	10	499,367
	20	193,706
	30	13,298
100	10	754,286
	20	441,951
	30	45,827

Case 3—Total Rent Dissipation by Ongoing Expenditures

Where the institutional form of a regulation impedes rent capitalization, up-front rent-seeking does not occur. Rather, rents are dissipated on a current basis, both by the incumbent monopolists and by those who seek to usurp their privileges in the rent protection, rent-seeking battle. Ongoing rent dissipation of this kind is institutionalized in the case of public utilities in the form of prescribed regulatory hearings over price adjustments, reporting procedures, audits, etc. Given major uncertainty concerning the composition of such regulatory commissions and the behavior of intervenors, rent capitalization is not feasible in this environment. Instead, rents are dissipated in periodic battles among the incumbent, its suppliers, its customers, and its potential competitors for control over the regulatory market. Politicians, lawyers, economists, and technical experts, as well as management, are diverted into socially wasteful activities in this adverse institutional environment. Table 14–2 indicates that a high percentage of monopoly rent that otherwise would be dissipated is returnable to consumers via deregulation in the ongoing rent dissipation case.

Case 4—Total Rent Dissipation by Mixture of Up-Front and Ongoing Expenditures

In this mixed case, the regulation market offers some rents in capitalizable form, which stimulates up-front rent-seeking, and other rents on a periodic basis, which give rise to ongoing rent-seeking. Table 14–2 presents a range of simulations for this case, varying the proportion of rents dissipated up-

Table 14–2. Proportional Gains from Deregulation Cases 3–5

Case	*Percentage of Rents Wasted Up-Front*	*Percentage of Ongoing Rents Retained by Incumbent*	*Gains from Deregulation % of Regulated Monopoly Revenue Per Period*		
			$n = 0.5$	$n = 1$	$n = 1.5$
3	0	0	37.7	40.55	44.95
4	0.25	0	26.79	28.77	30.94
	0.50	0	17.43	18.23	19.09
	0.75	0	8.51	8.70	8.89
5	0.50	50	14.29	16.27	18.44

front, and the price elasticity of demand in the regulated product market. Even in our worst case scenario, deregulation offers non-trivial net benefits via improved economic efficiency. This case retains the total dissipation assumption, with the incumbent receiving only a normal rate of return on rent seeking outlays.

Case 5—Less Than Total Dissipation of Available Rents

In this mixed case, imperfections in the rent-seeking market are assumed to allow the incumbent monopolist excess returns on its rent seeking outlays. In such circumstances, as table 14–2 indicates, sizeable efficiency gains are available from deregulation as well as additional wealth transfers from the monopolist to consumers.

Overall Implications

The qualitative implications for deregulation in Cases 3–5 as presented above are outlined geometrically in figure 14–3.

In figure 14–3, the competitive solution is output Q_C at price B. The regulated monopoly produces output Q_M at price A. In the absence of deregulation, the Case 3 one-period welfare loss comprises the Harberger triangle, CGF, and the rent-seeking loss ABGC. These losses are returnable to consumers, once transaction costs are deducted, via deregulation. The equivalent gain from deregulation in Case 4 is given by the area AB′F′C, which is less than that available in Case 3 by the magnitude B′BFF′ which reflects up-front sunk rent seeking expenditures by the incumbent monopolist. The net gain to deregulation in Case 5 is determined by subtracting the rent retained by the incumbent on an ongoing basis, A′B′E′E from the relevant area in Case 4, AB′F′C. This leaves a gain of AA′EC plus CE′F′ to deregulation.

Are Regulatory Rents Dissipated Up-Front?

The case advanced against deregulation is shown to be a special case where all rents are capitalized up-front and where the regulatory monopoly, once granted, is invulnerable to repeated attacks by rent seekers. We submit that this is not characteristic of the large majority of regulated monopolies within the U.S., and for good reasons.

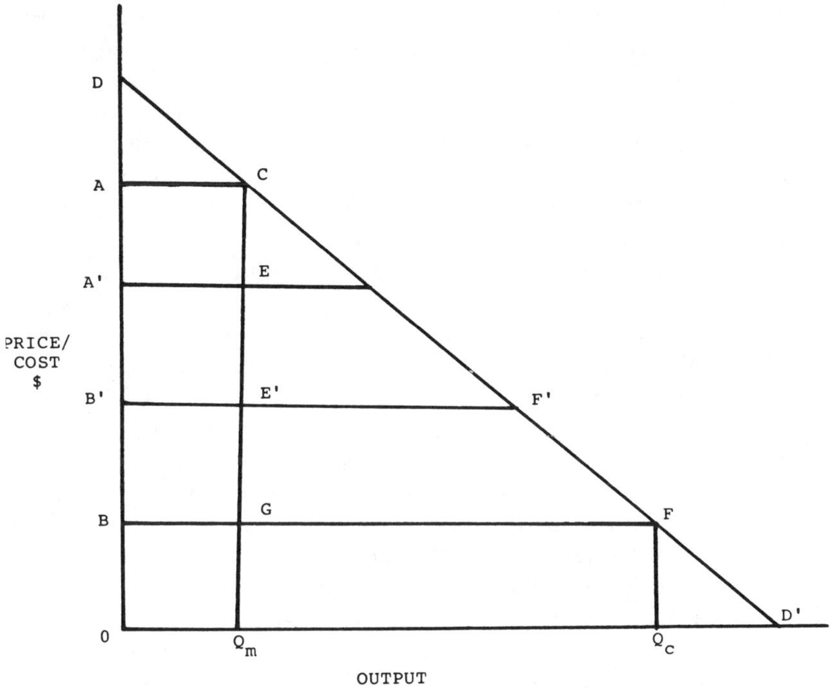

Figure 14–3.

First, as Higgins and Tollison (1984) have noted, competition for a regulated monopoly may not dissipate rents, but simply transfer them to those who manipulate the competition. For example, an auction in which the winning bid is the property of the politicians simply expropriates the original surplus and transfers it to politicians and/or bureaucrats. Further analysis then is required to determine whether the transferred rents are dissipated by rent-seeking in the political and/or bureaucratic markets. Alternatively, if rent seekers are obliged to court those who dispense regulatory monopolies with in-kind rather than with financial transfers, rents are not fully dissipated, although there is an excess burden which is a loss to society. Once again, secondary dissipation cannot be ruled out. In neither case are the production possibilities of the economy likely to be permanently reduced, as McCormick et al. suggest; however, since the resources are lost forever to the regulated industry, their case against deregulation is sustained.

Second, even granting McCormick et al. the paradigm in which monopoly rent-seeking is rent dissipative and, for example, court hearings, legal wrangles, expert testimonies, etc., eat into the potential surplus, it is still not certain that all rents will be dissipated. Early contributions by Tullock (1967), Krueger (1974), and Posner (1975) indeed suggested that rents were exactly dissipated. Subsequent contributions, however, cast doubt on the generality of that result: Tullock (1980) finding situations of under- or over-bidding when transfers probabilities were not a linear function of rent-seeking expenditures; Rogerson (1982) finding under-bidding when rent seekers faced differential start-up costs; and Hillman and Katz (1984) finding under-bidding when rent seekers exhibited risk-aversion and where the value of the transfer was large. The under-bidding results weaken the McCormick et al. prediction of disinterest in deregulation. However, they are derived from a theory in which both the value of the transfer and the number of the rent seekers is fixed. Higgins, Shughart, and Tollison (1984) have established that free entry into rent-seeking by risk-neutral competitors leads to the exact dissipation of available rents.

Third, even with free entry, bounded rationality may prevent the full dissipation of available rents. It is much more difficult for rent seekers to evaluate up-front the full present value of the available rents than it is for them to assess the size of the single-period rent-rectangle in the conventional neoclassical diagram. For they must take a view on the relevant discount rate; on the dynamics of the market into which they seek to enter; and on the likely behavior of the regulators under whom they are to seek their rents. Given risk-aversion, bounded rationality will lead to the under-dissipation of rents in the initial bidding competition.

Fourth, although further systematic research is required, evidence of an informal nature suggests that ongoing rent-seeking is an important feature of regulated industries. Indeed, many regulatory institutions appear to be designed to facilitate such ongoing rent-seeking. Utilities' profits are restricted, and they are regulated on a cost-plus basis giving them no great incentive to try to prevent rent-seeking (Daughety, 1984). Fair rate-of-return hearings, regulatory audits, regulatory decisions concerning potential new entrants, etc., provide ideal conditions for rent-seeking resource waste. Moreover, the regulatory bodies themselves are not budget-constrained in their interventions. In many instances, public intervenors are funded from utility revenues to oppose utility rate petitions. Almost always, regulatory commissions levy their utilities to fund their activities (Phillips, 1984). Crew and Kleindorfer (1985), in a recent study of regulatory costs and benefits in New Jersey, discovered that regulatory expenses were high in relation to potential benefits from regulation. They further discovered that costs of regulating smaller utilities were being covered by levies on larger utilities.

Hard evidence is difficult to come by, since it is in the interests of rent seekers to keep rents (and their dissipation) as invisible as possible. However, we are convinced that this is a potentially rewarding area of study. If ongoing rent-seeking is evident, the McCormick et al. paradigm clearly cannot hold. Ongoing rent-seeking constitutes a powerful *a priori* case in favor of deregulation.

Conclusions

Where ongoing costs occur in regulatory rent-seeking, political equilibrium is likely to be more fragile than in the situation posited by McCormick et al. The existence of ongoing rent-seeking is evidence of a net social loss to continuing regulation which does not exist in the up-front case. Such net losses may fuel a limited additional deregulation lobby among consumers. More important, however, is the enhanced contestability of regulated markets implied by the smaller sunk cost advantages of regulated incumbents. In such circumstances, a powerful producer interest in deregulation is predictable, raising the probability of an uprising in deregulation.

Underpinning the approach of McCormick et al. is a concept of *equilibrium* in regulatory markets. To the extent that regulation persists, equilibrium indeed must be inferred. It is important to note, however, that such equilibrium is determined politically and not just by the market. Changes in the preferences of constituency groups, and/or in coalition opportunities, within the political market may induce deregulation policies of the kind that are such a feature of the current U.S. scene. We conclude this paper, therefore, by reemphasizing that regulation equilibrium is a balance of constituent interests. In no sense does such a balance necessarily imply the absence of a significant interest in deregulation.

References

We are grateful to James M. Buchanan, Robert Elgin, Paul Kleindorfer, Robert D. Tollison, and Gordon Tullock for encouragement and helpful comments. Earlier drafts benefited from a Workshop Discussion at the Center for Study of Public Choice, George Mason University, and from the Rutgers University Advanced Workshop in Public Utility Economics and Regulation, held at Mohonk Mountain House, New Paltz, New York.

Baumol, W.J.; Panzar, J.C.; and Willig, R.D *Contestable Markets and the Theory of Industry Structure*. Harcourt Brace Jovanovich, Inc., 1982.

Buchanan, J.M. "Positive Economics, Welfare Economics, and Political Economy," *Journal of Law and Economics* 2 (October, 1959): 124–38.

Cherkes, M.; Friedman, J.; and Spivak, A. "The Disinterest in Deregulation: Comment." *American Economic Review* no. 3, 76 (June, 1986): 559–63.

Crew, M.A., and Kleindorfer, P.R. *The Economics of Public Utility Regulation*. Cambridge: MIT Press, 1986.

Crew, M.A., and Kleindorfer, P.R. "Governance Costs of Rate-of-Return Regulation." *Journal of Theoretical and Institutional Economics* (March, 1985).

Crew, M.A., and Rowley, C.K. "Deregulation as an Instrument in Industrial Policy." *Journal of Institutional and Theoretical Economics* 142 (1986): 52–70.

Daughety, A.F. "Regulation and Industrial Organization." *Journal of Political Economy* no. 92, 5 (October, 1984): 932–53.

Higgins, R.S.; Shughart II, W.F.; and Tollison, R.D. "Free Entry and Efficient Rent Seeking." (May, 1984).

Higgins, R.S., and Tollison, R.D. "Notes on the Theory of Rent Seeking." (November, 1984).

Hillman, A.L., and Katz, E. "Risk-Averse Rent Seekers and the Social Cost of Monopoly Power." *Economic Journal*, no. 94, 373 (March, 1984): 104–110.

Krueger, A.O. "The Political Economy of the Rent-Seeking Society," *American Economic Review* (June, 1974): 291–303.

McCormick, R.E.; Shughart II, W.F.; and Tollison, R.D. "Disinterest in Deregulation." *American Economic Review*, no. 74, 5 (December, 1984): 1075–79; and "Reply." *American Economic Review*, no. 3, 76 (June, 1986): 564–65.

Olson, M. *The Rise and Decline of Nations*. New Haven: Yale University Press, 1982.

Peltzman, S. "Toward a More General Theory of Regulation." *Journal of Law and Economics* 19 (1976): 211–240.

Phillips, C.F. *The Regulation of Public Utilities*. Arlington: Public Utility Reports, 1984.

Posner, R.A. "The Social Costs of Monopoly and Regulation." *Journal of Political Economy* 83 (August 1975): 807–827.

Rogerson, W.P. "The Social Costs of Monopoly and Regulation: A Game-Theoretic Analysis." *Bell Journal of Economics* 13 (Autumn, 1982): 391–401.

Rowley, C.K, and Elgin, R. "Toward a Theory of Bureaucracy." In: D. Greenway, and G.K. Shaw (eds.) *Public Choice, Public Finance and Public Policy*. Oxford: Basil Blackwell, 1985.

Rowley, C.K., and Tollison, R.D. "Rent-Seeking and Trade Protection." *Swiss Journal of International Relations* (1986): 141–66.

Stigler, G.J. "The Theory of Economic Regulation." *Bell Journal of Economics and Management Science* 2 (1971): 3–21.

Tullock, G., "Efficient Rent-Seeking." In J.M. Buchanan, R.D. Tollison, and G. Tullock (eds.) *Toward a Theory of the Rent-Seeking Society*. College Station: Texas A & M, 1980, 97–112.

Tullock, G. "Welfare Costs of Tariffs, Monopolies, and Theft." *Western Economic Journal* 5 (June, 1967): 224–232.

15 RENT EXTRACTION AND RENT CREATION IN THE ECONOMIC THEORY OF REGULATION

Fred S. McChesney*

Introduction

The economic theory of regulation has advanced considerably since Stigler's seminal piece explained government's ability to create rents by cartelizing private producers.[1] Because political action can redistribute wealth generally, it is now seen that private interest groups other than producers also have an incentive to organize, both to obtain the gains and to avoid the losses from a whole menu of government enactments.[2] The configuration of winners and losers depends on many factors, and it changes as the underlying demands for and costs of regulation shift. New

---

* John M. Olin, Visiting Fellow in Law and Economics, University of Chicago Law School; Associate Professor, Emory University School of Law. Many persons commented helpfully on earlier drafts of this paper, including participants in presentations at Emory University, Clemson University, the Federal Trade Commission, Holy Cross College, and the annual meetings of the Western Economic Association (July 1985), and the Public Choice Society (March 1985). My colleague David Haddock provided especially helpful comments. Henry Butler, Frank Easterbrook, Ernest Gellhorn, Mark Moran, Timothy Muris, Steven Salop, David Schap, and an anonymous referee also contributed much useful criticism.

technology, for example, may render existing government regulations undesirable to their prior beneficiaries or make current regulations useful to groups previously not benefited. Finally, "government" itself has come to be treated, not as a unit, but as a complicated network of individuals, each with an incentive to maximize his own interest.

The original economic theory of regulation thus has evolved into a more complex description of the various ways government regulatory power can be turned to private ends. Two limitations of the current economic model are noteworthy, however. First, despite the growing realization that "government" is not a monolith, the role of the politician has not been integrated satisfactorily into the model. The politician has remained a "mystery actor,"[3] a passive broker among competing private rent seekers.[4] Second, the economic theory, even in its post-Stiglerian form, remains one of rent creation. Observers note that creation of rents does not seem to explain many of the regulatory statutes that legislators have enacted.[5] But the opportunities for political gains from activities other than rent creation have not been considered.

This article focuses specifically on politicians. It views them, not as mere brokers redistributing wealth in response to competing private demands, but as independent actors making their own demands to which private actors respond. The conceptual reversal of roles in turn forces consideration of the ways other than rent creation that politicians can gain from private parties. A model is developed to show how politicians reap returns first by threatening and then by forbearing from extracting private rents already in existence. These private rents, as opposed to politically created rents, represent returns to their owners' entrepreneurial ability and firm-specific private investments.[6]

Political office confers a property right, not just to legislate rents, but to impose costs. A politician can gain by forbearing from exercising his right to impose burdensome restrictions on private actors. The passage of sharply focused taxes and regulations will reduce the returns that private capital owners receive from their skills and investments. In order to protect these returns, private owners have an incentive to strike bargains with legislators, as long as the side payments to politicians are lower than the expected losses from compliance with the threatened law. (The payments need not be bribes; they might be contributions to political campaigns or in-kind donations of service and property, for example.)

A politician thus can gain by forbearing—for a price—from exercising his right to impose costs on private actors that would reduce rents from capital they have created or invested themselves. Though the strategy has not been recognized heretofore, one in fact observes private producers being compelled to pay legislators to prevent private rents from being extracted. In a static sense the payments might seem to be simple transfers. But the transfers required to protect returns to private investments create disincentives to invest in valuable specific capital in the first place. The short-run view ignores the longer-run adverse consequences of threatened rent extraction for overall levels of wealth. In the end, the article suggests, existing estimates of the welfare costs of government regulation overlook the costs of inducing government *not* to regulate.

Rent Extraction and the Economic Theory of Regulation

Legislative Creation of Political Rents

The original (Stiglerian) interpretation of regulation is the traditional cartel model, but one in which government imposes and enforces the anticompetitive restrictions. If expected political rents net of the costs of organizing and procuring favorable legislation are positive, then producers will demand—pay for—regulation. Deadweight consumer loss is measured by the welfare triangle. Producers stand to gain the rent rectangle, but political competition for it produces additional social loss from rent-seeking.[7]

Industry-wide cartelization is not the only way politicians can create rents. More recent theoretical[8] and empirical[9] contributions have noted that regulation can create Ricardian (inframarginal) rents if it raises costs of some firms more than those of others. This "cost-predation" strategy differs from Stiglerian cartelization in that only some firms in the industry gain while others lose. Industry cooperation to obtain rents for all firms is replaced by rivalry among industry subgroups to benefit some firms at others' expense.

The cooperation and rivalry models of regulation are the same, however, in that both focus on private purchase of rents. Politician/brokers respond to private demands for rents with a supply of regulation but do not actively enter the market for rents with their own demands.[10] This is perhaps in keeping with the consumer-sovereignty model of private markets, but the applicability of that model to the political market is questionable. Clearly, a politician himself actively seeks votes, campaign contributions, and other forms of recompense, contracting to receive a supply of goods or services from private parties in response to his own demands.[11]

Modeled just as a broker among competing private demands, the politician has not been well integrated into the economic theory of regulation. His role thus far has been "subsumed,"[12] with little explicit consideration given to the ways in which the politician himself benefits from creating rents for private parties. More important, no attention has been paid to ways other than rent creation that a politician can obtain benefits from private individuals.

A politician has alternative ways to engage private parties in exchange. He may demand votes or money and offer the rent rectangle as consideration, as in the orthodox economic theory of regulation. But a politician may also make his demands on private parties, not by promising benefits, but by threatening to impose costs—a form of political blackmail. If the expected cost of the act threatened exceeds the value of the consideration that private parties must give up to avoid legislative action, they will surrender the tribute demanded of them. With constant marginal utility of wealth, a private citizen will be just as willing to pay legislators to have rents of $1 million created as he will to avoid imposition of $1 million in losses.

Once the politician is seen as an independent actor in the regulatory process, his objective function cannot be treated as single valued. He will maximize total returns to himself by equating at the margin the returns from votes, contributions, bribes, power, and other sources of personal gain. All these, in turn, are positive functions not only of private benefits he confers but also of private costs he agrees not to impose.

The political strategy of cost forbearance can assume several forms. Perhaps most obvious is the threat to deregulate an industry previously cartelized. Expected political rents created by earlier regulation are quickly capitalized into firm share prices. If politicians later breach their contract and vote unexpectedly to deregulate, shareholders suffer a wealth loss. Rather than suffer the costs of deregulation, shareholders will pay politicians a sum up to the amount of wealth threatened to have them refrain from deregulating. In fact, one routinely observes payments to politicians to protect previously enacted cartel measures.[13]

Subsequent payments to avoid postcontractual opportunism by politicians must be distinguished from contractual payments to guarantee rent permanence *ex ante*. Both politicians and rent recipients gain when the durability of regulation is increased by holding legislators to longer contracts. But new arrivals on both sides succeed to the interests of the original contracting parties. A legislator not party to the original bargain has less incentive to abide by the political rent-creation deal struck by his predecessors unless he too is compensated. Guaranteed rent durability is thus impossible. Among firm owners, subsequent purchasers of shares with expected rents capitalized into their prices are vulnerable to rent extraction on the part of opportunistic politicians. Payments to political newcomers to secure performance of previously negotiated contracts earn no rents. Rather, they protect against windfall losses that new legislators could otherwise impose.

Political Extraction of Private Rents

The durability problem for politically created rents has been discussed elsewhere[14] and is not the focus of this article. But recognition of the rent-extraction opportunities that capitalized cartel rents represent to politicians suggests that similar strategies may offer gains to politicians when other sorts of rents exist. In particular, it leads one to focus on the capital value of privately created rents and predictable political responses to their existence.

Figure 15–1 depicts an industry in which producers have differing amounts of entrepreneurial capacity or some firm-specific, fixed-cost asset. The industry supply curve in the absence of regulation (S_0) thus is upward sloping. Returns to entrepreneurship and specific assets come as rents out of producers' surplus, 0AD. Regulatory measures could be identified that would increase costs for all firms, but more for marginal firms, moving the industry supply curve to S_1.[15] To inframarginal producers regulation

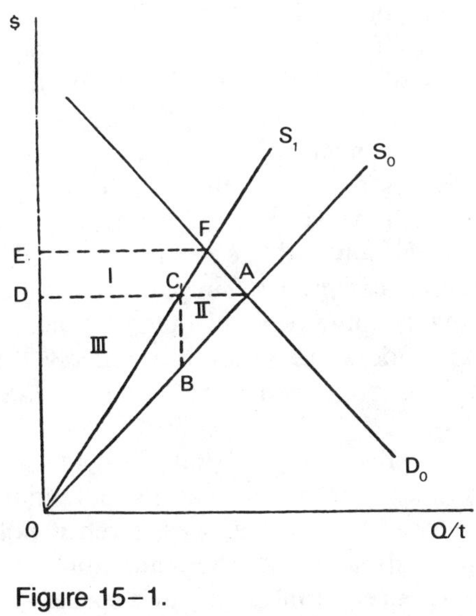

Figure 15–1.

is advantageous (that is, they would pay politicians to effect it) as long as there is a net increase in rents. In figure 15–1 area 1 is greater than area II (CDEF > ABC): the gains from higher prices exceed the losses due to fewer sales. The capitalized value of the increased rent flow defines the maximum payment producers would make to politicians in return for regulation.[16]

But rent creation by a governmentally mandated shift from S_0 to S_1 is not the only option open to politicians. *Existing* private rents rewarding specific assets are greater than the rents that can be created by regulation: 0AD > CDEF (area I). Regulatory measures can also be identified that would expropriate the producers' surplus, as explained below. Once such regulation is threatened, the price that producers would pay politicians in return for governmental nonaction would exceed any payment for rent-creating regulation.

Faced, then, with a choice between the two strategies, a regulator would maximize the benefits to himself by threatening to expropriate the existing private rents rather than by creating new political rents.[17] As with threatened deregulation of government cartels, payments must be made to protect rents. But unlike the cartel case, where rents were created by government itself, a legislator threatening to expropriate private rents is paid to let firms earn returns on capital they have created or invested for themselves. "Milker bills" is one term used by politicians to describe legislative proposals intended only to squeeze private producers for payments not to pass the rent-extracting legislation. "Early on in my association with the California legislature, I came across the concept of 'milker bills'—proposed legislation which had nothing to do with milk to drink and much to do with money, the 'mother's milk of politics.'... Representative Sam, in need of campaign contributions, has a bill introduced which excites some constituency to urge Sam to work hard for its defeat (easily achieved), pouring funds into his campaign coffers and 'forever' endearing Sam to his constituency for his effectiveness."[18] Milked victims describe the process simply as blackmail and extortion.[19] The threats are made quite openly. One reads, for example, that "House Republican leaders are sending a vaguely threatening message to business political action committees: Give us more, or we may do something rash."[20]

The producers' surplus compensating firm-specific capital is inframarginal, but this does not mean that its potential expropriation by politicians has no allocative consequences. Even if politicians eventually allow themselves to be bought off, their minatory presence reduces the expected value of entrepreneurial ability and specific-capital investments.

The possibility that government may reduce returns to their capital unless paid off reduces firms' incentives to invest in the first place. It also induces inefficient shifts to investment in more mobile or salvageable (that is, less firm specific) forms of capital as insurance against expropriation. In either event, the allocative losses from politicians' ability to extract the returns from private capital are measured by investments that are never made in the industry threatened.

In effect, an important similarity between capital expropriations in less-developed countries and "mere" regulation in developed nations has been overlooked. In both cases the very presence of a threatening government will reduce private investment.[21] The resulting welfare losses would be measured by the value of specific capital and other investments that firms would have made, but for the fear of subsequent expropriation and the cost of purchasing protection from politicians. The consequences are like those of ordinary theft: "One way of minimizing loss by theft is to have little or nothing to steal. In a world in which theft was legal we could expect this fact to lead to a reduction in productive activities."[22]

Rent extraction can succeed only to the extent that threats to expropriate private rents are credible. With any given firm or industry, producers and politicians may be locked in a "chicken" game: since legislators seemingly gain nothing if they actually destroy private capital, capital owners may be tempted to call politicians' bluff by refusing to pay. But a politician's demonstrated willingness actually to expropriate private rents in one situation provides a lesson for other firms or industries that will induce them to pay in their turn. To make credible expected later threats to destroy others' capital, politicians may sometimes have to enact legislation extracting private rents whose owners do not pay.[23] (And as discussed below, legislators can always enact statutes now and sell repeal later.)

The credibility and thus the political attraction of rent-extraction strategies also depend on the strength of constitutional rules that protect private property and contract rights against governmental taking. Legislative threats to expropriate returns to private capital will elicit fewer payments to politicians the more likely it is that capital owners later can have any legislation voided constitutionally in the courts. The level of constitutional scrutiny of legislative expropriations involving private contract and property rights has declined throughout the twentieth century.[24] The scope for credible legislative threats against private capital has expanded apace. In effect, as courts have retreated from affording consitutional protection against legislative takings, potential private victims have been forced to employ more self-help remedies by buying off politicians rather than submit to rent-extracting regulation.

Private Rent Extraction versus Political Rent Creation

Extraction of private rents and creation of political rents need not be mutually exclusive; maximum gains to politicians may involve a combination of the two. In figure 15–1, for example, politicians could create rents in area I (CDEF) by imposing regulation while threatening at the same time to expropriate the remaining producers' surplus in area III (0DC). The maximum private payment forthcoming from this combined tactic, I + III (0EF), would exceed that from merely threatening rent expropriation without regulation (0AD). But a combined strategy of rent creation and rent extraction is not necessarily optimal to politicians. Political rent creation (of either the Stiglerian or the inframarginal sort) requires restriction of output, which itself reduces the current stock of *expropriable* producers' surplus. *Ceteris paribus*, greater rent creation therefore means more forgone rent extraction. Particularly because the political processes of creating or extracting rents are not costless to legislators, the gains may justify using only one or the other strategy in a particular market.

The relative gains from the two strategies, and thus the optimal political mix of created and extracted rents, will depend on industry supply and demand conditions. The more inelastic industry demand is, the greater the relative attraction of political rent creation. Likewise, if industry supply is perfectly elastic, there is no producers' surplus and so no opportunity for rent extraction. On the other hand, when industry demand is perfectly elastic, extraction of private rents is the only plausible political strategy. Similarly, a large stock of specific (nonsalvageable) capital increases the relative attraction to politicians of private rent extraction. Of course, producers themselves would rather buy new rents than pay to protect their own existing rents. But in some markets, rent-creation opportunities may be slight as compared to the opportunities for extraction of returns to entrepreneurship and private capital. For example, ease of new entry into an industry may make rent-creating cartelization futile. At the same time, the presence of large specific-capital stocks would make the same industry vulnerable to rent extraction.

Information concerning demand and supply elasticities, entry costs, and the size and mobility of capital stocks is costly to politicians. The specter of rent extraction naturally will induce private owners of *expropriable* capital to try to hide the size of their capital stocks, which increases the costs to politicians of discovering how much producers would pay to avoid expropriation.[25] But political threats to act have the effect of instituting an auction market among private parties. "[L]egislatures work on the presence or absence of opposition. Legislation for which the claim can be made that some group will benefit, if only modestly, and which induces no opposition is almost certain to pass. Thus, introduction of a milker bill which does not generate the expected opposition to its passage, as evidenced by resources devoted to lobbying for its defeat, indeed will pass. By contrast, milker bills which generate the anticipated opposition will fail. Contrasting these outcomes usually makes an effective case for generating the lobbying resources."[26] An auction not only drives competitive bids for legislative favors higher but also reveals which firms stand to gain and which to lose and the magnitude of the respective effects.

The auction thus provides valuable information whether regulatory action or inaction will be more lucrative to politicians themselves; it helps to identify the likely payers and to set the amounts of the compensation to be paid. Particularly since legislators may not know the size of the rents potentially *expropriable*, they may prefer to make good their threat in order to elicit bids revealing the true size of the private capital stock. Actual enactment of legislation raises to unity the probability of rent-destroying measures being imposed, unless firms buy legislative repeal. Legislation that would destroy rents can be enacted with a delayed effective date to allow firms to mobilize and bid to remove or alter the statute.[27]

Because the maximum gains to legislators depend on knowledge of elasticities and the size of private rents, there may also be gains from specialization in identifying industries with expropriable producers' surplus and in determining how best to extract it. If so, legislators predictably would delegate cost-imposing functions to specialized bureaucratic agencies. By threatening or actually imposing costs, these outside agents create a demand for politicians to mitigate the costs. Use of specialized agencies to impose costs has a second advantage to politicians. While they may act at the behest of elected officials, bureaucrats will be perceived by at least some rationally ignorant voters as independent. Information about the regulatory process is costly to obtain, and so it may appear that misguided agencies rather than politicians themselves are responsible for the costs threatened.[28] Designation of institutions like the Federal Trade Commission (FTC) and the Securities and Exchange Commission as "independent agencies" may further the perception in some voters' eyes that politicians are less responsible for their activities.[29]

Methods of Extracting Private Rents

Having located private capital stocks whose returns will come out of producers' surplus, how can legislators extract that surplus? Two general strategies represent threats to private producers: reductions in price and increases in cost.[30]

Legislative Threats to Reduce Prices

Consider, for example, firms' fixed-cost investments in brand-name capital or reputation.[31] All firms may produce otherwise equivalent products, but some will have incurred greater costs in past periods (for example, by advertising) to make their names and quality familiar to consumers. Advertising creates a capital stock, returns from which are taken over time.[32] Once created, the capital is specific to the firm and enables the firm in a later period to incur lower costs to guarantee the quality of the goods or services that it sells. Rival firms without brand-name capital must incur higher costs in that same period to make their names and product quality as well-known and trustworthy to consumers.

This is shown in figure 15–2 for two representative firms. Industry supply and demand (from Figure 1) establish the equilibrium price, 0D. Firm X has been in business and advertised for years; firm Y has just started busines. Both firms provide identical products of equivalent quality at the same production cost ($MC_X = MC_Y$). But customers cannot evaluate product quality prior to purchase; hence there is uncertainty. Both firms guarantee quality, but in different ways. Firm X relies on its investment in brand-name capital in prior periods, its customers paying a

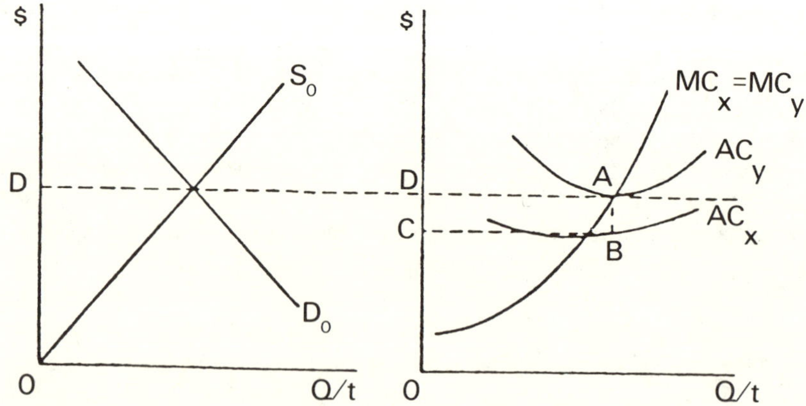

Figure 15–2

premium for the credible guarantee of quality that the reputation capital provides. To offer an equivalent guarantee, firm Y must incur other fixed costs in the current period, such as having an independent laboratory test its product quality and publicize the fact that it is just as good as X's, making its average costs higher ($AC_Y > AC_X$). The premium (AB) that firm X's customers pay for the reputational guarantee earns rents (ABCD).

But X's rents can be reduced or destroyed by government intervention. Politicians can pass legislation to have administrative agencies guarantee quality or truthful information by imposing minimum quality standards or mandatory information-disclosure regulations. Government agents then would police the market for quality and truth, substituting both for the brand-name capital invested earlier by firm X and for the current testing that firm Y would have commissioned to guarantee quality. To the extent it substitutes for private reputation capital, government regulation destroys the premium value of firm X's private capital while relieving the nonreputational firm, Y, of the need to incur new costs to warrant its own quality.

The threatened government intervention would lower price and increase the elasticity of industry supply, eradicating the producers' surplus available to compensate firms for their earlier fixed-cost investments. Rather than have politicians depreciate their capital stock, firm X would pay up to ABCD per period for nonintervention in the market. Even if regulation "only" substitutes for activities currently provided privately, it reduces the expected returns to private-reputation investments and so over time the amount of investment. Note also that in the new equilibrium firm Y would earn no rents from the regulation and so would offer politicians nothing for it. The only gains to politicians in this case come from threatening to extract X's rents.

The history of the FTC's "Used Car Rule" provides an example of the gain to politicians from threatening this type of regulation and later removing the threat for a fee. In 1975, Congress statutorily ordered the FTC to initiate a rulemaking to regulate used-car dealers' warranties.[33] The FTC promulgated a rule imposing costly warranty and auto-defect disclosure requirements, creating the opportunity for legislators to extract concessions from dealers to void the burdensome measures. In the meantime, in fact, Congress had legislated for itself a veto over FTC actions.[34] On promulgation of the rule, used-car dealers and their trade association descended on Congress, spending large sums of money for relief from the proposed rule's costs.[35] When the concessions were forthcoming. Congress vetoed the very rule it had ordered.[36]

It is noteworthy that conditions in the used-car industry conform closely to those hypothesized as conducive to a strategy of rent extraction. As

Stigler himself notes,[37] cartelization of the used-car industry would be difficult: start-up costs are low; there are no entry barriers (for example, licensing requirements); and units of the product have different qualities, making enforcement of cartel pricing difficult. By comparison, the industry is susceptible to a strategy of rent extraction. Quality uncertainty (the risk of getting Akerlof's "lemon")[38] is a problem, leading sellers to invest in reputation capital.[39] By requiring and policing seller disclosure of warranty and defect information, government would have substituted for sellers' investments in quality-assuring reputation. Rather than suffer the capital losses that regulation would entail, firms predictably would—and did—compensate legislators not to intervene.

Legislative Threats to Raise Costs

Just as proposals to institute price-lowering regulation imperil private rents, so do regulations that threaten to increase costs. Consider the situation portrayed in figure 15–3, in which legislators threaten to impose an excise tax or other per-unit cost of 0C. Rather than suffer a net loss in producers' surplus, area I–area II (0AEC–BDFE), firms earning rents will offer to compensate legislators to refrain from imposing the costs.

There are many examples of payments to politicians to purchase governmental inactivity in taxation.[40] Recently, the excise tax on beer has

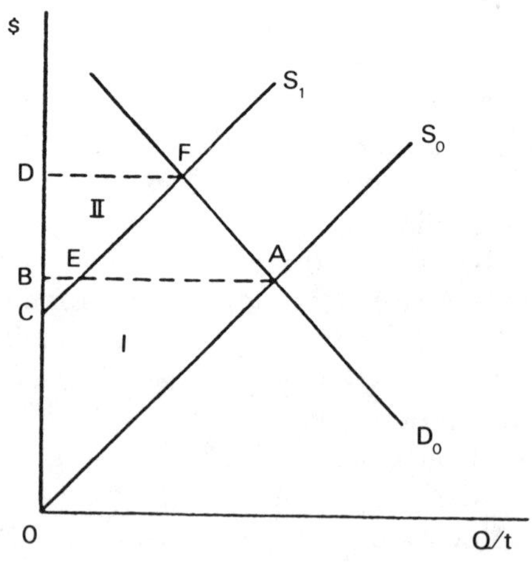

Figure 15–3

generated substantial revenue for legislators in return for their inactivity.[41] Of course, excise taxes are just one cost that politicians can threaten to impose on private firms. Other recent threats include proposals to require financial institutions to start costly reporting and witholding of taxes from depositors' interest and dividends (a measure that was passed and then repealed) and proposals to impose "unisex" premiums and benefit payments on insurance firms. Both episodes are difficult to explain using the standard economic model, as they consumed considerable political time but ended with no regulation at all being imposed. But even if the regulation was never actually imposed, each measure would be attractive politically as a device that might ultimately elicit private payments to legislators *not* to impose the threatened costs—which in fact each one did.[42]

Conclusion

This article extends the economic theory of regulation to include the gains available to elected politicians from alleviating costs threatened or actually imposed on private actors by legislators themselves and by specialized bureaucratic agencies. Status as a legislator confers a property right not only to create political rents but also to impose costs that would destroy private rents. Their ability to impose costs enables politicians credibly to demand payments not to do so. Even when politicians eventually eschew intervention, the mere threat and the payments required to remove it distort private investment decisions.

The model of rent extraction set out here in no way undermines the orthodox model of rent-creating regulation; rather it supplements it by recognizing alternative sources of political gains. Indeed, Stigler's original article foreshadowed a complementary rent-extraction model: "The state—the machinery and power of the state—is a potential resource *or threat* to every industry in the society. With its power to prohibit or compel, *to take* or give money, the state can and does selectively help *or hurt* a vast number of industries.... Regulation may be actively sought by an industry, *or it may be thrust upon it*" (emphasis added).[43] Conditions that make political rent creation relatively unattractive to politicians make private rent extraction more attractive. The relative attraction of rent extraction has also increased as constitutional protection of private rights has diminished.

Many of the insights from the rent-creation model of regulation will doubtless prove useful in further explorations of rent extraction. For example, the problem of double-dealing by opportunistic politicians that was discussed above in connection with deregulation raises equivalent issues for contracts with legislators not to extract private rents. As with rent creation, the rent-extraction model with be enriched by consideration of the need to assemble coalitions to obtain rent protection, the problems created by changes in coalitions' composition and power, and similar issues that arise once "government" is recognized as a collectivity of rational, maximizing individuals.

For the moment, howcvcr, it is sufficient to note that the problems of political opportunism and the imperfections in private-capital protection create disincentives for capital owners to buy off legislators. Yet several instances have been presented here in which private actors in fact have paid significant sums to induce government not to impose costs. Despite the political impediments to contract, then, the evident willingness of capital owners to purchase protection indicates that appreciable capital stocks are credibly imperiled by regulations that are never actually enacted.

If so, one cost of government regulation has been missed. Heretofore, the economic model has identified several different costs of government regulation: deadweight consumer loss, resources expended as private parties seek rents,[44] costs of compliance with regulation,[45] and diversion of resources to less valuable but unregulated uses.[46] To these should be added the costs of protecting private capital even when politicians ultimately are persuaded not to regulate. There is no such thing as a free market.

Notes

1. George J. Stigler, "The Theory of Economic Regulation," 2 *Bell J. Econ.* 3 (1971).

2. Sam Peltzman, "Toward a More General Theory of Regulation," 19 *J. Law & Econ.* 211 (1976); Gary S. Becker, "A Theory of Competition among Pressure Groups for Political Influence," 98 *Q.J. Econ.*371 (1983).

3. Robert D. Tollison, "Rent-Seeking: A Survey," 35 *Kyklos* 575, 592 (1982).

4. For example, Robert E. McCormick & Robert D. Tollison, *Politicians, Legislation, and the Economy* (1981).

5. "The 'consumerist' measures of the last few years...are not an obvious product of interest group pressures, and the proponents of the economic theory of regulation have thus far largely ignored such measures." Richard A. Posner. "Theories of Economic Regulation." 5 *Bell J. Econ.* 335 (1974). Migué also discusses regulations that are "difficult to reconcile with the economic theory of regulation." Jean-Luc Migué. Controls versus Subsidies in the "Economic Theory of Regulation." 20 *J. Law & Econ.* 213, 214 (1977).

6. Technically, some of the returns to private individuals are true economic rents (for example, the returns to entrepreneurial capacity), while others are more properly termed "quasi rents" (the returns to any fixed-cost investment). See Milton Friedman. *Price Theory:*

A Provisional Text 115–18 (1962). Often, however, the differences are of little operational significance. See, for example, Donald N. McCloskey, *The Applied Theory of Price 294* (1985) ("Producers' Surplus Is Economic Rent Is Quasi-Rent Is Supernormal Profit"). It is not the type of rent but its source that is of interest in this article. For expositional clarity, therefore, all profits created politically are described here as "political rents," while the returns to private capital are referred to as "private rents." Also, the term "capital" is used here to refer to both human (including entrepreneurial) and other types of capital.

7. Gordon Tullock, "The Welfare Costs of Tariffs, Monopolies, and Theft." 5 *W. Econ. J.* 224 (1967); Richard A. Posner, "The Social Costs of Monopoly and Regulation." 83 *J. Pol. Econ.* 807 (1975).

8. For a diagrammatic presentation of the theory, see Fred S. McChesney, "Commercial Speech in the Professions: The Supreme Court's Unanswered Questions and Questionable Answers," 134 U. Pa. L. Rev. 45, 74–100 (1985).

9. For example, Howard P. Marvel, "Factory Regulation: A Reinterpretation of Early English Experience." 20 *J. Law & Econ.* 379 (1977); R.H. Coase, "Payola in Radio and Television Broadcasting." 22 *J. Law & Econ.* 269 (1979); Michael T. Maloney & Robert E. McCormick. "A Positive Theory of Environmental Quality Regulation." 25 *J. Law & Econ.* 99 (1982); B. Peter Pashigian. "The Effect of Environmental Regulation on Optimal Plant Size and Factor Shares." 27 *J. Law & Econ.* 1 (1984); Ann P. Bartel & Lacy Glenn Thomas. "Direct and Indirect Effects of Regulation: A New Look at OSHA's Impact," 28 *J. Law & Econ.* 1 (1985).

10. "Regulation is. . . an instrument of wealth transfer—the extent of which is determined in a political market—where interest groups demand regulation and politician-regulators supply it." Migué, *supra* note 5, at 214.

11. For one of the few models based on political demands being made of private individuals, see William P. Welch, "The Economics of Campaign Funds." 17 *Pub. Choice* 83, 84 (1974) ("[t]he politician demands funds in exchange for political influence").

12. Robert E. McCormick. *The Strategic Use of Regulation: A Review of the Literature, in The Political Economy of Regulation: Private Interests in the Regulatory Process* 14 (Robert A. Rogowsky & Bruce Yandle eds. 1984).

13. Dairy interests pay handsomely for the continuation of congressional milk-price supports. Larry J. Sabato, *PAC Power: Inside the World of Political Action Committees* 133, 137 (1984). Physician and dentist "political action committees" (PACs) contribute large sums for continuation of self-regulation. *Id.* at 134–35.

14. Since more durable rent contracts are in the interest of both private parties and politicians, the intervention of third-party institutions predictably would be sought to hold legislators to their deals. The judiciary, for example, may help guarantee congressional rent-creation contracts, since courts can overrule legislators' attempted revisions of earlier contracts by holding the changes unconstitutional. William M. Landes & Richard A. Posner, "The Independent Judiciary in an Interest-Group Perspective," 18 *J. Law & Econ.* 875 (1975): Robert D. Tollison & W. Mark Crain, "Constitutional Change in an Interest-Group Perspective." 8 *J. Legal Stud.* 165 (1979). Executive veto of attempted changes in legislative deals is another way to increase the amounts private parties would spend for rent creation. W. Mark Crain & Robert D. Tollison, "The Executive Branch in the Interest-Group Theory of Government," 8 *J. Legal Stud.* 555 (1979). But neither guarantee system is perfect "since there will be some expectation that an independent judiciary will not support all past legislative contracts," Tollison & Crain, *supra*, at 167, and because newcomers to both the legislature and the executive office have less stake in continuing bargains made by their predecessors. Crain & Tollison, *supra*, at 561–66.

15. For an empirical demonstration of the harm to marginal firms from minimum-wage and union-pay increases; for example, see David E. Kaun, "Minimum Wages. Factor Substitution and the Marginal Producer," 79 *Q.J. Econ.* 478 (1965); and Oliver E. Williamson. "Wage Rates as a Barrier to Entry: The Pennington Case in Perspective." 82 *Q.J. Econ.* 85 (1968). For discussion of other regulatory measures with different effects on firms, see the sources cited in note 9 *supra*.

16. Maximizing payments to politicians would require, inter alia, that all producer beneficiaries be induced to pay and that consumer-voters exert no counterinfluence on the amount of regulation imposed. Relaxing these assumptions would not alter the fundamental implications of the rent-extraction model proposed here. See, for example, Becker, *supra* note 2: and Peltzman, *supra* note 2.

17. The conditions under which rent extraction is politically preferable to rent creation are explored further below.

18. W. Craig Stubblebine, *On the Political Economy of Tax Reform* 1, 2 (paper presented at the meeting of the Western Economic Ass'n 1985).

19. One PAC director describes congressional "invitations" to purchase tickets to political receptions as "nothing but blackmail." Sabato, *supra* note 13, at 86. Likewise, "[t]he 1972 reelection effort for President Richard Nixon included practices bordering on extortion, in which corporations and their executives were, in essence, 'shaken down' for cash donations." *Id.* at 5.

20. Brooks Jackson, "House Republicans Are Pressing PACs for Contributions." Wall St. J., June 27, 1985, at 36, col. 2. Further instances of how politicians pressure PACs for money are given in Sabato, *supra* note 13, at 111–14.

21. The effects of Third World government expropriations of private capital in diminishing the amount of investment made are analyzed in Jonathan Eaton & Mark Gersovitz. A Theory of Expropriation and Deviations from Perfect Capital Mobility, 94 Econ. J. 16 (1984).

22. Tullock, *supra* note 7, at 229 n.11.

23. The situation is thus a form of the "Samaritan's dilemma," in which a politician must convince private producers that he is willing to suffer losses in the short run in order to reap longer-run gains whose present value exceeds that of any immediate losses. See James M. Buchanan. *The Samaritan's Dilemma, in Altruism, Morality, and Economic Theory* 71 (Edmund S. Phelps, ed: 1975). Of course, to the extent that the political threats are convincing, private parties are more likely not to call a legislator's bluff, and he therefore will not actually suffer any short-run loss.

24. Richard A. Epstein, *Takings: Private Property and the Power of Eminent Domain* (1985); Terry L. Anderson & P.J. Hill, *The Birth of a Transfer Society* (1980).

25. See J. Patrick Gunning, Jr., "Towards a Theory of the Evolution of Government, in Explorations" in the *Theory of Anarchy* 22 (Gordon Tullock ed. 1972).

26. Stubblebine, *supra* note 18, at 2.

27. This was the pattern observed, for example, with the amendments to the Clean Air Act in the early 1970s, when the *Dept. Transportation* repeatedly delayed and altered standards on auto emissions in response to auto-firm lobbying.

28. The rent-extraction model thus sheds light on the recurring controversy whether bureaucratic agencies "run amuck," free of congressional or other constraints. The most recent study of the Federal Trade Commission (FTC), for example, concludes that "the Commission remains largely unconstrained from without." Kenneth W. Clarkson & Timothy J. Muris, *Commission Performance, Incentives and Behavior, in The Federal Trade Commission since 1970: Economic Regulation and Bureaucratic Behavior 282* (1981). But Weingast and Moran present evidence of systematic congressional influence over FTC

actions. Barry R. Weingast & Mark J. Moran. "Bureaucratic Discretion or Congressional Control? Regulatory Policymaking by the Federal Trade Commission." 91 *J. Pol. Econ.* 765 (1983). The rent-extraction model suggests that neither view may fully capture the essence of Congress-agency relations. A politician has less incentive to monitor specialized agencies ex ante while they consider and adopt cost-imposing measures more cheaply than Congress itself could. There is more incentive for legislative surveillance of agency action ex post, in order to locate opportunities for alleviating those costs (for a fee). For a discussion and evidence of politicians' intervention to remove the costs imposed by bureaucrats' antitrust investigations and prosecutions, see Roger L. Faith, Donald R. Leavens, and Robert D. Tollison, "Antitrust Port Barrel," 25 *J. Law & Econ.* 329 (1982).

29. Further, the appearance may not be purely illusory. Congressional monitoring of agencies is costly. See Isaac Ehrlich & Richard A. Posner. "An Economic Analysis of Legal Rulemaking," 3 *J. Legal Stud.* 257 (1974). Some of what agencies do, therefore, will not be known to a legislator until constituents bring it to his attention.

30. The purpose here is to illustrate how politicians acting collectively can induce private payments not to extract rents. This admittedly leaves unaddressed public-choice problems of achieving collective political action: how to assemble political coalitions when each politician maximizes his own interest, how to divide the gains from rent extraction among individual politicians, the role of the committee system in rent extraction, and so forth.

31. Benjamin Klein & Keith B. Leffler, "The Role of Market Forces in Assuring Contractual Performance," 89 *J. Pol. Econ.* 615 (1981); L.G. Telser, "A Theory of Self-enforcing Agreements," 53 *J. Bus.* 27 (1980).

32. See, for example, Yoram Peles, "Rates of Amortization of Advertising Expenditures." 79 *J. Pol. Econ.* 1032 (1971): Robert Ayanian, "Advertising and Rate of Return." 18 *J. Law & Econ.* 479 (1975).

33. The Magnuson-Moss Warranty–Federal Trade Commission Improvement Act of 1975 included an order to the FTC to initiate within one year "a rulemaking proceeding dealing with warranties and warranty practices in connection with the sale of used motor vehicles." 15 U.S.C. § 2309(b). For the FTC's initial rule, see 16 C.F.R. § 455 (1982).

34. Since Congress has always been able to annul any agency rule or regulation statutorily, the question arises why it would want a veto. Statutes to change agency action require the president's signature. If the president must sign the statute, he then is able to exact payment for his participation in rent-protecting legislation, lowering the payments available to Congress. In eliminating the executive role, the legislative veto is hardly a check on agency action. It is an attempt to avoid splitting fees with the executive. Indeed, if Congress has a veto, it then has an incentive to fund even more rent-threatening activities by independent agencies, *ceteris paribus*.

35. One study, cited in Sabato, *supra* note 13, at 134, found that, "[o]f the 251 legislators who supported the veto resolution and ran again in 1982, 89 percent received contributions from NADA (National Auto Dealers Association], which averaged over $2,300. This total included 66 legislators who had not been backed by NADA at all in 1980, before the veto resolution vote. Just 22 percent of the 125 congressmen who voted against NADA received 1982 money, and they averaged only about $1,000 apiece."

36. See the FTC announcement of the veto published at 47 Fed. Reg. 24542 (June 7, 1982). When the Supreme Court later invalidated the legislative veto. INS v. Chadha. 462 U.S. 919 (1983), and thus Congress's overruling of the FTC's rule. Process Gas Consumers Group v. Consumer Energy Council, 463 U.S. 1216 (1983), the FTC recalled its proposed rule and essentially gutted it. See 16 C.F.R. § 455 (1985).

37. Stigler, *supra* note 1, at 9–10.

38. George A. Akerlof, "The Market for 'Lemons': Quality Uncertainty and the Market Mechanism," 84 *Q.J. Econ.* 488 (1970).

39. "Both intuition and empirical data suggest that the used-car market attracts lemons. . . . A number of market mechanisms serve to alleviate these problems. The most visible solutions take the form of dealer guarantees and warranties, which recently have been beefed up with extended coverage backed by national insurers. Indirectly, dealers invest in brand-name maintenance (local television ads, for instance), which makes it more costly for them to renege on a reputation for quality. The reputation of the parent automakers is also laid on the line. All four domestic car manufacturers have certified the quality of the better used cars sold by their dealers. Two generations of Chevrolet dealers, for example, have designated better used cars with an 'OK' stamp of the dealer's confidence in the car's marketability." "Can Regulation Sweeten the Automotive Lemon?" *Reg.*, September, December 1984, at 7, 8.

40. "[M]embers of the tax-writing committees nearly tripled their take from political action committees during the first six months of this year, to $3.6 million, compared to the like period in the past two-year election cycle. . . . [T]he money is pouring in from. . .insurance companies that want to preserve tax-free appreciation of life insurance policy earnings, from horse breeders who want to keep rapid depreciation of thoroughbreds, from drug companies seeking to keep a tax haven in Puerto Rico, and from military contractors seeking to retain favorable tax treatment of earnings from multiyear contracts." Brooks Jackson. "Tax-Revision Proposals Bring Big Contributions from PACs to Congressional Campaign Coffers." *Wall St. J.*, August 9, 1985, at 32, col. 1.

41. One report notes that "there hasn't been an increase in the 65-cent-a-case federal tax on beer since the Korean War, and nobody is seriously proposing one right now." Yet the industry has organized a coalition of brewers and wholesalers to compensate key members of Congress anyway: "Members of House and Senate tax-writing committees regularly drop by the coalition's monthly meetings to talk about budge and tax trends, [and] pick up $2,000 appearance fees." Though new beer taxes "haven't. . .generated much interest in Congress," the president of the brewers' trade association says they "want to be prepared." Brooks Jackson, "Brewing Industry Organizes Lobbying Coalition to Head off Any Increase in U.S. Tax on Beer," *Wall St. J.*, July 11, 1985, at 48 col. 1.

42. The banking industry contributed millions of dollars to politicians in 1982 to obtain repeal of the statutory provision requiring banks to withhold taxes on interest and dividends. There are no precise figures on contributions to politicians to stop legislation banning gender-based insurance-rate and benefit schedules, but their magnitude may be inferred from the American Council of Life Insurance's media budget of nearly $2 million in 1983 and 1984 to defeat the legislation. Sabato, *supra* note 13, at 125.

43. Stigler, *supra* note 1, at 3.

44. Posner, *supra* note 7. See also Franklin M. Fisher, "The Social Cost of Monopoly and Regulation: Posner Reconsidered," 93 *J. Pol. Econ.* 410 (1985); W. P. Rogerson. "The Social Costs of Monopoly and Regulation: A Game-theoretic Analysis," 13 *Bell J. Econ.* 391 (1982).

45. Tullock, *supra* note 7.

46. James Alm, "The Welfare Cost of the Underground Economy," 24 *Econ. Inquiry* 243 (1985).

B *International Trade*

16 IDEOLOGY, INTEREST GROUPS, AND THE REPEAL OF THE CORN LAWS

Gary M. Anderson and Robert D. Tollison

Introduction

On March 27, 1846, the House of Commons voted to repeal the Corn Laws by a vote of 327 to 229 (Thomas, 1929, p. 57). The repeal of the import duties on corn (meaning cereals, including wheat, oats, and barley) was one of the most significant economic events of the nineteenth century. This action has long interested economists because it represents one of the few apparently unambiguous examples of the influence of economic theory, specifically, the theory of comparative advantage, on economic policy. Free trade policies were enacted by Parliament "in the end due to the devoted efforts of a few men who dedicated themselves to spread the message" of the relationship between free trade and economic efficiency (Hayek, 1978, p. 128).

There is no question that the repeal of the Corn Laws was consistent with classical economic analysis or that free trade policies in Great Britain increased economic efficiency in international markets. But despite the fact that "rivers of ink has been spilled on the repeal of the Corn Laws" (Kindleberger, 1975, p. 30), economic analysis has rarely been directed at the repeal campaign itself. While some writers have asserted a conflict between the manufacturing and agricultural classes, the organizational nexus of the repeal agitation—the National Anti-Corn Law League of 1838–1846—has escaped close scrutiny by economists.

The present paper seeks to redress this neglect. A body of work has recently emerged in economics which analyzes the origin and development of regulation using the tools of microeconomic theory and emphasizing the role of organized interest groups (Stigler, 1971; Peltzman, 1976; McCormick and Tollison, 1982; and Becker, 1983.) This paper adds to this literature a study of the origin and development of a movement which successfully *repealed* a significant body of economic regulation. The main argument is that the Anti-Corn Law League was the agent of a cohesive interest group, the cotton textile industry, which sought to prevent or to retard the passage of additional factory legislation and to repeal import duties on raw cotton. The issue of the Corn Laws was an effective means for achieving a political coalition to attain these ends rather than the primary goal of the Anti-Corn Law League.

The paper is divided into four sections. In section 2, alternative explanations of the repeal of the Corn Laws are reviewed, and the basis for the textile interest-group explanation is outlined. In section 3, the evidence pertaining to the lobbying efforts of the League in opposition to factory legislation is discussed. In section 4, the League's ultimately successful activities to repeal the import duty on raw cotton are presented. In Section 5, some odds and ends in the analysis, such as the financial rewards of Cobden and Bright, are covered. Finally, some concluding thoughts on the roles of ideology and economic interest in the repeal of the Corn Laws and a summary of the argument are offered.

Alternative Accounts of the Repeal of the Corn Laws

The most popular view of the repeal of the Corn Laws stresses the role of free trade ideology in animating the proponents of repeal. Gordon, (1971, pp. 200–201) puts this position this way:

> This explanation of the repeal is shared by most economists who have considered the issue (e.g., Mises [1966]; Kindleberger [1975]). Indeed, the defeat of the Corn Laws is often taken to be one of the best examples of Keynes' dictum that "it is ideas, not vested interests, which are dangerous for good or evil" (Keynes [1964], p. 384).

The problem with the ideological explanation of the activities of the Anti-Corn Law League is that it is difficult to state in a testable form. The costs and benefits of individual behavior do not seem to matter in such explanations of the political process as if, for example, partisans for a cause have a perfectly inelastic demand curve with respect to certain political goals. Tastes for a political result are inherently non-observable, and theories based on the explanatory role of forces such as tastes and ideas are difficult to formulate in a reliable manner. Of course, ideological explanations may be correct, but it would seem desirable to offer nontestable hypotheses only as a matter of last resort.

More important, however, there are empirical grounds for regarding the ideological theory with suspicion. The Anti-Corn Law League, which was virtually synonymous with the free trade movement form 1838 to 1846, was founded and led by manufacturers and other businessmen (Grampp 1960, pp. 84–86; McCord, 1968, p. 35). And the support of the manufacturing community for the Anti-Corn Law League was not merely reflected in the signing of petitions. The League was a well-financed and effective interest group. In 1843, the League, with apparent success, asked its contributors for 50,000 pounds to pay for its activities (McCord, 1968, p. 135). Calls for 100,000 pounds in both 1844 and 1845 were also successful. In fact, contributions in 1845 exceeded 116,000 pounds (McCord, 1968, p. 160–161). In February 1845, Bright estimated that the League had invested 250,000 pounds in the purchase of property qualifications (in essence, legally manufacturing votes for election of members of Parliament) in Lancashire, Cheshire, and Yorkshire (Prentice, 1968, p. 298).

While precise information on the sources of this funding does not exist, the bulk of the League's subscriptions were received in the form of large donations. For example, when the 1844 Fund was launched, 12,000 pounds was raised at a single meeting in Manchester (McCord, 1968, p. 160). In a single meeting in Manchester on December 23, 1845, almost 60,000 pounds was raised. This included twenty-four individual subscriptions of 1000 pounds or more (McCord, 1968, p. 200).

Moreover, the Anti-Corn Law League was the most advanced political organization that Britain had ever seen; "this machine was. . . a wonder to contemporaries" (McCord, 1968, p. 163). the League was administered from its headquarters in Newall's Buildings in Manchester, where a large staff was separated into a number of departments, the League Council, a cashier's office, a publication office, and an electoral office being the most important. The League's activities were highly centralized. All but the most routine expenditures were authorized by a vote of the League Council (McCord, 1968, p. 173). According to Prentice, (1968, p. 110), the League employed over 800 people in 1843 engaged solely in the publication and distribution of tracts. Also, numerous salaried lecturers were employed who addressed mass meetings (McCord, 1968, pp. 175–176).

The League substantially subsidized a number of newspapers in order to assure favorable reporting and editorials (McCord, 1968, pp. 109, 141). Most important were the League's extensive electoral activities. The legal qualification for voting was simply the presence of a man's name on the electoral register, reflecting the appropriate property-owning qualification. The League devoted enormous efforts and funds both to challenging the voting qualifications of protectionists and to padding the registers with the names of League members by purchasing qualifications (McCord, 1968, pp. 150–160). In short, the League functioned as a highly efficient, well financed, and pragmatic political organization.

The magnitude of the financial support for the League's activities and its highly organized lobbying efforts generate skepticism of purely ideological motivations on the part of its backers. This fact lends credence to Pincus' statement that "(it) cannot be accepted without argument that ideology, even the ideology of the Manchester School, is interest free" (Pincus, 1977, p. 130). Hence, it is unsurprising that a number of writers have argued (e.g., Halevy, 1961, pp. 111, 60ff.) that the manufacturing class constituted an interest group which sought the repeal of the Corn Laws because this action was thought to lead to the opening and expansion of markets (and in some versions, to the lowering of wage costs).

There are two main problems with this so-called "imperialism of free trade" argument (Semmel, 1970). First, Corn Law repeal is assigned the attributes of a public good, and yet the mechanism by which free riding is overcome in this case is not discussed. The "manufacturing class" was a large and diffuse group for whom the costs of organization were high and the per capita benefits of free trade low. Without an explanation of how this group impacted on the political process, the argument is inherently weak. Second, the manufacturing class was not in general in favor of repeal. For example, in his study of the voting patterns in Parliament on the repeal issue, Thomas, (1929, p. 58) found that with one noteworthy exception (the cotton textile representatives discussed below), there was no pattern to the votes of different manufacturing and commercial blocs in terms of "ayes" and "noes" (although in general a majority of manufacturers favored repeal).

The most economically plausible version of an interest-group theory of repeal running through the literature is that based on the "iron law of wages", or, more accurately, the theory which assumes the acceptance of this law on the part of manufacturers supporting repeal (see Grampp, 1960, p. 106; Bloomfield, 1978, p. 628). According to this argument, manufacturers believed that repeal would reduce food prices, which would in turn serve to reduce wages. Reduction of their wage-bills would reduce their costs of operation and increase their profits, supplying an economic motivation for involvement in the repeal campaign.

This argument suffers from several difficulties. First, very few manufacturers in this period had any degree of formal training in economics, and assuming an understanding and acceptance of Ricardian economic doctrine on a widespread basis is dubious. Grampp, (1982, p. 500) quotes Tooke and Newmarch to the effect that the merchants of London in 1820 (prominent advocates of free trade at that time) "understood little and cared less about the doctines and principles of Political Economy." It seems unlikely that this characterization would not fit the Manchester merchants and manufacturers twenty years later.[1]

Second, in any event the merchants and manufacturers who spoke for the Anti-Corn Law League appeared to offer the opposite argument—that repeal would tend to *increase* wages. For example, both Cobden and Bright consistently maintained that repeal would increase real wages (Grampp, 1960, p. 107). In specific reference to the Ricardian argument, Cobden (who unlike most League members was an able economist (see Fetten, 1980, p. 72)) proclaimed in 1841 that "the rate of wages (had) no more connection with the price of food than with the moon's changes" (Semmel, 1970, p. 162).[2] League literature also suggested that repeal would raise real wages.

Defenders of the Corn Laws claimed that repeal would reduce wages, which the League denied (Ward, 1962, p. 284). This points to the fact that the wage question became something of a political football in the repeal controversy. The League's appeal to the working class would certainly have been more difficult if they had proclaimed a linkage between repeal and lower wages. The fact remains, however, that "[those] who held the belief [that repeal would lower money wages] were a minority in the counsels of the League, and after a while their view counted for less than nothing" (Grampp, 1960, pp. 106–107).

Finally, there is reason to doubt that Ricardo himself held the simplistic position that repeal would raise profits by lowering wages. According to Hollander, (1979, p. 549), Ricardo thought that any attempt to raise profits by reducing current real wages was impossible; in a speech on May 9, 1822, Ricardo maintained that repeal would increase real wages (Hollander, 1979, p. 553).

For all of these reasons, the superficially plausible interest-group argument based on the acceptance of Ricardian theory by manufacturer-supporters of repeal seems highly unlikely.[3] There is little evidence that producers were generally organized and politically effective in any systematic fashion, and the issue of the impact of repeal on wage in manufacturing appears to have been mostly a tactical debating point, if anything.

There are, however, strong indications of a concentrated and well-defined interest group which is far more relevant to an understanding of the repeal campaign than the vaguely specified manufacturing class argument. This is the British cotton textile industry. The exception noted above in Thomas' accounting of votes for and against repeal were cotton-textile affiliated M.P.s, who voted 12 to 1 in favor of repeal. Cotton textile mill owners were the predominant group represented among the League's founders, leaders, and principal financial backers. Bright was a Lancashire cotton mill owner (Ausubel, 1966, p. 2). Cobden was the owner of a cotton mill that printed calicoes (Read, 1968, p. 10). Henry and Thomas Ashworth, owners of the large Ashworth mills, were League founders, and together contributed over 2000 pounds to the League (Boyson, 1970, p. 202). The Strutt family, textile mill owners, apparently were large contributors, donating 300 pounds in one recorded instance (McCord, 1968, p. 138). Generally, the cotton textile mill owners were the major participants and contributors in the League.

The cotton textile industry offers a plausible locus for an economic interest-group explanation of repeal. In the 1840s, it was concentrated, relatively small in numbers, and localized (roughly two-thirds of the industry was located in Lancashire in the 1840s). Moreover, there are some reasons to think that several factors minimized the probability of free riding and made the costs of organizing for political action low. While the industry was not highly concentrated, its geographical concentration was high, which made it easier to detect dilatory behavior with respect to political activities.[4] Moreover, the League kept careful records of its contributors, which made the identification of industry members who were not pulling their weight a simple matter (cf. Prentice, 1968, v. 1, pp. 91–93). We have no evidence about how free riding, to the extent that it existed, was sanctioned, but the important point is that the cotton textile industry did overcome the free rider problem, and "was largely united in the Anti-Corn Law Campaign" (Silber, 1966, p. 7). Thus, the costs of organization facing the textile owners were low, and the expected per capita benefits (discussed below) were high. For such reasons, the textile owners are a much better candidate than the manufacturing class in general for the motivating force behind the repeal campaign.

But what were the textile owners seeking? To argue that they were pursuing free trade in general suffers from the same weakness as the manufacturing class hypothesis. There is no particular reason to think that the textile firm owners would have sought the general public interest in this way. We believe that there is impressive evidence that the cotton textile industry perceived the Anti-Corn Law League as an effective vehicle for the achievement of two ends unrelated to the repeal of the Corn Laws—the prevention of further encroachment of government regulation in the textile industry in the form of factory legislation and the repeal of the import duty on raw cotton. In short, the support for repeal was a means for creating a political coalition which increased the effectiveness of the campaign in Parliament against the Factory Acts and the cotton duty. The purpose of the rest of this paper is to establish support for this interest-group explanation of the repeal of the Corn Laws.[5]

The Anti-Corn Law League and the Factory Acts

The most definitive modern study of the Anti-Corn Law League claims that the organization's activities were solely directed towards repeal of the Corn Laws (McCord, 1968, p. 23). In fact, the constitution of the League prohibited its taking on any other cause than repeal (Grampp, 1960, p. 101). Hence, claims of involvement by the League in opposition to the Factory Acts or any other cause would seem necessarily to be rejected.

However, upon closer examination it appears that the League did not restrict its activities to repeal. Apparently, from an early point in the League's history, opposition to factory legislation played a substantial role in its agitation. (McCord, 1968, p. 69), records a piece of League propaganda commissioned in the summer of 1839 portraying Lord Ashley (the leading Parliamentary advocate of increased factory regulation) as supporting the Ten Hours Bill for hypocritical and corrupt reasons.[6] In March 1841, the official organ of the League printed an editorial describing the Ten Hours Bill as a "monopolist" attack on industry, which would cause factory operatives to be "mulcted of a portion of their wages" (Ward, 1962, p. 303). In fact, until its dissolution in 1846, the Anti-Corn Law League served as the chief organization of opposition to the Factory Acts. Bright and Cobden were among the staunchest opponents to extension of factory legislation beyond the limits of the existing 1833 Act.

Bright, in particular, took a position on the Factory Acts which "was nearer to pure laissez-faire than (he took) on any other issue" (Grampp, 1960, p. 88). Soon after Bright entered Parliament in 1843, he became the leading opponent of the Ten Hours Bill (designed to limit the operations of textile mills to ten hours per day). Writing some years later, Lord Ashley described Bright as "ever my most malignant opponent" in the Ten Hours debate (Read, 1967, p. 211).

Cobden, too, was generally opposed to further factory legislation during this period, although he was not nearly so preoccupied as Bright with the controversy. In Parliament, Cobden "usually spoke against the acts, and his economic and political arguments were similar to Bright's" (Grampp, 1960, p. 91).

Cobden and Bright were the chief spokesmen for the Anti-Corn Law League, so that its opposition to a measure would naturally be observable to a large degree in their actions. However, the League more generally was an organization opposed to the Factory Acts—or at the very least, to their extension beyond the 1833 Act (which basically only limited the hours of children under 13). As Grampp, (1960, p. 91) concludes, "[the] new factory acts were passed over the opposition of the League."

Although seemingly disparate political goals, the repeal of the Corn Laws and the opposition to further extension of the Factory Acts were actually interdependent to a considerable degree. Many Parliamentary supporters of factory legislation were also defenders of the Corn Laws, and attacks on proposed factory legislation were made to serve the purpose of supporting repeal. For example, in the course of a particularly acrimonious debate with Lord Ashley in the House of Commons on March 15, 1845, Bright responded to an assertion regarding the alleged economic exploitation of cotton mill workers by maintaining that the conditions of agricultural laborers employed by Ashley and his fellow Corn Law supporters were much worse (Robbins, 1979, pp. 50–51). Joseph Hume, a founding member of the League (Smith, 1925, p. 148), argued on the floor of Commons on April 2, 1845, that if Parliament wanted to legislate against child labor, "let them begin with the farming children" (Fetter, 1980, p. 74).

In short, there appears to have been a substantial interdependency between repeal and opposition to Factory Act extension, at least on the level of Parliamentary strategy. But the opposition to the Factory Acts cannot be readily dismissed as merely a political ploy serving a limited tactical purpose in the campaign for repeal. For one thing, the Tories seem to have largely acquired their zeal for factory legislation in combination with agricultural protectionism in order to forge a coalition with the working class, as factory legislation was a popular nostrum among the working class population (see Ward, 1962, pp. 232ff). If the concern of the Anti-Corn Law League was exclusively with repeal, as its constitution maintained, support for further factory legislation would probably have increased the League's popularity among factory operatives. As it was, the League directed an enormous (and expensive) propaganda campaign aimed at generating working class support for repeal (see McCord,

1968, pp. 180–186). While the proportion of League resources devoted to opposition to factory legislation is unclear, much valuable time of what were surely its most important assets—Cobden and Bright—was devoted to this opposition.

Of course, much of the League's rhetoric was directed in favor of general free trade. A case could be made that support for free trade implied support for free labor markets and hence opposition to factory legislation. However, there are some serious empirical problems with this argument. By and large, the opposition of the League and its leaders to the regulation of labor markets was confined to the textile industry. Cobden *supported* Ashley's act of 1842 which prohibited child labor and limited the working hours of women in the mines. In 1864, the Factory Acts were extended to potteries and other manufacturing establishments, and Cobden took no part in the debate (Grampp, 1960, p. 91).

A more satisfactory alternative explanation is that the League's concern with the Factory Acts reflected one of the most urgent interests of many of its leading members and some of its principal financial backers in the textile industry. That these regulations raised costs to textile operators is clear.[7] And while the League was not successful at preventing further factory legislation applying to textiles, it must not be forgotten that forestalling costly regulation has a present value. And beyond this, the detail, enforcement, and design of subsequent regulation could have been far different without the League's political activities on this front.

The Anti-Corn Law League and Raw Cotton Import Duties

In addition to the prevention of the expansion of factory regulation, a second major goal of the Anti-Corn Law League appears to have been the repeal of the duty on imported raw cotton. This goal was never prominent in League propaganda or speech making, but there is considerable evidence that it was much on the minds of the leaders of the League from an early period. Robertson explains that "Bright interested himself in the supply of cotton to the manufacturing districts" at "an early point in his public career" (Robertson, 1889, p. 272). The raw cotton duty was imposed upon imports from outside the Empire and represented the principal impediment to this supply. This duty was enacted in 1798, was applied in terms of weight, and at 5 percent of assessed value represented an important source of revenue for the government. Farnie, (1979, pp. 38–39) explains that the abolition of the duty in 1845 "severed the last fiscal link" between the government and the cotton industry. According to McCloskey, the tariff revenue resulting from the cotton import duty in 1841 was 528,000 pounds; this sum was evidently an approximate annual average for the period from the mid-1830s to the mid-1840s (McCloskey, 1981, pp. 156–159).

Grampp, (1960, pp. 108–109) points out that opposition to the raw cotton duty was undertaken by the Manchester Chamber of Commerce in the mid-1830s, prior to the formation of the Anti-Corn League. The League continued this opposition. In a speech delivered by Bright on May 15, 1844, he concluded with the statement:

> That [cotton] trade was not long ago an infant, struggling into life. It is now great and powerful...it has sprung up into a giant of enormous proportions, and yet that giant, powerful as it is, lies well-nigh prostrate under the fetters and shackles which a benighted, ignorant, and thoughtless policy has formed around its muscular form (quoted in Robertson, 1889, p. 187).

By 1841, Henry Ashworth—by all accounts one of the leading lights of the League—was attempting to convince workers in his cotton mill of the connection between repeal of the cotton duty and their own continuing prosperity (Boyson, 1970, pp. 205–206). The Operative Cotton Spinners Provincial Association of Bolton is on record as agreeing with Ashworth on the necessity of repealing the raw cotton duty on several occasions in 1844–1845 (Boyson, 1970, p. 206). Halevy notes the Anti-Corn Law League's work on behalf of repeal of the raw cotton duty (Halevy, 1950, v. 4, p. 122), and mentions that agricultural interests in the American South were strong moral, if not financial, supporters of the League. In the period 1841–1845, Britain imported 2,491 million pounds of cotton from the U.S., and only 69 million pounds from all other countries (Scheiber, Vatter, and Faulkner, 1976, p. 121).[8]

That the cotton textile industry and its spokesmen in the League had a strong, simple, and direct economic self-interest in lobbying for removal of the cotton duty is clear. In this case, unlike that of factory legislation, they were completely successful. In 1845, the duty on cotton was removed by Parliament on the initiative of Peel, and the Anti-Corn Law League's agitation surely played an important role in this achievement, as both Halevy (1950, v. 4, p.122) and Grampp, (1960, p. 109) imply.[9] Therefore, bundled in the movement to general free trade was an important economic benefit for the textile mill owners. One does not have to question the ideological commitment to free trade on the part of League members and contributors in order to recognize a straightforward economic motivation behind a large bloc of this support.[10]

The Dissolution of the League, the Payoff of Cobden and Bright, and the Chartists

This section briefly addresses three points related to the discussion. First, why was the League disbanded in 1846? Second, what exactly did Cobden, Bright, and other League agitators receive for their services? Third, why were the Chartists so strongly opposed to the League when members of both organizations supported repeal of the Corn Laws?

The Anti-Corn Law League was the preeminent political action organization of the nineteenth century, achieving "a more important place in national life that any previous Radical body" (McCord, 1968, p. 15). There would seem to have been no impediment preventing the ready transferability of the League's organizational resources, as well as its numerous political and social connections—in short, its political capital structure—to other related causes after the repeal of the Corn Laws. Its leaders, Cobden and Bright, became active proponents of reform in the realms of public finance, electoral reform, and foreign policy in the years after 1846. But instead of being transferred to the support of other causes, the organizational investment of the League was scrapped soon after repeal.

The League dissolved basically because by 1846 its financial support had begun to dry up (McCord, 1968, p. 204). The League leaders and agitators did not suddenly lose interest in political issues, but many of them lost pay checks as employees in League offices. The rapid reduction of financial support is consistent with the interest-group theory of the League. Parliament repealed the duty on raw cotton in 1845. The League had been unable to defeat an extension of the Factory Acts in 1844, and the Ten Hours Bill was passed in stages beginning in 1847. The tide had turned in Parliament with respect to factory legislation, as evidenced by the fact that the new Prime Minister (after the resignation of Peel), John Russell, came into office as the "first Prime Minister pledged to support factory reform", that is, as a committed supporter of the Ten Hours Bill (Ward, 1962, p. 326). These developments and not the repeal of the Corn Laws were most likely the reasons for the end of the League's financial support.

There is also the matter of the returns to agitation sometimes mentioned, but usually dismissed by historians. It turns out that the major participants in the League "did very well by doing good". Following the cessation of active operations by the League in 1846, Richard Cobden (its acknowledged leader) received a cash payment of over 75,000 pounds (Prentice, 1968, p. 444). Cobden received another payment of 40,000 pounds (made up of a "private subscription" chiefly in Lancashire, Glasgow, and Birmingham) in 1860, which was apparently in honor of his work with the League (Apjohn, (1881), p. 222).[11] George Wilson, the League's secretary, received a payment of 10,000 pounds from the organization's Council (McCord, 1968, p. 204). McCord adds that "[m]assive gifts of plate were voted to the more active members of Council." There is no record of Bright having received a cash payment, but Ausubel, (1966, pp. 24–25) explains that in 1846, following the repeal of the Corn Laws, he "wanted as his reward the privilege of sitting in the House of Commons as Member for Manchester". The remnants of the League "went to work and rallied the right people" with the result that Bright secured the nomination and subsequently won the seat.

Finally, a minor mystery of the Anti-Corn Law agitation is the fierce opposition of the Chartists to the League. Members of the Chartist movement—advocates of universal manhood franchise, combined with a number of secondary demands—worked vigorously from an early period to break up League meetings, frequently shouting down League speakers and even on some occasions violently disrupting them. The mystery arises from the fact that the Chartists evidently agreed with the ostensible major premise of the League, namely that the Corn Laws should be repealed. Slosson, (1968, p. 156–157) explains that the Chartists opposed the League, but not Corn Law repeal. The first speaker of the Manchester Anti-Corn Law League (the immediate precursor to the National League) was A.W. Paulton, who was apparently very sympathetic to Chartist demands, so much so, in fact, that some popular confusion arose between the League and the Chartists based on his lectures (McCord, 1968, pp. 37–38.) The League did not strongly object to being confused with the Chartists. J.B. Smith, the Manchester League's Treasurer, "consoled himself that at any rate being confused with the Chartists might at least bring them in more working-class support" (McCord, 1968, p. 38). The League made strenuous efforts to improve its relations with the Chartists, and supported their principal demand for democratic suffrage (Ausubel, 1966, pp. 10–11). Both the League and the Chartists campaigned on a platform based on the need for reducing the cost of food (Slosson, 1968, p. 156; McCord, 1968, p. 27). Yet despite these apparent similarities and bases for alliance, the Chartists bitterly opposed the League on a consistent basis.

A common explanation for this opposition among historians has been that the League and the Chartists were direct competitors for the hearts and minds (and contributions) of the working class (Read, 1968, pp. 36–37; Witmer, 1968, pp. 160–161; Slosson, 1968, pp. 156–157). However, this explanation is ad hoc and unconvincing. The League and the Chartists on the surface appeared to agree on most matters of substance. An alliance would have helped to further the interests of both organizations.

The real reason appears to have been that there was basic disagreement between the Chartists and the League on one major matter of substance: the Factory Acts. The Chartists were proponents of the Ten Hours Bill and other extensive factory regulations, which the League strongly opposed. According to West, (1920, p. 176), "...in practice the Charter was too closely associated with the demand for factory legislation—to give the crucial instance—to be entirely compatible with the Anti-Corn Law agitation".

Conclusion

Our argument is simple and can be briefly summarized. The movement to repeal the Corn Laws has been commonly treated in the literature as an example of the power of non-self-interested ideology to influence economic policy. Without denying that ideology played a role, there is ample evidence to question the dominance of ideology in motivating the repeal campaign. Specifically, we have presented considerable evidence to support two propositions: (1) the Anti-Corn Law League, despite its name, devoted substantial efforts towards preventing and impeding the passage of further Factory Acts in the cotton textile industry and towards the repeal of the raw cotton duty; and (2) the principal financial suport for the League came from the cotton textile industry, which had a strong economic interest in these activities (if not repeal of the Corn Laws per se). A concentrated and localized industry group, sharing very specific common interests, invested heavily in promoting the League and its activities.

We do not pretend that this is a complete theory of Corn Law repeal. We agree, for example, with those writers who have stressed the importance of the 1832 Reform Act, which extended the franchise to the middle classes and reduced the influence of the agriculturalists in Parliament.[12] Our intention has been to explain in simple terms that a substantial proportion of the financial and organizational support for the Anti-Corn Law League resulted from economic interests motivated to support other goals. General free trade appears to have been gained as a by-product of these activities. Popular support for the League was undoubtedly synonymous with support for Corn Law repeal. But the main sources of financial and popular support appear to have been basically distinct. Ideas in this case mattered, but there is reason to believe simple economic self-interest actually dominated. Finally, this was a case where competition among interest groups tilted the economy toward more efficient arrangements, a result that will not seem so surprising in light of Becker's (1983) recent results.

Notes

1. Grampp (1960, p. 107) adds: "It is not to the Ricardian system that one can trace the promptings of the businessmen or those of most others in the free trade movement."

2. Semmel (1970, p. 161) points out that in 1835 Cobden had argued that the reduction in the price of corn would tend to reduce wages. But Cobden consistently made the opposite argument during his involvement with the repeal movement.

3. Stigler (1982, p. 64) argues that "if Cobden had spoken only Yiddish, and with a stammer, and Peel had been a narrow, stupid man, England would have moved toward free trade in grain as its agricultural classes declined and its manufacturing and commercial classes grew".

4. Gatrell, (1977, p. 99) reports that in 1841 in Manchester the top 10 percent of textile firms, assessed in terms of horsepower, employed 36 percent of all power in primary processes and 31 percent of all labor. Unfortunately, data on industry concentration do not exist, and Gattrell's calculations may not be good proxies for underlying concentration by, for example, market share. However this may be, Gattrell's data are the most reliable available. See also Lloyd-Jones and LeRoux (1980).

5. Before proceeding further, we should consider another argument in the literature (Barnes, 1965, p. 267; Demsetz, 1982, p. 112) which suggests that the driving force behind the Anti-Corn Law League was the principle of *retortion*: only through free trade in corn could Great Britain persuade other nation states to introduce free trade themselves and thereby increase the export market share of the British cotton textile manufacturers. Hence, the cotton textile manufacturing interests had a direct interest in Corn Law Repeal, regardless of any concern with other issues (e.g., opposition to Factory Act extension) which may have been "bundled" with this main goal.

It is a fact that Cobden endorsed this argument quite explicitly; for example, declaring in 1846: "I believe that if you abolish the Corn Law honestly, and adopt Free Trade in its simpliciy, there will not be a tariff in Europe that will not be changed in less than five years to follow your example" (Barnes, 1965, p. 268). The main difficulty with concluding that this statement was an honest statement of actual economic motivation, and not simply a rhetorical flourish, is that Cobden's prediction was falsified by events. Nations on the European continent began to dismantle their protective and prohibitive trade restrictions only after the Anglo-French Treaty of 1860 (Kindleberger, 1975, p. 40). Furthermore, Corn, Law repeal was undertaken unilaterally—apparently at no time did the Anti-Corn Law League propose any linkage be negotiated with any foreign government between Corn Law repeal and foreign tariff reduction, on British textile exports or any other exports. For these reasons we conclude that "retortion" was probably not a significant economic motivating factor behind Corn Law repeal.

6. This poster portrays Lord Ashley as a villain stealing a piece of bread from a starving child, saying, "I will never rest until the poor factory child is protected by a ten hours bill from the tyranny of the *merciless and griping mill owners*" (McCord, 1968, p. 69).

7. There is an argument in the literature which suggests that some mill owners have profited from factory regulation. This argument is neither very convincing nor germane to the present discussion. See Marvel, (1977) and Anderson and Tollison, (1984).

8. Grampp, (1960, p. 104) explains that the duty on raw cotton had apparently been enacted at the behest of British owners of West Indian cotton plantations.

9. At the same time as repeal of the cotton duty, duties on glass, wool, and the importation of Baltic staves were repealed, as well as duties on 430 other items which yielded only

"nominal amounts". The cotton duty involved by far the most revenue (Smith, 1926, p. 149).

10. There was another interest group which gained from the repeal of the raw cotton duty and which may have contributed financial support to the League with this end in mind. This group was composed of cotton brokerage firms engaged in the raw cotton re-export trade. These firms were heavily concentrated in Liverpool and Manchester by the 1840s. Farnie (1979, p. 16) cites statistics indicating that 23.3 percent of raw cotton imported by England in the period 1833–1853 was subsequently re-exported. The cotton brokerage firms surely gained as a result of the duty's repeal, and there is tangential evidence that they were involved in the League's activities. This group of firms was small and geographically concentrated in Liverpool and nearby Manchester. Ellison, (1968, p. 182) lists the names of ninety firms which comprised the Liverpool Cotton Brokers' Association in 1841. A comparison of the lists of names on the League Council with those in the Cotton Brokers' Association reveals two possible cotton brokers on the former roster (J. B. Smith and Charles Edward Rawlins), as well as several other possible relatives of cotton brokers (in particular, P. A. Taylor and James Kershaw, perhaps kins of John Taylor and William Kershaw). While this evidence is speculative, the economic incentive for participation in an anti-duty lobbying effort by the cotton brokers appears to have been simple and plausible.

11. Historians who mention this payment to Cobden usually explain that it was intended to cover the debts which his business had accumulated during his tenure as leader of the League (McCord, 1968, p. 206; Prentice, 1968, p. 444). However, this explanation turns out to be dubious; Apjohn, (1881, p. 222) explains that Cobden "*invested and lost a considerable portion of this money in American railway speculations*, so that...his circumstances were again embarrassed", occasioning the additional subscription for him of 40,000 pounds (emphasis added).

12. Repeal of the Corn Laws was not a pure loss on the part of cereal producers in Britain. In 1846, Parliament created a fund of 2,000,000 pounds in Britain and 1,000,000 pounds in Ireland to finance below-market interest rate loans to farmers for drainage projects. The fund was established "to coat the bitter pill of repeal" and to compensate the agricultural lobby. See Hueckel, (1981, p. 194).

References

Anderson, G. M., and Tollision, R. D. "A Rent-Seeking Explanation of the British Factory Acts." In: D.C. Collander, (ed.), *Neoclassical Political Economy*. Cambridge, Mass., 1984.

Apjohn, L. *Richard Cobden and the Free Traders*. Glasgow, 1881.

Ausubel, H. *John Bright: Victorian Reformer*. New York, 1966.

Barnes, D.G. *A History of the English Corn Laws from 1660–1846*. New York, 1965.

Becker, G.S. "A Theory of Competition Among Interest Groups for Political influence." *Quarterly Journal of Economics* 98 (1983): 371–400.

Bloomfield, A.I. "The Impact of Growth and Technology on Trade in Nineteenth Century Britain." *History of Political Economy* 10 (1978): 608–635.

Boyson, R. *The Ashworth Cotton Enterprise: the Rise and Fall of a Family Firm, 1818–1880*. Oxford, 1970.

Demsetz, H. *Economic, Legal, and Political Dimensions of Competition*. New York, 1982.

Ellison, T. *The Cotton Trade of Great Britain*. New York, 1968.

Farnie, D. A. 1929. *The English Cotton Industry and the World Market. 1815–1896*. Oxford, 1929.

Fetter, F. W. *The Economist in Parliament, 1780–1868*. Durham, N.C., 1980.

Gatrell, V. A. C. "Labour, Power, and the Size of Firms in Lancashire Cotton in the Second Quarter of the Nineteenth Century." *Economic History Review* 30 (1977): 95–139.

Gordon, H. S. "The Ideology of Laissez-Faire." In: A. W. Coats (ed.), *The Classical Economists and Economic Policy*. London, 1971.

Grampp, W. D. *The Manchester School of Economics*, Stanford, Ca, 1960.

—— "Economic Opinion when Britain Turned to Free Trade." *History of Political Economy* 14 (1982): 496–520.

Halevy, E. *A History of the English People in the Nineteenth Century—Vols. 3 and 4*. New York, 1961.

von Hayek, F. A. *Denationalization of Money*. London, 1978.

Hollander, S. *The Economics of David Ricardo*. Toronto, 1979.

Hueckel, G. "Agriculture during Industrialization." In: R. Floud, and D. McCloskey (eds.). *The Economic History of Britain Since 1700, Vol. 1*. Cambridge, 1981.

Keynes, J. M. *The General Theory of Employment, Interest, and Money*. New York, 1964.

Lloyd-Jones, R., and LeRoux, A. A. "The Size of Firms in the Cotton Industry: Manchester 1815–1841" *Economic History Review* 33 (1980): 72–82.

Kindleberger, C. P. "The Rise of Free Trade in Western Europe, 1820–1875." *Journal of Economic History* 35 (1975): 20–55.

Marvel, H. P "Factory Regulation: A Reinterpretation of Early English Experience." *Journal of Law and Economics*. 20 (1977): 379–402.

McCloskey, D. M. *Enterprise and Trade in Victorian Britain*. New York, 1981.

McCord, N. *The Anti-Corn Law League, 1838–1846*. London, 1968.

McCormick, R. E., and Tollision, R. D. *Politicians, Legislation, and the Economy*. Boston, 1982.

von Mises, L. *Human Action*. New York, 1966.

Peltzman, S. "Toward a More General Theory of Regulation." *Journal of Law and Economics* 2 (1976): 211–240.

Pincus, J. J. *Pressure Groups and Politics in Antebellum Tariffs*. New York, 1977.

Prentice, A. *History of the Anti-Corn Law League, Vol. 2*. New York, 1968.

Read, D. *Cobden and Bright*. New York, 1968.

Robbins, K. *John Bright*. London, 1979.

Robertson, W. *The life and Times of John Bright*. New York, 1889.

Scheiber, H. N.; Vatter, H. G.; and Faulkner, H. U. *American Economic History*. New York, 1976.

Semmel, B. *The Rise of Free Trade Imperialism*. Cambridge, 1970.

Slosson, P.W. *The Decline of the Chartist Movement*. New York, 1980.
Silver, A.W. *Manchester Men and Indian Cotton 1847–1872*. Manchester, 1966.
Smith, G.B. "Free Trade." In: H. Higgs (ed.), *Palgrave's Dictionary of Political Economy, Vol. 62*. London, 1925.
Stigler, G.J. "The Theory of Economic Regulation." *Bell Journal of Economics and Management Science* 2 (1971): 3–21.
—— "Do Economists Matter" In: *The Economist as Preacher and Other Essays*. Chicago, 1982.
Thomas, J.A. "The Repeal of the Corn Laws, 1846." *Economica* 9 (1929): 53–60.
Ward, J.T. *The Factory Movement, 1830–1855*. London, 1962.
West, J. *A History of the Chartist Movement*. New York, 1920.
Witmer, H.E. *The Property Qualifications of Members of Parliament*. New York, 1968.

17 RENT-SEEKING AND TRADE PROTECTION*

Charles K. Rowley and Robert D. Tollison

Introduction

For some thirty-five years following the end of the Second World War, successive U.S. governments proved to be reasonably consistent supporters of freer international trade and opponents of trade protection, irrespective of the political balance between the Democrats (historically the free trade Party) and the Republicans (historically the Party of protection). As an active supporter of the General Agreement on Trade and Tariffs (GATT), as a major participant in the "Kennedy Round" and the "Tokyo Round" of tariff reductions,[1] and as a reasonably resolute defier, especially at presidential level, of persistent protectionist special interests within its own domestic economy, these U.S. governments played an invaluable role in extending international trade, and with it associated

* We are grateful to Richard Blackhurst. James M. Buchanan, Bruno Frey and Gordon Tullock for encouragement and helpful comments. Earlier drafts benefited from a Workshop Discussion at the Center for Study of Public Choice, George Mason University and from The Conference on Protectionism and Structural Adjustment, St. Gallen, Switzerland, both held in September 1985. We are also indebted to Heinz Hauser and Hansjorg Herzog for helpful comments.

comparative advantages, across the Western World. In so doing, they offered an important counter-example to the logic of collective action,[2] wherein it is predicted that special interest producer groups typically dominate the generalized consumer interest in political markets, despite the underlying balance in the vote motive of those concerned.

Since 1980, the situation has dramatically changed, with Congress markedly more deferential to protectionist special interests and with the president, rhetoric to the contrary ignored, actively engaged in protectionist measures, most especially targeted against Japanese imports[3] Protectionism, moreover, is not confined to traditional Republican sources, but manifests itself with yet greater force within the Democratic Party. The only presidential candidate to run in 1984 on an explicitly free trade manifesto (Senator Gary Hart) was eliminated in the Democratic Party primaries in favor of a candidate (Walter Mondale) whose special interest credentials were unassailable[4] The spatial fixity of the opposition candidate on "protectionism" enabled the incumbent (Reagan) to shift perceptibly away from free trade without fear of sacrificing the median consumer vote. If present tendencies persist, the viability of the GATT itself may fall under question, and the West may retreat once again, as it did so disastrously in the 1930s, into a process of competitive exchange rate depreciation, and/or tariff and quota impositions, in a prisoner's dilemma situation for which the U.S. would be largely responsible.

This paper centers attention on one important determinant of trade protection policy, namely the process of rent-seeking by special interests whose monopoly rents would be transferred to consumers by free international trade. The relevant concepts of rent-seeking and rent protection are carefully defined, together with their social cost implications. The interrelationship between perceived rent durability and the level of rent-seeking outlays is explored. Public choice restrictions on moving from a once-established protectionist to a free trade environment are outlined. The paper ends on a note optimistic for free trade, by detailing important historical examples of the breakdown of protectionist forces in the face of an institutional change and countervailing special interest attacks. In this exercise, the stability or otherwise of protectionist equilibrium moves centerstage, as policy outcomes are evaluated by reference to a public choice rather than to a welfare maximizing theory of government.

The Durability of Monopoly Rights

The nature and extent of T-costs expended in pursuit of a monopoly right is related both to the environment in which rent-seeking occurs and to the *ex ante* perception of the durability of the protection that is sought.[5] Suppose, to take one extreme, that the political environment is such that rent-seeking must take the form of resource dissipation rather than of costless transfers of wealth from the rent seekers to their sovereign. Further suppose that the monopoly right, once granted, is perceived to be perfectly durable over an indefinite future. In such circumstances, T-costs will be completely dissipated upfront: resources equal to the present value of all future rents associated with the "right" will be sunk into the rent-seeking competition and will be lost forever to society.[6]

In this scenario, the normative case for deregulating, once the monopoly right has been purchased, is slight, since only that part of the H-costs that can be recouped represents a net welfare gain to society. All other benefits to consumers are transfers, reflected in the capital losses of producers who mistakenly had engaged in up-front rent-seeking investments. If the monopoly is perceived by consumers to be durable, they are unlikely to engage in costly deregulation lobbying within the political process. Thus, the minimal *normative* case for deregulation may coincide with a *positive* disinterest in deregulation based upon a rational calculus of expected costs and benefits.[7] The logic of collective action, which predicts the dominance of producer over consumers' interests in any special interest group competition for political favours, tends to confirm the likelihood of such a coincidence.

It is important to note that a perceived political equilibrium in support of durable monopoly rights will deter secondary rent-seeking, even where the monopolist earns positive rents. Suppose, for example, that our earlier example obtains, with the winning bidder making $90,000 on its $10,000 outlay. The rent so earned is the outcome of an equilibrium game, in which rent-seeking outlays reflect a durability assumption. Only in such circumstances will complete up-front rent dissipation occur. However, unless prior perceptions are subsequently falsified, the winner, despite residual rents, must be safe from secondary rent-seeking competition, without further outlays in defense of its rights.[8]

Two important implications for trade protection policy can be derived from this analysis. First, there may be existing areas in which protectionist policies qualify as evidently durable political investments. In such cases, the theory infers that it is not worth a great deal to reverse policy, since resources will have been wasted upfront in prior rent-seeking competition. Thus, an old tariff really may be a good tariff and an old tariff may evidence a generalized disinterest in its removal. Second, where potentially durable monopoly rights are under prior political consideration, an ounce of prevention is worth a pound of cure. Those who stand to lose from trade protection, in such circumstances, stand to lose heavily and early if they fail to counteract the perception of its durability and to cast doubt upon the inevitability of its imposition.

Our analysis so far has assumed that producers perceive complete success in creating a durable monopoly right and that they determine their individual rent-seeking outlays on that basis. Consumer outlays in defense of existing surpluses either do not occur at all or are rendered politically ineffective as a consequence of the free rider problem inherent in the logic of collective action. Evidence disputes the general validity of that assumption, however, since consumers frequently lobby, sometimes successfully, against potential regulatory monopolies.

Suppose, following Stigler (1971) and Peltzman (1976), that the market in regulation responds even-handedly to the precise balance of dollar-votes expended in the battle over an available right.[9] Further assume that the consumer interest is not eroded by free-riding. In such circumstances, the durable right defined by the regulation market will not secure maximum available rents for the successful rent seeker. Equilibrium will confirm output in excess of, and price less than, the full monopoly potential, reflecting the marginal impact of consumer outlays. Figure 17–1 illustrates such an outcome.

In figure 17–1, producers rent seek a full monopoly right, at price OA and output OQ_m. Consumers defend the competitive solution, at price OE and output OQ_c. All such expenditures represent social waste. The regulator chooses an equilibrium price along AE weighting equally the dollar votes of producers and consumers. In this example, the political price is set slightly above: OF, the midpoint of AE. This follows because producers outlay the present value of FCIE to lift price from OE to its expected value of OF. Consumers, operating on the same expected value, OF, as producers, outlay the present value of ABCF to hold price below the monopoly level OA. Since FCIE exceeds ABCF, the political price is set slightly above OF.

In this example, the social cost of the established partial monopoly, on the dissipation assumption, is identical to that of full monopoly without consumer competition (i.e., the area ABCF + FCIE + CID is exactly equivalent to the area ABDE).[10] This result is particular to the assumptions employed and should not be generalized to all regulation markets.

Some Implications of Non-durable Monopoly Rights

Not all monopoly rights provided by government can be viewed as durable, even if the regulation market is completely dominated by producer interests during the initial rent-seeking exercise. Political market equilibria

Figure

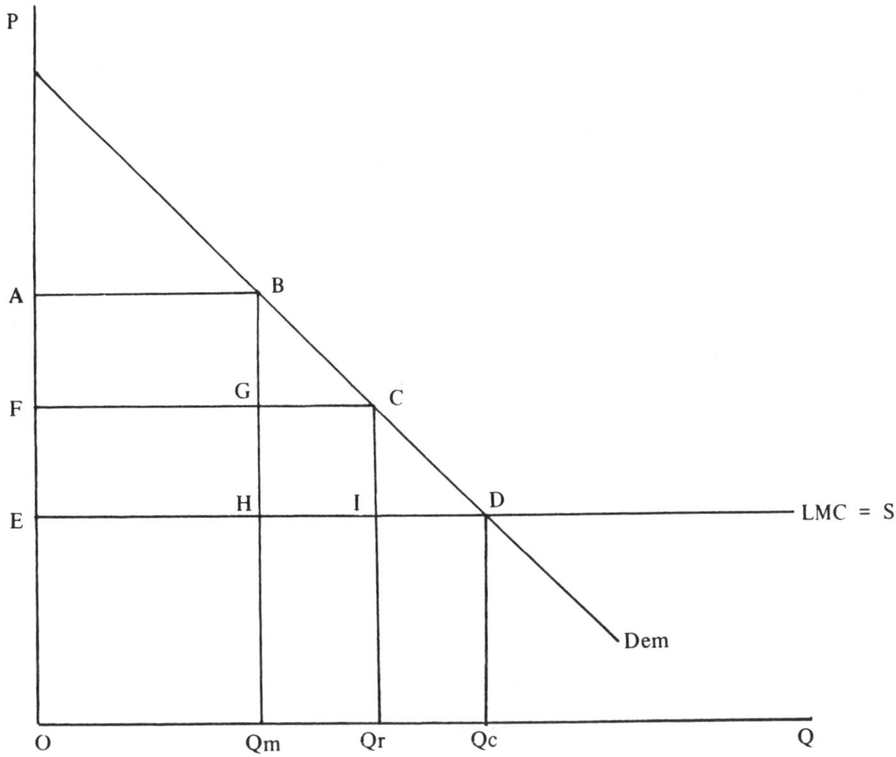

Figure 17–1

change, in some cases markedly, over time, as a consequence of shifts in the preferences of the various agents, and/or of technological and other supply adjustments. Regulators may be completely bought out by rent seekers but they do renege, get fired, change jobs, or retire. Eventually, of course, they always die. These features of any regulation market, of course, are known when initial rent-seeking is initiated and, inevitably, are reflected in upfront expenditure decisions.

Once the durability assumption is relaxed, potential monopolists, recognizing the instability of incumbency, abate up-front rent-seeking expenditures to reflect the present value of future rents suitably discounted for subsequent ongoing rent protection outlays. In essence, the prediction of complete up-front rent dissipation gives way to a prediction of limited upfront rent-seeking supported by subsequent ongoing outlays designed to protect the incumbent from secondary rent-seeking by outside producer and consumer interests (Crew and Rowley, 1986). Such a solution reflects an expectation that equilibrium in regulation markets is an ongoing response to dollar outlays and cannot be bought out once-for-all save under the most unusual of institutional circumstances.

If ongoing rent-seeking *is* an important feature of regulatory monopoly, the welfare economics case for deregulation is fueled by more than the present value of future H-costs. For society can now also escape the present value of future ongoing rent-seeking by introducing a durable deregulatory reform. Furthermore, if the monopoly right is vulnerable, outside producers and consumers may well expend resources to induce deregulation, as a pure transfer process, thus dispelling the disinterest in deregulation that is an inevitable consequence of acknowledged durability. Trade protection measures of this more vulnerable nature are both more justifiable targets of reform, and much more likely to attract deregulating attention than are those with less vulnerable characteristics.

Rent-Seeking: A Public Choice Perspective

An important implication of rent-seeking into monopoly rights is the increase in the identifiable social cost of monopoly, where rent-seeking outlays dissipate rather than simply transfer resources. This additional cost manifests itself entirely up-front, at the time of monopoly right establishment, in the case of completely durable rights. It occurs throughout the life of less durable rights, although even in these cases it will tend to peak out during the initiation phase, when "first-mover" advantages are subject to rent-seeking competition. Clearly, societies characterized by widespread monopoly and dissipative rent-seeking will, *ceteris paribus*, be significantly less wealthy than those that are not.[11] It becomes important, therefore, to identify public choice restrictions on the dissipative rent-seeking society.

Consider the public choice implications of perfect rent dissipation in a society with unspecialized inputs in rent-seeking and thus an absence of rents in the rent-seeking supply function. With perfect dissipation, there exist no excess returns on any margin for rent-seeking investments. Neither the potential monopolist nor the government earns more than a normal expected return from monopolizing behavior. In such circumstances, the market in monopoly rights is likely to be limited, both in terms of demand and supply, to opportunity cost considerations alone. There is no special incentive, in such a system, for governments to create monopoly.

Furthermore, in such circumstances, a self-seeking political sector has strong incentives to minimize rent-seeking losses associated with the conferment of monopoly rights. Transfers are much preferred to dissipation, even if the transfers in large part are in-kind rather than income-based, with the excess burden that such former transfers imply. Political entrepreneurship will be dedicated to restricting dissipation and encouraging transfers from those who seek to those who supply rent-creating monopoly rights.

Now compare and contrast two types of society: one in which T-costs per unit for monopoly are high (perfect dissipation), and the other in which they are zero. Which society, *ceteris paribus*, will be wealthier? The answer cannot be unambiguous. In the former society, there will be high social costs per instance of monopoly, but few monopolies, since monopoly creation and regulation attracts only a normal return. In the latter, there will be low social costs per instance, but much more monopoly, and thus greater H-costs, because the incentive to creat monopoly is strong. At some level of monopoly, H-costs in the non-dissipative society will exceed the T- and H-costs combined in the dissipative society. But it is impossible to generalize this level across different societies.

Public choice analytics predict, unfortunately, that majority vote systems of government are conducive to high social costs from monopoly. The level of T-costs per instance of monopoly is controlled via the political market to ensure that transfers to politicians rather than dissipation, dominate the rent-seeking process. Thus contributions to campaign finances, bribes, and in-kind benefits tend to be more effective than media advertising, direct lobbying, and other public relations exercises in purchasing monopoly rights. Dissipation then occurs at the secondary level as potential politicians and their advisers rent seek their way into office. In such a system, instances of monopoly tend to be high while the social cost per instance, correctly measured, is also high. Given the open rent-seeking nature of the U.S. Congressional system of politics, it is a mark of private enterprise's entrepreneurial success that almost all Americans do not live in caves, painted in wode, and exist on a subsistence diet of berries and root vegetables. In socialist systems, where transfer activities dominate, such latter outcomes are not outlandish hypotheticals.

Trade Protection and Public Choice

The pure theory of international trade unequivocally states that a unilateral shift to free trade will increase overall real income in a country unless it induces a significant (i.e., counter-balancing) deterioration in that country's terms of trade (Johnson, 1965). The theory concludes that once governments are informed of the clear net benefits of unilateral trade liberalization, they will do away with trade protection, compensating losers, if necessary, via a non-distortionary tax/subsidy intervention. Much of the international trade literature seems to be dedicated to this process of information transmission. However, governments patently do not respond as the pure theory predicts they will. Public choice explains theoretically why governments accept generalized wealth destruction by maintaining and even extending trade protection policy even in a well-informed political market.

The public choice explanation for trade protection centers on predictable distortions in the vote motive surrounding the trade liberalization issue. For, in the informed situation, if all citizens determined tariffs by a direct single majority vote in an assembly, the median voter would cast his vote in favor of free trade. Since he does not do so, an explanation is in order. The following five modifications (Frey and Schneider, 1984) help resolve this paradox:

1. Those who lose from specific reductions in tariffs or other terms of trade protection are not compensated. Where such losses constitute a decisive voter set, their uncompensated votes will be cast effectively against trade liberalization (Baldwin, 1976).
2. Prospective beneficiaries from trade liberalization have less incentive to inform themselves on the issue, to organize and to support pressure groups, even to vote, than do the losers. The benefits from trade liberalization have strong public good characteristics and are derived in an uncertain future, whereas the associated costs are concentrated, immediate, and highly visible (Downs, 1957; Olson, 1965; Becker, 1983).
3. Where the beneficiaries of trade protection are geographically concentrated, a geographically-orientated, first-past-the-post vote system may provide them with differential vote representation in the legislature (Frey and Schneider 1984).
4. Where those who benefit from trade protection evince differentially intense preferences on the issue, logrolling or vote trading within representative political systems may overrule an underlying majority vote, even though it results in an overall net loss of welfare to society (the paradox of logrolling).[12]
5. Where trade protection is a source of immediate government revenue (e.g., tariffs), governments may trade off a future generalized loss of political support for current revenue, especially

where the latter can be diverted to purchase specific votes among favored constituencies.[13]

It is not our purpose in this paper to offer more than a thumb-nail sketch of the overall public choice perspective on trade protection. Suffice it that the theory is plausible, that a growing econometric literature does not dispute its central predictions,[14] and that unilateral trade liberalization is not evident in the Western world (and certainly not evident in the Eastern bloc). (OECD, 1985) Our interest centers upon the relationship between trade protection and rent-seeking behavior in the advanced Western democracies.

Although it represents a simplification of the full public choice analytical framework, the Stigler/Peltzman regulation model, suitably adjusted to allow for rent-seeking as social cost, provides a relevant mechanism for trade protection analysis. The model assumes that the regulators, who make the market in monopoly rights, seek to maximize a vote majority. They do so by selecting the size of the beneficiary group, the amount that they require the group to outlay for mitigating opposition, and the amount that they transfer to the beneficiaries. An important implication of this model is that the losers must be taxed less than the interests of the winners would dictate. Equilibrium in the regulation market requires that the marginal political return from a transfer must equal the (positive) marginal political cost of the associated tax.[15]

Thus even if a single interest dominates the regulation market, the rents that it can secure (even ignoring rent-seeking losses) will be less than those potentially available from privately monopolising a non-contestable market. Political equilibrium, which may or may not be durable, occurs at a point of tangency between the gross profit hill available from monopoly, and an iso-majority curve relevant to the regulators. Only in the somewhat unlikely event that there is no political opposition to higher prices would such a tangency occur at the peak of the profit hill. Only in the equally unlikely event that the slopes of the relevant iso-majority curves remain constant over time will the initial political equilibrium prove to be durable.

It is a further implication of this regulatory model that the actual equilibrium achieved is the consequence of rent-seeking interventions by all potential rent recipients, *not least with respect to the selected instrument of protection that is to be marketed*. This is extremely important for trade protection, where different instruments offer a different balance of rents to separate beneficiaries in the international community. Failure to recognize this simultaneous *ex ante* resolution of the level of protection *and* the instrument of protection significantly weakens otherwise interesting earlier analyses of rent-seeking and trade protection (Bhagwati and Srinivasan, 1980).

Trade Protection, Monopoly Rights, and Rent-Seeking

Trade protection is designed to protect domestic industry from international competition. Where domestic-supply elasticities in affected markets are less than infinite, such protection defines monopoly rights which give rise to future rents. Inevitably, therefore, trade protection has a domestic rent-seeking constituency, prepared to devote resources to its creation and/or to its retention. In certain circumstances, trade protection may also have a foreign constituency. Rent-seeking interactions between such constituencies will determine the precise instrument of protection traded in the political market-place. In this section, the rent-seeking characteristics of tariffs, quotas, domestic subsidies, and other specific forms of trade protection are evaluated.

Tariffs

The tariff was the first government-imposed monopoly right to be exposed to the rent-seeking insight (Tullock, 1967). Following a lengthy period of subsequent neglect as the rent-seeking literature expanded, the recent reemergence of trade protectionist lobbying, especially in the U.S., has reawakened the public choice interest in the market for tariff protection (Bhagwati and Srinivasan, 1980; Frey and Schneider, 1984).

The rent-seeking constituency in support of tariff protection predictably extends beyond that of the domestic industry exposed to foreign competition. It encompasses additionally those who seek to divert the revenues accruing from tariffs to the central government and those who perceive rents from illegal evasion of the tariff barrier (smugglers). The interests of these constituencies are not identical since the revenue maximizing tariff will differ from the tariff required for total trade diversion. The smuggling influence also clearly competes both with the trade protection and with the tariff revenue constituencies, eroding rents otherwise available to both from any adopted level of tariff protection. The smuggling constituency inevitably is more restricted than the others in its opportunities to lobby in favor of protection.

The amount of effective protection offered to domestic production cannot be ascertained simply by examining nominal tariff rates[16] Effective protection is measured, not by the extent to which a tariff raises the final value of the finished imported good, but rather by the extent to which the domestic producer can increase the value added to a particular stage of production without altering the competitiveness of domestic production. The tendency for industrial nations to impose low or zero tariffs on imported raw materials, while maintaining tariffs on manufactured goods, implies that effective rates typically exceed nominal rates of tariff protection.

The present value of the differential value added is available as a rent to the domestic producer(s) only where that differential is not eroded or eliminated by subsequent domestic output expansion. In this sense, the tariff is *not* equivalent to an output restricting domestic monopoly right. Domestic producers can take full advantage of the tariff only where they are non-contestable[17] single-firm monopolies or non-contestable cartels, shielded from new entry by government-imposed protection. Otherwise, output expansion will occur to the point where normal returns only are achieved by the marginal firm, with rents available only to relatively low-cost suppliers. If free entry combines with homogeneous, constant-cost supply, there are no equilibrium rents available even from durable tariff protection. If tariffs are viewed as non-durable in the international market for free trade versus protection, much of the rent-seeking will be ongoing rather than up-front, when it occurs at all.

Domestic rent-seeking into tariffs *is* predictable on the part of those sheltered by the tariff. Firms typically are not completely homogeneous. The inframarginal rent recipients thus are motivated to rent seek. Entry barriers typically are not zero, most especially in industries that are organized to rent seek via government, nor is internal output expansion completely uncontrollable. Disequilibrium is often persistent, with rents extractable over lengthy adjustment periods. Factor inputs restricted in industry supply and specialized in production (e.g., unionized labor) may extract rents where commodity suppliers themselves cannot. The scope for direct rent-seeking thus is likely to remain non-trivial.

Potential smugglers have an identifiable, criminal, rent-seeking interest in establishing and maintaining tariffs (and indeed quotas), since trade protection offers rents to those who successfully evade the law and (potentially) expected net rents even when the private expected cost of apprehension, conviction, and punishment is accounted for. Smuggling has been analysed within the trade protection literature (Bhagwati and Hansen, 1973; Bhagwati and Srinivasan, 1973), but only as an *ex post* response to specific instruments of trade protection. Smuggling here is noted, more fundamentally, as a potential rent-seeking constituency in the regulatory market itself, with its outlays reinforcing the thrust towards high levels of protection.

However, a pronounced—and identifiable—smuggling interest will deter rent-seeking by others, since smuggling, *ex post*, will erode both the available rents from tariff protection and the revenues available to government. The smuggling constituency, which may be domestic or international, is unlikely to be easily identifiable, since its expenditures will be laundered through apparently legal special interest channels.

A characteristic of trade protection measures is that they offer protential rents to a constituency significantly more broadly based than that of the protected domestic industry. Tariffs generate revenues for central government which may prove to be an important source of rent-seeking activity. Quotas create rents for those who successfully lobby for import licenses within the protected market. Once again, Bhagwati and Srinivasan (1980) recognize the phenomena while failing to note implications for the market in regulation.

Specifically, if wider constituency rent-seeking into quotas is more effective than such rent-seeking into tariffs, as Olson's logic of collective action suggests, the market in regulation will be disturbed in favor of the quota solution. Predictably, if tariff levels systematically are reduced via international bargaining, quotas will become increasingly apparent as a consequence of the rising relative importance of this wider constituency demand. Instruments of trade protection are market determined, and *not* exogeneously imposed.

Quotas

In 1965, Bhagwati introduced an equivalence definition for a tariff and its quota counterpart into a theory of international trade then uninfluenced by rent-seeking notions. In essence, the equivalence criterion rested on the provision of identical levels of protection to some pre-designated domestic industry. As such, it was readily assimilated into the pure theory of international trade, confirming the robustness of overall real equilibrium to the two alternative forms of intervention. For almost a decade thereafter, international trade theory centered attention upon protection levels rather than upon the nature of protection instruments.

In 1974, Krueger, utilizing Tullock's concept of rent-seeking with respect to quotas only, disturbed the Bhagwati equivalence theorem, establishing firstly that quantitative restrictions were always inferior to tariffs because of rent-seeking resource losses, and secondly that overall real equilibrium must therefore differ within the context of Bhagwati equivalence. Bhagwati and Srinivasan (1980) responded to this criticism by emphasizing the rent-seeking implications of tariff revenues as a counterpart to rent-seeking into quota licenses. Even on the assumption that both forms of rent-seeking were fully competitive, however, overall equilibrium in the two outcomes might well differ as a consequence of differing capital/labor ratios in the alternative rent-seeking industries.

In our view, the debate between Krueger and Bhagwati/Srinivasan essentially misses the point of the rent-seeking insight, namely the latter's contribution to understanding the mechanics of the regulation market. The relevant issue is not whether Bhagwati-equivalent tariffs and quotas provide identical economy-wide equilibria in real resource allocations. Rather it is whether the differential rent-seeking behavior in the trade protection market will influence the public choice decision on the instrument of protection. Olson's logic of collective action suggests that such indeed will be the case, with rent-seeking predictably biasing the regulation market in favor of domestic quota restrictions, which offer rents to more narrowly-based and better organized special interests than do tariffs.

Quotas offer a number of potential advantages over Bhagwati-equivalent tariffs to the various rent-seeking interests involved. To the domestic industry seeking out protection, they guarantee the outer-bound of import penetration against unforeseeable shifts in underlying conditions of supply and demand, whereas tariffs clearly do not. Given *ex ante* equivalence, risk averse domestic suppliers clearly prefer the quota. Foreign suppliers who obtain quotas are protected against export expansion by rival foreign suppliers.

To the secondary rent seekers, they offer more specialized rents in the form of domestic import quota licenses often unavailable to new entrants. This limits the free rider problem associated with rent-seeking into tariff revenues. To the relevant government department they offer a more complex system of administrating and hence a larger budget.[18] To central government, auction revenues compensate for lost tariff revenues. To the smuggler, the existence of well-organized interests in import restriction offers an alternative source of rent, since such interests will expend protection outlays against the significant erosion of their monopoly rights via illegal importations.

The combination of such factors unequivocally biases the regulation market in favor of quotas, even when the latter are applied in accordance with the GATT criteria of global, non-discrimination. Once the GATT constraints are discarded, as is the case with "voluntary export restraint" agreements, the rent-seeking bias becomes yet more accentuated with foreign governments and foreign producers entering the picture as potential rent seekers and rent recipients.

Voluntary Export Restraints

Voluntary export restraints (VERs), together with other kinds of bilateral quantitative restrictions, such as orderly marketing agreements (OMAs), differ from global import quotas in two important respects. Firstly, they tend to discriminate between nations, in contravention of the most-favored nation principle enshrined in Article 1 of the GATT as well as in Article XIII, which governs the use of quantitative restrictions. Secondly, they render the exporting country responsible for administering the quota system via export licenses distributed to participating companies.

Thus VERs offer monopoly rights to the protected domestic industry similar to, but presumably less invulnerable than, those established by global import quotas. The direct rent-seeking implications, therefore, are approximately the same. Like import quotas, there are no rents immediately available to domestic taxpayers or to the secondary rent seekers who prey upon the revenues of government. Unlike import quotas, however, VERs offer no secondary rents to domestic import agencies. In consequence, they are unlikely to dominate in a regulation market exclusive to domestic interests.

Once trade protection becomes an argument in international diplomacy, however, and the regulation market assumes an international dimension, VERs become viable market outcomes. The quota rents, now appropriated by foreign governments in compensation for a direct loss of export markets, can be auctioned off to rent seekers in the form of export licenses. Any expected net receipt of quota rents by established exporters, now protected from new entry competition from native competitors, creates a rent-seeking vested interest in the VER solution. This foreign interest counteracts domestic private rent-seeking in favor of global import quotas and consolidates diplomacy-based government rent-seeking in the trade protection market, designed to force VER agreements via the threat of discriminating domestic tariff impositions.[19]

Can the Rentiers Be Routed?

Trade protection has been practiced throughout the history of international trade, long before the rent-seeking literature was available to offer insights into the resource dissipation that it induces. The importance of special interest groups in seeking factional benefits from trade protection at a net loss of welfare to the wider citizenry was well known in the eighteenth century, as is clear from Smith's attack on mercantilism in *The Wealth of Nations*.

It has been argued by many economists that Smith's writings were the major influence in routing the mercantilist rentiers, in shifting England to a free trade policy, and in returning available surpluses to entrepreneurs and to consumers. Skeptics, however, doubt the power of ideas alone and point to efficacious institutional adjustments and to the emergence of countervailing special interest groups as major factors in the development of free trade policy in England. It is instructive to review two detailed case studies on this issue (Baysinger, Ekelund, and Tollison, 1980; Anderson and Tollison, 1985), both of which emphasize a consistent rent-seeking story.

Baysinger, Ekelund, and Tollison evaluate mercantilism (as it evolved over the period 1500 to 1776 in England and France) as a rent-seeking society, with the balance-of-trade objective a mere derivative of the effective demand for regulatory rents by domestic economic agents. Their model explains the rise and fall of mercantilism in terms of the costs and benefits accruing to the participants "in the often deadly game of mercantile rent-seeking". Merchants, the monarch, and the public, as represented by the legislature and the judiciary, are featured as self-interested protagonists.

The rise of mercantilism is modelled as a market response to the demand for trade protection rights by rent-seeking merchants and the supply of such rights by a revenue-seeking monarch essentially secure from competition, ruling ultimately by divine right. In such circumstances, with consumer interests virtually irrelevant, movement to the "contract locus" was unimpeded, and mercantilist trade protection flourished. Prior to 1500, transaction costs had been much higher, since potential rentiers had to negotiate with numerous, vulnerable feudal rulers, individually incapable of enforcing protection contracts.

The eventual decline of mercantilism is modelled as the trade protection market response to rising transaction costs. As absolute monarchy gave way during the eighteenth century in favor of representative democracy, so the cost of lobbying for protection rights increased and the durability of such rights diminished. As the king's courts faced increasing competition from the common law courts, the legal validity of existing trade protection rights became less certain and ongoing rent-seeking and rent-protection outlays eroded the net benefits to the rentiers of their monopoly rights.

In consequence, trade protection gave way to the consumer interest in free trade, fueled by the H-costs of trade protection and accentuated by the increasing T-costs of resources dissipated by rent-seeking competition. Cromwell's contemptuous dismissal of the English Rump Parliament in essence was no more than a "monarchical" response to rent-seeking waste in early Parliamentary democracy and an attempt to replace such waste with rent transfers to support a military dictatorship.

Mercantilism slowly gave way during the late eighteenth and early nineteenth centuries in England in favor of freer trade policies. It received the "coup de grace" on March 27, 1846, when the House of Commons voted to repeal the Corn Laws by a majority of 327 to 229. This action is widely viewed (even by such normally perspicacious commentators as Hayek, (1978)) as a triumph of economic theory over special interests in a country where comparative manufacturing advantage provided a compelling economic motive for free trade. An alternative interpretation, by Anderson and Tollison (1985), however, interprets the repeal as a regulation market response to counter-rent-seeking by the National Anti-Corn Law League of 1838–1846.

The Anti-Corn Law League was in reality a mouthpiece not of Smithian economics, but of a cohesive interest group, the cotton textile industry, which sought (unsuccessfully) to prevent or to retard the passage of additional factory legislation and (successfully) to repeal import duties on raw cotton. The Corn Laws issue offered an effective opportunity for Cobden and Bright to forge a political coalition of textile and other manufacturing interests designed to rent seek in a quite different political market.

The league was a well-financed and effective interest group, organizing petitions, distributing propaganda, lobbying Parliament, and purchasing property qualifications to extend the franchise of citizens supportive of its primary objectives in Lancashire, Cheshire, and Yorkshire, where textile interests were located. With the Factory Acts (1844) and the Ten Hours Act (1847) evading its defenses, and with the duty on raw cotton successfully repealed (1845), the rationale of the League evaporated and, with it, the financial support. The League was disbanded in 1846, to the last proclaiming its free trade pretensions, and its devotion to a non-self-interested ideology.

The demise of mercantilism and the repeal of the Corn Laws in England categorically support the view that trade protection rentiers can be routed. Significantly, however, equilibrium in the trade protection market was in both cases not disturbed by consumers rent-seeking in search of rent transfers and of lost Harberger triangles of consumers' surplus. Free trade was a regulation market response to shifting rent opportunities perceived by producer special interest groups. Rectangles rather than trapezoids dominated the free trade/protection conflict.

Can the Trapezoids Ever Win?

Rent-seeking analysis suggests that producer rectangles typically dominate consumer trapezoids in regulation markets resistant to rent dissipation. This occurs, despite the greater size of the trapezoids, because of public choice factors outlined above. Where rent opportunities are extensive and the margins high, rent-seeking will therefore, flourish, and monopoly rights will be marketed extensively, despite severe aggregate deadweight losses of consumers' surplus and major wealth transfers from consumers to rentiers. The logic of collective action offers little scope for an effective trapezoid counter-attack on the regulation market equilibrium. Mercantilism represented the supreme example of enduring rectangle domination in the trade protection market.

The rectangles are weakened, however, in regulation markets conducive to rent-seeking resource dissipation, where rent margins tend to be low or even non-existent. In such circumstances, monopoly rights will not be extensively marketed, overall H-costs will be relatively low, but T-costs will be high per instance of monopoly. This outcome, although evidently representing trapezoidal triumph, is a consequence of rectangle self-mutilation. It does not really constitute an Olson-defying victory of general over special interests. In such circumstances temporary trapezoidal gains will be swiftly eliminated if the rectangles recover and rent margins once again appear high. The 300 trade protection bills presently dormant in the U.S. Congress, awaiting the regulation market judgment on textile protection, are testament to the fragility of any free trade equilibrium.

If the trapezoids are to stand any real chance of direct victory in the free trade versus protection struggle, both a high level of transparency within the regulation market and a generalized rather than a case specific counter-attack are essential. It is much harder for special interests to persuade U.S. Presidents than to persuade the U.S. Congress that there are net advantages in trade protection. It is harder for them to persuade Congress than it is to activate "administrative mechanisms" such as the "Escape Clause" of the 1974 Trade Act or the "Less-than-Fair Value" criteria of the Treasury Department and the ITC.[20]

The rectangles thrive on secrecy and complexity in regulation markets and on the vulnerability to well-organized rent-seeking of pluralistic political markets. The trapezoids fare best when the issues are clear and well-publicised, an advantage exploited wherever feasible by the GATT in its negotiations with national governments. Public choice warns, however, that political market institutions are endogeneous and not exogeneous, biased predictably to the advantage of the better organized special interests. Transparency is not widespread in trade protection markets and trapezoids are always vulnerable. If general interests typically are to dominate, political institutional reform is necessary. The issue of how such reform can be effected through a biased policy is an important but as yet unresolved problem in public choice.

Notes

1. Although world trade in manufactures encounters lower tariff obstacles than at any time since the outbreak of World War One, the rising tide of protectionism during the 1970s manifested itself in severe non-tariff barriers and districting subsidization. High nominal and effective tariffs still affect more than a quarter of world trade in manufactured goods (OECD, 1985, pp. 11–12).

2. The logic of collective choice was first formally expounded by Olson (1965). It was extended and generalized in Olson (1982).

3. For example, restricted imports as a share of total manufactured imports into the U.S. increased from 6.2 percent to 12.72 percent between 1980 and 1983 (OECD, 1985, p. 31). These results are based on a narrow definition of non-tariff barriers. The level of domestic subsidies to specific industries (notably automobiles and shipbuilding) also rose dramatically.

4. More recently, released from the spatial constraints of his Primary Campaign. Mondale has become a Born Again Free Trader!

5. See Landes and Posner (1975) for a discussion of the durability of legislative contracts with special interest groups.

6. See McCormick, Shughart, and Tollison (1984). As they indicate, because of the impact of rent-seeking on specialized resources, not all even of the H-costs can be regained by deregulation in such circumstances.

7. As Crew and Rowley (1986) indicate, however, such positive disinterest is a function of perceived durability of regulation. Consumers do not concern themselves over sunk investments of monopolists. Bygones are bygones in the competition for wealth transfers.

8. See. Hillman and Katz (1984) for a discussion of the effects of uncertainty in the theory of rent-seeking.

9. In reality, it does not do so for reasons outlined by Olson (1965, 1982).

10. This is not erroneous double-counting BCG is wasted in consumer rent-seeking and CDI in H-costs when the regulator sets price at F.

11. Private entrepreneurs, for the most part, move resources from lower to higher valued uses. Political entrepreneurs, for the most part, move resources from higher to lower valued uses.

12. Bernholz (1973, 1978) has demonstrated that logrolling does not avoid the Arrow paradox and problem of cyclical majorities.

13. This is especially true in less developed countries where, due to the inefficiency and corruption of the tax system there is little acknowledged tax revenue.

14. See Caves (1976). Frey and Schneider (1984). Magee and Brock (1980), and Pincus (1975, 1977).

15. This result itself makes it unlikely that the full present value of a future monopoly rent will be wasted upfront in rent-seeking (Crew and Rowley 1986).

16. On this complicated issue see Wells (1968).

17. In the sense of Baumol. Panzar and Willig (1982).

18. For an account of how even Adam Smith succumbed to the sirens of bureaucracy see Anderson and Tollison (1985).

19. For a detailed analysis see Blackhurst (1985). See also Godek (1985) who concludes a detailed empirical analysis with d.p. 701; "In the cross-section of U.S. manufacturing industries, the ratio of tariffs to total protection decreases as total protection increases. This pattern suggests that quotas are indeed used to compensate foreign suppliers and include them in the redistributive process".

20. An illuminating account to these protectionist routes is provided by Blackhurst (1985).

References

Anderson, G., and Tollison, R.D. "Ideology, Interest Groups, and the Repeal of the Corn Laws." *Journal of Institutional & Theoretical Economics*, June (1985): 1971–212.

Anderson, G.; Shughart, W.F.; and Tollison, R.D. "Adam Smith in the Customhouse." *Journal of Political Economy*, 4, 93 (1985): 740–759.

Baldwin, R.E. "The Political Economy of U.S. Trade Policy." *The Bulletin* (1976).

Baumol, W.J.; Panzar, J.C.; and Wilig, R.D., *Contestable Markets and the Theory of Industry Structure*. Harcourt, Brace Javanovitch, 1982.

Baysinger, B.; Ekelund, R.B.; and Tollison, R.D. "Mercantilism as a Rent-Seeking Society." In: J.M. Buchanan, R.D. Tollison, and G. Tullock (eds.), *Toward a Theory of the Rent-Seeking Society*. College Station: Texas A&M University press, 1980.

Baysinger, B., and Tollison, R.D., "Evaluating the Social Costs of Monopoly and Regulation." *Atlantic Economic Journal* 8 (December, 1980): 22–26.

Becker, G. "A Theory of Competition among Pressure Groups for Political Influence." *Quarterly Journal of Economics* 98 (August, 1983): 371–400.

Bernholz, P. "Logrolling, Arrow Paradox and Cyclical Majorities." *Public Choice* 15 (1973): 87–95.

Bernholz, P. "On the Stability of Logrolling Outcomes in Stochastic Games." *Public Choice* (1978): 65–82.

Bhagwati, J.N. "On the Equivalence of Tariffs and Quotas." In: R.E., Caves P. Kenen, and H.G. Johnson (eds.), *Trade, Growth, and the Balance of Payments*. Rand McNally, 1965.

Bhagwati, J.N. *Illegal Transactions in International Trade: Theory and Measurement*. North-Holland, 1974.

Bhagwati, J.N., and Hansen, B. "A Theoretical Analysis of Smuggling." *Quarterly*

Journal of Economics (May, 1973): 172–187.
Bhagwati, J.N., and Srinivasan, T.N. "Smuggling and Trade Policy." *Journal of Public Economics*, November (1973): 377–389.
Bhagwati, J.N., and Srinivasan, T.N. "Revenue Seeking: A Generalization of the Theory of Tariffs." *Journal of Political Economy*, no. 61, 88 (1980): 1069–1087.
Blackhurst, R. "The Economic Effects of Different Types of Trade Measures and their Impact on Consumers." In: OECD, *Symposium on Consumer Policy and International Trade*, 1985.
Buchanan, J.M. "Rent Seeking and Profit Seeking." In J.M. Buchanan, R.D. Tollison, and G. Tullock (eds.), *Toward a Theory of the Rent-Seeking Society*. College Station: Texas A & M University Press, 1980.
Buchanan, J.M.; Tollison, R.D.; and Tullock, G. (eds.) *Toward a Theory of the Rent-Seeking Society*. College Station: Texas A & M University Press, 1980.
Caves, R.E. "Economic Models of Political Choice: Canada's Tariff Structure." *Canadian Journal of Economics* 9 (1976): 278–300.
Corcoran, W.J. "Long-Run Equilibrium and Total Expenditures in Rent-Seeking." *Public Choice*, no. 1, 43 (1984): 89–94.
Cowling, K., and Mueller, D.C. "The Social Costs of Monopoly Power." *Economic Journal*, 88 (December, 1978): 727–748.
Crew, M., and Rowley, C. "Dispelling Disinterst in Deregulation." Unpublished manuscript (1984).
Crew, M.A., and Rowley, C.K. "Deregulation as an Instrument in Industrial Policy." *Journal of Institutional and Theoretical Economics* (March, 1986).
DiLorenzo, T.J. "The Domain of Rent-Seeking Behavior: Private or Public Choice." *International Review of Law and Economics* 4 (December, 1984): 131–35.
Down, A. "An Economic Theory of Democracy." Harper, 1957.
Finger, J.M.; Hall, H.K.; and Nelson, D.R. "The Political Economy of Administered Protection." *American Economic Review* (June, 1982): 452–66.
Fisher, F.M. "The Social Costs of Monopoly and Regulation: Posner Reconsidered." *Journal of Political Economy* 93 (April, 1985): 410–416.
Frey, B.S., and Schneider, F. "International Political Economy: A Rising Field." *Economia Internazionale*, no. 3–4, 37 (Agosto–November, 1984): 3–42.
Godek, P.E. "Industry Structure and Redistribution Through Trade Restrictions." *Journal of Law and Economics*, Vol. 27 (October, 1985): 687–703.
Harberger, A.C. "Monopoly and Resource Allocation." *American Economic Review* 44 (May, 1954): 77–87.
Higgins, R.; Shughart, W.F.; and Tollison, R.D. "Free Entry and Efficient Rent Seeking." *Public Choice*, no. 3 (1985): 247–58.
Higgins, R., and Tollison, R.D. "Life Among the Triangles and Trapezoids: Notes on the Theory of Rent-Seeking." Unpublished manuscript (1985).
Hillman, A.L., and Katz, E. "Risk-Averse Rent Seekers and the Social Cost of Monopoly Power." *Economic Journal* 94 (March, 1984): 104–110.
Johnson, H.G. "An Economic Theory of Protectionism, Tariff Bargaining, and

the Formation of Customs Unions." *Journal of Political Economy* 73 (1965): 256–83.

Krueger, A. O. "The Political Economy of the Rent-Seeking Society." *American Economic Review* 64 (June, 1974): 291–303.

Landes, W. M., and Posner, R. A. "The Independent Judiciary in an Interest-Group Perspective." *Journal of Law and Economics* 18 (December, 1975): 875–901.

Lee, D. R., and Tollison, R. D. "Optimal Taxation in a Rent-Seeking Environment." Unpublished manuscript (1985).

Magee, S. P., and Brock, W. A. "A Model of Politics, Tariffs, and Rent-Seeking in General Equilibrium." *International Economic Association* (1980).

McCormick, R.E.; Shughart, W.F.; and Tollison, R.D. "The Disinterest: in Deregulation." *American Economic Review* 74 (December, 1984): 1075–79.

OECD. *Costs and Benefits of Protection*. Paris, 1985.

Olson, M. *The Logic of Collective Action: Public Goods and the Theory of Groups*. Washington, D.C.: Howard University Press, 1965.

Olson, M. *The Rise and Decline of Nations*. New Haven: Yale University Press, 1982.

Peltzman, S. "Toward a More General Theory of Regulation." *Journal of Law and Economics*, no. 1, 19 (Spring, 1971): 3–21.

Pincus, J.J. "Pressure Groups and the Pattern of Tariffs." *Journal of Political Economy* 83 (1975): 757–778.

Posner, R. A. "The Social Costs of Monopoly and Regulation." *Journal of Political Economy* 83 (August, 1975): 807–827.

Rogerson, W.P. "The Social Costs of Monopoly and Regulation: A Game-Theoretic Analysis." *Bell Journal of Economics* 13 (Autumn, 1982): 391–401.

Stigler, G.J. "The Theory of Economic Regulation." *Bell Journal of Economics and Management Science* 2 (Spring, 1971): 3–21.

Tollison, R. D. "Rent-Seeking: A Survey." *Kyklos* 35 (fasc. 4): 575–602.

Tullock, G. "Efficient Rent-Seeking." In: J. M. Buchanan, R. D. Tollison, and G. Tullock (eds.) *Toward a Theory of the Rent-Seeking Society*. College Station: Texas A&M University Press, 1980.

Tullock, G. "Long-run Equilibrium and Total Expenditures in Rent-Seeking: A Comment." *Public Choice*, no. 1, 43 (1984): 95–98.

Tullock, G. "The Welfare Costs of Tariffs, Monopolies, and Theft." *Western Economic Journal* 5 (June, 1967): 224–232.

Wells, S.J. *The Shape of Britain's Tariff*. Institute of Economic Affairs. Research Monograph 17 (1968).

C *Political Markets*

18 VOTERS AS INVESTORS: A RENT-SEEKING RESOLUTION OF THE PARADOX OF VOTING

W. Mark Crain, William F. Shughart II, and Robert D. Tollison

Introduction

Although the economic approach to politics has generated many insights into the workings of the political process, economists have not made much headway toward providing a satisfactory explanation for observed voting behavior in democracies. Downs (1957) and Tullock (1976), for example, have analyzed the voting decision within the context of a simple benefit-cost model. Put in these terms, it is astonishing that anyone ever bothers to vote. The probability that any one vote will be decisive in an election is vanishingly small, and so the expected benefits of voting cannot exceed the costs of registering and going to the polls for more than a few citizens. In order to account for the relatively high voter turnouts that do occur—more than 80 million ballots were cast in each of the three most recent U.S. presidential elections, for instance—an alternative hypothesis has been put forward emphasizing the consumption rather than the investment aspects of voting (see, e.g., Riker and Ordeshook, 1968). The main idea

* We benefited from comments by Kenneth Greene, Dwight Lee, and Michael Munger. Remaining errors are our own.

here is that utility may be derived from participating in an election that is independent of the outcome (for example, from the exercise of one's "civic duty"). Peer pressure and other "sociological" factors have also been suggested as influential in the decision to vote.[1]

Stigler (1972, p. 98) has observed that the gap between the principles applying to economic versus political competition arises from the tendency to treat (incorrectly) political success as an all-or-none proposition, for example, labeling "the winning of 51 percent of legislative seats a victory and 49 percent a defeat." In Stigler's view, political competition occurs more or less along a continuum. Although only one party can "win" an election, the "losers" are not powerless to affect public policy decisions. In particular, he notes that the representatives of electoral minorities can, by trading votes in the legislature, secure enactment of some of their own programs and can impose costs on the majority in enforcing policies to which the minority is opposed. Moreover, "these costs will be larger, the larger the minority and the more intense its opposition." (Stigler, 1972, p. 100)

Stigler's point is that it is premature to abandon the hypothesis that voting behavior is explained by investment rather than by consumption motives. He offers empirical support for this proposition by showing that expenditures per pupil in public schools decline as the minority that opposes such spending becomes larger. In other tests of the investment motive, Barzel and Silberberg (1973) found that voter turnouts increase in gubernatorial elections that are expected to be close. Crain and Tollison (1976) found that candidates from the minority party running for the U.S. House of Representatives spend more on marginal seats than candidates from the majority party. The value of an incremental seat is predictably higher for the minority if legislative proportions are subject to diminishing returns.

In this paper we present additional evidence on the investment approach to political otucomes. Specifically, we test whether the returns to voting are continuous rather than all-or-none. The experiment we propose is to examine the impact of the share of the popular vote cast for the winning presidential candidate on the enactment of legislation in subsequent congressional terms. The main product of political competition is public policy, and executive and legislative approval are both required to produce the bulk of such policies. If political competition is more-or-less, not all-or-none, then political productivity should be larger when presidents receive larger pluralities.

Using data covering the period 1824 through 1980, our empirical results show consistently that an increase in the president's popular majority increases the number of bills enacted into law during his term of office, all other factors being equal. This supports the view that votes cast in presidential elections have positive marginal products. On the one hand, a vote for the candidate who wins raises his majority and accordingly makes him more effective in obtaining legislative approval of his policy agenda. On the other hand, a vote for the candidate who loses reduces the winner's majority, constraining the latter's political effectiveness.

The traditional way of looking at the paradox of voting is in terms of the benefits and costs of voting to one individual. We reject this approach. In interest-group terms, what matters is the cost of getting a block of marginal vote suppliers to the polls. Put another way, what is the number of additional votes necessary for an interest group to have an impact on bill production in the legislature? We use here the term "impact" to mean raising either the probability that legislation transferring wealth to the group will be enacted or that legislation transferring wealth from the group will be defeated. Rent-seeking and rent extraction are opposite sides of the same coin, and any particular piece of legislation that is proposed can cause the various interest groups within the polity to line up differently. Producing votes as investments in future bill production accordingly seems like a quite feasible economic activity for interest groups. Indeed, our estimates suggest that 6,000 marginal votes can invoke the passage of one additional bill. Viewed from an interest-group perspective and compared with the benefits and costs of voting to one individual, the investment motive for explaining voting behavior thus appears to have empirical content.

The paper is organized as follows. Section 2 contains a description of the empirical model and presents the results. Some concluding remarks are offered in section 3.

Empirical Model and Results

The U.S. Congress is the body that authorizes the taxing, spending, regulatory, and other policy initiatives that are the final products of political competition. We therefore want to test whether a party's degree of competitive success (in terms of votes for the party's presidential candidate) is one of the factors that influence the output of such policies. To do so, we adopt a legislative production function that is based on the interest-group theory of government (see Stigler, 1971; Peltzman, 1976).

Extensions of the interest-group model by McCormick and Tollison (1981) suggest that the institutional characteristics of the legislature—its size and degree of bicameralism—affect the cost to interest groups of obtaining legislation. Empirical estimates using data from state legislatures by McCormick and Tollison (1981), Crain (1979), and Crain and Tollison, (1980) support a legislative production function of the following form:

$$\begin{aligned}Q_t = {} & a_0 + a_1\text{SIZE}_t + a_2\text{HSR}_t + a_3\text{POP}_t + a_4\text{TURN}_t + \\ & + a_5\text{WPCT}_t + a_6\text{D}_t + a_7\text{DUM24}_t + a_8\text{DUM72}_t + v_t\end{aligned}$$

where Q_t = the number of bills enacted during a four-year presidential term;
SIZE_t = total legislative size (U.S. House plus U.S. Senate membership);
HSR_t = the ratio of U.S. House size to U.S. Senate size;
POP_t = total population of the U.S.;
TURN_t = total votes cast in the Presidential election as a percent of total population;
WPCT_t = the popular vote share of the winning Presidential candidate;
D_t = 1 if the party of the President and the majority party in the U.S. House and U.S. Senate are the same, and zero otherwise;
DUM24_t = 1 for the years 1924 and beyond, and zero otherwise;
DUM72_t = 1 for the years 1972 and beyond, and zero otherwise;
v_t = the regression error term.

The coefficient on SIZE must be determined empirically. That is, a_1 will be positive if increases in legislature size result in lower costs to interest groups of obtaining votes in Congress. This would be the case if, for example, having more legislators per voter makes it easier for interest groups to monitor their representatives, or if more legislators mean that the "price" of a vote falls sufficiently so that the cost of influence to interest groups falls. In contrast, if larger legislatures make it more difficult for legislators to reach agreement, a_1 will be negative.

The interest-group theory of government unambiguously predicts $a_2 < 0$. Specifically, as HSR rises (the House and Senate become more disparate in size), the cost of obtaining a majority in both legislative chambers increases (Crain, 1979; McCormick and Tollison, 1981, pp. 44–45). The reasoning here is straightforward. For a given total size of the legislature, more unequal chamber sizes raise the price of influence in the larger chamber more than the price of influence falls in the smaller chamber. Overall, the cost of influence rises as chamber sizes become more disparate. Such increased costs should be associated with fewer bills enacted, *ceteris paribus*.

More legislation is predicted to be forthcoming with a growing population ($a_3 > 0$). As POP increases, each voter will have a smaller influence on public decisions. In addition, individual incentives to lobby against bills that reduce wealth weaken because larger populations lower the per capita costs of these transfers.

Voter turnout, TURN, controls for the absolute sizes of majorities and minorities. In other words, a slim victory with a large turnout may translate into more political effectiveness than a similar victory with a small turnout. We make no *a priori* conjecture about the sign on a_4, however.

Our basic test of the investment hypothesis about voting focuses on the sign and significance of the coefficient on WPCT. If political effectiveness is indeed an increasing function of the size of the winner's majority, then one would expect legislative output to be increased by larger popular vote shares ($a_5 > 0$). Alternatively, a finding that a_5 is not significantly different from zero would be evidence against the investment hypothesis.

The dummy variable D controls for the separate effects of voting for the president versus voting for members of Congress. Specifically, D is set equal to unity when the party of the winning presidential candidate is the same as the majority party in the U.S. House and U.S. Senate during the two congressional sessions coinciding with his term of office, and zero otherwise. Such circumstances should increase the president's political effectiveness, and we therefore expect the sign of the estimated coefficient to be positive. Moreover, including this variable allows us to assess whether or not a vote for the president has value apart from a vote cast for the members of his party in the legislature.

Finally, two separate dummy variables, DUM24 and DUM72, are used to control for periods in which the number of potential voters changed. In particular, DUM24 controls for the advent of women's suffrage and DUM72 controls for the lowering of the voting age to eighteen. In each of these cases, the supply of voters shifted to the right, and this may have altered the degree to which presidents can transform winning margins into political outcomes. As in the case of voter turnout, however, we make no predictions about the signs of the coefficients on the two dummy variables.

Our data cover the 39 presidential elections from 1824 through 1976 (popular votes are not available for earlier contests).[2] For each election we calculate the winning candidate's popular vote as a percentage of the total votes cast for all candidates.[3] Although we considered using Electoral College results as a measure of political support for the president, we discarded the idea because electoral vote margins depend on the distribution of popular votes across states. We note that popular and electoral majorities are highly correlated.[4] The observations on the dependent variable are the total number of public and private laws enacted during the two congresses that coincide with each presidential term. SIZE, HSR, and POP were calculated as the averages of their respective values at the beginning and at the midpoint of the president's term. The dependent variable was transformed by taking its natural logarithm.

The results from estimating the legislative production function by ordinary least squares are presented in table 18–1. Of central interest are the strongly positive signs on WPCT in all of the specifications. Voting matters in the sense of Stigler. Historically, a 1 percent increase in a president's share of the popular vote leads to approximately a 1 percent increase in the amount of legislation enacted over the course of his term. This suggests something like a continuous underlying political effectiveness function—in effect, a supply curve of legislation that rises proportionately to the winning percentage of the vote.

The consistently positive and significant coefficients on D have two

Table 18–1.

	Dependent Variable: Log of Bills Enacted by Presidential Term, 1824–1980			
Intercept	4.0638	5.5148	3.8356	5.3569
SIZE	0.0037	0.0042	0.0047	0.0053
	(2.35)**	(2.53)**	(2.27)**	(2.46)**
HSR		−0.3587		−0.3800
		(−1.01)		(−1.08)
POP			−0.0040	−0.0044
			(−0.71)	(−0.78)
TURN	2.9481	2.3441	4.2069	3.6307
	(1.22)	(0.94)	(1.47)	(1.25)
WPCT	2.5448	2.4809	2.2922	2.1990
	(2.57)**	(2.51)**	(2.12)**	(2.04)**
D	0.3190	0.3056	0.3258	0.3116
	(2.59)**	(2.47)**	(2.58)**	(2.47)**
DUM24	−0.6583	−0.5138	−0.6621	−0.4922
	(−1.55)	(−1.15)	(−1.54)	(−1.08)
DUM72	−0.6686	−0.6793	−0.4907	−0.4846
	(−1.94)*	(−1.97)*	(−1.14)	(−1.12)
$\hat{\varrho}$	0.4365	0.4394	0.4042	0.4089
R^2	0.533	0.547	0.556	0.571

Notes: *t*-statistics; $\hat{\varrho}$ is the estimated first-order autocorrelation coefficient. Asterisks denote significance at the 5 percent (**) and 10 percent (*) levels.

implications. First, the president is more successful in obtaining approval of his legislative agenda when his party dominates both houses of Congress during his term of office. Second, holding the party composition of Congress constant, an increase in the president's popular vote share still leads to greater legislative output. This result suggests that even if the President is confronted by a legislature controlled by the opposition party during some or all of his term, having received a larger plurality makes him more politically effective.

The other results in table 18–1 turn out more or less as expected. In particular, increases in legislature size lead to increases in legislative output. (The coefficients on SIZE are significantly different from zero in all cases.) This suggests that as the total size of the legislature increases, the effect of competition between legislators on the price of influence more than offsets the tendency for transactions costs to rise. On balance, interest groups find it easier to obtain legislation in a larger Congress, perhaps because each representative is better able to specialize in narrower constituent concerns.

In general, an increase in the disparity of House and Senate sizes reduced the output of laws, and more legislation was produced as population grew over time. The coefficients on HSR are negative but not different from zero at standard levels. Similarly, the coefficients on POP are not significant. (These results are indicative of the presence of multicollinearity in our data set.) The voter turnout variable does not show an effect on bills enacted, which suggests that, as in markets, it is margins that matter in politics. The franchise extension variables likewise do not impact on the production of legislation, although in both cases the estimated effect is in the direction of reducing legislative output.

Overall, the model performs reasonably, explaining more than half of the variation in bills enacted by the U.S. Congress over the past 156 years. The legislature appears to read the election returns.[5]

Concluding Remarks

In this paper we have reported evidence supporting the hypothesis that political outcomes range more or less continuously from failure to success. In particular, using data covering the quadrennial elections held from 1824 through 1976, we found that the legislative output of the U.S. Congress is influenced by the size of the president's popular vote majority. This result suggests that a vote for president has value, either by raising the political effectiveness of the voter's candidate if he wins or by constraining the opposition's effectiveness if the voter's candidate loses. The president and vice-President are the only officeholders elected nationally, and the winning ticket's share of the popular vote apparently serves as an input into the production process for legislation.

What do our results mean in more practical terms? We find that, other things equal, a 1 percent increase in a president's winning margin leads to a 1 percent increase in legislation. This implies that at the means of our data, a 1 percent larger victory was associated with about 22 more bills passed during the following four years. A 1 percent increase over the mean winning popular vote share in the data translates into about 132,000 votes. At the margin, then, 132,000 additional voters could invoke the passage of 22 more bills, or one bill for each 6,000 marginal voters. And the issue is *not* that 1/6,000 is still a small number. This is the traditional way of looking at the paradox of voting, i.e., in terms of the value of voting to one individual out of many. We reject this approach; alternatively, we interpret our results in terms of how much it costs interest groups to get marginal vote suppliers to the polls, by our estimate to increase voter turnout by 6,000 votes. Viewed in this way and compared to, say, the costs of turning out 500,000 voters, producing votes as investments in bill production seems like a quite feasible economic activity for interest groups. A marginal vote supply of 6,000 votes is not that many votes to round up, most particularly where bill production in the legislature can be tailored to marginal vote suppliers (geographically, for example). So it would seem to us that Stigler was correct. It is indeed premature to abandon the investment motive for explaining voting behavior, all the more so when this point is understood in terms of the interest-group theory of government.

Notes

1. See Tollison and Willett (1973) for a summary.

2. The basic voting data were taken from Congressional Quarterly Inc. (1975); the observations on all other variables were obtained from U.S. Department of Commerce (1975). All of the series were updated through 1980 with data from U.S. Department of Commerce (1981). We would be happy to supply our data set upon request.

3. This enables us to avoid negative signs on three observations. In the elections of 1824 (Adams-Jackson), 1876 (Hayes-Tilden), and 1888 (Harrison-Cleveland), the winning candidate received fewer popular votes than his main rival. On average, however, 51.4 percent of the popular vote was cast for the person elected to the Presidency.

4. The simple correlation coefficient between WPCT and the winning candidate's electoral vote share is 0.772 in our data set; this correlation is significantly different from zero at the 1 percent level. In addition, WPCT is significantly correlated (at the 1 percent level) with the winner's popular vote (r^2 = 0.645) and electoral vote (r^2 = 0.690) pluralities.

5. We also ran the six specifications of the legislative production function shown in table 18–1 for a subperiod, 1888–1980, over which observations on real income were available. Although the resulting estimates suffered from severe multicollinearity, the coefficients on WPCT were positive and significant in five of the cases. Moreover, our results held up in specifications omitting TURN and the two dummy variables.

In addition, we estimated several variants of the legislative production function employing as an explanatory variable the predicted values from a regression of the log of bills introduced by presidential term on SIZE, TURN, WPCT, and the two dummy variables. When we used the instrumental variables technique to account for the possible nonindependence between bills enacted and bills introduced, the estimated coefficients on WPCT in the production function were generally of the same magnitude and significance level as those reported in table 18–1.

References

Barzel, Y., and Silberberg, E. "Is the Act of Voting Rational?" *Public Choice* (1973): 51–58.

Congressional Quarterly Inc. *Congressional Quarterly's Guide to U.S. Elections*. Washington, D.C.: Congressional Quarterly Inc., 1975.

Crain, W. M. "Cost and Output in the Legislative Firm." *Journal of Legal Studies* 8 (June, 1979): 607-21.

Crain, W.M., and Tollison, R. D. "Campaign Expenditures and Political Competition." *Journal of Law and Economics* 19 (April, 1976): 177–88.

Downs, A. *An Economic Theory of Democracy*. New York: Harper and Row, 1957.

McCormick, R. E., and Tollison, R. D. *Politicians, Legislation, and the Economy: An Inquiry into the Interest-Group Theory of Government*. Boston: Martinus Nijhoff, 1981.

Peltzman, S. "Toward a More General Theory of Regulation." *Journal of Law and Economics* 19 (August, 1976): 211–240.

Riker, W. H., and Ordeshook, P. C. "A Theory of the Calculus of Voting." *American Political Science Review* 62 (March, 1968): 25–42.

Stigler, G. J. "Economic Competition and Political Competition." *Public Choice* 13 (1972): 91–106.

Stigler, G. J. "The Theory of Economic Regulation." *Bell Journal of Economics* 2 (Spring, 1971): 3–21.

Tollison, R. D., and Willett, T. D. "Some Simple Economics of Voting and Not Voting." *Public Choice* 16 (1973): 59–71.

Tullock, G. *The Vote Motive*. London: Institute for Economic Affairs, 1976.

U.S. Department of Commerce, Bureau of the Census. *Historical Statistics of the United States, Colonial Times to 1970*, 2 vols. Washington, D.C.: USGPO, 1975.

U.S. Department of Commerce, Bureau of the Census. *Statistical Abstract of the United States*. Washington, D.C.: USGPO, 1981.

19 COMMITTEES AND RENT-SEEKING EFFORT

Roger D. Congleton*

Introduction

Committees are widely used by nearly all social organizations as a means of developing and implementing policies that often have clear distributive implications. Applications range from academic committees responsible for conferring minor student awards to corporate, congressional, and party committees responsible for decisions that have substantial effects upon the allocation of national resources. Such a state of affairs must be more than a little puzzling to those familiar with the modern literature on committee deliberations. Committee deliberations fall prey to all the problems of majority rule decision-making: the obvious diseconomies of multi-person decision-making, the possible absence of unique equilibria, the potential for intransitive rankings of alternatives and the implied arbitrariness of decisions noted by Arrow (1951), Black (1958) Buchanan and Tullock (1962), and Usher (1981). These weaknesses would seem to

* The author would like to thank Fred Menz, Paul Downing and the anonymous referees for helpful suggestions on earlier drafts of this paper.

suggest that allocative decisions would be better made by single individuals than by committees.

There are many possible defenses of committees, from democractic values and economies of sampling to differences in information possessed by participating individuals. Unfortunately, few, if any, of these ideas seem to account for the widespread use of committees by cultures and institutions that apparently place little value of majority rule procedures, per se.[1] This paper provides an explanation that may be more broadly applicable. Namely, the use of committees may reduce rent-seeking waste. This paper suggests that fewer resources may be used to affect the deliberations of committees than those of single individuals with equivalent authority. To the extent that such efforts at influence constitute wasteful rent-seeking, committees may be expected to out perform and out survive the institution of one-person allocation wherever the economics of reduced rent-seeking waste more than offset the additional costs of majority-rule decision-making. The paper thus provides a rare, if limited, efficiency based defense of majority rule institutions.

In order to demonstrate the potential economies of committees, the methodology of rent-seeking as developed by Tullock (1967), Krueger (1974), and in Buchanan, Tullock, and Tollison (1980) is applied to the task of analysing competitive games of influence under committee and one-man decision-making regimes. Our intent is to contrast the resource commitments made to influence committee decisions with those which would have occurred under one-person administration.

Because our interest is essentially a comparison of institutions, all other sources of variation are to be rendered as small as possible. Administrators are assumed to be drawn from the same homogeneous pool of individuals, and so have identical tastes and skills at decision-making. The agenda for both committee deliberations and one-man administration is presumed to be given at the outset. A fixed award or grant is to be distributed between two possible recipients according to the dictates of a particular allocative rule. Potential recipients are assumed to have equal skills at influencing the various decisions of the award allocating body. And since our interest is the level of resources utilized in the award-seeking process, we shall ignore the particular methods by which award-seekers influence the decisions of award administrators. All such mechanisms are to be included under the broad umbrella of what might be called the influence production function or the "application process." For our purposes, it is enough that influence varies directly with the value of resources committed to the application process.

The analysis focuses on cases where there are but two award-seekers in order to facilitate analysis and because it is often possible to characterize the award-seeking efforts of more than two individuals as competition between two coalitions. Each of two decision-making methods (one-man and committee) will be paired with two allocative rules (all-or-nothing and proportionate-share rules) which allows comparison of four administrative structures. We first examine the effects of committee versus one-man administration of all-or-nothing rules and then proceed to a similar analysis of proportionate-share rules.

Award-Seeking Effort under All-or-Nothing Allocative Rules

Administration of all-or-nothing rules requires the selection of deserving grantees from a pool of applicants. Under such rules, some applicants will be conferred awards and so find themselves among the "most worthy", while others will receive no award at all. As a consequence, there is a clear incentive for potential grantees to attempt to influence the allocative decision of the administrative body so that they might be included among those "honored." Our analysis suggests that there is a tendency for fewer resources to be employed in the resulting competitive game of influence if selections are made by committees rather than by single administrators.

One-Man Administration of All-or-Nothing Rules

When resource grants are to be made by a single administrator, the task of influencing one's future award is straightforward. Would-be recipients simply devote effort to influence the administrator's evaluation of their own merit vis-à-vis others. Because worthiness is assumed to be an increasing function of the resources employed demonstrating or manufacturing the properties of interest to the administrator, successful award-seekers will be those who have invested the greatest award-seeking effort. (In the unlikely event of a tie, the award will be granted arbitarily to one of the applicants.) Potential recipients will undertake this effort—play the rent-seeking game—if the anticipated gain exceeds the sacrifice incurred by actively participating in the game. If e is the opportunity cost of the minimum recognizable effort, then the smallest prize that might attract individual award-seeking effort is $P > e$.

The optimal strategy for an award-seeker in this game is to devote just a bit more effort to the process of lobbying than other applicants. By minimizing the cost of success, the net advantage of winning is maximized. The problem with this ideal strategy is that it requires the award-seeker to know the level of resources that will be devoted by other competitiors. Unfortunately, it is not possible for each supplicant to devote more resources than all others. As a result, there are no dominant pure strategies. Award-seekers will choose strategies based upon their *judgement* of the effort levels forthcoming from their competitiors rather than an objective determination of the net-payoff maximizing commitment. Thus little can be said regarding the level of resources that will be employed in a single round of the application process beyond noting that it will never pay to devote resources as valuable as the sought award.[2]

This ambiguity is an important feature of games of influence in all of the institutional settings explored by this paper. Deterministic allocation rules do not necessarily imply deterministic strategies. Nor are mixed or random strategies particularly attractive alternatives in settings where a game is to be played only a few times. A variety of methods for choosing strategies have been suggested for such circumstances, although none is universally accepted. One possibility which is widely used, but less widely accepted, is to choose strategies that maximize one's payoff given some expectation about the play of other game-players. This paper explores the implications of the simplist of the conjectural variation schemes, attributed to Antoine Augustin Cournot. Under the Cournot rule, a player chooses a strategy based on knowledge of the previous round of the game and the expectation that other players will not alter their strategies. In the small-number setting of interest here, it is assumed that strategic planning is based upon information obtained about competitor intentions rather than previous rounds of the game of influence.

In the two-party game of influence characterized above, Cournot interaction generates a pattern of adjustment often associated with competitive settings, namely escalation. If player A anticipates some level of effort from player B, A will devote a bit more effort than that in order to obtain a favorable decision from the administrator. If player B learns of this intention, a strategy involving a bit more effort than planned by A becomes B's optimal strategy. A's reaction to B's new strategy will again require efforts beyond those planned by B. The deterministic nature of the grant-allocating regime, together with information concerning competitor intentions, allows each competitor to believe that his own commitment will be a winning strategy. Cournot interaction causes each competitor's effort at influence to move toward upper bound P, the maximum effort that can ever be a reasonable strategy. As this limit is approached, the total effort committed to the game of influence approaches 2P.[3] At this limit, resour-ccs approaching twice the award granted are consumed in the competitive game of influence.[4]

Committee Administration of All-or-Nothing Rules

Under committee administration, grants are awarded to individuals considered to be the most deserving by the majority of committee members. Because the number of awards is assumed to be smaller than the pool of potential recipients, there will again be clear incentives for would-be grantees to attempt to influence the decisions made by the administrative body. If a particular committee member may be influenced only to the extent that specific resources are devoted to that end, then successful award-seekers will be those who have devoted the greatest effort to a majority of individual committee members. A committee having three members will reward the efforts of those successfully targeting two of the three administrators.[5]

The smallest prize capable of attracting award-seeking effort under committee administration will be somewhat larger than that required under one-man administration. If e is the opportunity cost of minimal efforts targeted at a single committee member, then the minimum commitment required to influence a committee having three members is the amount required to be noticed by a majority of committee members, or $2e$. Thus, the minimum grant sufficient to attract award-seeking effort under committee administration will exceed $2e$, rather than e, the minimum under a single administrator. Fewer award-seeking games will be played under committee administration since some prizes will be sufficient to attract the active participation of award-seekers under one-man administration but not under committees. However, many awards will be sufficient to overcome the participation thresholds for both committees and single administrators.

Under committee administration, active award-seekers have the dual problems of determining appropriate investment levels and properly distributing that effort among committee members in a manner which gains majority approval for their preferred resource allocation. To maximize net advantage, an award-seeker should identify the minimally sized majority of administrators who will receive the least attention by the competition and submit applications to that majority which embody just a bit more effort. Unfortunately, this ideal strategy suffers from the same sort of practical defect posed under one-man administration. In this case, the award-seeker must know both the extent and the distribution of the efforts of other prospective grantees. Because it is always possible for a competitor to be successful by altering his applicative efforts given this information, there are no pure strategies that dominate all others. Award-seekers are once again left to uncertainties of judgement in any single play of the grant-seeking game.

However, in contrast to the situation under one-man arbitration, there is no clear tendency for pre-application Cournot adjustment to increase overall effort levels in two-party games of influence. Mr. A's ideal strategy given Mr. B's intent *never* requires more resources than those committed by B. For example, suppose that A has learned of B's intention to distribute relatively large efforts across all committee members, as in a pattern of (100, 100, 100). A can dominate B's strategy by concentrating a smaller overall effort on a simple majority, as in a pattern of (101, 101, 0). Concentrating one's efforts on a minimally sized majority coalition will generally prove to be a cost-effective strategy. Unfortunately for A, B can respond to this plan by focusing still smaller total efforts on the neglected minority and a small portion of A's majority coalition, as with (0, 102, 1). This strategy requires just a bit more than half of the resources put forth by A. A could respond to B's new intent with a similar strategy, as with a pattern of (1, 0, 2) which establishes a very cost-effective majority. In this game, a process of Cournot adjustment leads to a de-escalation, rather than escalation, of competitive efforts. As this process continues, patterns of effort converge toward $(e, 0, e + d)$, where e is the resource cost of the smallest effective application, and d is the smallest increment of effort above e that allows a committee member to distinguish an application based upon an effort level of $e + d$ from one fashioned from effort level e. Once at this limit, further adjustment will cause potential majorities to change in cyclic pattern. Other strategies are possible, but none is consistent with the Cournot method of choosing strategies, that is, with maximizing the net pay-off of successful application given competitor strategies.

While convergence of the adjustment process does not allow us to predict a particular winner or loser, it does allow us to predict the total resource commitments that will be made at the limit, namely $4e + 2d$. To the extent that minimal efforts are small relative to the propective award, the investment limit for committees, $4e + 2d$, will be less than the limiting case for one-man administration, 2P. Perhaps more important than these limiting cases is the contrast between the escalation of competitive efforts under one-man administration and the potential for de-escalation under committees.

These tendencies suggest that fewer games of influence will be played under committee administration, and the games that are played tend to be played with relatively fewer resources. Committee administration itself may reduce the extent that resources are utilized in competitive games of influence.

Award-Seeking Effort under Proportionate-Share Rules

All-or-nothing distributive rules are by no means the only means of allocating a pool of resources between competing parties. They explore the possibility that the results obtained above are peculiarities of the all-or-nothing rule, we now modify that administrative structure by changing the allocative rule to be implemented. Rather than restrict awards to a specific subset of all potential grantees, awards will now be distributed across all eligible parties according to some criteria of relative merit or "grant-worthiness." Merit raises and governmental grants are often apportioned among applicants according to some criteria of relative performance rather than restricted to a select few. The alternative rule will be called a proportionate-share rule.

Under a proportionate-share rule, some pool of awards is to be distributed across all applicants according to *relative* merit. If A is twice as deserving as B, A will receive a grant twice as large as that given B. If P is the total value of the pool of awards to be apportioned, E_j is the level of effort put forth by the *j*th individual, and demonstrated merit is produced via such efforts with constant returns to scale, then the award received by the *j*th individual can be written as:

$$A_j = \left[\frac{E_j}{\sum E_i}\right] P. \tag{19.1}$$

As might have been expected, the adoption of this more equitable rule changes the incentives for competitive efforts.

Before we proceed, a few differences between all-or-nothing and proportionate-share rules should be noted. First, under proportionate-share rules any level of applicative effort will guarantee the applicant some non-zero award, whereas there is no similar guarantee under all-or-nothing rules. Second, proportionate-share rules require a divisible pool of rewards, whereas all-or-nothing rules do not. Third, administration of proportionate-share rules requires a cardinal measure of worthiness, whereas all-or-nothing rules require only ordinal measures. As a consequence of the last two characteristics, it will not always be possible to replace all-or-nothing allocative rules with proportionate-share rules. Some awards are intrinsically all-or-nothing, as there can be only one ambassador to the United Nations or but few Nobel laureates. In some settings, the required cardinal measure of worthiness may not be available, or possible. Thus, comparisons across allocating rules must be limited to those areas in which a change can be readily made.

One-Man Administration of Proportionate-Share Rules

Under one-man administration, awards are determined by the administrator's perception of relative merit. If we assume that demonstrated merit is produced by a process exhibiting constant returns to scale, then relative merit amounts to the relative value of the resources invested by each competitor. In this setting, the net advantage of application is the award received less the cost of applicative efforts, or

$$N_j = A_j - E_j. \tag{19.2}$$

If we return to our two-applicant world and let individual A's effort level be E_a and let E_b represent the effort level of B, eq. (19.2) becomes:

$$N_a = \left(\frac{E_a}{E_a + E_b}\right)P - E_a. \tag{19.3}$$

The first-order conditions for maximizing A's net return is satisfied in:

$$\frac{\partial N_a}{\partial E_a} = P\left(\frac{E_b}{(E_b + E_b)^2}\right) - 1 = 0. \tag{19.4}$$

Solving this condition for E_a in terms of E_b gives us A's optimal strategy function:

$$E_a = -E_b + \sqrt{PE_b}. \tag{19.5}$$

This function specifies the pay-off maximizing effort for A given B's effort and the size of the award pool, P. Once again, the best strategy for A depends on the level of effort chosen by B. Symmetry implies that B's strategy will be based upon a similar rule. Because no single effort level proves optimal independent of the actions of one's competitors, the resource level embodied in any single application will again be the result of active judgement rather than an objective process of optimization.

However, if it is possible for each competitor to learn the intended effort levels of the other and to adjust accordingly, there is a tendency for effort levels to converge to equilibrium levels. Figure 19–1 depicts the

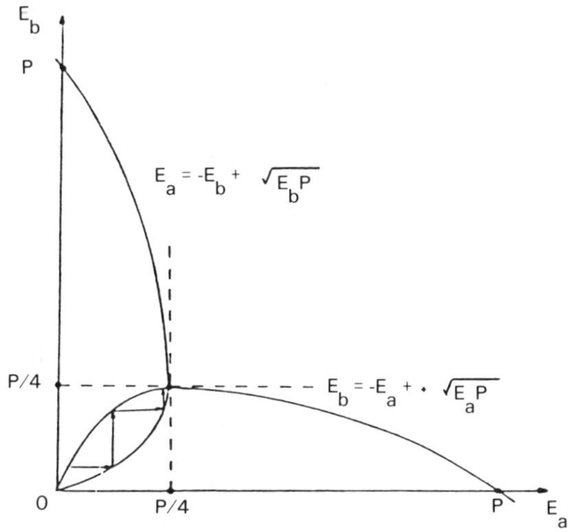

Figure 19.1

optimal strategy functions (or reaction functions) of the two players. Note that selection of any strategy requiring fewer than P resources leads to a series of adjustments that converge to P/4, P/4, which constitute equilibrium levels of effort.

Thus, one-man administration of proportionate-share rules differs from the previous examples in that equilibrium strategies do exist. At this equilibrium, fewer resources are devoted to the competitive game of influence than under a similar administration of all-or-nothing rules at or near their escalation limit. P/2 will always be less than 2P.

Committee Administration of Proportionate-Share Rules

Committees charged with administering proportionate-share rules will tend to allocate the pool of resource grants in accordance with the median administrator's evaluation of relative merit. Because the administrators are assumed to be homogeneous, both the median voter and his inclinations regarding relative merit will be determined by the distribution of efforts across members of the decision-making body. For convenience, it will again be assumed that the allocating committee has three members.

Grant-seekers facing this administrative structure have the threefold task of (1) determining optimal levels of grant-influencing effort, (2) distributing that effort across members of the decision-making body so as to generate a particular median voter, and (3) demonstrating the optimal level of merit to that median voter. In our two-applicant world, Mr. A's net gain for an effort level of M_a focused on the median voter is:

$$N_a = \left(\frac{E_n}{E_a + E_b}\right) P - E_a - S_a. \tag{19.6}$$

where P is the size of the award fund. M_b is B's effort level toward the committee member that A determines to be the best median voter, and S_a is the level of resources required to assure a particular median voter. Needless to say. S_a should be as small as possible since it does not directly affect the grant ultimately received by A. Allocating no effort to one of the committee members efficiently assures that he will be an extreme and not the median. Similarly, allocating some very small amount of effort to members neglected by one's competitor assures that they will be the other extreme (in this case, of the view that essentially all of the award should go to A). Thus, a typical pattern of applicative effort will look like $(0, S_a, M_a)$.

An optimal award-seeking effort function can be derived from eq. (19.6) in a manner similar to that used above for proportional share rules under one-man administration. The resulting function is:

$$E_a = -E_b + \sqrt{PE_b}. \tag{19.7}$$

This equation does not dictate a total level of effort, but rather the optimal level of effort to direct at the median voter given the efforts of B. Note that the cost of assuring this particular median. S_a, is irrelevent at this point, it being a fixed cost. A similar function can be determined for B:

$$E_b = -E_a + \sqrt{PE_a}. \tag{19.8}$$

Eqs. (19.2) and (19.8) indicate that the optimal level of resources to be directed toward the median voter varies with the efforts of one's competitor. Again, there are no dominant pure strategies in the game of influence.

If the competitors confront a stable median voter, then eqs. (19.7) and (19.8) represent reaction functions similar to those developed above for one-man administration of similar rules. However, the presumed homogeneous character of the administrators implies that the median committee member is endogeneously determined by the relative effort levels of the competitors. Instead of following the dictates of eq. (19.7) or (19.8), competitors will generally find it cost-effective to alter the distribution of their efforts and generate a new median voter. For example, were Mr. B to learn of Mr. A's intent to distribute his efforts in a pattern like $(0, S_a, M_a)$, B's best response would be to ignore committee member 3 (A's intended median) and attempt a strategy like (S_b, M_b, 0). This strategy makes administrator number 2 the median voter. Unfortunately, B's strategy renders A's plan sub-optimal. Were A to learn of B's new plan, he would be inclined to adopt a pattern like (M_a, 0, S_a). This revision in turn renders B's strategy sub-optimal. In contrast to one-man administration of proportionate-share rules, Cournot adjustments do not converge to stable strategy pairs. There are no equilibrium pure strategies under committee administration.

However, a series of Cournot adjustments will converge to stable levels of resource commitment. As was mentioned above, both S_a and S_b should be as small as possible in order to minimize the cost of establishing a particular median administrator. If e is the smallest effective effort level, then eq. (19.7) implies that optimal strategies will involve patterns of effort like (e, 0, $-e + \sqrt{eP}$), where e is the minimum discernible effort and $-e + \sqrt{eP}$ is the level of effort focused on a median voter who is the target of e efforts from one's competitor. Strategic revision at this point requires changes in the distribution of efforts rather than the level of resources committed.

To the extent that minimal effort, e, is "small", fewer resources will tend to be used in the competitive game of influence under committee administration of proportionate-share rules than under one-man administration. This parallels our result under all-or-nothing rules. However, since $-e + \sqrt{ep}$ must be at least as large as $e + d$, the resource investments made under committee administration of proportionate-share rules will be at least as large as those committed under a similar administration of all-or-nothing rules.

Conclusion and Summary

In admittedly abstract and highly simplified circumstances, committee administration has been shown to reduce the extent to which scarce resources are utilized by would-be recipients to influence the deliberations of administrators. Two properties of committee administration are responsible for this result. First, the minimum award necessary to induce participation in a game of influence is greater for committees than for single administrators. There are simply more people to be influenced under committee administration than under one-man administration and thus the participation threshold tends to be greater. Second, two-party games of influence have a tendency to de-escalate under committee administration, whereas such games tend to escalate under one-man administration within the environment explored. Games of influence played under majority rule institutions are not simply a matter of resource commitments but of coalition building. The usually undesirable absence of stable majority coalitions allows award-seekers to economize on efforts devoted to influencing committee deliberations by targeting alternative majority coalitions.

Table 19–1 summarizes the resource commitments made at the respective Cournot limit points under the four allocative regimes examined. Both decision-making method and allocative rules have substantial effects on the extent to which resources are utilized in award-seeking games. Fewer resources were committed to games of influence under committee administration than under one-man administration of either allocative rule. Casual empiricism tends to support these theoretical results. Lobbying efforts directed toward committees do seem to be somewhat smaller than those directed at single individuals with similar allocative authority. It should be noted that the effects of allocative rule changes were not decision-method invariant. Under one-man administration, a shift from all-or-nothing rules to the more equitable proportionate share rules tended to greatly reduce competitive efforts, whereas a similar shift under committee administration tended to increase effort levels.[6]

The question of whether all competitive efforts at influence should be classified as counter-productive rent-seeking has not been explored and is beyond the scope of this paper. A reasonably thorough characterization of the sorts of competitive efforts that do tend to be wasteful can be found in the previous work of Tullock (1967) and Congleton (1980). It is presumed here that minor efforts to influence decisions may be productive in so far as more informed choices might be made, but that greater efforts tend to have little, if any, positive effect on the decision reached. These supra-

Table 19–1.

Administrative structure	*Limiting case or equilibrium strategy*	*Grant-seeking effort rank*
1. All-or-Nothing		
(a) One administrator	P	1
(b) Majority rule administration	$(0, e, e + \delta)$	4
2. Proportionate-share		
(a) One administrator	P/4	2
(b) Majority rule administration	$(0, e, -e + \sqrt{eP})$	3

productive efforts may properly be regarded as wasteful rent-seeking if they neither generate positive externalities nor represent the simple transfer of resources to others.

In this context, the above analysis implies that committees themselves tend to reduce rent-seeking waste. To the extent that these economies more than offset the generally higher decision costs of multi-party deliberations, committees may serve as efficiency enhancing instruments despite their cumbersomeness.

The scope of this conclusion is limited by the institutional environment explored and by the mechanism used to generate competitor strategies. The Cournot method of modeling individual choice and interdependency has a limited appeal in settings where decision-makers are considered to be well-informed and interaction extensive, although even here the Cournot assumption provides substantial insight into the operation of auctions and other important market processes. On the other hand, if individuals are presumed to be less than completely informed and social institutions largely the result of evolutionary tendencies, then the convergence properties of relatively simple choice mechanisms may be of greater relevance. To the extent that Cournot adjustments are accepted as a reasonable first approximation of actual decision-making procedures, committees might be used because of a conscious awareness of the economies developed above. Or, more likely, they may, in Hayek's (1973) terms, be examples of *kosmos* or social evolution; institutions created by chance and perhaps maintained for incorrect reasons, but nonetheless reasonably efficient social mechanisms.

Notes

1. Buchanan and Tullock (1962) provide an individualistic rationale for the adoption of majority rule institutions that requires no ethical commitment to democratic principles. They suggest that individuals may prefer majority decision rules over rules requiring unanimity or minority approval because of a trade-off between achieving successful authorization of policies that benefit particular individuals and avoiding collective actions that damage those same interests. This line of reasoning can be used to explain the adoption of majority rule procedures by a committee of the whole, even if individuals have no allegance to majoritarian norms, per se. Representative committees similarly may be defended as a transactions-costs-reducing means of accomplishing the same ends. However, the existence of committees that are not intended to be representative or are too small to represent a statistically useful subsample of the population cannot easily be explained by the Buchanan and Tullock theory of constitutional choice.

An alternative explanation of the use of small representative committees is that such committees reduce incentives for individuals outside the deliberating body to invest in award-seeking effort, since those efforts may tend to needlessly duplicate the efforts of the committee members themselves.

2. The process of judgement, itself, may be open to analysis. For example, Foster (1981) suggests that judgement may be modeled as an exercise in subjective probability calculus. Note that the presumed deterministic nature of the allocative rule implies that the only probabilistic aspect to be modeled is the behavior of one's competitors. Thus, under this model of judgement, a typical competitor forms priors concerning the efforts of his opposition and, if risk neutral, invests the level of effort that maximizes the expected net payoff. If a competitor were risk averse, he would invest somewhat more than this amount of zero (and not play the game). Unfortunately, the range of plausible subjective probability distributions allow optimal investment levels over the entire 0 A interval.

Another possible representation of judgement is to consider it a mechanism for implementing optimal mixed strategies. Shiffman (1953) established that games with mathematical structures similar to the ones of interest here have equilibrium *mixed* strategies, although the optimal density functions to be employed by the players cannot always be determined.

Such models do not eliminate the role of judgement, but rather reduce it to the determination of prior probabilities and the probability-event space. I or our purposes, the lack of a deterministic choice is the matter of interest rather than analysis of particular representations of the process of judgement itself.

3. The P, P strategic pair is not a stable equilibrium, merely the upper bound toward which Cournot adjustment tends to converge.

4. Other games in which players jointly 'over-invest' relative to prospective rewards are, of course, not uncommon. State-run lotteries and private gambling establishments are, for the most part profitable ventures.

5. Personalized applications are often the only means of influence available to would-be recipients in the informal setting typical of games of influence. Without the assumed private character of applications, homogeneous committee members would have always acted in unison and so been equivalent to one-man rule. In cases where applications efforts are limited to the production of public goods or their equivalents, the escalating tendencies of one-man administration are also implied for committee administration of all-or-nothing games.

6. It may also be worth noting that to the extent that administrators are beneficiaries of competitor efforts, one expects committees to prefer the more equitable proportionate-share rules because of the above competitive propensities alone. Thus, to the extent that equity, itself, is of general interest, our analysis suggests that committees may be a preferred method of decision-making because they may tend to adopt more equitable distributive procedures.

References

Arrow, K. *Social Choice and Individual Values*. New York: John Wiley and Sons, Inc., 1951.

Black, D. *The Theory of Committees and Elections*. Cambridge: Cambridge University Press, 1958.

Buchanan, J.M.; and Tullock, G. *The Calculus of Consent* Am Arbor: University of Michigan Press, 1962.

Buchanan, J.M.; Tollison, R.D. and Tullock, G. (eds.) *Towards a Theory of the*

Rent-seeking Society College Station: Texas A & M Press, 1980.

Congleton, R. D. "Competitive Process, Competitive Waste, and Institutions. In: J. M. Buchanan, R. D. Tollison, and G. Tullock (eds.), *Towards a Theory of the Rent-seeking Society College Station:* Texas A & M Press, 1980.

Foster, E. "Competitively Awarded Government Grant." *Journal of Public Economics* 13, 105 (1981): 111.

Hayek, F. A. *Law, Legislation, and Liberty*. Chicago: University of Chicago Press, 1973.

Krueger, A. O. "The Political Economy" of the Rent-seeking Society. *American I Economic Review* 64, 291 (1974): 303.

Shiffman, M. "Games of Timing" In: H.W. Kuhn and A.W. Tucker (eds.) *Contributions to the Theory of Games II*, Annals of Mathematical Studies, 28. (Princeton: Princeton University Press, 1953.

Tullock, G. "The Welfare Costs of Tariffs, Monopoly, and Theft. *Western Economic Journal* 5 (1967): 224–232.

Usher, D. *The Economic Prerequisites to Democracy* New York: Columbia University Press, 1981.

20 GOVERNMENT AND ITS BUREAUCRACY: A BILATERAL BARGAINING VERSUS A PRINCIPAL-AGENT APPROACH

Charles K. Rowley and Robert Elgin

Introduction

Early theories of bureaucracy tended to be dominated by Weberian[1] notions of impartial, efficient service by government officials concerned to serve the public interest as interpreted by their elected governments. Economists for the most part took little account, in analyzing market failure and recommending bureaucratic interventions, of the undercurrent of popular criticism of bureaucrats on grounds of laziness, insensitivity to citizen preferences, and of self-seeking behavior assumed in the theory of the firm.

Early challenges to this *nirvana* model stemmed from Tullock[2] in 1965 and from Downs[3] in 1966. Both analyzed the internal organization of bureaucracy, subjecting bureaucratic agents to critical scrutiny and noting the inevitable control loss associated with this form of economic organization. However, it was not until 1971, with the publication of Niskanen's[4] text, that bureaucracy was subjected to a comprehensive analysis predicated on the universal self-seeking assumptions of public choice. Niskanen's theory quickly dominated existing Weberian theories of bureaucracy, all but supplanting models based on vague notions of the public interest.

For some fifteen years, Niskanen's theory of bilateral bargaining between budget maximizing bureaucrats and elected government dedicated to satisfying the preferences of median voters has dominated the public choice literature. With few exceptions, scholars researching the Niskanen paradigm have exaggerated his early insight of bureau domination in the bilateral bargaining process, for the most part ignoring the role of elected representative governments in monitoring the supply of public services. Only recently, with a resurgence of interest in the role of property rights, and with developments in principal-agent theory, has the relationship between government and its bureaucracy begun to attract significant attention among scholars of public choice.

Bureaucracy is a concept that can be defined broadly or narrowly, with some, like Breton and Wintrobe[5], extending its domain even to include private corporate organizations which raise their revenues by selling commodities at a per-unit price. It is the thesis of this paper, however, that the concept should be narrowly drawn in the sense of Niskanen[6], indeed even more tightly than his definition, since we wish to exclude from consideration private, non-profit organizations which otherwise satisfy his criteria. Thus bureaus are here defined as public sector organizations in which "owners" and employees cannot appropriate any part of the difference between revenues and costs as direct personal income and in which a significant part of the recurring revenues derive from other than the sale of output at a per unit price.

This paper surveys recent contributions to the theory of bureaucracy within the monopoly/bilateral monopoly framework established by Niskanen[7]. This approach is then contrasted with the competitive, exchange-oriented theory of bureaucracy developed by Breton and Wintrobe[8]. The issue of input preference also is analyzed[9]. Finally, the paper surveys the relevant literature on property rights and principal-agent theory, evaluates existing applications of this literature in economic analyses of political-bureaucratic behavior, and develops a more fully articulated theory useful in explaining relations between elected governments and their bureaus. The paper is designed to provide a basis for subsequent empirical testing of such relationships within the context of the U.S. federal government.

The Monopoly/Bilateral Monopoly Theory of Bureaucracy

Niskanen's theory of bureaucracy and representative government (he stresses the importance of the dual relationship)[10] is predicated on the self-seeking generative assumption associated with all senior bureaucrats who exercise responsibility over bureau budgets. Of the several variables which enter the bureaucrat's utility function—salary, perquisites of office, public reputation, power, patronage, output of the bureau, ease of making changes and ease of managing the bureau—Niskanen suggested that all except the last two were a monotonic increasing function of the total budget of the bureau. Thus he employed budget maximization as a relevant proxy for utility maximization by senior bureaucrats, predicting that bureaucrats produce output levels yielding the highest possible budgets rather than, for example, those output levels which maximize the difference between revenues and costs.

Niskanen further assumes[11] that government bureaus possess supply monopolies and, for the most part, bargain against governments or their appropriations committees over their budgets from positions of information advantage. Given that they trade a total output for a total budget, this enables them to exercise monopoly power in a manner comparable to perfect price discrimination, extracting the total consumers' surplus from their commodity provisions.

Niskanen's model posits a senior bureaucrat acting under a budget constraint given by;

$$\mathrm{B} = a\mathrm{Q} - b\mathrm{Q}^2 \tag{20.1}$$

Where B is the budget which the government is willing to grant the bureau for a given expected level of output, Q. Niskanen further assumes an increasing marginal cost function of the form:

$$\mathrm{TC} = c\mathrm{Q} + d\mathrm{Q}^2 \tag{20.2}$$

If the total cost is less than or equal to the total budget at the budget-maximizing output (the case of the demand-constrained bureau), the choice of output by the bureau head will be $\mathrm{Q} = \frac{a}{2b}$ where the budget is maximized. If the total cost exceeds the budget at that output (the case of the budget-constrained bureau), the bureau will settle for a constrained maximum which assures equality of total cost with budget, namely $\mathrm{Q} = \frac{(a - c)}{(b + d)}$.

These solutions suggest to Niskanen that a primary problem with bureaucracy is oversupply in the sense that output exceeds (in his example by a factor of two) that which would maximize net value to the government sponsor. Note that this concept is remote from that of Pareto optimality, since the government and not individual citizens have articulated demand. A second problem, save only in the limiting case of budget-constrained output, is that output will be supplied at above minimum possible cost. A third problem, sensed rather than fully articulated by Niskanen, is that bureaus will tend to overemploy capital in order to boost the present value of the budget. In general, therefore, Niskanen-type bureaus diverge sharply from the Weberian ideal.

Although a number of commentators, for example Orzechowski[12] and Miller[13], criticize Niskanen for his emphasis upon bureau monopolies in the context of sponsor passivity, this criticism is only justified in connection with his "basic model". For, in the relatively neglected Part V of his text, Niskanen models the review process in representative government, utilizing the median voter theorem in this connection, albeit concluding that "although the interests of the review committee and the bureau are not identical, they are often (maybe generally) consistent."[14] He also relaxes the assumption of bureau monopoly to explore bureaucratic behavior in a competitive environment, emphasizing the beneficial effects of such competition upon the cost-effectiveness of supply in the demand-constrained environment and upon the provision of supply information to government sponsors.

In an important paper which retained the monopoly assumption of Niskanen's basic model, Migue and Belanger[15] challenged Niskanen's budget maximization hypothesis as internally inconsistent in that it fails to differentiate between bureau output and all other perquisites of office attainable via budget discretion. The Niskanen bureaucrat is seen to derive zero utility from fiscal residue. Instead, he pursues the productive efficiency of the competitive firm without any regard for taking rents from the bureau himself.

Migue and Belanger[16] suggest that bureau heads may value rewards of office independently from bureau output and may expend less than the total budget on output in order to retain a discretionary budget, given by:

$$D = aQ - bQ^2 - cQ - dQ2 \tag{20.3}$$

where the symbols are as above defined.

Thus, the output level which maximizes the discretionary budget, in this example is:

$$Q = \frac{(a - c)}{2(b + d)} \tag{20.4}$$

The level of output here achieved is that preferred by the sponsor but it is supplied inefficiently with the total surplus appropriated by the bureau. As Migue and Belanger recognize, this is the alternative polar case to that posited by Niskanen, and intermediate cases are anticipated in which bureau heads maximize a utility function of the form:

$$U = f(Q, D) \tag{20.5}$$

The comparative statics of the Niskanen and the Migue and Belanger models also differ since the Niskanen model predicts that bureaus respond to a demand increase by expanding both output and budget in *pro rata* terms, whereas the Migue/Belanger model predicts a relatively large budget increase associated with an increase in unit cost. Since Migue and Belanger do not specify the particular input preference of the bureaucrat, their model is silent on the issue of bureaucratic bias in resource utilization.

Both models leave little role for the legislature, or its representatives, concerning the final output of the bureau, other than in budget negotiations which are seen in any event to be dominated by the bureau. Thus, overproduction and/or successful rent-seeking by bureau heads is not viewed as provoking a legislative response. Both models ignore property rights and their delineation as a basis for analysing bureaucracy. They consequently take no account of the principal-agent relationship which is central to an understanding of bureau behavior.

Bureau Behavior in a Competitive Environment

Although Niskanen is best known for his monopoly theory of bureau behavior, in fact he devoted a chapter of his book to an analysis of bureaucratic behavior in a competitive environment. At the local government level, he noted the importance of exit as a mechanism for imposing competitive discipline on bureaus offering alternative service-tax packages, with the inference that even "monopoly" bureaus would supply near-optional levels of output at near-minimum production cost. At national government levels, however, he suggested that the effect of competition among bureaus must depend on the nature of the review process and the political structure of the government.

Bureau competition is encouraged in certain areas of public good provision, notably among the armed forces of the U.S. Niskanen analyzes a case in which two bureaus supply the same services to national government under somewhat different cost conditions. The budget-output proposals are jointly reviewed by a committee, dominated by representatives of a group with a relatively high demand for the service. The committee then forwards a total budget and output for approval by a majority of the entire body of representatives.

Niskanen establishes that such a review committee would select the same total output and budget from the competing bureaus as would a monopoly bureau, in a budget-constrained situation. Under such conditions, bureau competition does not increase efficiency in supply nor does it reduce service oversupply. However, in the demand-constrained situation, the difference between the budget and the minimum production cost of monopolistic bureau may be considerable. Competition will then induce efficiency in two ways: firstly, by increasing demand elasticity for the services of each bureau; and secondly, by providing the review committee with a contemporary basis for comparison. However, bureau competition does not reduce the general problem of bureau oversupply, but rather reduces total expenditure without affecting output.

In 1982, Breton and Wintrobe,[17] while explicitly recognizing the importance of demand forces via the legislature or its review committees for the overall determination of bureaucratic outputs, nevertheless concentrated upon the development of an exchange-based theory of supply with significant internal trading and competitive characteristics. Although their theory is utilized to determine bureaucratic behavior in both government and corporate organizations, it is reviewed here only from the former perspective. Their theory, which continues to provide a role for authority, emphasizes the importance of trade, and thus breaks both with Weberian traditions of bureaucracy as rational and efficient and with the early public choice perspective that bureaus are inherently inefficient in their provision of outputs.

Relationships between superiors and subordinates are viewed in general as being governed by exchange and trade, with superiors purchasing obedience from their subordinates, and with subordinates competing and trading among themselves. To assist their task, the authors introduce three notions essentially ignored by the early public choice approach, drawn from the conventional literature on bureaucracy.

The first such notion is trust. Trade essentially requires the existence of property rights which for the most part cannot be supported by legal instruments[18] in the case of bureaucratic relationships. Instead, therefore, in the bureau they are supported by trust. The existence of trust—confidence in some degree by one bureaucrat that another will effect his promise—enables trade to take place where otherwise it would be impossible. Trust networks thus are the analogues of markets, just as trust is the analogue of law and law enforcement. The structure of networks in the organization is referred to as the informal structure and is treated as a variable, the extent, complexity, and influence of which are all under bureaucratic control. In particular, trust networks are accumulated by rational individuals who wish to trade with one another over time.

The formal structure, in contrast, is seen to be important essentially as a significant determinant of the cost of accumulating or maintaining networks rather than for its authority role. Breton and Wintrobe (in our view incorrectly) reject the relevance for bureaucracy of principal-agent analysis. They argue firstly that monitoring the behavior of agents in the context of contractual, enforceable law is necessarily different from monitoring in the context of relationships based on trust. Secondly, they contend that since monitoring typically is conducted by bureaucrats, the problem remains as to who should monitor the monitors. For Breton and Wintrobe, monitoring is definitely ancillary to trust.

The second concept employed by Breton and Wintrobe is that of selective behavior, the essence of which is that bureaucrats choose whether to be efficient or inefficient within the limits of their capacity. Selective behavior is viewed as the outcome of a trading process—a set of explicit or implicit negotiations conducted via bureaucratic networks between superiors and subordinates on the one hand and among subordinates on the other. The outcome is determined by forces of demand and supply, with the price offered by superiors for efficient service compared with rewards available to subordinates from inefficiency. These forces are determined themselves by the cost of monitoring and by the distribution of trust in the network.

The third concept introduced is that of bureaucratic competition (in the modern Austrian sense)[19], which Breton and Wintrobe claim to be a dominant feature of bureaucracy, both within and between specific bureaus. Within bureaus, there is competition for jobs, together with a less well-recognized form of competition for network ties. Between bureaus, there is territorial competition. For Breton and Wintrobe these various forms of competition are viewed as substitutes, with imperfections in one form compensated for by competition in others. Somewhat unconvincingly, they claim that the world of bureaucracy essentially is a world of competition.

On the basis of these concepts, Breton and Wintrobe develop a theory of bureaucracy which is logically self-contained and, given careful attention to the definition of observable proxies for "trust", one capable of generating testable predictions.[20] They claim to have developed a model in which both competition and bureaucratic behavior play important roles in the structure and the provision of bureaucratic output. Competition, in their theory, does not eliminate selective behavior, whether efficient or inefficient—hence the authors' recognition of a role for direct monitoring, reorganization and regulation by sponsors to combat inefficient behavior. Yet these latter concepts play only a peripheral role in their text and operate essentially outside any notion of property rights as usually defined.

In our view, these serious deficiencies are likely to relegate the theory to a peripheral position in the literature on bureaucracy and representative government.

Issues of Bureaucrat Input Preference

Even the competition oriented theories of bureaucracy do not deny the possibility of residual discretionary power which may give rise to inefficiency in supply while analyses based on the superior monopoly advantages of bureaus suggest that a relatively large fiscal residuum arises from which senior bureaucrats indirectly may extract wealth. The manner in which such wealth is extracted, however, is not classified either by Niskanen or by Migue and Belanger, or indeed by Breton and Wintrobe.

Orzechowski[21] attempted to remedy this deficiency by employing the notion of Migue and Belanger that bureaucrats indeed divert the fiscal residuum generated by their agencies for their own purposes in a model of bureau behavior which incorporates explicitly the resource preferences of bureaucrats. He noted the emphasis placed by C.N. Parkinson[22] in early studies of bureau behavior upon the strong internal preference for staff (the so-called Parkinson's Law that the growth rate of staff in public bureaus approximates a positive constant over time). He noted also the confirmation of this preference by O.E. Williamson[23] for utility maximizing managers of firms imbued with non-trivial discretionary power. He noted further the contributions of Borcherding and Bush and Spann,[24] which emphasized the vote motive for bureaucrats to extend their bureaus and thereby enlarge the political base for their activities, and which indeed demonstrated statistically for the U.S. that voter participation rates were highest among bureaucrats. In contrast, he noted the view of De Alessi[25] that bureaus may tend to favor relatively capital-intensive production methods since these draw in a larger proportion of supply cost over a shorter time horizon. Orzechowski then derived a model of bureaucracy capable of incorporating elements of both approaches, but which, in his application, assumes that labor is the dominant preference variable.

Thus the Orzechowski model defines a utility function for senior bureaucrats containing two variables, namely output (following Niskanen) and the size of labor input. Bureaus are assumed to maximize this function:

$$\text{Max } U = U(Q, L) \tag{20.6}$$

Subject to a to budget constraint B = R(Q)

$$R[f(K, L)] = wL + rK \tag{20.7}$$

Using the Lagrangian method and substituting $f(K, L)$ for Q to convert the choice problem into one involving two variables, Orzechowski manipulates the first order conditions to yield an expression which indicates the pattern of resource usage by bureaus, namely:

$$\frac{f_K}{f_L} = \frac{r}{w - \dfrac{U_2}{\lambda}} \tag{20.8}$$

With λ and U_2 (the marginal utility of labor) both greater than zero, the implication derived is that:

$$\frac{f_K}{f_L} \neq \frac{r}{w} \tag{20.9}$$

On this basis, Orzechowski established that the bureau will employ factor inputs inefficiently, with the ratio of marginal products not equal to their price ratio, and (on his assumptions) with labor the overemployed factor input, for any linear-homogeneous or homothetic production function.

The comparative static implications of this model also differ from those of standard profit maximization. For example, the bureaucrat's response to a decrease in the price of capital will have an ambiguous effect on the labor-capital ratio, possibly inducing the use of more labor relative to capital. Moreover, the response of the bureau to demand shocks also is ambiguous with the Migue/Belanger thrust suggesting greater inefficiency as the bureau budget expands, but with the Parkinson thrust suggesting that staff size expands as budgets experience significant cuts.

Peacock[26], while judging Orzechowski's model a distinct improvement over those based upon the budget maximization generative assumption, suggested that it fails to encapsulate two widely recognized features of bureaucratic leadership—caution and laziness. Peacock denied that the taste for leisure by senior bureaucrats appropriately was captured by employing labor input as a preference variable, since staff enlargement in his view tends to be associated with an increase in managerial and administrative responsibilities.

Thus Peacock specified a utility function as follows for senior bureaucrats with no expectation of further promotion:

$$\text{Max } U = U[N, L, S] \; (U_n, U_L, U_s > 0) \tag{20.10}$$

where N represents the number of administrative grade officials under his command, L represents "on-the-job leisure", and S represents the surplus (fiscal residuum) over and above the wages and emoluments payable to administrative grade staff.

Peacock retained the bureau-monopoly assumption of Niskanen, but introduced as an objective constraint the inability of the senior bureaucrat to fix salary rates within the bureau. Assuming (for simplicity) that all administrators are of the same grade and receive identical salaries the budget constraint is

$$B = \bar{w}N + S \tag{20.11}$$

The leisure constraint upon senior bureaucrats is:

$$L = L(N) \text{ with } L_n < 0 \text{ and } L_{nn} < 0 \tag{20.12}$$

implying a Lagrangian of the form:

$$W = U(N, L, S) + \lambda 1, [L - L(N)] + \lambda 2(B - {}_nN - S] \tag{20.13}$$

The first-order conditions for utility maximization simplify to:

$$U_n + UL \cdot L_n = U_x \cdot \bar{w} \tag{20.14}$$

Thus the bureaucrat maximizes utility where the marginal utility derived from increasing administrative manpower is equated with the marginal utility derived from using the wages of the marginal administrator for surplus activities. Once N is determined L is too, on Peacock's assumptions. Given the exogenous determination of the cost of labor input, the limitation on the demand for labor is determined by the maximum size of the budget. The upper limit on output expansion is determined by the loss of utility from leisure marginally induced by an expansion in administrative staff. In Peacock's model output may lie below the level of the perfectly competitive industry, in contrast both to the Niskanen and the Orzechowski models. Technical inefficiency via excessive leisure and fiscal residuum objectives clearly is a predictable outcome of this bureaucratic monopoly model.[27]

The Role of the Legislature

At best, the legislature is seen to exercise only a shadowy role in bureau surveillance in the important analyses of bureaucracy so far reviewed. At worst, legislatures are seen to exercise no role at all. Since we shall argue that this is an important weakness, a brief survey of the relevant perspectives is provided in this section.

Niskanen[28], in his basic model, noted that most bureaus are financed by a single or dominant collective organization which, in turn, is financed by tax revenues or by compulsory contributions. The officers or representatives of the collective are usually elected by a wider constituency but are often effectively self-perpetuating.[29] These officers review (in single or in multi-stages) the bureau's proposed activities and budget, approve the budget, monitor the performance of the bureau, and usually approve the appointment of the bureau head. Given the monopoly nature of Niskanen's bureau, the relationship between bureau head and the review officers is viewed as one of bilateral monopoly characterized "by both threats and deference, by both gaming and appeals to a common objective."[30]

However, because the officers typically are more concerned with reelection issues than with bureau-monitoring, and are aware that their constituencies are ill-informed of their committee contributions and in any event vote for a "package" of policies, Niskanen argues that they tend to be diverted from their bureau-monitoring responsibilities. Given the differential access to relevant information by bureau heads, the bureau is provided with "overwhelmingly dominant monopoly power."[31] Niskanen suggests that this monopoly model is probably more applicable to national and state governments than to local governments, where committee responsibilities are presumably more central to the reelection issue, and where constituent exit costs are significantly lower in response to bureau alienation.

Even in subsequent analysis of the review process in representative government, where Niskanen departs from the passive sponsor assumption, he remains very skeptical about significant sponsor control, especially at the national government level, as the following passage indicates:

> Under such conditions, the committee review process is a farce. The bureaus estimate the largest budget that will be approved by the larger body of representatives and add a few percent based on the historical record of reductions made by the committee. The review committees oblige by making the expected reductions. The larger body of representatives dutifully approve the budget recommended by the committee. Most of the participants in this process, I suppose, believe that they are acting in the public interest.[32]

Niskanen claims as his most important conclusion the notion that, although the interests of the review committee and the bureau are not identical, they are often (indeed perhaps generally) consistent, not least because the committees tend to be backed by "special interest" legislators. Even when they are inconsistent, the low incremental benefits to the review committee and the high cost of an effective review often will induce the committee to accept the bureau's budget-output proposals.

For the most part, Migue and Belanger accept without question Niskanen's notion of the passive sponsor, which is central to their own model. They relax the assumption only at the conclusion of their paper when they adjust the bureau financing mechanism from block grant budgets to per-unit subsidies for local bureaus otherwise enjoying complete autonomy. In such circumstances, the central government must exercise initiative in defining the level of the subsidy to be granted, since local bureaus simply respond competitively, albeit without new entry threats, to the subsidy on offer. However, the notion of per-unit subsidies extends the concept of bureaucracy beyond the definitional scope of this paper.[33]

Breton and Wintrobe downplay the importance of sponsors in their book, not because they accept the notion of the passive review committee, but because they are concerned more centrally with the competitive exchange paradigm of bureau behavior. They note in passing, however, that politicians are aware that bureau information indeed is distorted and incorrect and leads to the financing of inefficient production. In consequence, sponsors are seen to allow fewer resources to bureaus than would be the case if such distortions could be policed without cost. In this view, the budget of the bureau will be smaller than would be the case if bureaucrats did not attempt to maximize it by information distortions. If true, this creates a real dilemma for the Niskanen bureaucrat!

In an earlier note,[34] Breton and Wintrobe specifically addressed the problem of the legislature, arguing that the assumption of the passive sponsor was "the basic flaw" in Niskanen's theory. Politicians, concerned about their prospects for reelection, obviously would attempt to exploit their monopsony power as purchasers of bureau output. At some cost, information concerning bureau production and cost functions can be obtained from bureau heads. In such circumstances, the legislature may well gain access to some of the surplus created by bureau outputs. Under these conditions, the actual budget will fall between the total cost curve and the total valuation curve, with part of the surplus retained by the agency head, part retained by the legislature, and part dissipated in monitoring costs.

In a more recent paper, Niskanen[35] concedes that this model provides a starting point for analyzing the review process but notes correctly that it incorporates neither the specific institutions of the review process nor the incentives of legislators. He reemphasizes the importance of the review committee rather than the entire legislature in bureau monitoring, and reaffirms his view that most such committees are dominated by legislators with higher demands for the services under review than the median demand in the legislature. In support of this view, he cites studies of the committee assignment process—by Rohde and Shepsle[36], by Shepsle[37], and by Cohen[38]—which establish that most legislators receive the committee assignments they request and that requests are correlated with services that are most important to their respective constituencies. He confirms that committee decisions are rarely amended or reversed by the entire legislature. In such circumstances, he claims, bureau and review committee objectives are consistent and cannot be rejected out of hand, with the implication that more consumers' surplus will be siphoned off by bureau heads in the form of oversupply than Breton and Wintrobe would allow.

Of course, a high-demand committee has the same incentives to control inefficiency in supply as a randomly selected committee. Indeed, given the cost of control instruments to reduce oversupply and to control inefficiency in supply, the high-demand committee will utilize more control instruments over the latter than would the randomly selected committees, unless supply inefficiency manifests itself in the purchasing of high-cost factor inputs from those constituencies represented in the review committee itself.

Furthermore, Niskanen argues that the monitoring function is a public good within the legislature, in that the benefits accrue to whole populations as a function of their tax costs. In consequence, a substantial free-rider problem exists, with the implication that monitoring activities will be undersupplied. Modelling this situation, Niskanen suggests that a legislator will spend time on activities specific to his constituents and contributors as a negative effect of the vote effect of taxes paid, of the time-cost of reducing bureau-costs, and of the share of taxes paid by his constituents.

Niskanen emphasizes the role of the party leadership in monitoring individual legislators to limit the size of efficiency losses. However, in political systems such as the U.S., party leadership cannot deny membership in the legislature as a sanction. In consequence, a substantial free-rider problem exists in the monitoring function, even for the party leadership, but in much more pronounced form for individual voters.

Orzechowski[39], for the most part, restricted discussion to internal bureau maximands, implicitly accepting in this respect the Niskanen bureau monopoly solution. However, in explaining the Parkinson bureau output expansion path, he relied on the notion of incremental budgeting, suggesting that bureaus typically experience only small changes in their budgets. An explanation of this is the high relative cost of attempts by appropriations committees in reviewing an entire budget, save perhaps only in the case of the largest bureaus, where the review benefits may be substantial.

Miller[40], in his review of some of the literature surveyed in this paper, was critical of Niskanen, Migue and Belanger, and Breton and Wintrobe for their respective emphases upon one-sided equilibrium, whether as a consequence of passive sponsors or of passive bureaus. Instead, he argued that both the agency head and the party in power determine the output of the agency, the latter by its appropriations decisions, the former by its output response. This approach leads to an analysis based on games with an infinite but countable number of pure strategies—games which are not easy to handle. Moreover, such games may well not offer unique solutions, but instead may result in multiple equilibria, unstable equilibria, divergent games, mixed strategy solutions, or even prisoners' dilemmas. Miller then proceeeded to explore likely game solutions under specified hypothetical conditions.

The governing party, following Niskanen, is designated an evaluation function:

$$MG = aQ - bQ^2 - B$$

and the agency head, following Migue and Belanger, is designated a maximand made up of output and managerial discretionary profit:

$$M_h = M_h(Q, MPD)$$

If, as is the case with Niskanen, Mg is concave in G and M_h is concave in H, then at least one pair of equilibrium strategies exists. If Mg should be convex in H and if M_h should be convex in G, then equilibrium would be unique. However, this condition will not hold in the likely event that the governing party maximizes net benefit and has a decreasing marginal valuation of Q. The resulting concavity of Mg in H thus precludes a unique equilibrium in the bureaucratic game.

Peacock[41], although essentially endorsing the monopoly bureau hypothesis, clearly was aware of the reward-cost structure as a monitor of bureaucratic behavior. For example, the relevance of job security for senior bureaucrats in encouraging their pursuit of leisure is outlined, as is the likely pressure for monitoring constraints in response to negative externalities from the bureaucrats' "busy loafing".

Peacock suggested that the problem of bureau monitoring is more appropriately studied via a framework which displays the interdependencies between bargaining groups within the economy rather than via the legislator-bureaucrat confrontation model central to the post-Niskanen literature. As such, legislators are seen to offer "facilitation services" to consumers and firms, particularly those in their respective constituencies. The prospect of collaboration between legislators and bureaucrats also cannot be denied. Of course, recognition of such interplays takes the theory of bureaucracy well away from the partial equilibrium analysis of Niskanen. Whether the loss of precision is justified by the increase in generality is a complex methodological issue.

Property Rights and Principal-Agent Theory

Notable for its absence in the literature reviewed thus far is the notion of property rights and their influence upon sponsor-bureau relationships. Those analysts who rely on the bureau monopoly or the sponsor monopoly models clearly obviate all discussion of contractual relationships. Most extreme of all is the view advanced by Breton and Wintrobe[42] that property rights cannot be supported by legal instruments in the case of bureaucratic relationships and therefore do not exist, and that trust networks replace rights as the basis for exchange relationships.

It is a central thrust of this paper that neglect of property rights considerations, with a few recent exceptions in the economic analysis of bureaucracy, simply has mirrored much earlier work in the theory of the firm, potentially with very similar disadvantages.

The theory of the firm prior to the important contribution in 1972 by Alchian and Demsetz was essentially not a theory of the firm at all; rather it was a theory of markets with the firm operating as a "black box" to satisfy relevant marginal conditions with respect to inputs and outputs in pursuit of specified objectives. For the most part, the mechanism through which the conflicting objectives of individual participants were reconciled within the firm was not defined. Not surprisingly, the theory of the firm disintegrated during the later 1960's into a series of special cases lacking generality and even simple testability.[43]

Following Alchian and Demsetz[44], a more general approach to the theory of the firm has reemerged with classical behavior on the parts of agents within the firm forming a central assumption. The firm is viewed as a set of contracts between factors of production, with each factor motivated by self-interest. The specification of individual rights, by reference to the contract nexus, determines the input-output relationship and the allocation of costs and rewards among individual participants. The early property rights literature focused attention on the survivorship characteristics of alternative sets of contracts for firms engaging in team production in competitive capitalistic markets.

Given the free-rider problem in team production, with incentives for individuals to divert activity excessively from productive to leisure pursuits, incentives exist for the selection of a centralized contractual agent to monitor performance on behalf of all factor inputs. Thus the entrepreneur (manager/risk-bearer) was central to Alchian and Demsetz' property rights approach:

> The essence of the classical firm is identified here as a contractual structure with: (1) joint input production; (2) several input owners; (3) one party who

> is common to all the contracts of the joint inputs; (4) who has the right to renegotiate any input's contract independently of contracts with other input owners; (5) who holds the residual claim; and (6) who has the right to sell his central contractual residual status. The central agent is called the firm's owner and employer.[45]

As Alchian and Demsetz recognized, however, the classical capitalist firm is no longer dominant as an organization form in advanced Western economics. Its position has been eroded by the relative advance throughout the twentieth century of corporate enterprise, of public enterprise, and of government bureaucracy. Such changes in organizational form have severely attenuated property rights in the central residual status. The monitoring relationship has changed and a principal-agent problem created.[46] Since 1972, research has integrated principal-agent analysis into the property rights literature on the theory of the firm.[47] Only very recently, however, has such analysis been extended to the theory of bureaucracy.

The early literature on agency relationships developed independently of that on property rights, even though it was concerned with closely related problems. An agency relationship is defined as a "contract under which one or more persons (the principal(s)) engage another person (the agent) to perform some service on their behalf which involves delegating some decision-making authority to the agent".[48] All parties to such a contract being utility maximizers, agents will not always act in the interests of their principals. Principals can limit the extent of the agency problem via suitable reward-cost incentives, but monitoring is costly and will be applied only to the cost-effective margin.[49] Residual losses to principals are predictable.

In 1976, Jensen and Meckling defined the relationship between stockholders and management in corporate enterprise as a pure agency relationship. They noted that the level of agency costs depends, among other factors, on statutory and common law and on human ingenuity in devising contracts. They interpreted the law and the sophistication of contracts relevant to the modern corporation as the products of an historical process in which powerful incentives exist for individuals to minimize agency costs. In a somewhat sanguine judgment on the efficiency of the agency solution in practice they concluded that "whatever its shortcomings, the corporation has survived the market test against potential alternatives."[50] Nevertheless, their contribution provided a fulcrum for subsequent, more critical discussion of the role of the capital market as an agency relationship monitor.

Fama (1980) rejected the notion of equity stockholders as owner-principals in the modern corporation. With management and risk-bearing now treated as factors of production, it is by no means clear that the capital market exercises the dominant monitoring role ascribed to it by both Alchian and Demsetz[51] and Jensen and Mechling.[52] Within a nexus of contracts perspective, the firm is "just a set of contracts covering the way inputs are joined to create outputs and the way receipts from output are shared among inputs."[53] Ownership of the firm thus becomes an irrelevant concept, and the concept of the entrepreneur is finally laid to rest, with management and risk-bearing viewed as separate factors of production.

In such circumstances, it is not obvious that the risk-bearers have any *special* interest in the viability of the corporate team. Of course, as residual claimants, risk-bearers suffer from the failure of teams with which they are associated. However, capital markets allow them to shift among teams at relatively low cost and to hedge against potential failures by diversifying their holdings across teams. Indeed, optional portfolios for risk averse investors are likely to be widely diversified, with individual stockholders having little or no incentive to oversee the detailed activities of any single firm.

In contrast, the managers of any one firm rent a substantial portion of their wealth (their human capital) to that firm. The rental rates for that capital are signalled by the managerial labor market, depending on the relative success or failure of the firm. For it is the function of management to oversee the contracts among factors and to ensure the viability of the firm. Moreover, the transaction costs of shifts across teams are considerably higher for management than for investors. Thus, it is argued, management has the greater incentive to monitor.

The outside managerial labor market exerts direct pressure on the firm to evaluate and reward managers according to performance. Potential new managers seek information about the responsiveness of the firm to performance in its reward-structure and react accordingly. If the reward system is not responsive to performance the firm will lose managers, with the best predictably the first to leave. There is also internal monitoring of managers by managers, both in the upward and in the downward direction, given the jointness of managerial marginal products inherent in team production. Upward monitoring occurs where lower managers attempt to step over less competent managers above them in bids to increase their own marginal productivities and rewards.

The monitoring of management in corporate enterprise becomes more problematic at the highest echelon, however, where the relationship between top management and the board of directors assumes major importance. Where top managers compete against themselves, in an uneasy team coalition, monitoring may be effective, whatever the composition of the board of directors. This will be particularly true when top management remains concerned to maximize its opportunity wage in the outside labor market, and where the board of directors retains the right to engage in *ex post* "settling up" of managerial wages, in the light of *ex post* marginal productivity.[54]

Early non-contractarian theories of the firm suggested that discretionary behavior by management was feasible only where products markets were characterized by monopoly and then capital markets were inefficient.[55] As we have noted, the latter contribution, but not the former, is necessary for the principal-agent problem to exist; neither condition, singly or jointly, is sufficient. Product market competition may not protect stockholders from aberrant management in a world replete with agency problems and in which monitoring costs are non-trivial. In such circumstances, resolution of the problem must await institutional innovations which effectively lower monitoring costs in the agency relationship without countervailing cost disadvantages.

Most commodities can be produced by a range of organizational forms—corporations, proprietorships, partnerships, mutuals, non-profits and government bureaus. In the absence of government fiat, there is competition among these forms for survival. The important factor in such survival is control of agency problems. Fama and Jensen[56] have argued that the characteristics of residual claims are important (at least within the private sector) in explaining the survival of specific organizational forms in specific activities by reference to the agency problem and its resolution. Since this issue is relevant to our later discussion of bureaucracy, conclusions in the case of corporate enterprise are here outlined.

The common stock residual claims of open (non-financial) organizations are unrestricted in the sense that (1) stockholders are not required to exercise any role in the organization, (2) the residual claims of stockholders are freely alienable, and (3) the residual claims are rights in net cash flows for the life of the organization. The unrestricted nature of the residual claims, in the sense here defined, allows for almost complete separation and specialization of decision functions and residual risk-bearing. If agency problems are ignored, this organizational form is able to deliver products at lower prices than organizations with restricted residual claims.[57]

However, agency problems associated with the separation of ownership and control in open corporations cannot be ignored. The agency costs of mechanisms for separating decision management from decision control constitute part of the price that open corporations pay for the benefits of unrestricted stock residual claims. For this reason, unrestricted common stock residual claims predictably will exist when there exist significant economics of scale that (1) are realizable only within a complex decision hierarchy utilizing specialized decision skills, (2) generate large aggregate risks to be borne by residual claimants, and (3) demand large amounts of wealth from residual claimants to purchase risky assets and to bond the payoffs promised to a wide range of agents in the organization. Fama and Jensen contend that agency costs are controlled in such circumstances by decision structures that separate the management and control of important decisions.

A Principal-Agent Theory of Government and Its Bureaucracy

The early bargaining models of bureaucracy ignored completely the implicit contracts that exist between governments and their bureaucracies and the principal-agent problems that arise as a consequence of the severe attenuation of property rights involved. Indeed, as late as 1975, Niskanen[58] continued to develop a bargaining theory of the relationship between bureaus and the political process, albeit now more sophisticated than his original theory of bureau monopoly, but still without any recognition of contract relationships based upon property right allocations.

McCormick and Tollison,[59] in an early application of principal-agent analysis, were concerned not with the issue of bureaucracy, but with the articulation of an interest-group theory of politics. They defined the political setting as a nonproprietary situation in which individual agents were not always confronted with the full economic consequences of their decisions. Thus, political agents faced different constraints on their behavior than private agents because the principals in the two situations (for example, voters and stockholders) confronted different incentives to control the behavior of the agents. Specifically, managers of political firms faced lower incentives to control costs since they could not personally recoup any cost savings that they achieved for their agencies. Moreover, the means available to voters to delimit shirking by political managers were low, and were costly to implement, while expected returns were minimal by comparison with those available to stockholders in private enterprise.

The principal-agent theory of government and its bureaucracy, as expounded in the extant literature, is outlined in this section. To date, however, most of the relevant contributions in the field have emphasized empirical testing rather than theoretical elaboration.[60]

Bureaus are viewed, in the post-Niskanen literature, as institutions operating within an environment significantly different from that of corporate enterprise.[61] Firstly, the indivisible nature of their budget-output contract rules out significant marginal adjustment within a given budgetary time period, irrespective of changes in supply or demand conditions. Secondly, the absence of any profit signal makes it difficult for monitors to evaluate bureau performance. Thirdly, the nebulous characteristics of most bureau outputs make it difficult for monitors to assess the underlying production function and thus to evaluate technical efficiency of production. Fourthly, the statutory protection of bureau from competition eliminates an important signal available to monitors within the unregulated corporate sector.

These characteristics of the bureau environment influence the behavior of expected wealth maximizing bureaucrats. The absence of a capital market renders it difficult if not impossible to motivate bureaucrats by providing them with shares in the present value of future fiscal residua. The absence of a clearly-defined production function impedes monitoring via the outside labor market in terms of marginal productivity criteria, as well as upward and downward marginal productivity monitoring within the bureau itself. In these important respects, property rights are attenuated within the bureau by comparison with those exercised by senior corporate management within the market sector. In such circumstances, three distinctive characteristics of bureaus are evident. Firstly, bureaucrats' remuneration is fixed and not related to performance criteria, save for periodic settling-up via promotion procedures which themselves tend only loosely to be performance-related. Secondly, bureaus tend to be organized hierarchically on the basis of carefully defined spheres of authority, via rules based upon procedure rather than upon performance, with discretion strictly limited at levels below the top. Thirdly, both bureau principals and customers seek to regulate bureau behavior, the former through investigation, oversight hearings and budgetary controls, the latter through a system of administrative appeal and via the courts.

Bureaus are monitored by legislators who are assigned (or assign themselves) to relevant oversight committees or subcommittees. As such, legislators themselves serve as agents to constituencies whence they seek and/or receive electoral support.[62] Motivated by a combination of expected wealth maximization and vote-seeking objectives, legislators provide a flow of policy benefits to interest groups with whom they are identified. Given the differential political impact of well-organized interest groups, it is unlikely, in practice, that legislators will reflect the preferences of the median voter in their oversight capacities. Rather, they will serve the interests of their predictably high-demand (highest-bidding) constituents.[63]

Within this political framework, legislators may be viewed as principals monitoring their bureaucratic agents on the basis of a network of complex implicit contracts. In the U.S., congressional institutions are tailored to facilitate this process, with committees forging the essential contracts nexus between interest groups and benefit provisions of bureaus. As Weingast[64] has argued, the assumption that bureaus depend on Congress, like the assumption that firms depend on customers, is the key to understanding the principal-agent relationship. However, the property rights available to legislators in their relationship with bureaus are severely attenuated by comparison with those available to stockholders in their relationship with management in the case of corporate enterprise.[65]

Firstly, the residual claims of legislators, via constituencies, on the outputs of bureaus are not freely alienable. Constituent interests represent costly investments which cannot be freely sold to release resources for more attractive electioneering and expected wealth-seeking elsewhere in the political marketplace. Furthermore, legislators cannot move costlessly across oversight committees in response to changes in relative bureau residuals, even if their constituency relationships are highly malleable.

Secondly, the residual claims of legislators from their bureaus do not constitute rights in net cash flows, or in votes, for the expected life of the bureau. Elections intervene and relationships may be terminated by unforeseeable shifts in voter allegiance. Inevitably, therefore, the relationship between legislator and bureau is more myopic than that between stockholder and enterprise. Myopia is exacerbated by inability to capitalize future residuals into present values.

Thirdly, as a consequence of the above-mentioned property right restrictions, maximizing legislators must exercise a more direct monitoring role than is required of stockholders in corporate enterprise. For self-seeking bureaucrats, in the absence of such monitoring, may confront inadequate incentives to tailor bureau performance to the time-preferences of the legislator and his constituents.

Thus, important distinctions exist between the risk-taking stockholder in corporate enterprise and the risk-bearing, reelection-seeking legislator in a bureau-oversight capacity. The former is indifferent as to the precise composition of his portfolio as long as its mean-variance values satisfy his attitude toward risk. If he is risk-averse, the stockholder will diversify his portfolio rather than concentrate his holdings, thus increasing his vulnerability to risk. In contrast, legislators are forced by procedural rules and constituent interests to specialize within committees, diversifying across subcommittees and involving themselves directly in the oversight process, albeit relying upon constituent interests to advise them of bureau performance characteristics and to forewarn them of bureau activities which are prejudicial to their reelection prospects. Broad diversification, appropriate for the risk-averse stockholders, would leave the legislator with very little control over bureau behavior and thus less capable of addressing constituent concerns. Hence, greater concentration in bureau-team holdings will characterize the legislator's portfolio, leading to a more active role in the monitoring function.

Notes

This paper stems from two earlier papers prepared by the authors: the first, "Towards a Theory of Bureaucracy," was presented at the Festschrift Conference for Alan Peacock held at the University of Buckingham, September 5–7, 1984 and was subsequently published in Greenaway, David and G.K. Shaw, *Public Choice, Public Finance and Public Policy* (Oxford: Basil Blackwell, 1985): pp. 31–50; the second, "Representative Government and its Bureaucracy" was presented at the Southern Economics Association Meeting, November 1984.

1. M. Weber. *The Theory of Social and Economic Organization* (Edinburgh: W. Hodge, 1947).

2. G. Tullock. *The Politics of Bureaucracy* (Washington, D.C.: Public Affairs Press, 1965). Here Tullock employs a model of a maximizing bureaucrat to examine the personal relations and advancement procedures within the bureau.

3. A. Downs. *Inside Bureaucracy* (Boston: Little Brown & Co., 1967). In this book, Downs developed a comprehensive theory of management processes within bureaus but made no attempt to relate this theory to budget and output performance.

4. W.A. Niskanen. *Bureaucracy and Representative Government* (Chicago and New York: Aldine—Athortan, 1971).

5. A. Breton and R. Wintrobe. *The Logic of Bureaucratic Conduct* (New York: Cambridge University Press, 1982).

6. Op. Cit. at Chapter 1.

6. Ibid.

8. Op. Cit.

9. Niskanen offered no theory explaining the input preferences of senior bureaucrats. It is relatively easy, however, to assimilate such preferences into his theory.

10. Although a number of commentators collapse his analysis into the bureaucracy dimension alone.

11. In the development of his basic model he relaxes this assumption subsequently to incorporate notions of bureau competition.

12. W. Orzechowski, "Economic Models of Bureaucracy: Survey, Extensions, and Evidence," in T.E. Borcherding (Ed.) *Budgets and Bureaucrats: The Sources of Government Growth* (Durham: Duke University Press, 1977): pp. 229–259.

13. G.J. Miller, Bureaucratic Compliance as a Game on the Unit Square," *Public Choice* XXIX, Spring, 1977.

14. Op. Cit at p. 153.

15. J.L. Migue and G. Belanger, "Towards a General Theory of Managerial Discretion," *Public Choice* XVII, Spring, 1974.

16. Ibid.
17. Op. Cit.
18. In our view, unjustifiably.
19. A notion in sharp contrast to the otherwise neoclassical thrust of their text.
20. They claim that trust, both vertical and horizontal, is endogenous, dependent on such facts as the amount of turnover, the amount of perquisites, such as bonuses for subordinates and the frequency of promotions. These latter variables are measurable; thus, productivity per employee can be evaluated against variables that affect the amount and distribution of trust.
21. Op. Cit.
22. C.N. Parkinson. *Parkinson's Law and Other Studies in Administration* (New York: Ballentine Books, 1957).
23. O.E. Williamson. *The Economics of Discretionary Behavior: Managerial Objectives in a Theory of the Firm* (Englewood Cliffs: Prestice Hall, Inc., 1964).
24. T.E. Borcherding, W.C. Bush and R.M. Spann, "The Effects on Public Spending of the Divisibility of Public Outputs in Consumption, Bureaucratic Power and the Size of the Tax Sharing Group," in T.E. Borcherding (Ed.) *Budgets and Bureaucrats* Op. Cit.
25. L. De Alessi, "Implications of Property Rights for Government Investment Choices," *American Economic Review* March, 1969.
26. Op. Cit.
27. Peacock does not incorporate the budget-constrained bureau as a polar case in his own analysis.
28. Op. Cit.
29. At least within a specific election period.
30. Op. Cit. at p. 24.
31. Ibid. at p. 30.
32. Ibid at p. 153.
33. In fact, the per unit subsidy notion extends the concept well beyond any of the recent literature concerning the economics of bureaucracy.
34. A. Breton and R. Wintrobe, "The Equilibrium Size of a Budget Maximizing Bureau," *Journal of Political Economy* 1975.
35. W.A. Niskanen, "Bureaucrats and Politicians," *Journal of Law and Economics* December, 1975.
36. D. Rohde and K.A. Shepsle, "Democratic Committee Assignments in the House of Representatives: Strategic Aspects of a Social Choice Process," *American Political Science Review 1973*.
37. K.A. Shepsle, "A Model of the Congressional Committee Assignment Process: Constrained Maximization in the Institutional Setting," *Public Choice* Summer, 1975.
38. M.D. Cohen. *The Importance of Member—references in Committee Assignments: An Assessment Against Optional Standards and a Simple Process Model* (Mimeo, 1974).
39. Op. Cit.
40. Op. Cit.
41. Op. Cit.
42. Op. Cit., 1982.
43. This unfortunate development was triggered by an excessive emphasis on the separation between ownership and control in corporate enterprise. With management cut loose from direct monitoring, the way was open for economists to experiment with variations in utility functions and constraints in a sequence of special case modelling. See for example, W.J. Baumol, "On the Theory of Oligopoly" *Economica* 1966, pp. 1–16; O.E. Williamson,

The Economics of Discretionary Behavior (New Jersey: Prentice-Hall, 1964).

44. A. Alchian and H. Demsetz, "Production, Information Costs and Economic Organization," *American Economic Review* December, 1972: pp. 777–795.

45. Ibid. at p. 794.

46. Alchian and Demsetz anticipated this transition but did not articulate their analysis in principal-agent terms.

47. See for example, M.C. Jensen and W.H. Meckling, "Theory of the Firm: Managerial Behavior, Agency Costs and Ownership Structure," *Journal of Financial Economics* 3, 1976: pp. 305–360; E. Fama, "Agency Problems and the Theory of the Firm," *Journal of Political Economy* Vol. 88, 1980: pp. 288–349; E. Fama and M.C. Jensen, "Separation of Ownership and Control," *Journal of Law and Economics* Vol. 26, 1983: pp. 301–325.

48. Jensen and Meckling, Ibid. at p. 308.

49. For an early version of the monitoring problem not couched in principal-agent terms, see M.A. Crew, M.W. Jones-Lee and C.K. Rowley, "X-Theory Versus Management Discretion Theory," *Southern Economic Journal* Vol. XXXVIII, October, 1971: pp. 173–184.

50. Op. Cit. at p. 357.

51. Op. Cit.

52. Op. Cit.

53. Op. Cit. at p. 289.

54. Op. Cit., 1980: p. 305. Here Fama claims that *ex post* settling up "is at least one of the ingredients in the survival of the modern large corporation characterized by diffuse security ownership and the separation of security ownership and control, as a viable form of economic organization."

55. Op. Cit. O.E. Williamson, 1964.

56. Op. Cit., 1983.

57. Here the usual *ceteris paribus* conditions apply.

58. Op. Cit.

59. R.E. McCormick and R.D. Tollison, *Politicians, Legislation and the Economy* (Boston: Martinus Nijhoff, 1981): p. 6: "Political agents will face different constraints on their behavior than private agents because principals in the two cases (e.g., voters and stockholders) for different incentives to control the behavior of the agenda."

60. See, R.L. Faith, D.R. Leavens and R.D. Tollison, "Antitrust Pork Barrel," *Journal of Law and Economics* Vol. XXV, October 1982: pp. 329–342; B.A. Weingast and N.J. Moran, "Bureaucratic Discretion or Congressional Cortel? Regulatory Policy Making by the Federal Trade Commission," *Journal of Political Economy* Vol. 91, 1983: pp. 765–800; B.A. Weingast, "The Congressional Bureaucratic System: A Principal-Agent Perspective," *Public Choice* Vol. 44, 1984: pp. 167–192; Also see K.B. Grier, "Congressional Preferences and Federal Reserved Policy: A Principal-Agent Approach," (*Mimeo*: June 1984).

61. On this see, C.K. Rowley, "Efficiency in the Public Sector," in C. Bowe (Ed.) *Industrial Efficiency and the Role of Government* (London: HMSO, 1977): pp. 7–28.

62. This is the link back to the McCormick/Tollison approach, Op. Cit.

63. On this, see B.L. Benson, "Why Are Congressional Committees Dominated by 'High-Demand' Legislators?" *Southern Economic Journal*, 1981.

64. Op. Cit., 1984.

65. On this, see C.K. Rowley and R.S. Elgin, "Towards a Theory of Bureaucratic Behavior," in D. Greenaway and G.K. Shaw. (Eds.) *Public Choice, Public Finance and Public Policy* (Oxford: Basil Blackwell, 1985): pp. 31–50.

21 DEMAND REVEALING, TRANSFERS, AND RENT-SEEKING[1]

Gordon Tullock

A recurring objection to the demand revealing process is that the Clarke tax it entails is apt to be very high when the interests of the parties are strictly opposed. Thus it has often been said that it doesn't work very well for transfers.[2] The point of this article is to argue Clarke taxes would be high only where rent-seeking would be likely. This high Clarke tax in many rent-seeking situations is a positive advantage, as it prevents transfers with no social value.

Let us begin with a simple situation. A group of people, let us say farmers, wish to use the government to obtain transfers from another group, let us say all taxpayers. This is, of course, characteristic of substantially every modern democratic country.[3] Figure 21–1 shows the net social cost of the transfer (per dollar transferred) by the line CC and the benefit the farmers receive by the line BB. It is assumed that the demand by the farmers for their transfer is literally its dollar value. This seems reasonable.

The line BB or the social benefit of re-transfer must of necessity lie below line CC if there is any administrative cost in making the transfer at all. Since there always is, the demand revealing process which would sum the demand of the farmers, together with a zero demand of the

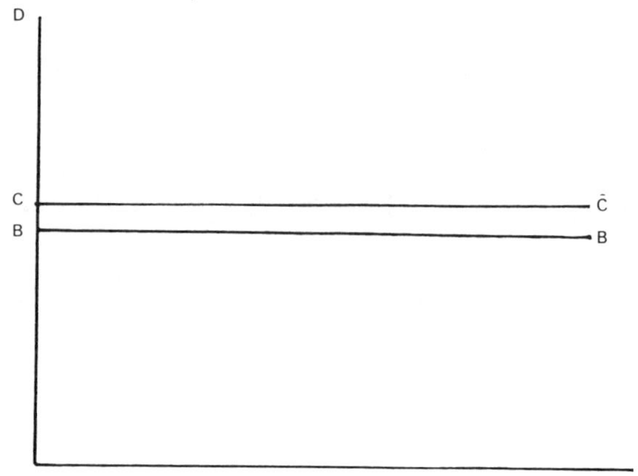

Figure 21–1

non-farmers for this particular procedure, would show its appropriate size as zero.[4]

The Clarke tax here is probably nonexistent. The reason for this is that it seems likely in any realistic case that the costs of administering a transfer and hence the distance between line CC and BB would be greater than the taxes paid by any individual taxpayer. Under these circumstances the removal of any individual for the purpose of computing the Clarke tax would make no change in the outcome. Hence there would be no Clarke tax. If this were not true, i.e., if some individuals' tax burden were larger than the entire cost of administering the transfer, then the outcome is indeed strange. No transfer would be made to the farmers, but every taxpayer whose potential tax burden exceeded the administrative cost would pay a Clarke tax equivalent to the amount that he would have paid had the transfer proposed by the farmers gone through. In theory, although not probably in any realistic case, the sum of these Clarke taxes paid by the various objecting taxpayers could be equal to the total transfer which would otherwise have been made. The farmers would not receive any benefit from this however, and it seems very dubious that they would even propose the transfer unless we were in a society with a really ferocious class struggle.

Farm aid programs frequently, however, take the form of administrative rules which implicitly transfer resources from the general citizenry to the farmers. The American system, for example, consists of both a tax subsidy

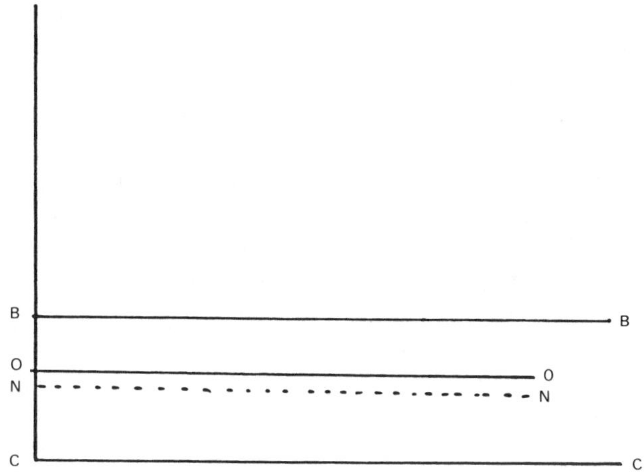

Figure 21–2

and a price support program.[5] There is, in so far as it is a simple administrative rule, no direct tax cost.

Such administrative regulations can be dealt with by the expedients shown on figure 21–2. The individuals are permitted to indicate the loss that they receive through the administrative rules. Thus, line BB is the benefit the farmers receive, line O is of course zero, and the victims suffer the cost shown by line CC. When we add these lines together, we get the dashed line marked NN which is below zero. Hence again there is no program. This figure could be made a little more complicated by drawing another line which shows the administrative cost slightly above the zero line. Here again, rent-seeking is eliminated.

Once more, there is at least a theoretical chance of significant Clarke taxes falling on the potential victims, but there would be no transfer.

The general policy of permitting people to cast such negative votes through the demand revealing process seems to be a desirable one. After all we can be damaged by things other than taxes. The alternative of course would be to compute the implicit tax involved, but that would require a government bureaucracy making decisions as to how much things cost people. It is better to let people make these decisions themselves.

There would, however, be in this case a small problem of education. One can readily understand an individual who objects to a particular government policy solely because it will cost him some tax money, mistakenly feeling that he should cast a negative vote instead of a zero vote. This would be unwise, because it increases his chances of paying a Clarke tax. There is of course no reason why the demand revealing system could not be converted so that the tax always showed itself as a negative amount below zero, but the system would be less elegant.

So far we have been dealing with pure transfers in which the victim is injured and the beneficiaries gain less than the injury. Most economists do not like such transfers, but there are certain cases in which at least some of them would be favored by economists. If the majority of voters wished to tax a particular minority (e.g., millionaires or Jews, to take two groups of which this apparently was true in certain countries in recent times), then the result of demand revealing process would be radically different from that of majority voting. There is of course no reason why, if we have two different ways in making decisions—majority voting, and the demand revealing process[6]—they should always lead to the same conclusion. The decision between them must be made on extrinsic grounds.

Let us now turn to cases in which there is a genuine public good involved. In figure 21–3, we show the situation which would arise if it were proposed to put a bridge across some part of the Puget Sound, with A and B being people who would benefit from that bridge, and C being a resident

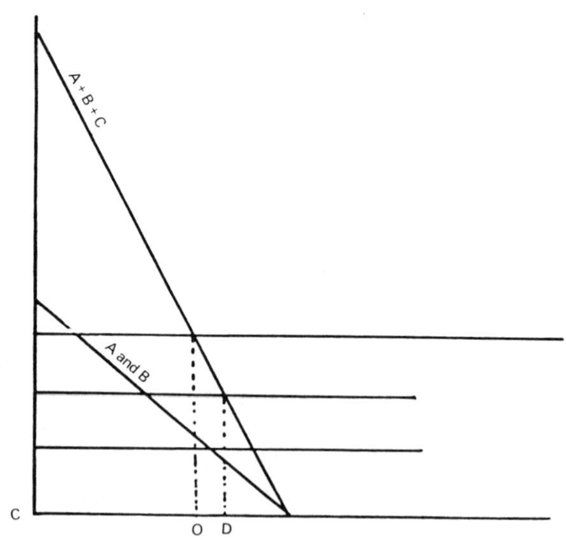

Figure 21–3

in New York who never intends to visit the far west. I assume for simplicity that A and B have exactly identical demands for the bridge. Their demands are then shown by the line A and B. The man living in New York, C, has a zero demand shown by the horizontal axis. The sum of the three is shown by A + B + C and is of course identical to the line which could be shown A + B. A socially optimum amount of bridge building is O. If we use Lindahl pricing (one of the advantages of the demand revealing process is that it permits close approximation of Lindahl pricing),[7] the cost of the bridge would be evenly split between A and B. C would pay nothing. Indeed, with Lindahl pricing, simple majority voting, which in this case might well be unanimous, would show as much bridge purchased as the demand revealing process.

If we assume that A and B, making up the majority, would like to exploit C a bit and hence decide that the cost of the bridge would be evenly divided among the three of them, then they would choose to purchase D bridge. If they decided to use their majority to exploit him even further, and hence put the entire cost of the bridge on him, they would of course buy out to the point where their two demand curves reached the horizontal axis.

Here again, majority voting, with the majority also permitted to vote on the tax, leads to an outcome which is different from the demand revealing process. I have difficulty believing that there will be many economists who in this particular case prefer the majority voting outcome.

I have not drawn in the mechanism for determining the Clarke tax, because in real world situations there are many, many more voters. The total size of the Clarke tax shrinks as the number of voters rises, and in fact becomes very small eventually. It will always be larger than it would be, however, if C's interests were not strictly opposed to those of A and B.

There is another case in which the interests of the two parties are opposed, but where there is at least some desire to produce the good on the part of all of them. Suppose A and B are well off, and C is poor. A and B have a demand for aid to C as shown by the line A and B in figure 21–4. C's demand is of course the line CC showing what he will receive. Adding the two well off demands, we get the line A + B, and O shows what could be argued was the social optimum. C, however, has a demand for the transfer which is exactly the same as the transfer itself. If we add C to A + B, we get the line A + B + C, which I have shown falling below the cost line at O′ on the theory once again that there is at least some administrative cost. It can easily be argued that O′ is the social optimum.

Note that in this case a simple majority vote with A and B splitting the cost of the transfer between them, which is of course the Lindahl tax price,

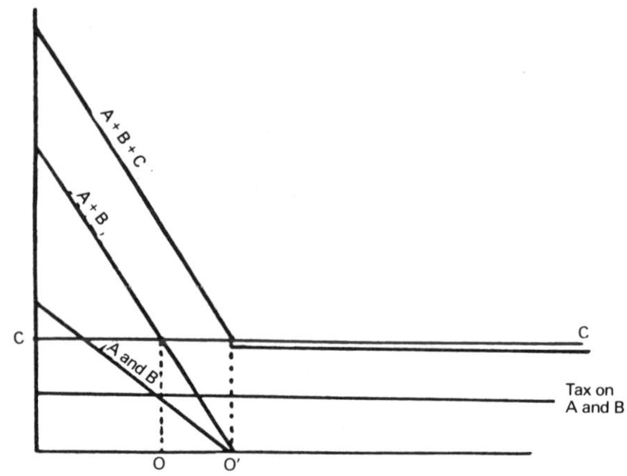

Figure 21–4

would generate O. This is, however, merely an artifact of this particular example. With a larger number of voters, the poor making up a minority of the voters, the demand revealing process would normally lead to more redistribution than simple majority voting. The exact amount would of course depend upon whether the poor did or did not vote.

The problem here, as can be seen, is one of the franchise. If we look at the real world, we find that sometimes beneficiaries of charitable activities are permitted to vote and sometimes not. At the moment, the ones who are not permitted to vote are mainly those foreigners to whom we give aid, but historically it has not been particularly uncommon for domestic recipients of charity being automatically deprived of their vote. Dicey, in fact, was quite upset when England, breaking a precedent, provided that certain old age pensioners should retain the vote while receiving their pensions.[8] If you look at the real world, it is not obvious that it makes much difference whether the poor are permitted to vote or not. *A priori*, one would assume that the poor would do better when they vote on the amount they will receive. What little empirical evidence we have, however, seems to indicate it makes little difference.[9] In any event, if the recipients of charity are not permitted to contribute their vote, the demand revealing process should transfer to them somewhat more than they would obtain under simple majority vote. If they are permitted to cast their vote, it should transfer more.

In sum, my initial feeling that the demand revealing process would not work very well in transfer cases turns out to be largely misplaced. The

Clarke tax prevents a number of transfers where the transfer itself is not welfare enhancing. In other cases where it does not actually prevent such transfers, it at least reduces them. In those cases where the transfers are welfare enhancing, i.e., charitable transfers where the donors obtain at least some benefit from the charity, the demand revealing process will lead to somewhat more transfer than simple majority vote and quite possibly considerably more. It depends on franchise.

Thus, what I think has been the most important argument against demand revealing is, in actuality, a result of comparing the demand revealing with perfection. When you compare it with other realistic voting methods, it works better in transfers as well as in other areas.

Notes

1. The author benefitted from very helpful comments by T. Nicholas Tideman and Ed Clarke.

2. Mainly this has been part of the oral discussion, but see "Revealing The Demand For Tansfers" in Richard D. Auster (ed), *American Re-evolution, Papers And Proceedings* (Tucson: University of Arizona 1977), pp. 107–23.

3. In this example, and in all others in this article, we will assume that the amount is a continous variable. Adjustment of the models to deal with discontinous outcomes is simple.

4. This same result can be obtained by two other ways. We could assume that the transfer is intrinsically inefficient as all farm transfer programs in fact are, with the result that the line BB lies much farther below CC than it does in figure 1. Secondly, we could assume probably correctly, that the donors of this gift not only do not want to pay their taxes at the value of those taxes, but actually were somewhat annoyed by the whole procedure. Under these circumstances their demand curve, instead of lying along the horizontal axis would lie somewhat below it and when we summed the demand curves line BB would be once again moved down.

5. The system is even more complicated than that. The bulk of the tax subsidy is used to fund the price support program.

6. Or any other way which insures that only pareto optimal decisions are made.

7. See "A New And Superior Process for Making Social Decisions", T Nicholas Tideman and Gordon Tullock *Journal of Political Economy* (October 1) pp. 225–73.

8. *Law And Public Opinion In England*, A. V. Dicey, London, Macmillan, 1962 p. xxxv.

9. This subject is discussed at great length in my, *The Economics of income Redistribution*, Gordon Tullock, Kluwer-Nijhoff, Boston, 1983.

22 COMPETING FOR AID

Gordon Tullock

Economists have known for a very long time that most social states have more than one equilibrium. In particular, there is the agreement equilibrium that corresponds to some point on the Pareto optimal frontier, and that represents cooperation among the members of the society. There is a second, well-known equilibrium—the independent adjustment equilibrium—which occurs when, for one reason or another, agreement is not possible. The independent adjustment equilibrium is normally less satisfactory to the parties than the cooperative equilibrium. Ideally, the role of the state is to affect this independent adjustment equilibrium in ways that lead to superior outcomes. Economists, although occasionally dealing with the independent adjustment equilibrium, have normally confined their research to the cooperative equilibrium.

The independent adjustment equilibrium can be used to analyze a number of very unpleasant situations that have been relatively little considered by economists. In this article, however, I shall deal with a special application in the field of politics. The point is to indicate that the independent equilibrium analysis *has* value and to encourage other scholars to apply it.

Let me begin with an incident that occurred in Blacksburg, Virginia some time ago. The local paper ran an article explaining the town's plan for road repair and construction. About two weeks later, the same paper reported the letting of a large number of contracts for road repair. It was notable that none of the roads in the road repair "plan" were included among those for which bids had been let. At first, I was puzzled by this phenomenon, but with a little thought I realized that the roads covered by the plan were, on the whole, important enough so that there was a fair chance of getting the Commonwealth of Virginia to pay all (or a good part) of the cost. The town, therefore, had set up a plan that it was now negotiating with the Commonwealth. On those roads where it was crystal clear the Commonwealth would *not* make any contribution, the city was going ahead on its own.

Note the phenomenon. A "plan" had been constructed not for the purpose of guiding the city's action, but for the purpose of persuading the Commonwealth to act. Further, the repair of the more important roads was actually being delayed, while that of the less important roads was to be undertaken immediately. It is, of course, possible that the unimportant roads had been permitted to deteriorate to a poorer state than the important roads before the bids were let. However there are good reasons why the most important roads might be left unrepaired, even if they were in very bad condition. Repairing the important roads immediately would have cost the town the full amount; with some delay, they stood a finite chance of getting someone else to pay all or part of the cost. Hence, it was wise to take the delay. With respect to the less important roads, the opposite situation existed.

Let us, however, look at this matter a little more formally. On figure 22–1 the vertical axis represents simply dollars (either cost or gain); the horizontal axis is time shown as years from some arbitrary starting point. In our particular case, we assume that some road was completely resurfaced in year one. The cost of resurfacing the road again in any given year is shown by line R. The cost is somewhat simplified. I assume that the actual physical cost of repairing the road is not affected by wear and tear on the road, nor is it expected to change in the future. Further, I assume that the road is eventually to be repaired, i.e., it is not to be permitted to simply deteriorate. The more general (and complicated) model, in which these two restrictions were not included, could be constructed without any great difference in the conclusions. Nevertheless, with these two assumptions, the cost of repairing the road in any given year becomes simply the interest on the money which is foregone by not waiting until the following year. If the cost of resurfacing would be \$100,000 and the current interest rate is 10 percent, it costs the county \$10,000 to do it this year instead of next

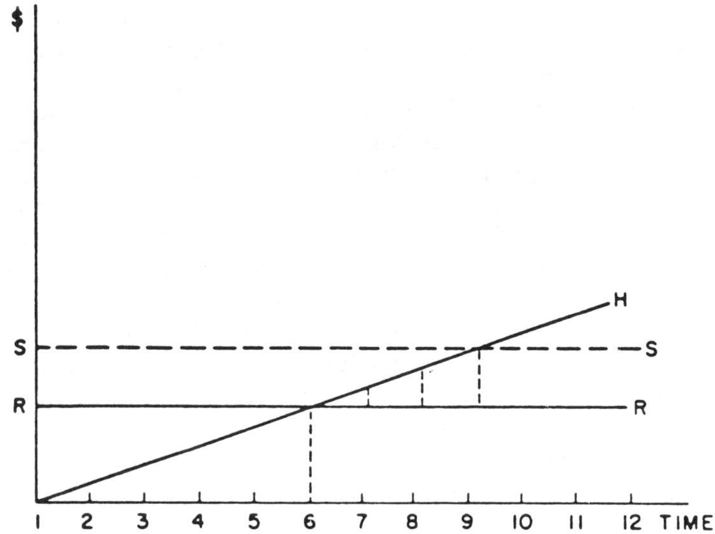

Figure 22–1

year. If the county contemplates a delay of several years, then of course the interest would be compounded. Unfortunately, it is not possible to represent this on a simple diagram but, once again, introducing this complication would not make any significant difference in the line of reasoning or in the conclusion.

Line H shows the cost to the community (wear and tear on vehicles, delay, etc.) of leaving the road unrepaired for one more year. It should be noted that, in Blacksburg, repairs must be made during the summer, and this breaks the time-stream down into a series of discontinuous one-year periods. Line H continuously slants upward. In the early period, the inconvenience, discomfort, and possible physical damage to the cars from holes and other defects in the pavement is very small. With time, it grows. If we assume that the community is left entirely to itself, and that the local town council perfectly represents the interests of its citizens, then the road would be resurfaced at the end of the sixth year. At this point, the cost of waiting one year to resurface the road rises above the cost of repairing it. The assumption that the town council perfectly expresses the preferences of its citizens is, of course, an improbable one, but the town council (more than any higher-level government agency) is more likely to represent the preferences of the citizens of Blacksburg.

Assume, however, that there is a state program for rebuilding roads. Assume, further, that the amount of money appropriated by the state for road repair is not sufficient to actually satiate demand for road repairs (a not unlikely assumption), and that the road commission spends this money on those roads where the need for repairs is greatest. Once again, this is a not unlikely assumption, although political considerations would be important, of course. Under these circumstances, the town council must make some calculations. If the amount of road repair funds and the degree of repair of other roads in the Commonwealth is such that the Commonwealth will repair the road during year six, then there is no problem. The town is able to pass the entire burden onto the shoulders of the Commonwealth. This is, however, on the whole a rather unlikely coincidence. Normally one would assume that the road funds would be either in shortage or in excess.

Let us begin by assuming that the total road funds are now supplied in shortage; hence the community realizes that the repair of its roads will not be undertaken by the Commonwealth in year six because there will be other roads that are already more deteriorated. Under these circumstances, the community must make an estimate of the likely delay which will follow if they decide to depend upon the Commonwealth. Assume that the Commonwealth road funds are available in a quantity that makes it possible for the Commonwealth to see to it that all roads are repaired when the cost of further use of them for one more year is at line S, rather than at line R. Under these circumstances, the community would anticipate that the road would be repaired in year nine. This means a wait for the Commonwealth through three more years of gradually deteriorating roads and, in this particular case, I have drawn the diagram in such a way that the cost to the community of these three additional years of delay for the town is approximately the same as the cost to the community of repairing the road itself now.[1]

Thus, the community would choose to repair the road itself at the end of the sixth year if it thought the Commonwealth standard for repairing roads was higher than S, i.e., the delay would be more than three years; but it would depend upon the Commonwealth if it thought the delay would be less than three years. From the local community standpoint, this would be a profit-maximizing decision. Note, however, that the town might have made a misestimate. Perhaps the funds available for road building will not be great enough, so that three years after year six (in year nine) roads deteriorated to the extent to which this particular road will then have deteriorated will be repaired. If the road funds are very restricted, they may be confined to roads that are in even poorer condition. Under these circumstances, in year nine the town would once again have to make an estimate. The cost it has already incurred from not repairing its road is, of course, a sunk cost and it would have to decide whether it is likely that further delay of a year or two would lead the state to repair the road. With my particular diagram, a year's delay from year nine would still be sensible for the town; but if prospective delay expected in year nine was greater than a year then it would be better for the town to repair the road itself. If this contingency occurred, even if the road was repaired in year ten the town would end up in a worse situation than it would be had it repaired the road in year six. Further, if in year nine the town came to the conclusion that a year's delay would not lead to enough deterioration of the road so that the state would repair it, then it would undertake the repair itself and the losses incurred from leaving the road unrepaired for three years would be a net loss to the community.

This problem does not occur only on the local level. In the early years of the Eisenhower administration, there was a vast expansion of divided center, limited access highways paid for by tolls. The development of these roads was extremely rapid and appeared likely to continue at a similar rate. This is particularly remarkable because the gasoline taxes, which pay for a good part of road building, were collected on gas used on these roads and not used to finance them. The individual using these roads had to pay the usual taxes to support the highway system, *plus* the toll. The speed with which these roads would have developed had the federal and state governments decided to rebate the taxes on gasoline consumed upon them to the toll authorities is hard to overestimate.

Unfortunately, this development did not occur. President Eisenhower got the idea that the federal government should introduce the interstate system at the cost of *all* drivers by way of a special tax on gasoline. When this new program was announced, all the local projects for building toll highways were dropped. As a result, development of divided center, limited access highways was markedly retarded, since the federal government adopted a schedule rather like the one I have specified for the higher authority dealing with Blacksburg, and long delays in construction of such highways resulted. To keep the matter on a local note, Blacksburg itself only achieved full integration into the nationwide interstate system in 1972.

Blacksburg has had another striking example. Fifteen years ago Blacksburg was a very small town which depended for hospital facilities on the country seat, about ten miles away. With the rapid expansion of Virginia Polytechnic Institute and State University, Blacksburg has grown to the point where it is now much the largest town in the county. The establishment of a hospital in Blacksburg seemed desirable, particularly since the hospital in the county seat was becoming obsolete. The town attempted to obtain federal government funds for a new hospital and spent several years in the effort. Eventually, it was decided that the prospects for federal financing were poor, and the town put up a hospital which it partially financed by a bond issue, but which is basically a private, profit-making hospital. The delay of several years was clearly the cost of the effort to obtain federal funds. It was an attempt to obtain a transfer and this attempt had costs.

Nevertheless, the individual city is rational in making its decision to delay provision of some facility because there is a finite chance of a higher authority providing the facility free (or, of course, providing a subsidy). The only question is the present discounted value of the two income streams, and it will frequently be higher if costs are absorbed in the immediate future in order to receive a grant from higher authority later. It should be noted, of course, that a desire to "help" the local city is not by any means the only motive that may inspire a higher level government to make such payments. Highway construction, for example, has very distinct externalities. The Commonwealth of Virginia does have a legitimate interest in seeing to it that the Town of Blacksburg provides somewhat more in the way of street repair than it would on its own. This is because the Town of Blacksburg will not take into account those noncitizens of Blacksburg who use its streets.

The ideal situation with respect to street repair, of course, would be Vickrey's scheme in which each person driving over a street is charged—by way of an elaborate electronic device—for his use of that particular segment of the street at an appropriate fee. Toll roads approximate this ideal. When this is not possible, payments from higher level authorities to lower level organizations may be a rational way of internalizing the externality. Normally, it is not possible to arrange these payments in such a way that the local government cannot partially distort its behavior pattern in order to increase its payments, but the problem is not a desperate one. The basic transfer problem arises when the motive inspiring higher level payments to local governments is a desire to "help" these local governments. Under these circumstances, the local governments are thrown into competition to receive the transfers and problems of the sort that we discussed in connection with figure 22–1 will arise.

Note that, provided only the amount of money supplied by the central government for street repair pulls the line S low enough to make it profitable for the community to delay repair, the community itself gains from the receipt of this transfer. If, however, we realize that the average community must be paying out as much in taxes to support the gifts as it is receiving in payments, and that the result of competition among the communities to receive such payments is a general delay in road repair, then the net effect of this central government provision of subsidies is actually to injure the citizens of the separate communities. They end up in a worse situation than they were in before the program was begun.

One solution for this problem would, of course, be to appropriate enough money to satiate the demand for whatever public service is being subsidized. As a step in this direction, if the amount of money provided by the state were exactly the amount needed to lower line S to line R, then our particular community would end up with the same road repairs it would have if there were no state program. Assuming it is an average community, it would be paying the same amount of taxes, also. Unfortunately, this solution is unlikely because different communities have different demands for road services, and hence would normally aim at different levels. At the very least, the central program will provide an equal level of service throughout its jurisdiction, which is inefficient.

The central government funds may be more than enough to fully replace the local expenditures. Suppose, for example, that the central government appropriated enough money so that line S was lowered to the point where it intersected line H at 4. Under these circumstances, the community would resurface its roads every four years. Clearly the community would be better off under this arrangement than it would be if it were resurfacing the road every six years, provided one disregards the tax cost. The community, however, would be still better off if the state simply gave it the entire cost of the road resurfacing every four years, and then the community in fact resurfaced the roads every six years. This overrepair of the roads leads to social waste just as does the underrepair discussed before.

So far, however, we have assumed that the state, in deciding to help a given community, simply observes how great the "need" for the particular type of service in that community is. Under these circumstances, the communities are well-advised to create "need," and hence produce a lower level of satisfaction. The desire on the part of the state to help communities which "have inadequate hospital facilities" actually generates inadequate hospital facilities. That community which has the worst hospital facilities will receive the aid.

In passing, I may note an amusing plaque which, at least some years ago, was set in the cement at the entrance to the Toledo, Ohio airport. This plaque was a letter from President Eisenhower to the City of Toledo in which he congratulated the city on having built their airport entirely on their own without federal funds. He made it clear that he thought this was a highly meritorious, and even noble, act. In order not to raise any misunderstanding in other parts of the country, however, he then went on to say that, of course, those communities which could not provide their own airport must receive federal aid. I take it that the citizens of Toledo never again found it possible to build their own airport.

The alternative, providing enough resources so that communities are able to provide the service before they would themselves regard it worthwhile, must also lead to net social loss, albeit of a different nature. The result, then, of this type of program is always loss, and this loss comes from the competition among the potential recipients of the benefit for its receipt. The community that lets its hospital run down because it feels that the federal government will replace it is in the same situation as the Chinese beggar who mutilates himself to obtain funds from passersby. In both cases, the individual action is rational, and in both cases the net effect is to lower welfare.

So far our analysis has proceeded in terms of one possible technique which higher authority might use in making transfers among local communities. There are, of course, other methods. Basically, however, I think these methods can be classified into three general categories. The first of these, which we have already discussed, is distribution of the manna according to need. As we have pointed out, this leads to a competition among the potential recipients in generating need. The second is simply to make direct income transfers on some arbitrary basis. This, together with the third method, to attempt to second-guess the local communities, will be discussed below.

To begin with simple income transfers, they have somewhat the same attractions as negative income tax. Suppose, for example, that a higher level government allocates to local governments a fund of so much per head, which can be used in any way the local government wishes. Clearly the effect of this allocation is simply to permit the local government to reduce its taxes. Since the average local government will be paying as much in taxes as it is receiving in its allocation, there will be no income effect, and hence it will purchase about the same services and goods it would purchase without this transfer. Those communities which receive more income than they pay in taxes will have a wealth increase, and hence they will spend more; while those who pay more than they get will have a wealth decrease and will spend less. Basically, however, this leaves the decision as to what should actually be done with the money to local authorities, and has only modest tendencies toward inefficiency.

There is one significant disadvantage of this system, however, which is that it makes it impossible for communities to experiment with the combination of very low taxes and a very low bundle of services. Perhaps these experiments are undesirable, but we must at least note that this procedure makes them impossible. In any event, there is no competition among communities to get funds under this procedure, and hence this type of conflict we have been describing above does not occur.[2] Note that it is not necessary that the subsidy be distributed on a per head basis, only that it be distributed in such a way that the individual communities cannot obtain increased subsidies by changing their behavior. There may, of course, be a good deal of investment in lobbying, etc., in order to get the higher level government to adopt a particular method of distributing the subsidy which is of advantage to a particular local community.

The third method, and at the moment the most widely used method, consists of a variety of efforts to prevent the local government from either spending the money exactly as it wishes which it would do under, the second method, or deliberately generating needs, as it would do under the first method. These methods are complex and not terribly efficient. Basically, they involve either some kind of incentive payments which are intended to lead the local government in which the central government regards as the correct direction, or direct administrative controls over the way the local government spends the central government's money.

The problem is rather similar to that which has led most major corporations to decentralize managements. It is simply impossible for the central government to know as much about the situation in any local community as the local government does. Thus, if the central government attempts to set up specific regulations or detailed administration, it simply leads to local government activities aimed at taking advantage of this central administration. Indeed, it is probable that it is far less efficient than local administration of the money, because the central government bureaucracy of controllers is offset by a massive local government bureaucracy of planners, city engineers, assistant superintendents, all of whom in fact exist almost solely for the purpose of obtaining as much central government money as can be obtained, granted the restrictions.

The proliferation of local officials that has occurred in areas where central government grants are available is normally discussed in terms of desirability of "planning." This is a misunderstanding. These officials are there for the purpose of assisting the community in obtaining central government funds, partly by preparing plans which are not intended for local use, but for the central government inspection. As an example that will impress almost all academics, VPI, like most universities, now has a "Dean of Research." According to the table of organization, he is in charge of research in the university. His actual duties are to assist the university in obtaining research grants from Washington and from the foundations. As part of these duties, he does, indeed, exercise some influence on research actually carried on at the university. He makes efforts to push it in directions that will lead to increased funds. He also makes judgments as to whether a particular possible area of research would cost more in terms of university research allocations than it is worth in terms of funds likely to come in. His presence has little or nothing to do with actual research on campus and a great deal to do with raising money.

Not only are such specialized officials as planners and deans of research basically engaged in attempting to get money from higher authorities, but many standard administrators have become specialists in this field. The present-day school superintendent of a large system is apt to be more concerned with attempting to raise money from Washington, or perhaps from the state or private foundations, than with actually running the school system. Surely this must, over time, lead to less efficient supervision of the local activity, together with a higher administrative cost. The local community that hires at high price a very competent school superintendent, in the sense that he is good at getting money from Washington, does well in its competition with other local communities. The existence of this competition, however, means that a great deal of resources are devoted by various local communities to essentially offsetting sales efforts in Washington.

The situation can be illustrated by figure 22–2. On the vertical axis we have a dollar amount, and on the horizontal axis we have probable receipts in grants from Washington. Note that a certainty of $100 would be shown at the same location on the horizontal axis as a 50-50 chance of $200, a one-in-three chance of $300, etc. In other words, no risk factor is shown. In the real world, the community would also have risk aversion, and hence this simple diagram would have to be complicated. A community investing resources in efforts to obtain grants from Washington is assumed in this diagram to make simple, straightforward cash payments, perhaps for additional members of its "planning" bureaucracy. The cost is shown as line C.

As a beginning, we represent the receipts as constant in value; that is, each unit of receipts on the horizontal axis is shown as a certain number of dollars by the horizontal line PP. The community faces declining returns on its investments in efforts to get transfers, and the cost and return lines cross at A. Thus, the community would invest the total amount shown by the rough triangle under line C and to the left of A, and receive a gross return equivalent to the rectangle to the left of A. The operation would be profitable from the standpoint of the community. If we consider that the national government has some bureaucracy to supervise the distribution of

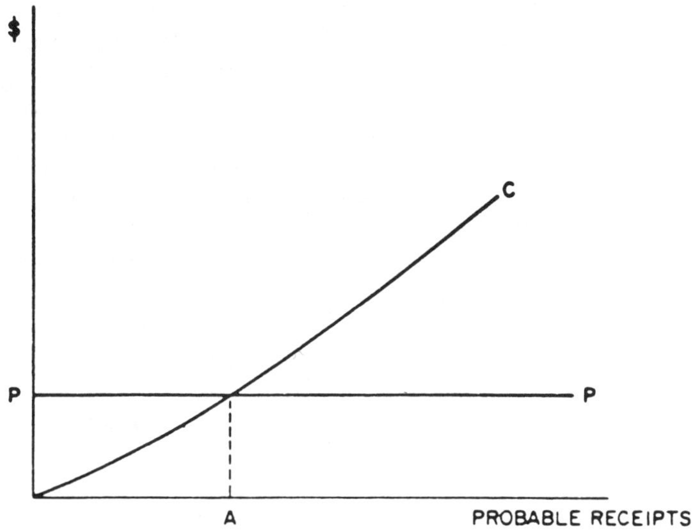

Figure 22–2

funds, it may or may not be profitable from the standpoint of this one local community plus the national government. Surely, however, from the standpoint of society as a whole, it would be desirable that the funds used to generate this grant and the funds used by the national government to supervise such generation be dropped. It is the competition between this local community and other communities, together with the national government's role as referee over this competition, that causes the waste.

Frequently, however, the national government does not simply make straightforward payments to the local government. The funds delivered must be spent in particular ways or the local government must take certain types of activity in order to receive them. I recall hearing the president of the University of South Carolina explain a project to tear down a neighboring black slum and build some playing fields for the university as part of a federal government urban renewal project. He remarked on the amount of money we would receive for this purpose, but then said this was not all "clear." It would be necessary to spend approximately 25 percent of the grant to develop plans, etc. These plans were not necessary for the development of the playing field, they were entirely part of the federal government's program. The university had hired an expert at getting this kind of money, and the expert had said that it would be necessary for the university to spend a fairly large amount of money on some planning and research documents which were of no interest to it. They were probably not of much interest to the federal government, either. The reasons why the federal government required them will be discussed below.

When the federal government does not make the gift free and clear, then line PP on figure 22–2 has a somewhat different form. Suppose the federal government has a program that provides some opportunity for the Town of Blacksburg to receive some money. This money, however, must be spent on something which the Town of Blacksburg does not regard as of first priority. If the federal government simply gave them the cash, they would spend it, let us say, on street improvements; but the grant can only be spent on improved recreational facilities. Under these circumstances, the grant is worth less to us than its dollar cost to the federal government, and the line PP would thus be lower than if they were simply making cash payments.[3]

Not only does the tying of the grant lower its value to the local government, it is probable that the line PP should be downward slanting to indicate that the local government will first attempt to get money under those programs that are of greatest value to it, and then under programs of a lower value, etc. This is not sure, however. The local government should be uninterested in the actual dollar cost of the funds to the federal government, and only interested in the benefit to themselves and the cost of generating it. Thus, suppose that there are two government programs, one of which will cost the federal government $500,000 and provide a benefit which the local authorities believe is worth only $50,000, and another which will cost the federal government $50,000 and provide the local government with a benefit which they think is worth only $40,000. If, in the town's estimate, the cost of obtaining these two grants is the same, the city fathers would prefer the first.

The fact that the government grants to a local community are normally accompanied by special requirements, and that the community's behavior is to a considerable extent adjusted to the desirability of obtaining these grants, means that the grants are always worth less to the community than their cost to the central government. Once again, competition among communities for these grants may lead to very large costs to the community and the nation. Note, however, that the fact that the grant is of lower value to the community than cash does not necessarily indicate that the community should be permitted to disperse the money in an unhampered way. If the objective of the central government is not to aid the local community but simply to internalize certain externalities which would otherwise be ignored by the community, then, although the grant will be worth less than its dollar value to the community, restrictions may be sensible.

If the grant to the local community, however, is motivated by a desire to simply benefit the local community, then the costs which we have been describing are net offsets against the benfits to be obtained from the grant and there is clear social waste. This is particularly true since in many cases the restrictions put on the expenditure of the grant do not represent any general concensus as to values. The central government bureaucrats, allocating funds among a number of competing clients, are likely to develop standards for delivery of these funds which in part are an expression of their own tastes, and in part are designed to reduce their decision problem. Bureaucrats in general, although they like power, normally do not like the business of finally turning down applicants. Thus, the introduction of essentially arbitrary requirements in the review process by reducing the number of applicants is an improvement in the well-being of the bureaucrats. This is particularly so since the imposition of these requirements is as good an expression of their power as the individual decisions would be. Many of the restrictions put on local communities who wish central funds are arbitrary and complying with them is pure social waste, except insofar as individual bureaucrats are benefited by them by reduction in their subjective decision costs.

Notes

1. Note that I ignore compounding on both sides of the equation. In the real world, a decision for three years would presumably have to take a compounding effect into account, and hence would be more complicated.

2. In special circumstances, this is not entirely true. The Town of Blacksburg is expanding and quite deliberately taking in the university campus on the grounds that a certain amount is paid to local governments on a per-head basis by the Commonwealth of Virginia, while the students in fact consume relatively little in the way of government services. The county government, which may lose this asset, is naturally angry.

3. It is possible for the value of the grant to be higher for the federal government or for the rest of the nation, even though it is lower from the standpoint of the local government. This point will be discussed further below.

D *The Firm*

23 MANAGERIAL RENTS AND OUTSIDE RECRUITMENT IN THE COASIAN FIRM

Roger L. Faith, Richard S. Higgins, and Robert D. Tollison*

In the corporation, decision making about the use of capital by managers and risk taking by the owners of capital are specialized activities. Various institutional mechanisms have been analyzed as forces disciplining the opportunistic behavior of management under these conditions. We maintain that no single mechanism, such as wage revision in the managerial labor market or an internal device that relies on influencing incentives by making executives residual claimants in the firm, is sufficient to solve problems of managerial incentives. Instead, the margins of several control devices are extended simultaneously to maximize the value of the firm, net of the cost of control. In this context we will emphasize one means of managerial control which has not been fully analyzed to date—the impact of outside hiring on the behavior of incumbent managers.

---

* The opinions expressed in this paper are solely our own and do not necessarily reflect the views of the Federal Trade Commission, its staff, or any individual Commissioner. We are grateful to James Buchanan. Mark Crain, Robert McCormick, Dennis Mueller, Roger Sherman, and William Shughart for helpful comments on earlier drafts. The usual caveat applies.

Our analysis is developed in terms of the neoclassical theory of the firm, as exposited by Ronald Coase (1937), and extended by Armen Alchian and Harold Demsetz (1972), Michael Jensen and William Meckling (1976), Eugene Fama (1980), and others. In this tradition the firm is seen as an institution that economizes on transaction costs. It is defined as a collection of contracts between input owners and the owner(s) of the firm where multilateral contracting among resource owners is replaced by bilateral contracting between each resource owner and the firm. This contractual structure reduces transaction costs because it reduces the number of formal contracts required for productive activity.

Alchian and Demsetz extend the theory of the firm by analyzing the substitution of hierarchical organization for market organization—the productivity of team production outweighs the cost of monitoring individual marginal value contributions. Firms deal with the monitoring problem by establishing a specialized monitoring input that is common to all input contracts and that can renegotiate individual contracts. The incentives of this specialized input are controlled by making it a residual claimant. Alchian and Demsetz appreciate the value of further specialization in the modern corporation, which requires substantial capital to take advantage of available economies of scale. The classical owner-entrepreneur is replaced by numerous owners, who hold diversified portfolios of ownership claims and who delegate decision-making authority to management. In Alchian and Demsetz, the problem of separation of ownership and control is dealt with in numerous ways. Their emphasis, however, is on the internal and external control mechanisms related to the transferability of voting shares.

The ownership-control problem is a major theme in Jensen and Meckling. They recognize that efficient allocation of risks calls for the specialization of risk-bearing and decision-making activities within the firm, and that efficient allocation is achieved at a cost of reduced control over management by the firm's owners. They emphasize various mechanisms devised in the interest of the firm's owners to control opportunistic behavior by management—contingency clauses in shareholders' contracts, the composition of managerial pay, proxy fights, stockholders' derivative actions, and so on. They are also sensitive to the internal and external mechanisms of control based on efficient valuation of shareholder claims in the capital market, a process that also plays a paramount role in Henry Manne's (1965) takeover model of corporate control.[1]

Fama argues that the ownership-control problem can be resolved by wage revision in the managerial labor market. His thesis parallels that of Alchian and Demsetz, which also relies heavily on external markets to achieve internal managerial discipline. We agree with Fama that the degree of discipline imposed by the managerial labor market is an empirical question, but a priori, we are inclined toward an eclectic hypothesis which accommodates several margins of internal and external control.

Specifically, we present a model of the determination of a firm's outside hiring rate. Just as the firm externally substitutes hierarchical organization for market organization and internally adjusts the organizational form until returns are equalized at the margin, the firm also utilizes external and internal markets for managerial services until net gains are exhausted. Our thesis is similar to Fama's in its emphasis on the external labor market, but unlike Fama we stress the impact of outside hiring on the matrix of internal managerial incentives, not just on the incentives of the manager(s) replaced.[2]

We will describe how managers can appropriate rents in the firm through informal (unwritten) contracts, and suggest how such behavior can be controlled through outside hiring. Next, we present a formal model of the informal contracting idea. We derive implications about the relationships between firm-specific factors and the tenure and pay of the firm's chief executive officer. We provide a test of the major implications of the model and present some concluding remarks, stressing other implications of the analysis.

Informal Contracting

A contract is an allocation of rewards over states of the world and over actions of the contracting parties. An efficient contract will assign rewards based on joint action-state contingencies in order to provide incentives for value-maximizing actions, provided that the costs of contracting (costs associated with enumerating states and state-contingent actions, verifying states and actions, and enforcing judgments) are not prohibitive. An efficient contract maximizes the expected net gains from trade.

Because it is costly to write and enforce completely specified contracts, many contract terms are left implicit. To the extent that some terms of contracts are implicit, appropriate actions for given states of the world are not expressly stated. Instead, they are assessed *ex post*, with costs and rewards assigned accordingly.

A contract can be enforced in two major ways: either a penalty is imposed by a third-party in the event of breach, or the prospect of gain from continued dealing is withheld from the breaching party. In the case of a self-enforcing agreement, no outside party is required to detect violations, assess damages, and enforce judgments. Rather, the parties to the contract continue to abide by the agreement so long as the expected net gains exceed the current gains of violating it. Monitoring activities may still go on within self-enforcing agreements since the value of an agreement is greater the more quickly violations are detected. Parties will exhaust the marginal gains of more rapid detection through monitoring.

Another important distinction is that between exogenous and endogenous enforcement. When contracts are multilateral, the term "third-party enforcement" is ambiguous. The mutual responsibilities of two agents in a multilateral agreement can be enforced by another contracting party. We refer to this situation as endogenous third-party enforcement to distinguish it from court enforcement, where the enforcer is outside the agreement, and from self-enforcing contracts, where no third-party enforcer is necessary. We use the term informal contract to denote any behavioral agreement among two or more managers which is self-enforcing or enforced endogenously.

As a by-product of management's putative role in monitoring team production, managers are well placed to capture a portion of the firm's value through informal contracting. Legitimate monitoring devices can be used to detect incipient and recent violations, encouraging self-enforcing agreements that serve managerial goals at the expense of the firm. The internal organization established to discipline managerial discretion provides a system of checks, which empowers managers to penalize actions that violate informal agreements, as well as to enforce the formal contracts that define the firm. For example, manager C may be in a position to penalize manager A for violating a provision of an informal agreement governing the duties of manager A and manager B. In turn, manager B may be in a position to enforce the subcontract between managers C and A, and so on. This is endogenous third-party enforcement of informal contracts as defined above.[3]

When there are potential gains from trade inside the firm and some agents are situated to control the magnitude and distribution of these gains, informal contracting will compete with other mechanisms devised to control the actions of the agents on behalf of the owner(s). These latter mechanisms—formal contracts, internal organization, and external market price adjustment—are not established in a vacuum, but evolve interdependently with the informal contracting activity of management, and the mechanism of control based on internal organization provides a means of facilitating informal agreements.

Of course, mechanisms of control will respond to informal contracting. One method of control, which has large potential for constraining informal contracting, is hiring outside managers. In this respect our emphasis is different from that of Fama. Full *ex post* "settling up" is not necessary in our model. What is important is that outsiders replace key managerial personnel, thereby upsetting the informal contracts established by incumbent managers. Our emphasis is not on replacing a manager with a more productive outsider, but on raising the net productivity of the entire management team by dissolving informal contracts.

Theory and Implications

We analyze the problem of control of the management team by the owner(s) of the firm through resort to the market for managers. We consider both profit-maximizing firms and firms in which ownership rights are attenuated.

The Market for Managers

Every currently employed manager is an "insider" with respect to his current employer and an "outsider" with respect to other firms. A competitive labor market implies that the marginal return to working for any particular employer will be equalized. This return is made up of both the contractual wage, W, and the rents, R, accruing to the manager. Assuming a competitive labor market and using subscripts 1 and 0 to denote insiders and outsiders, we can write

$$W_0 + R_0 = W_1 + R_1 = MP(V), \tag{23.1}$$

where V is a vector of variables which affect managerial marginal productivity or performance.

To the firm, there is a difference in the costs of employing an inside manager for another period or promoting an insider to a higher position versus bringing in an outside manager. If the firm goes outside, it incurs a cost equal to $W_0 + R_0 + OH$, where OH is the cost of outside hiring. The firm gains $W_1 + R_1 + R_S$, where R_S represents the rents appropriated by management through informal contracts, *throughout the organization*, destroyed by bringing in an outsider.

In equilibrium, the firm will equate the marginal benefits and marginal costs of outside hiring:

$$W_0 + R_0 + OH = W_1 + R_1 + R_S, \tag{23.2}$$

or

$$W_0 - W_1 = R_1 - R_0 + R_S - OH.$$

Given (23.1), the firm goes outside until $R_S = OH$, but we will find it useful to concentrate on net managerial rents, $R_N = R_1 - R_0 + R_S$. Thus, given market wages, the basic cost relationship facing the firm is a tradeoff between net managerial rents R_N, and the cost of outside hiring OH.

Profit-Maximizing Firms

The firm's tradeoff is derived from a pair of cost functions relating managerial rents R_N, and the cost of outside hiring OH, to the rate of outside hiring, h.

The managerial rent function is assumed to be an increasing function of managerial tenure in the firm, T, and it is assumed that $R_0 < R_1(T)$ for all positive values of T. That is, the appropriable rents of a new manager, R_0, are less than the appropriable rents of a current inside manager with positive tenure. Since average tenure is inversely related to the outside hiring rate, managerial rent declines in h. This is because the outside candidate is not bound by and does not receive private benefits from the informal agreements that the inside managers have made. Since the marginal gain of outside hiring will eventually be dominated by losses caused by too frequent interruption of legitimate lines of communication among members of the managerial team, the marginal reductions in managerial rent appropriation decline.[4] Thus,

$$R_N = f(h, X),\ f_h < 0 \text{ and } f_{hh} > 0, \tag{23.3}$$

where X is a vector of other exogenous variables which affect RN.

The cost of outside hiring is primarily the cost of bringing the outsider's productivity up to the level of the insider. This cost arises because insiders have been trained in firm procedures and own specific capital which is valuable to the firm. The greater the rate of outside hiring, the greater these training costs. In addition, there are costs of finding the outside manager. It is costly to detect fakers (low-productivity types) in the supply of outside candidates. It is assumed that the marginal cost of error (higher training costs to offset lower productivity) rises the more the firm resorts to the outside market. Therefore,

$$OH = g(h, Y),\ g_h > 0 \text{ and } g_{hh} > 0, \tag{23.4}$$

where Y is a vector of other exogenous variables which affect OH.

Equations (23.3) and (23.4) represent the benefits and costs of hiring on the outside. As the outside hiring rate goes up, the managerial team is subjected to stricter discipline, and managerial rent appropriation is reduced. At the same time, the firm incurs a loss in value because there is a cost of outside hiring. A profit-maximizing owner will choose an outside hiring rate that minimizes the sum of R_N and OH because he is indifferent to the source of the costs that diminish the firm's value.

Analytically, the R_n–OH tradeoff is constructed by eliminating *h* between (23.3) and (23.4). The resulting opportunity locus is denoted $OH = F(R_N; X, Y)$, where $F' < 0$ and $F'' > 0$. The constraint F is depicted in figure 23–1. The value of *h* is implicit in F; as one moves from right to left along F, *h* increases.

The profit-maximizing owner's objective is to minimize $R_N + OH$. A \$1 increase in outside hiring cost that is accompanied by a \$1 reduction in managerial rent seeking leaves the value of the firm unchanged and also leaves the owner's utility unchanged. In figure 23–1, the owner's indifference lines over R_N and OH, denoted by C, have slopes equal to -1 everywhere; he is indifferent to the composition of MR + OH.

The actual position of the constraint F will depend upon the exogenous factors X and Y, such as the size of the management team, the level of output, the effectiveness of other managerial monitoring devices, and so on. For example, an increase in the efficiency of internal auditing would shift F toward the origin, implying a lower level of $(R_N + OH)$ at the optimal hiring rate.

The marginal condition defining the minimum cost combination of OH and R_N (given F) is

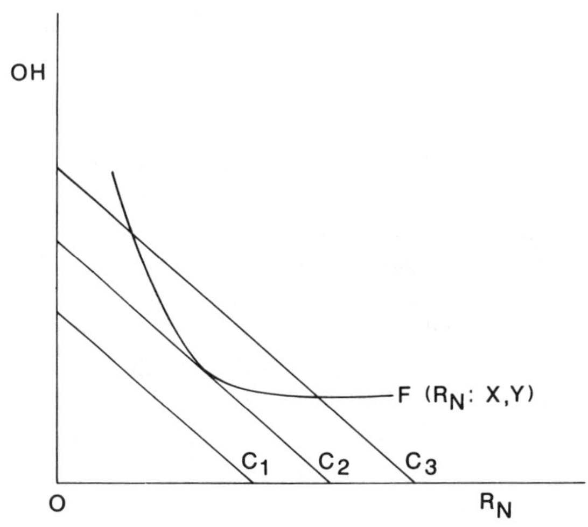

Figure 23–1

$$\partial OH/\partial R_N \quad g_h(h^*;X,Y)/f_h(h^*;X,Y) = -1,$$

or
$$g_h(h^*;X,Y) = |f_h(h^*;X,Y)|. \tag{23.5}$$

At the optimal rate of outside hiring, h^*, implicit in (23.5), the rate at which a dollar of managerial rent can be saved per dollar of outside hiring cost expended is equal to unity. A positive level of managerial rents and outside hiring costs at h^* imply, from (23.2), that the firm's contractual wage for insiders declines, relative to the outsider's wage, with increasing tenure in the firm. Further, since $R_0 < R_1[T(h^*)]$, for $h^* > 0$, it follows from (1) that $W_0 > W_1$.

Derivation of the CEO Pay-Tenure Relation

The chief executive officer (CEO) of a corporation shares in the rents created through the cooperation of the managerial team. This is the reason that the owners of the firm will sometimes resort to the outside market for a CEO. In the market for managerial services, however, total returns (rent and nonrent) are equalized across managerial positions requiring equal abilities. As discussed above, the market equilibrium relationship between nonrent pay and pay received as rent is negative, holding constant such factors as firm performance and the composition of managerial compensation.

Substituting the individual firm's equilibrium relationship between managerial rent and outside hiring, $R_N^* = f(h^*, X)$, into the equilibrium pay equation (2), we obtain a relationship between CEO nonrent pay and the variables h^* and X. Based on the qualitative informative presumed about the managerial rent function ($f_h < 0$), we predict, *ceteris paribus*, that h^* impacts on W positively. An increase in reliance on the market for managers reduces managerial rent, and lower managerial rent is associated with higher managerial nonrent pay.[5]

Two important exogenous variables, included in X, directly and indirectly (through h^*), affect CEO nonrent pay: the size of the management team, N, and the amount of potential rent appropriable by managers. For each of these variables, the overall impact on CEO nonrent pay is ambiguous, although the effects on pay are predictable a priori, holding h^* constant. In the case of the size of the managerial team, informal contracting will be more difficult the larger the number of managers whose cooperation is necessary for rent creation, that is, $\partial R_N^*/\partial N < 0$. Consequently, holding h^* constant, W is predicted to be positively related to N. The second factor is the potential rent that management can appropriate through informal contracting. An increase in the amount there is to appropriate will raise R_N^*; hence, in the CEO nonrent pay equation, W will be negatively related to appropriable rents, holding h^* constant.

We do not have separate measures for the size of the managerial team and the amount of appropriable rents. In our empirical test we use a measure of firm size as a proxy for these factors—on average, the greater a firm's size, the larger its managerial team and its capital in jeopardy. Additionally, if greater ability is required to manage large firms effectively, firm size may also affect CEO nonrent pay positively through MP(V) in (23.1). The net impact of firm size on CEO pay is ambiguous.

The market equilibrium pay condition in equation (23.1) implies a *ceteris paribus* relationship between W and V, the vector of parameters that affect managerial marginal productivity. One element of V is the extent that management is remunerated with contingent pay. The composition of pay is important in controlling managerial behavior. It is a substitute for outside hiring to some extent because the interest of owners in maximizing the firm's value can be imposed on the manager by compensating him through stock options and bonuses. Pay composition is not a perfect substitute for other control devices, however; the manager requires a pay package with a larger expected value because diversification is restricted and risk increased. In our approach, the firm will operate on both the outside hiring and contingent pay margins. Since managerial rent seeking will be negatively related to contingent pay compensation, we predict that CEO nonrent pay will be positively related to the contingent pay variable.

Another component of V is firm performance. Because firm performance is an *ex post* indicator of the CEO's productivity, a measure of firm performance should be positively related to nonrent pay.

Attenuated Property Rights

There are firms in which the property rights of owners are limited by law as in the case of firms subject to rate of return regulation. There are also firms and nonprofit organizations in which the transferability of property rights is limited. That managers in public utilities, labor unions, and universities engage in expense preference is not controversial. What has not been generally analyzed is the role of outside hiring in enterprises with attenuated property rights. In this section we are concerned with the effect of property rights attenuation on the organization's use of outside hiring to

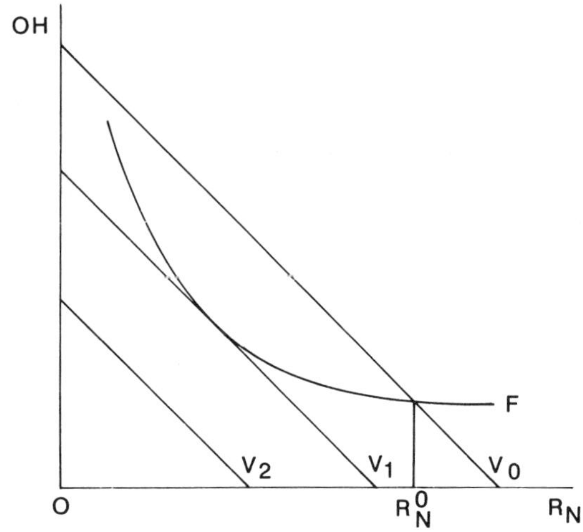

Figure 23–2

discipline management.[6] Specifically, we contrast the CEO pay relation and CEO turnover policy in firms with and without rate of return regulation.

In firms subject to a rate of return constraint, management is prohibited from maximizing firm value. Additionally, a profit restraint can alter input prices. We focus on the impact of a rate of return constraint on the value to management of managerial rents in terms of the firm's profit, which affects the firm's tenure policy. For example, in figure 23–2, if the rate of return constraint limited the value of the firm (the owners' maximand) to V_0, which is below its maximum value V_1, outside hiring to discipline managerial rent seeking would be redundant for R_N less than R_N^0. In effect, the CEO's indifference curves in figure 23–2 would be vertical for all points below V_0. Although this illustration conveys our basic result—that the relative value of outside hiring as a means of managerial control is lower for regulated firms, resulting in greater CEO tenure—it is unrealistic in supposing that there is some maximum value of the firm subject to a regulatory restraint that is independent of the firm's turnover policy. Below we construct a model of managerial rent seeking in which regulation induces expense preference according to a neoclassical utility function and in which firm value is endogenous.

We suppose, in general, that the firm maximizes a utility function with arguments R_N and the actual value of the firm V^a: $U(R_N, V^a)$. We further

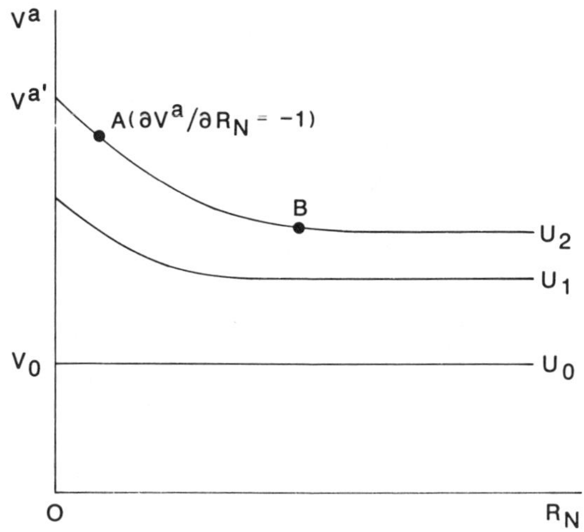

Figure 23–3

suppose that $V^a = V^p - (R_N + OH)$, where V^p is the potential value of the firm. For a proit-maximizing firm, $\partial U/\partial R_N \equiv 0$, and maximizing U is equivalent to maximizing V^a or minimizing $R_N + OH$. But for a regulated firm, $\partial U/\partial R_N$ is not identically equal to zero. For firms under a regulatory constraint, we assume that the indifference curves have the form illustrated in figure 23–3.

In figure 23–3 there is a threshold value of the firm under a regulatory constraint, V_0, below which the CEO's marginal valuation of rents in terms of profits is zero. In effect, the probability that the CEO will be fired (on account of disciplinary action by stockholders or other firms) is one. For firm values greater than V_0, disciplinary action is less certain. Specifically, we assume that disciplinary action is less likely the greater is V^a relative to V_0, *ceteris paribus*, and given V^a, the lower is R_N. Thus, for $V^a > V_0$, the CEO's marginal valuation of rents in terms of profit rises as V^a increases, and the marginal valuation falls as R_N rises, *ceteris paribus*. These assumptions imply smooth substitution of rents for profit with diminishing marginal valuation exhibited along an indifference curve up to some value of R_N.

Given a utility function of this form, we next derive indifference curves in R_N–OH space in order to contrast the turnover policies of unregulated and regulated firms. Solving $U[R_N, V^p - (R_N + OH)] = U^0$ for OH as a function of R_N, we find that $\partial OH/\partial R_N = (\partial U/\partial R_N - \partial U/$

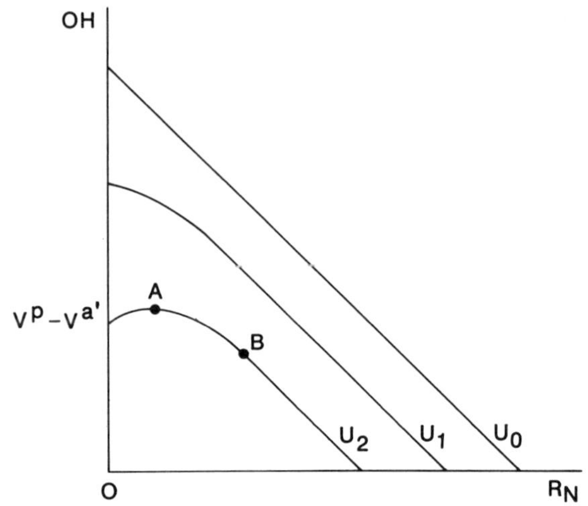

Figure 23–4

$\partial V^a)/(\partial U/\partial V^a)$. Based on the second-order properties of U illustrated in figure 23–3, we depict the preference map over R_N–OH in figure 23–4. In contrast to figure 23–3 utility decreases towards the northeast in figure 23–4.

The preference map in figure 23–4 is found by choosing a point in R_N–V^a space of figure 23–3 and mapping it to the point $(R_N, V^p - V^a - R_N)$ in figure 23–4, with slope equal to $\partial OH/\partial R_N = (\partial U/\partial R_N/\partial U/\partial V^a) - 1$. Thus, all the points on the flat indifference curve, U_0, in figure 23–3 are mapped to U_0 in figure 23–4 where $\partial Oh/\partial R_N = -1$. Similarly, the points on U_2 in figure 23–3 map to U_2 in figure 23–4. Specifically, the point $(0, V^{a'})$ in figure 23–3 maps to $(0, V^p - V^{a'})$ in figure 23–4, with slope equal to $(\partial U/\partial R_N/\partial U/\partial V^a) - 1 > 0$. As R_N is substituted for V^a along U_2 in figure 23–3, $(\partial U/\partial R_N/\partial U/\partial V^a)$ approaches unity so that point A in figure 23–3 corresponds to point A in figure 23–4 where the slope of the indifference curve is $1 - 1 = 0$. Beyond point B along U_2 in figure 23–3 the slope of the indifference curve for the corresponding points in figure 23–4 equals −1.

With the regulated-firm CEO's preferences defined on R_N–OH space in figure 23–4 we can readily compare the unregulated firm's choice of turnover policy and managerial rents with the regulated firm's decision. (Recall that for the unregulated firm the indifference curves in R_N–OH space are all linear with a slope of −1.) In figure 23–5 we depict the

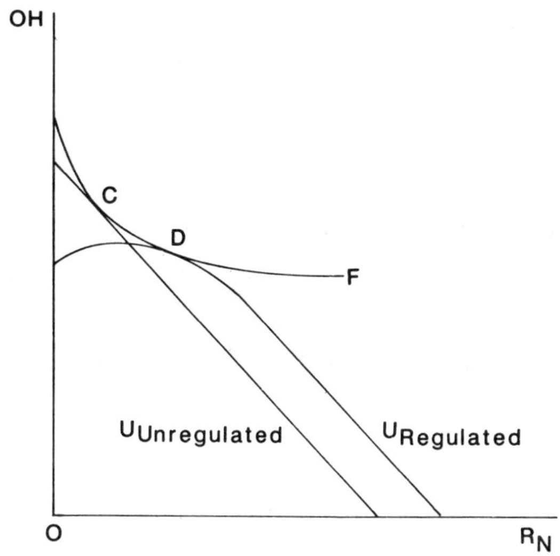

Figure 23–5

respective solutions, C and D, to the managerial control problem for an unregulated and a regulated firm. The sum of R_N and OH is greater (since we know that R_N + OH is minimized at C) at D than at C. Furthermore, we see that R_N is larger at D than at C; the firm with attenuated property rights chooses an outside hiring policy that allows more rents to be captured internally by management. And, based on the derivation of the constraint F, we know that the outside hiring rate is lower a: D than at C. Thus, if we distinguish firms by presence of rate of return regulation, we expect to find lower outside hiring rates where ownership rights are attenuated.

The model has implications for managerial pay as well. Competition in the market for managers will assure that managers in profit-restrained firms receive lower total pay, excluding rents, than managers in unrestrained firms where rents are lower. In a pay equation with CEO tenure, pay composition, firm size, firm performance, and a dummy variable indicating the presence of rate of return regulation as arguments, we predict that tenure will affect pay negatively. Moreover, a negative relationship between regulation and pay is consistent with our argument that all margins of managerial control are worth less in a regulated environment. We discuss this point in more detail below.

Empirical Results

Regression Model

We estimated the parameters of the following CEO pay equation to test the predictions of our model about tenure and regulation:

$$\begin{aligned}\text{CEOPAY} = {} & a_0 + a_1\text{CTGPAY} + a_2\text{COYRS} + a_3\text{CEOYRS} \\ & + a_4(\text{CEOYRS})^2 + a_5\text{SIZE} + a_6\text{AGE} \\ & + a_7\text{FPERF} + a_8\text{D} + u. \end{aligned} \tag{23.6}$$

The variables in (23.6) are defined as follows:

CEOPAY is CEO compensation;

CTGPAY is contingent remuneration plus stock options divided by total compensation;

COYRS is the number of years a CEO has been with a company;

CEOYRS is the number of years the CEO has been a company's CEO;

SIZE is firm size measured by net sales;

AGE is CEO age;

FPERF is a measure of short-run firm performance;

D is a dummy variable for the presence of rate of return regulation which equals 1 if regulated and 0 otherwise; and

u is a stochastic error term with the usual properties.

This empirical model of CEOPAY yields several *ceteris paribus* predictions. The effect of tenure in the company on *CEOPAY* is paramount. We predict a negative sign on COYRS because outside hiring frequency (the inverse of tenure) disciplines informal contracting and because nonrent compensation is inversely related to pay as rent.

Second, we predict a positive sign for CEOYRS as an indication of a learning effect among CEOs. However, this argument interacts with our tenure prediction. As CEOYRS increases, there is both learning and reduced managerial discipline with respect to informal contracting. To capture these effects we include both a linear and quadratic term for CEOYRS. We predict a positive linear (learning) and a negative quadratic (as informal contracting becomes more pronounced) effect.

Third, our model predicts less CEOPAY in regulated firms. However, this prediction is not a *ceteris paribus* prediction because CEOPAY is affected by regulation through firms' tenure policies. Our model is silent about the direct effects of regulation on CEOPAY, holding tenure constant, although a negative regulation effect is consistent with our basic argument. The essence of our analysis is that the firm operates on several margins to control informal contracting by management. Since all margins of owner control are worth less in a regulated environment, and since we are unable to control for all of these disciplinary margins in our empirical specification, it is likely that the regulation variable will have some separate negative impact on CEOPAY.

Fourth, we can make a priori predictions about the impact of the remaining control variables. CTGPAY should impact on CEOPAY positively because there is less incentive for informal contracting the more an executive is compensated on the basis of short-run performance. To the extent that sales are positively related to the size of the management hierarchy, which retards rent seeking, the predicted effect of SIZE is positive. Also, because more managerial ability is required in large firms to achieve equal performance between small and large firms, SIZE will be positively related to CEOPAY. To the extent that sales are positively related to the firm's appropriable capital, SIZE will be negatively related to GEOPAY. Thus, the net impact of SIZE on CEOPAY is uncertain. Further, we expect a positive sign on AGE as a reflection of nonspecific human capital in CEOs. Finally, FPERF, a measure of the recent performance of the CEO, should impact on CEOPAY positively.

The Data

We estimated the regression model using data on executive pay and tenure from a survey of executive compensation published by *Forbes* (1981) and on firm size from *Compustat* (1980). The sample from *Forbes* included 818 U.S. firms chosen on the basis of magnitude of total compensation; we were able to match firm data from *Compustat* for 814 firms.

We estimated several specifications of (23.6), depending on how much CEOPAY reflected contingent pay components. The *Forbes* survey separated total compensation into four categories: salary and bonuses, benefits, contingent remuneration, and stock options.[7] The data on COYRS, CEOYRS, and AGE were taken directly from *Forbes*. As a measure of firm size, we used the net sales figure from *Compustat*. Firm performance (FPERF) was measured by the average of the rates of return on equity for 1978, 1979, and 1980. More specifically, we calculated annual rates of return based on beginning-of-the year and end-of-the-year stock prices and on dividends paid during the year, and we averaged these rates over the three years prior to and including the year for which we had observations on CEOPAY. Finally, regulated firms were defined as public utilities. There were fifty-two public utilities in the sample.

The Results

For each of the alternative measures of CEOPAY, we estimated regression models with a complete set of regulation-interaction terms. None of the interaction terms was statistically significant. We subsequently dropped the interaction terms and computed the following least squares estimates.[8]

$$\begin{aligned} \text{CEOPAY1} = \; & \underset{(-7.85)}{-459.84} + \underset{(3.14)}{6.49}\text{CEOYRS} - \underset{(-2.46)}{0.17}(\text{CEOYRS})^2 \\ & - \underset{(-4.13)}{2.17}\text{COYRS} + \underset{(22.74)}{107.35}\text{SIZE} + \underset{(1.39)}{1.31}\text{AGE} \\ & + \underset{(1.75)}{50.51}\text{CTGPAY} + \underset{(4.67)}{87.24}\text{FPERF} - \underset{(-6.42)}{138.41}\text{D} \\ R^2 = \; & 45;\ \text{F-statistic} = 77.9;\ N = 814. \end{aligned} \tag{23.7a}$$

$$\begin{aligned} \text{CEOPAY2} = \; & \underset{(-7.56)}{-518.54} + \underset{(3.49)}{8.43}\text{CEOYRS} - \underset{(-2.77)}{0.23}(\text{CEOYRS})^2 \\ & - \underset{(-4.10)}{2.53}\text{COYRS} + \underset{(21.07)}{116.39}\text{SIZE} + \underset{(1.31)}{1.45}\text{AGE} \\ & + \underset{(2.52)}{85.13}\text{CTGPAY} + \underset{(4.73)}{103.32}\text{FPERF} - \underset{(-5.68)}{143.14}\text{D} \\ R^2 = \; & 42;\ \text{F-statistic} = 68.4;\ N = 814. \end{aligned} \tag{23.7b}$$

$$\begin{aligned} \text{CEOPAY3} = \; & \underset{(-7.52)}{-673.61} + \underset{(3.28)}{10.37}\text{CEOYRS} - \underset{(-2.62)}{0.28}(\text{CEOYRS})^2 \\ & - \underset{(-4.02)}{3.24}\text{COYRS} + \underset{(18.43)}{132.99}\text{SIZE} + \underset{(1.68)}{2.43}\text{AGE} \\ & + \underset{(9.64)}{426.49}\text{CTGPAY} + \underset{(3.11)}{88.78}\text{FPERF} - \underset{(-4.64)}{152.95}\text{D} \\ R^2 = \; & 42;\ \text{F-statistic} = 69.8;\ N = 814. \end{aligned} \tag{23.7c}$$

The first remarkable result is that the regressions uniformly explain a substantial amount of the variation in CEOPAY, and each of the regression coefficients is usually highly significant.

The major prediction of our model that CEO pay and company tenure are inversely related is corroborated. *Ceteris paribus*, and specifically holding CEOYRS constant, each year of company tenure reduces CEOPAY by \$2,170, \$2,530, and \$3,240, respectively. This is the central result for the informal contracting hypothesis.

The variables CEOYRS and $(\text{CEOYRS})^2$ have the predicted signs, with estimated crossover points at 12.7, 12.8, and 12.7 years.[9] This does not mean that informal contracting and rent capture do not occur until 12.7 years of CEO tenure. It means that, on average, it takes 12-plus years for the effects of informal contracting to overcome the effects of experience on the various forms of CEO pay.

The predictions about the effects of CEO experience (AGE), firm size (SIZE), and firm performance (FPERF) are also corroborated. In the case of size, we used two specifications, net sales and the natural logarithm of net sales. Assuming that changes in CEOPAY are proportional to percentage changes in firm sales has substantially more explanatory power than assuming sales has a linear effect on pay. The results reported in (23.7a), (23.7b), and (23.7c) are based on the logarithm of sales. The R^2 is as much as 50 percent lower when the linear specification is adopted. Firm performance as measured by the three-year average of annual rates of return on equity has a positive and statistically significant effect on CEOPAY. We also experimented with a model specification in which the three annual rates of return were jointly included as separate regressors. Typically, all three were not statistically signficant, but their overall contribution was about the same as the three-year average which we have reported.

We find that CTGPAY, which is defined as the ratio of contingent pay and stock options exercised to total CEO compensation, is significant in all three specifications. There is little surprise in discovering the substantial significance of CTGPAY in (23.7c), but apparently, judging by its coefficient size and significance in (23.7a) and (23.7b), contingent pay is heavily relied on to discipline managerial behavior.

The estimated coefficients of D reveal that regulation has a negative effect on CEOPAY which is independent of tenure and contingent pay. We interpret this to mean that there are several other control margins besides tenure and pay composition, the value of which is reduced by rate of return regulation. Furthermore, the magnitude of coefficients of D are noteworthy; *ceteris paribus*, managers in rate of return regulated firms receive on average approximately \$150,000 less pay than their counterparts in unregulated corporations.

Conclusion

Our model implies several relationships which are different from theories of corporate control articulated by Oliver Williamson (1975) and Williamson, Michael Wachter, and Jeffrey Harris (1975) and based on the concept of an internal labor market. First, the internal labor market theory suggests that in order to economize on the production of costly firm-specific information, firms will provide fewer ports of entry to outside managers in the higher eschelons of the management pyramid. While it is conceded that long periods of exposure in the office environment is an ideal way to gather valuable firm-specific information, it is also a fertile breeding ground for intermanager agreements which need not serve the interests of the firm. Our theory suggests that although hiring managers from the outside entails costs, the gains to hiring outside managers rises as one moves up the management hierarchy.

Second, our model implies that across firms at a fixed level in the management hierarchy, managerial compensation is inversely related to tenure. This proposition is contrary to that suggested by the internal labor market theory.

Third, our model implies that property rights, including rights of market access, affect the demand and supply of monitoring and control. In other words, differences in property rights may have a wealth or substitution effect, or both. For example, rate of return regulation reduces the value to shareholders of all methods of controlling managerial rent seeking without differentially affecting the cost of any one method. Thus, our model predicts that all control margins will be contracted in a regulated environment, including CEO tenure. As a consequence, managerial compensation will be lower in firms subject to rate of return regulation.

Ownership differences may also affect the costs of monitoring and control as well as the gains. Some margins of control will be differentially affected by ownership form. Consider, for example, the use of hiring policy and performance-based remuneration of management. It is easier to judge the performance of a firm when shareholders can transfer their shares than when shares are nontransferable. Consequently, judging the performance of managers will be more costly in a publicly owned than a privately owned firm. Our model predicts both a wealth and a substitution effect in this instance. For public firms, all margins of control are less valuable, but at the same time controlling management by hiring more frequently from the outside will be easier than controlling management with incentive pay schemes.

Although our empirical test is confined to assessing the effects of tenure on executive pay for regulated and unregulated U.S. corporations, we think our model has wider applicability. The competitiveness of the "markets" that affect organizational performance is linked to both the value and the cost of controlling managerial rent seeking. For example, business firms in Japan are noted for their paternalistic policies toward employees, and there is no highly developed external managerial labor market. Because of the high cost of utilizing an outside hiring policy to control managerial rent seeking, we observe the predictable use of substitutes. Compared to experience in U.S. corporations, executives in Japanese firms wind their way through *all* the firm's divisions as they climb up in the firm. Beside acquiring knowledge about the firm's operations, this policy assures that would-be CEOs have less opportunity and incentive to invest in informal contracts within a given division or functional part of the firm.

Our model also has implications for the behavior of nonprofit bureaucracies. The military, for example, has a policy of moving personnel around frequently. In this way opportunities for internal rent-seeking are reduced by limiting the potential development of friendship capital with subordinates. At first this appears to contradict our model and to support the internal labor market theory. However, our model predicts that in public organizations, both the value and cost of controlling rent seeking are affected. In some cases, the effect of public ownership is to raise the relative productivity of tenure as a means of control, even as the value of all methods of control is reduced.

Lest the reader infer that our model is tautological, we observe that in the case of the military, our model predicts that during wartime, when output is more easily monitored, there will be less movement of managerial personnel. Similarly, Christian church organizations vary between totalitarian centralism and individualistic atomism. In the Roman Catholic Church, there is more cross subsidization than there is in the Baptist Church, and hence monitoring of clerical rent seeking by parishioners is costly. Rent-seeking in hierarchial churches is controlled to a large extent by planned turnover of the local pastors. Within Congregational Churches, rent seeking is controlled more through tenure based on church-specific performance evaluation.

Notes

1. Benjamin Klein, Robert Crawford, and Alchian (1978) provide further analysis of the putative conflicting interests in agent-principal relations. They cite the role of appropriable quasi rents in creating incentives for *ex post* opportunistic behavior, and they highlight various

methods of market contract enforcement with an emphasis on vertical intergration. The cost of contracting and the limits of market contract enforcement are also major themes in Lester Telser's (1980) paper on self-enforcing agreements.

2. It is also important to note that because market participants are rational, management interests are also served by effective control devices. Rational investors will anticipate managerial discretion, and contracts governing managerial rewards will be adjusted to compensate for any anticipated exercise of expense preference by management.

3. Suppose that A, B, and C comprise a pool of inside candidates for a position at a higher level in the firm. Rather than compete for promotion by "overworking" or informing on the rent-seeking activities of others, the candidates may collude not to destroy the rents of one's former colleagues if they are promoted. The competition to be promoted will take place in terms of informal contracts that are made with one's colleagues in return for support in the internal reviews or audits necessary for promotion. These informal contracts can take many forms—larger raises in the future, better office and support facilities, increased subsequent influence in the firm, and so on. Alternatively, managers may trade damaging inside secrets about one another's rent-seeking behavior, with a commitment to blow the whistle on any manager (including the one promoted) who seeks to use similar information to improve his future promotion probabilities.

4. An alternative categorization of costs and benefits would treat the negative impact of greater outside hiring on informal contracting as an element of outside hiring costs. The destruction of the legitimate ability to communicate occasioned by management instability could be treated as depreciation of firm-specific capital.

5. Our model also predicts that managerial pay will be greater at all levels of management as the frequency of hiring outside managers increases because expected managerial rent appropriation falls throughout the firm. Further, lower-level managers will revise their *ex ante* expectations regarding promotion probabilities as the observed outside hiring rate increases. In order to prevent more than the optimal rate of voluntary turnover (quits), the firm will have to compensate existing and entering managers for the increased risk of slower promotion. However, the firm alternatively could compensate lower-level managers by reducing the size of internal candidate pools, thereby maintaining the probability of promotion and expected utility.

6. Attenuating property rights may have the effect of reducing the demand and supply of internal and external mechanisms for controlling managerial rent seeking. Moreover, the various control mechanisms may be affected differentially. In other words, there are "wealth" and "substitution" effects associated with attenuating property rights. In our model, we focus on the wealth effect; we analyze the effects of regulation as if the value of all control mechanisms were reduced.

7. Benefits include imputed monetary values for items such as club dues, company-paid life insurance premiums, and the value of past stock bonus awards which vested during the year. Contingent remuneration "includes the amounts expensed for deferred compensation agreements. . . under performance related long-term incentive plans" (*Forbes*. p. 114).

8. CEOPAY1 is salary and bonuses; CEOPAY2 is CEOPAY1 plus benefits; CEOPAY3 is CEOPAY2 plus contingent remuneration. We also estimated the regression coefficients in an equation for CEOPAY that included stock options and achieved results that are not very surprising or interesting. In this specification the SIZE and CTGPAY variables explained almost all of the variation in CEOPAY, and the significance of the remaining coefficients was drastically reduced. The primary reason for this result is that the stock options component comprises such a large percentage of total pay that CEOPAY3 plus stock options is naturally correlated with CTGPAY. Furthermore, on a priori grounds we are uninterested in

explaining variation in total compensation where the latter variable includes the realized value of stock options and not their price (i.e., their value *ex ante*).

9. The linear component of the marginal effect of CEOYRS on CEOPAY is not given simply by the coefficient on CEOYRS. The reason is that COYRs includes both company tenure as non-CEO and CEO. Thus, strictly speaking, we must add the coefficients of CEOYRs and COYRS to get the appropriate linear component. For example, to find the crossover point in (23.7a), we must solve the marginal condition, 2 × (0.17)CEOYRS = 6.49 − 2.17, for CEOYRS.

References

Alchian, A.A., and Demsetz, H. "Production, Information Costs, and Economic Organization." *American Economic Review* 62 (December, 1972): 777–95.

Coase, R.H. "The Nature of the Firm." *Economica* 4 (November, 1937): 386–405.

Fama, E.F. "Agency Problems and the Theory of the Firm." *Journal of Political Economy* 88 (April, 1980): 288–307.

Jensen, M.C. and Meckling, W.H. "Theory of the Firm: Managerial Behavior, Agency Costs, and Ownership Structure." *Journal of Financial Economics* 3 (October, 1976): 305–60.

Klein, B.; Crawford, R.G.; and Alchian, A.A. "Vertical Integration, Appropriable Rents, and the Competitive Contracting Process." *Journal of Law and Economics* 21 (October, 1978): 297–326.

Manne, H.G. "Mergers and the Market for Corporate Control. *Journal of Political Economy* 73 (April, 1965): 110–20.

Telser, L.G. "A Theory of Self-Enforcing Agreements." *Journal of Business* 53 (January, 1980): 27–44.

Williamson, O.E. *Markets and Hierarchies: Analysis and Antitrust Implications*. New York: The Free Press, 1975.

——; Wachter, M.C.; and Harris, J.E. "Understanding the Employment Relation: The Analysis of Idiosyncratic Exchange." *Bell Journal of Economics* 6 (Spring 1975): 250–78.

Forbes, June 8, 1981.

Standard and Poor's Compustat II Services, Inc., Compustat, 1980.

E *Taxation*

24 OPTIMAL TAXATION IN A RENT-SEEKING ENVIRONMENT

Dwight R. Lee and Robert D. Tollison

Introduction

A basic proposition in public finance is that, other things being equal, the less the price elasticity of demand for a good or service the smaller the welfare loss from imposing an excise tax on it. More generally, when considering the optimal pattern of excise taxes on a number of commodities, an inverse relation exists between the tax and the price elasticity of demand. This inverse relation holds in both partial equilibrium models (Hicks, 1947) and general equilibrium models (Baumol and Bradford, 1970; Sandmo, 1976).

It is the purpose of this paper to argue that the connection between the optimal pattern of excise taxes and demand elasticities is, to the contrary, quite tenuous. The standard analysis of taxation rests on a questionable assumption, but one which is so ingrained in the mindset of economists that it is seldom made explicit. The assumption is that the revenue raised by a tax is simply a transfer and is thus neutral with respect to economic efficiency. As taxpayers people are worse off, but as beneficiaries of government programs, they are better off. The only allocative distortion seen to result from the tax is represented in the welfare triangle, which the wedge of taxation prevents economic agents from exploiting. It is this excess burden of taxation which a regime of optimal taxes is aimed at minimizing, subject to a revenue requirement.

Rent-seeking will be included in a model of excise taxation in this paper.[1] As a preliminary step, we present an optimal taxation model with the assumption that the supply curve is horizontal. Next, the implications of rent-seeking for the optimal tax pattern are examined; the case where marginal costs are increasing in output is developed, and the efficiency implications of excise taxation and rent-seeking in both a competitive and monopoly environment are considered. No claim is made for the sophistication of the model, since indeed it is developed in a very simple partial equilibrium setting. Such a setting, however, is adequate for the purpose of pointing out that the standard view on the relation between optimal taxation and demand elasticities rests on a naive view of political behavior. Some concluding remarks are offered in section 5.

A Conventional Model

It is assumed that n goods are subject to an excise tax, with each good supplied at a constant marginal cost and priced accordingly. Therefore, if the per unit tax on good i is T_i, the price of i will increase from the constant P_i to $P_i + T_i$. The demand for good i will be given by the function $Q_i = Q_i(P_i + T_i)$. The excess burden imposed by excise taxes T_i, $i = 1, \ldots, n$ is given by

$$\sum_{i=1}^{n}\left[\int_{P_i}^{P_i+T_i} Q_i(\tau)\,d\tau - T_iQ_i(P_i + T_i)\right]. \tag{24.1}$$

The objective of optimal taxation is to choose the pattern T_i which minimizes (24.1) subject to the tax revenue constraint, or

$$\sum_{i=1}^{n} T_iQ_i = R. \tag{24.2}$$

Ignoring the extraneous complexity of corner solutions, the necessary conditions for this minimization are

$$T_i\frac{dQ_i}{dT_i} + \lambda\left[T_i\frac{dQ_i}{dT_i} + Q_i\right] = 0,\ i = 1, \ldots, n \tag{24.3}$$

where λ is the Lagrangian multiplier arising from constraint (24.2) and represents the marginal cost, in terms of excess burden, of increasing tax revenue. With a little manipulation equation (24.3) can be rewritten as

$$\lambda = -(1 + \lambda)\frac{T_i}{Q_i}\frac{dQ_i}{dT_i}, \; i = 1, \ldots, n \tag{24.4}$$

which can be expressed as

$$E_i = \frac{\lambda}{1 + \lambda}, \tag{24.5}$$

where $E_i = -\frac{T_i}{Q_i}\frac{dQ_i}{dT_i}$ is the tax elasticity of demand for good i.[2]

Since λ is independent of i, condition (24.5) requires that the tax elasticity of demand be the same for all goods. This is easy to interpret as yet another version of the inverse elasticity rule which is a standard result of the optimal tax literature (Lerner, 1970).

This equalized tax elasticity rule finds inelastically demanded commodities attracting more taxation than elastically demanded commodities, which follows from the fact that any violation of (23.5) calls for shifting taxation from the latter commodities to the former. If the tax portion of the demand curve is less elastic for good i than it is for good j, then, assuming the same pre-tax quantities for both goods, the optimal tax on good i will be higher than on good j.[3]

In the case of linear demand curves the uniform tax elasticity condition implies that the tax pattern be such that the amount demanded of each commodity be reduced by the same proportion of the pre-tax quantity.[4] In the general, non-linear case this proportional decrease result holds only when an arbitrarily small amount of tax revenue is required, since only in this case are changes in quantity demanded sufficiently small that linear approximations of the demand curves are justified. This result is known in the optimal tax literature as the Ramsey rule (Ramsey, 1927; Sandmo, 1976).

Another implication of (24.5) concerns the limits on increasing tax revenue. As the marginal cost of tax revenue approaches ∞, the tax elasticity of demand for each commodity approaches 1. This result has obvious intuitive plausibility since it becomes impossible (infinitely costly) to raise more tax revenue once the tax elasticity of demand for all commodities has been increased to unity.

Excise Taxation and Rent-Seeking

We now introduce rent-seeking into the above model of optimal taxation and examine the resulting implications. Because of rent-seeking, some proportion of the burden (both the revenue payment and the excess burden) imposed by a tax will be wasted through political efforts to lighten the burden or keep it from increasing further. We let γ_i, where $0 \leq \gamma_i \leq 1$, represent the proportion of the burden imposed by tax i that is wasted by rent-seeking activities. The social cost resulting from taxes T_i is now given by adding the following expression to (24.1):

$$\sum_{i=1}^{n}\left[\gamma_i \int_{P_i}^{P_i+T_i} Q_i(\tau)\,d\tau\right],$$

which yields

$$\sum_{i=1}^{n}\left[(1+\gamma_i)\int_{P_i}^{P_i+T_i} Q_i(\tau)\,d\tau - T_iQ_i\right]. \tag{24.6}$$

The objective is to minimize (24.6) with respect to the T_i, subject to constraint (24.2).

Considering in this case the possibility of corner solutions, the necessary conditions to this minimization problem are given by

$$(1+\gamma_i)Q_i - (1+\lambda)Q_i - (1+\lambda)T_i\frac{dQ_i}{dT_i} \geq 0 \tag{24.7}$$

where λ remains the marginal cost, now in terms of both excess burden and rent seeking, of increasing tax revenue. With a slight amount of manipulation (24.7) can be rewritten as

$$E_i \geq \frac{\lambda - \gamma_i}{1+\lambda},\ i = 1, \ldots, n \tag{24.8}$$

where, as before,

$$E_i = -\frac{T_i}{Q_i}\frac{dQ_i}{dT_i}$$

is the tax elasticity of demand for good i. If the strict inequality holds, for example, because $\lambda < \gamma_i$, then (24.8) calls for $T_i = 0$.[5] Obviously, the larger the rent-seeking cost that is associated with a tax on a particular commodity, the more likely the optimal tax on that commodity will equal zero. This opens the possibility that a commodity with a demand curve which is quite inelastic should not be taxed, while a commodity with a demand curve which is quite elastic would be taxed. Even in the absence of corner solutions, the possibility now exists that the optimal tax pattern will find the tax to be less on the inelastically demanded product than on the elastically demanded one.

In figure 24–1, an example is illustrated for two of the n commodities,

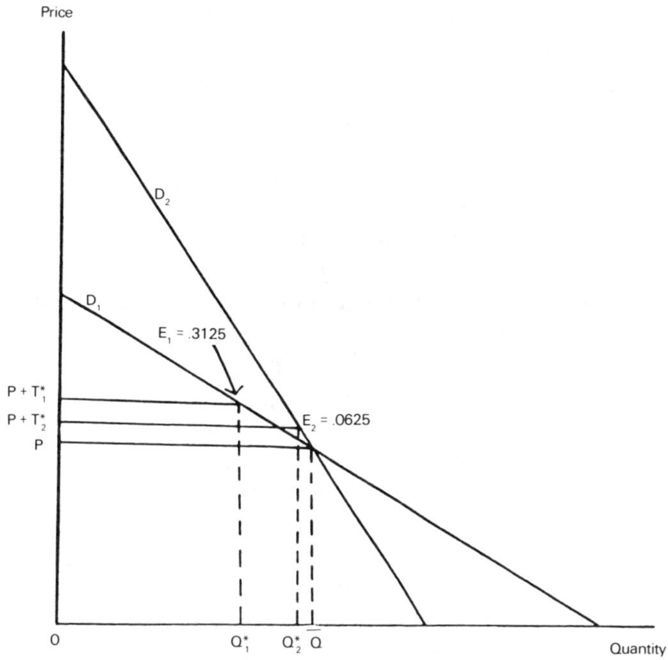

Figure 24–1

1 and 2. The demand curves for commodities 1 and 2 are given by D_1 and D_2, respectively. As constructed, the pre-tax price and quantity, P and Q, are the same for both commodities. In order to be as realistic as possible with respect to parameter values, we turn to several studies on the marginal excess burden cost of commodity taxation. Assuming no influence on labor supply, Browning (1976) estimated the marginal excess burden cost of excise taxes in the United States at .26. This is similar to the .24 estimate in Campbell's (1975) study of commodity taxes in Canada. More recently, Ballard, Shoven, and Whalley (1985) estimated the marginal excess burden cost of consumer sales taxes in the U.S. at .256 (assuming no effect on savings and labor supply). So a reasonable estimate for the λ (considered as just the cost of the excess burden) is .25.

Given this estimate, we now arbitrarily assume that the marginal rent-seeking cost associated with the optimal taxation of all n commodities is .35, which yields a value of .60 for λ in the rent-seeking model. It is further assumed that $\gamma_1 = .1$ and $\gamma_2 = .5$.

With these parameter values and condition (24.8), which holds as a strict equality for commodities 1 and 2, we obtain $E_1 = .3125$ and $E_2 = .0625$. With the linear demand curves D_1 and D_2 in figure 24–1, this requires that T_1 reduce the quantity demanded of commodity 1 by 31.25 percent of the post-tax quantity, and T_2 reduce the quantity demanded of commodity 2 by 6.25 percent of the post-tax quantity. These post-tax quantities are shown in figure 24.1 at Q_1^* and Q_2^*, respectively.

The taxes on commodities 1 and 2 which yield these post-tax quantities are shown at T_1^* and T_2^*. The important thing to notice is that $T_1^* > T_2^*$, or the optimal pattern of excise taxes requires the lower tax on the relatively inelastically demanded tax base. Obviously, this example only shows the possibility that the size of social cost minimizing excise taxes can be related positively with demand elasticity. While this possibility is not particularly surprising once one recognizes the costs of rent-seeking, it is a possibility worth notice given the long standing acceptance of the proposition that under the most general conditions the optimal excise tax is inversely related to demand elasticity.

For our confounding result to materialize, rent-seeking has to be more pronounced for inelastically demanded than for elastically demanded commodities. It is not unreasonable to expect this to be the case. Purchasers of inelastically demanded products are more vulnerable to exploitation by increased commodity taxation (and have more to gain from reduced commodity taxation) than are consumers of elastically demanded products. Therefore, lobbying against increases or for reduction in excise taxes can be expected to be more intense the less elastic the demand for the product being taxed.

A final observation on the implications of condition (24.8) points to a situation in which there is no effective difference between a setting characterized by rent seeking and a setting without rent seeking. Consider a Leviathan government which has the objective of maximizing its take from taxation. In this case the authorities will continue to raise tax revenue as long as the marginal social cost, λ, of doing so is finite. Political equilibrium occurs when $\lambda = \infty$, which, as can be seen from (24.8), implies that $E_i = 1$ for all i. As in the case without rent-seeking, tax revenues are maximized when the tax elasticity of demand is unity for all commodities. Given a Leviathan model of government, all social costs associated with raising tax revenue, including rent-seeking costs, are ignored, so not surprisingly the difference between the models developed in sections 2 and 3 disappears.

Because of the simplifying assumption that all goods are supplied competitively at constant marginal costs, the burden of taxation in the present model falls entirely on consumers, a group which typically is considered not to be organized for effective political action because its interests are diffused. The current model has more force if one considers the possibility of concentrated input purchasers resisting excise taxation. However, a more realistic model allowing for producer surplus would strengthen our results. In the next section a model of excise taxation in which the marginal cost curve is upward sloping is developed.

Increasing Marginal Cost and Monopoly

The standard analysis of an excise tax is presented in figure 24–2. Demand curves, D_I and D_E, are relatively inelastic and elastic, respectively, at any given quantity. MC is an upward sloping marginal cost curve common to both demand curves. P and Q are the pre-tax price and quantity for both

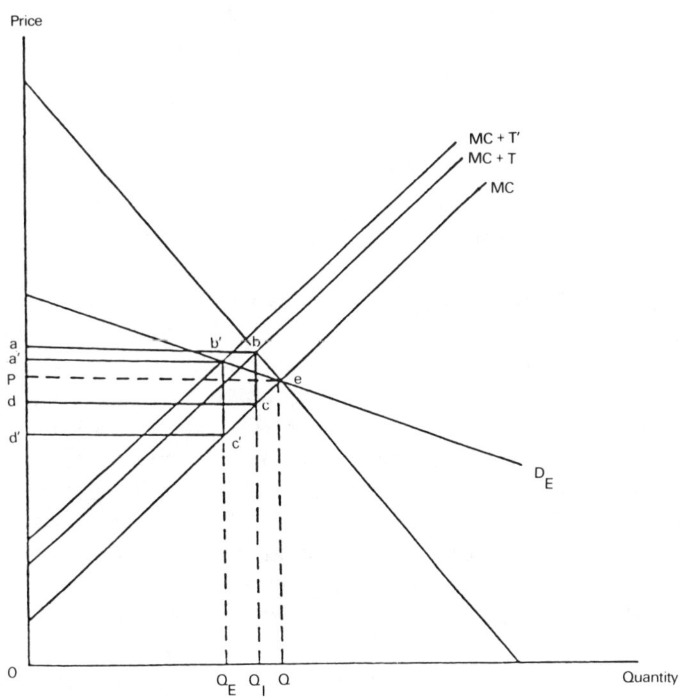

Figure 24–2

demand situations. Along D_I an excise tax of T will raise revenue equal to *abcd* and impose an excess burden of *bec*. Along D_E, a tax of $T' > T$ is required to raise $a'b'c'd' = abcd$ in revenue. Excess burden in this case equals $b'ec'$. Since $b'c' > bc$ and $Q_EQ > Q_IQ$, $b'ec' >$ bec; the excess burden is greater along D_E than along D_I.

Rent-seeking with Well-specified Demand and Supply Curves

Assume that the industry facing D_I has organized to lobby against the tax and that the industry facing D_E has not. This means that industry I will spend resources to avoid the loss of producer surplus caused by the tax, and industry E will not. In order to simplify the analysis we invoke the standard argument about the high costs of organizing the diverse interests of consumers and assume that the loss of consumer surplus will motivate no opposition to the tax in either industry.

Under these assumptions, what is the social cost of the excise tax in industry I? The traditional analysis establishes an excess burden of *bec*. Rent-seeking implies that in addition the industry could spend as much as *pecd* (the lost producer surplus) to avoid the tax. Thus, in the limit the tax imposes a social cost of *bec* + *pecd* on industry I.[6] Our main result is thus clear: In figure 24–2, $bec + pecd > b'ec'$. This means that rent-seeking causes the social cost of an excise tax which raises the same revenue to be greater in the inelastic than the elastic demand curve case.

This result depends on the assumption that industry I is organized and industry E is not. Our rationale for this assumption comes from the theory of cartels. The likelihood that an industry will organize for the purpose of acting collectively depends on the costs and benefits of doing so. An important influence on the cost of organizing is the number of firms in the industry. There is no clear basis for predicting how this consideration will vary as between industry I and industry E. On the benefit side, however, there is a clear difference in the position of the two industries. The industry with the more inelastic demand curve can realize relatively more profits by reducing output and behaving like a monopolist. So it is not at all unreasonable to expect industry I to be organized, and although it may be organized for some other reason, such as cartelization, a by-product of its organization will be an ability and interest in lobbying against taxes on industry wealth. The differences between two industries with respect to lobbying is surely more pronounced than the lobbying differences between the consumers of industry I's product and the consumers of industry E's product. It is true that the consumers of I will have more to gain from lobbying against the tax on I than consumers of E will have to argue against the tax on E. But the difference in motivation will more likely be swamped by considerations of organization costs in the case of consumers than in the case of producers.

Monopoly

An objection can be raised that if industry I is organized to exploit the inelastic demand curve it faces, the above analysis is not relevant, since it begins from a pre-tax situation in which both industries are operating where marginal cost equals price. In the case of an industry I cartel, the analysis must incorporate the marginal revenue curve to D_I. Under these circumstances, however, the result obtained earlier is strengthened, because it is easily shown that the introduction of monopoly increases the social cost of an excise tax.

In figure 24–3, we consider the same demand curve, D_I, and marginal cost curve, MC, as given in figure 24–2. We also show the effect of imposing an excise tax of T on the pre-tax competitive equilibrium where $P = MC$, just as we did earlier. How does the result in the competitive case compare to the situation where industry I acts as a monopolist, i.e., operates where $MC = MR$ with an output of Q_M and a price of P_M? It now takes an excise tax of $T_M (T_M > T)$ to raise the same revenue as excise tax T raised in the competitive setting; that is, *pfgh* = *abcd*. The excess burden associated with the tax, T_M, is given by *jkmg*, which is significantly greater than the excess burden of *bec* associated with the tax, T. Even though the monopoly output is less responsive to an excise tax than the competitive output (the MR curve is steeper than D_I), the larger excess burden is explained by the fact that (1) the required excise tax is larger in the monopoly setting, and (2) the distortion generated by T_M begins with $P > MR$ because of the pre-existing monopoly distortion.

The maximum amount of rent-seeking cost the monopolist would be willing to incur to oppose the tax is given by *hfmgi* in figure 24–2, which is more than the maximum amount that would be spent if the industry were acting as if it were competitive (*pecd*). It follows, then, that the total social cost associated with the monopoly excise tax, T_M, is greater than the total social cost associated with the competitive excise tax, T.[7]

Therefore, the fact that industry I was motivated to organize for the purpose of exploiting the monopoly profit potential of the inelastic demand for its product reinforces our result. Once it is recognized that transfers can beget rent-seeking, the well-accepted proposition that excise taxes should

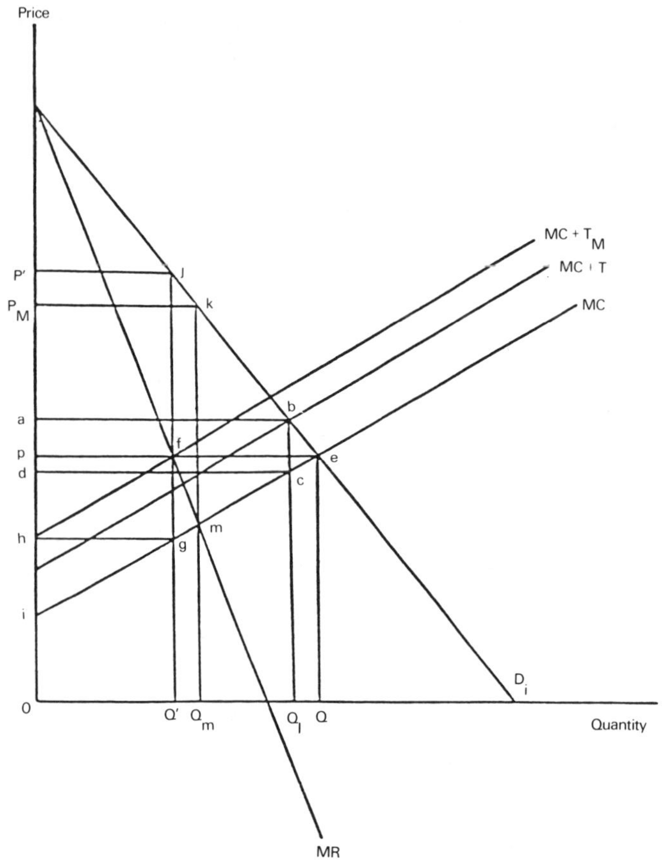

Figure 24–3

be imposed on inelastically rather than elastically demanded products may not be true. The distinct possibility exists that the entire social cost (excess burden plus rent-seeking cost) of an excise tax will be greater when applied to a product with an inelastic demand curve than to a product with an elastic demand curve.

Conclusion

In the context of a model of optimal excise taxation, we have looked at the implications of an important but almost entirely overlooked factor in the social cost of taxation—rent-seeking. Once it is recognized that the private burdens imposed by taxation may motivate resource-using political activities either to reduce this burden or to prevent it from being made heavier, a basic proposition in public finance theory is called into question. In particular, the well known inverse elasticity rule which calls for concentrating excess taxation on inelastically demanded commodities in order to minimize the social cost of acquiring a given amount of tax revenue is altered by the existence of rent seeking. Rent-seeking increases the marginal social cost of excise taxation across commodities in such a way as to confound the traditional result. It can easily follow that the correct pattern of excises is to tax relatively more elastic demand curves first.

It is easy to conceive of more complicated models than the ones developed here. No doubt putting our model in a general equilibrium setting or considering non-zero cross elasticities would change the particulars of our results. But there can be no doubt that the introduction of rent-seeking into any model of optimal taxation will undermine many of the normative propositions which public finance specialists have come to accept in their roles as economic theorists and policy advisors. For example, from the point of view of welfare economics, the specific taxation of such commodities as cigarettes and liquor may not be appropriate.[8]

Notes

* We are grateful to James M. Buchanan and Gordon Tullock for helpful comments. Faults are our own.

1. Contributions to the rent seeking literature are collected in Buchanan, Tollison, and Tullock (1980), and Colander (1984).

2. The tax elasticity of demand for good i is the same as the price elasticity of demand for that portion of the demand curve over the horizontal line at P_i which will be referred to as the tax portion of the demand curve.

3. Here we would have to be measuring the quantity of all commodities in terms of the same units, say pounds. This is, of course, not necessary for condition (24.4), but it does assist in the interpretation.

4. This follows directly from the fact that, in the linear case, the price elasticity of demand at any quantity is equal to the distance from that quantity to the horizontal intercept of the demand curve divided by the quantity. If, for example the common tax elasticity of demand is 1/2, then the post-tax quantity demanded of each good will be 1/3 less than the intercept (pre-tax) quantity.

5. The right hand side of (24.8) does not have to be negative for T_i to equal zero; it just has to be less than the tax elasticity of demand for commodity i at $T_i = 0$.

6. While it may appear that we are double counting here, this is not the case. The excess burden, *bec*, and the value of the resources devoted to rent seeking, *pecd*, are both separate social costs, even though they overlap graphically at *bec*.

7. We omit antitrust considerations from our analysis. The monopoly situation that we

discuss can be seen as analogous to the behavior of a highly concentrated industry that is legitimate under prevailing antitrust laws. The issue of whether one should tax such industries is therefore relevant.

8. Note also that our analysis leads to larger potential gains from the abolition of certain excises. If the tobacco industry, for example, spends $50 million each year to oppose prevailing excise taxes on its products, abolition of these taxes not only recoups the usual deadweight costs but also the present value of the $50 million spent on rent protection each year.

References

Ballard, L.; Shoven, B.; and Whalley, J. "General Equilibrium Computations of the Marginal Welfare Costs of Taxes in the United States." *The American Economic Review* 75 (March, 1985): 128–38.

Baumol, W.J.; and Bradford, D.F. "Optimal Departures From Marginal Cost Pricing." *American Economic Review* 60 (June, 1970): 265–83.

Browning, E.K. "The Marginal Cost of Public Funds." *Journal of Political Economy* 84 (April, 1976): 283–98.

Buchanan, J.M., and Brennan, H.G. *The Power to Tax*. Cambridge: Cambridge University Press, 1980.

Buchanan, J.M.; Tollison, R.D.; and Tullock, G. (eds.) *Toward a Theory of the Rent-Seeking Society*. College Station: Texas A&M University Press, 1980.

Campbell, H. "Deadweight Loss and Commodity Taxation in Canada." *Canadian Journal of Economics* 8 (August, 1975): 441–46.

Colander, D.C. (ed.) *Neoclassical Political Economy: The Analysis of Rent-Seeking and DUP Activities* Cambridge, MA: Ballinger Publishing Company, 1984.

Hicks, U.S. *Public Finance*. Cambridge: Cambridge University Press, 1947.

Lerner, A.P. "On Optimal Taxes with An Untaxable Sector." *American Economic Review* 60 (June, 1970): 284–94.

Ramsey, F.P. "A Contribution to the Theory of Taxation." *Economic Journal* 37 (March, 1927): 47–61.

Sandmo, A. "Optimal Taxation: An Introduction to the Literature." *Journal of Public Economics* 6 (July/August, 1976): 37–54.

Tullock, G. "The Welfare Costs of Tariffs, Monopolies, and Theft." *Western Economic Journal* 5 (June, 1967): 224–32.

F *The Environment*

25 RENT-SEEKING AND ITS IMPLICATIONS FOR POLLUTION TAXATION*

Dwight R. Lee

Introduction

One of the fundamental insights gained from the study of economics comes from an understanding of how market prices, arising from private property and exchange, can motivate efficient responses to the problem of scarcity. Not surprisingly, when private property rights and market exchange are deemed not to be feasible, for either technological or political reasons, economists have overwhelmingly recommended that politically imposed prices be employed as surrogates for market prices. The most extensively discussed example of this in the literature is the use of pollution taxation as a means of motivating polluters to take the full cost of their polluting activities into account.[1]

There are important differences, of course, between politically imposed prices and market prices, and these differences need to be considered when assessing the desirability of imposing any tax incentive program. In the

---

* The comments of an anonymous referee were helpful in the preparation of this paper. Any mistakes, of course, are the sole responsibility of the author.

absence of market exchange, for example, information crucial to choosing the appropriate price simply is not available. In the case of pollution control the best that can be done is to arrive at a politically acceptable level of pollution and to realize that level as efficiently as possible.[2] An effective way of realizing this limited efficiency, according to much of the literature, is by imposing the pollution tax that discourages pollution beyond the politically acceptable level.[3] Another problem, however, is that many political objectives can be realized by establishing "acceptable" pollution standards and many of them have little to do with protecting the environment.[4]

In this paper the problems of determining the charge that is conventionally considered to be efficient and getting the political process to impose it, will be ignored. This allows full attention to be devoted to another problem with political prices in general, and pollution taxation in particular, that has received no attention as far as this author is aware. This problem arises from a fundamental difference between a politically imposed price and a market price that has important implications for the efficiency of political prices. Simply stated, a market price generates revenue that is privately owned while a political price generates revenue that is commonly owned.

The claimants against revenues raised by market prices are generally well-specified, as is the extent of their claims. This is not true with revenue raised by government through political prices. Additional monies raised by government generally go into the common pool of general revenue. The allocation of these revenues among rival interests is determined through competition for political influence, a competition which requires the use of real resources. To a large extent this represents pure waste, since what is being motivated is zero-sum, rather than positive-sum, competition.

It is true that not all of the cost associated with this zero-sum, or rent-seeking, behavior represents pure waste. Some of what is perceived as cost by rent seekers will be, from a broader perspective, a costless transfer. But the setting within which the distribution of political benefits are determined will typically motivate a significant amount of resource dissipation, rather than resource transfer, and will therefore be waste.

The rent-seeking waste that is generated by the revenues raised through political prices has obvious implications for the efficiency of pollution taxes. The purpose of this paper is to analyze these implications in some detail. In the next section a simple model of efficient pollution taxation will be developed under the assumption that some proportion of the pollution tax revenue raised will be wasted through rent-seeking. In section 3, particular cases will be investigated with graphical analysis guided by the conditions developed in section 2. It will be shown that the efficient pollution tax may be either above or below the tax conventionally accepted as efficient. The potential importance of the total benefits relative to the total costs of unrestrained pollution in determining the efficient pollution tax will be examined in section 4. Some concluding remarks are offered in section 5.

A Rent-Seeking Model of Pollution Taxation

In order to abstract from problems that are extraneous to the primary concern of this paper, it will be assumed that complete information is given on the marginal benefit and marginal cost curves associated with pollution. Under this assumption, there is no need to experiment with different tax rates in order to realize an acceptable pollution level. The efficient pollution level, as conventionally determined, is immediately given by the intersection between the two marginal curves, and the full force of self-interest is brought to bear in achieving this level of pollution by imposing the marginal pollution tax which is also determined by this intersection. Even under these ideal conditions, however, there are still problems encountered with the use of pollution taxation. For example, the marginal cost curve may shift rather dramatically due to changes in the assimilative capacity of the environment and sudden adjustments in the pollution tax will be called for. There is also the enforcement problem of making sure that polluters do not evade the tax. But these are problems that have received at least brief attention elsewhere,[5] and they will be ignored here.

The concern of this paper revolves around the question: what happens to the revenue that will be raised by a pollution tax? On the one hand it may seem surprising that this question has not been considered since any serious attempt to confront pollution with pollution taxes would generate enormous revenues.[6] Yet it is not surprising that economists have failed to concern themselves with the efficiency implications of these revenues given the conventional view that tax payments are nothing more than transfers of wealth with no significance for efficiency. This widespread but politically naive view ignores the fundamental insight of the rent-seeking literature: in the political arena there is no such thing as a free transfer.

It is with this background that a rent-seeking model of pollution taxation is justified. Proceeding with the development of this model, we let the private benefits from polluting at rate P be given by function B(P). The marginal benefit from polluting is positive over the interval $(0, \bar{P})$, and decreasing throughout: $B'(P) > 0$, $0 \leq P < \bar{P}$, and $B''(P) < 0$. The pollution cost, which is external to those doing the polluting, is given by

C(P), and this cost is increasing in P at an increasing rate; $C'(P) > 0$ and $C''(P) > 0$. Faced with a tax on emissions of T per unit, polluters will respond by reducing pollution until

$$B'(P) = T. \tag{25.1}$$

Equation (25.1) establishes P as a function of T, P(T), with

$$dP/dT = 1/B'' < 0. \tag{25.2}$$

The revenue raised through this pollution tax, TP(T), will motivate rent-seeking activity, and δ is used to represent the proportion of the revenue wasted by this activity.

Determining the efficiency pollution tax, given these considerations, requires choosing the T that maximizes

$$B(P(T)) - C(P(T)) - \delta TP(T). \tag{25.3}$$

The efficient tax. T*, necessarily satisfies the condition

$$[B'(P) - C'(P)](dP/dT) - \delta[T(dP/dT) + P(T)] \leq 0. \tag{25.4}$$

This necessary condition can be usefully rewritten by dividing through by dP/dT and transposing terms to obtain,

$$C'(P) - B'(P) \leq -\delta[T + P(T)(dT/dP)]. \tag{25.4'}$$

The left hand side of (25.4′) equals the gain realized from a tax increase sufficient to reduce the pollution rate by one unit. The bracketed term on the right hand side is the marginal tax revenue associate with an increase in the pollution rate, and thus this term time $-\delta$ represents the rent-seeking waste when the pollution rate is reduced one unit.[7] If necessary condition (25.4′) holds as an inequality, the marginal benefit from reducing the pollution below $\bar{P}$ (where $B'(\bar{P}) = 0$) is less than the marginal rent-seeking waste from doing so, and the efficient tax is zero. If the efficient tax is positive, then (25.4′) holds as an equality with the marginal benefit and marginal rent-seeking waste from reducing pollution equal.

The second-order, or sufficient, condition for the maximization of (25.3) will play an important role in subsequent analysis. The sufficient condition in the present model is satisfied when the derivative of (25.4), with respect to T, is negative, or

$$[B''(P) - C''(P)](dP/dT)^2 - 2\delta(dP/dT) + [B'(P) - C'(P) - \delta T](d^2P/dT^2) < 0. \tag{25.5}$$

This condition, and the subsequent analysis, will be greatly simplified by assuming that the marginal benefit curve is a straight line, which implies

$d^2P/dT^2 - 0$. with this assumption, and using (25.2) to substitute for dP/dT condition (25.5) can be rewritten

$$1 - 2\delta > C''/B''. \tag{25.6}$$

Making the additional assumption that the marginal cost curve is also a straight line, the right hand side of (25.6) is a negative constant, K, and we can express the sufficient condition

$$1 - 2\delta > C''/B'' = K < 0. \tag{25.6'}$$

Graphical Analysis of Particular Cases

The efficient pollution tax, as determined by the conditions developed in the previous section, can be greater than or less than the tax conventionally considered to be efficient; the tax determined by the intersection between B″(P) and C′(P). The easiest way of establishing the range of possibilities is by considering different cases with the aid of graphical analysis.

Case 1

$$B(P) = C'(P) \text{ when } P > 1/2\bar{P}, \text{ where } B'(\bar{P}) = 0.$$

In this case the intersection between B′(P) (the demand for pollution) and C′(P) occurs where the tax elasticity of demand for pollution, ϵ_T, is less than unity.[8] While there is no limit to possible subcases that could be considered here, it will be shown in the appendix that the only important consideration for our purpose concerns the elasticity of B′(P) when it intersects C′(P). Therefore, without any important loss of generality, it is assumed that the slopes of B′(P) and C′(P) are equal in absolute value (K = −1), and that C′(P) = 0 when P = 1/4$\bar{P}$. This case is shown in figure 25–1. With K = −1, it follows from (25–6′) that the sufficient condition will be satisfied for all realistic values of δ. As long as not all tax revenue is wasted as a consequence of rent-seeking (δ< 1), inequality (25.6′) is satisfied.

The marginal revenue from the pollution tax is shown as MR(P) in figure 25–1. For all P ≥ 1/2$\bar{P}$, the absolute value of this marginal revenue, −MR(P), is the additional revenue that will be raised when a tax increase reduces pollution by a marginal unit. Assuming a δ of 3/4, for example, it follows that the marginal rent-seeking cost of reducing pollution below $\bar{P}$ is given by −3/4 MR($\bar{P}$). As is shown in figure 25–1, in the case under consideration this marginal rent-seeking cost is exactly equal to the

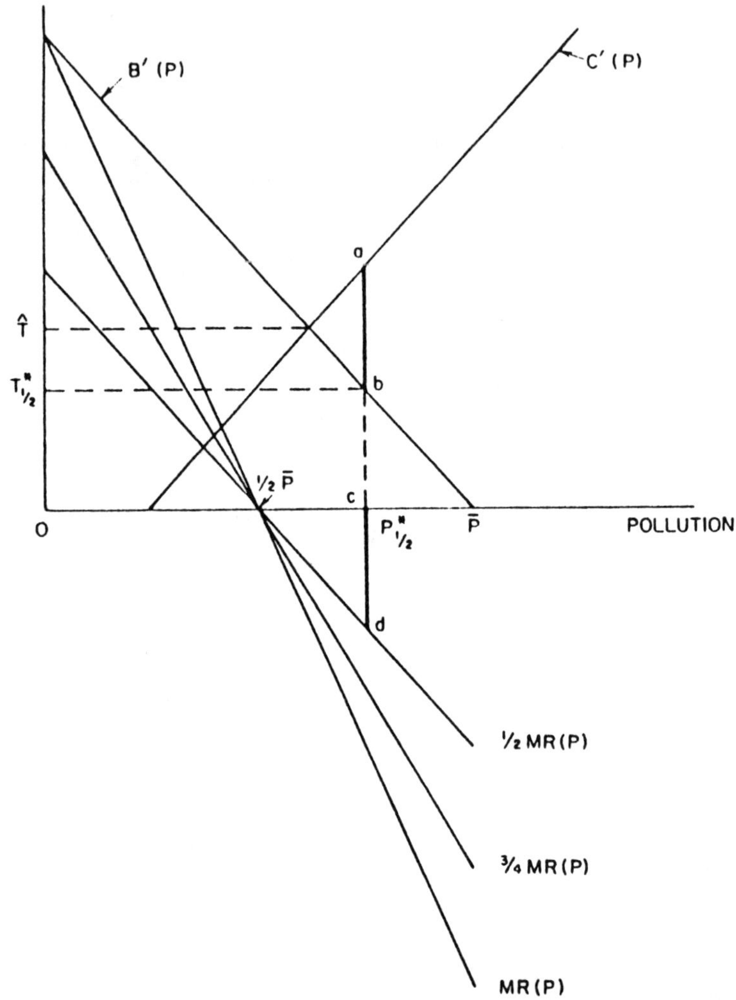

Figure 25–1

marginal benefit from reducing pollution below $\bar{P}$; $C'(\bar{P}) = -3/4MR(\bar{P})$. In this subcase the necessary condition (25.4′) is satisfied as an equality and the efficient tax is given by the corner solution, $T^* = 0$. For any $\delta > 3/4$, the corner solution is still called for, with condition (25.4′) being satisfied as an inequality. Only when $\delta < 3/4$ will there be an interior solution with $T^* > 0$.

For example, if $\delta = 1/2$ it is seen from figure 25–1 that $C'(\bar{P}) > -1/2\,MR(\bar{P})$, and the marginal benefit from reducing pollution by increasing the tax above zero exceeds the marginal rent-seeking cost from doing so. This remains true until the tax has been increased to $T^*_{1/2}$ and pollution has been reduced to $P^*_{1/2}$, at which point $C'(P) - B'(P) = -1/2\,MR(P)$ (the distances *ab* and *cd* in figure 25–1 are equal). It is easily seen that the lower the proportion of tax revenue wasted through rent-seeking activity, the higher the efficient pollution tax. But only if $\delta = 0$ will the efficient tax be determined by the intersection $B'(P)$ and $C'(P)$. In all other cases, the efficient pollution tax is lower then that conventionally considered efficient; represented as $\hat{T}$ in figure 25–1.

Case 2

$$B'(P) = C'(P) \text{ when } P = 1/2\bar{P}$$

In this case the intersection between $B'(P) = C'(P)$ occurs where $\epsilon_T = 1$. It is again assumed that the horizontal intercept of $C'(P)$ occurs at $P = 1/4\bar{P}$. In order to satisfy the elasticity condition assumed in this case, the slope of $C'(P)$ has to exceed the absolute value of the slope $B'(P)$. This being the case, $K < -1$, and the sufficient condition (6′) will be satisfied for all reasonable values of δ; i.e., $\delta \leq 1$. As seen in figure 25–2; $C'(P) - B'(P) > -\delta MR(P)$ for all $\delta \leq 1$ as long as $P > 1/2\bar{P}$, and the marginal gain from increasing the tax is positive. At $P = 1/2\bar{P}$, $C'(P) - B'(P) = -\delta MR(P)$ for all δ and the objective function (3) is maximized by the tax conventionally considered efficient, $T = \hat{T}$.

Case 3

$$B'(P) = C'(P) \text{ when } P < 1/2\,\bar{P}$$

In this case the intersection between $B'(P) = C'(P)$ occurs where $\epsilon_T > 1$. The $B'(P)$ curve in figure 25–3 is the same as in the two previous figures, but, still without loss of generality, the $C'(P)$ curve is assumed to have a vertical intercept equal to $1/2\bar{T}$, where $B'(0) = \bar{T}$, and the slope of $C'(P)$ is 1/4 the absolute value of the slope of $B'(P)$; $K = -1/4$.

Consider first a δ of 3/4. As can be seen in figure 25–3, under the above assumptions the pollution rate $\bar{P}$ satisfies the necessary condition (25.4′) as an equality; $C'(\bar{P}) = -3/4\,MR(\bar{P})$. But with $K = -1/4$, it follows from (25.6′) that the sufficient condition is not satisfied unless

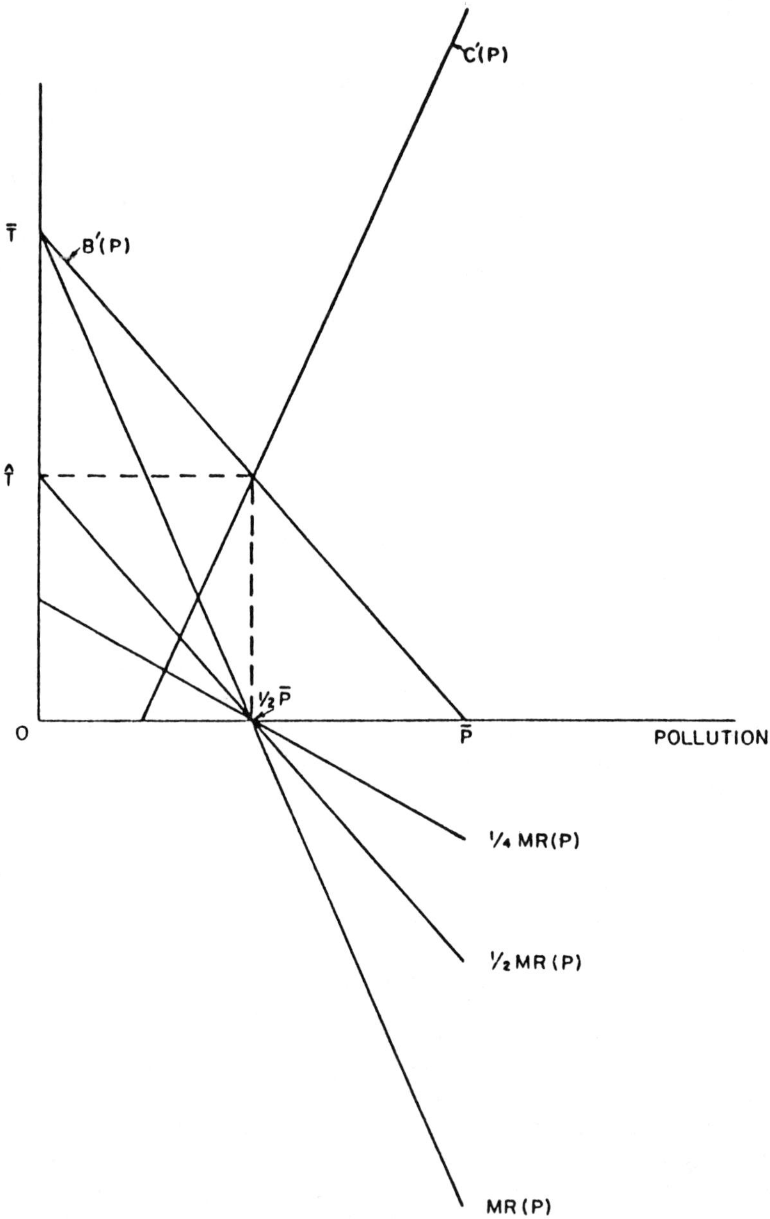

Figure 25–2

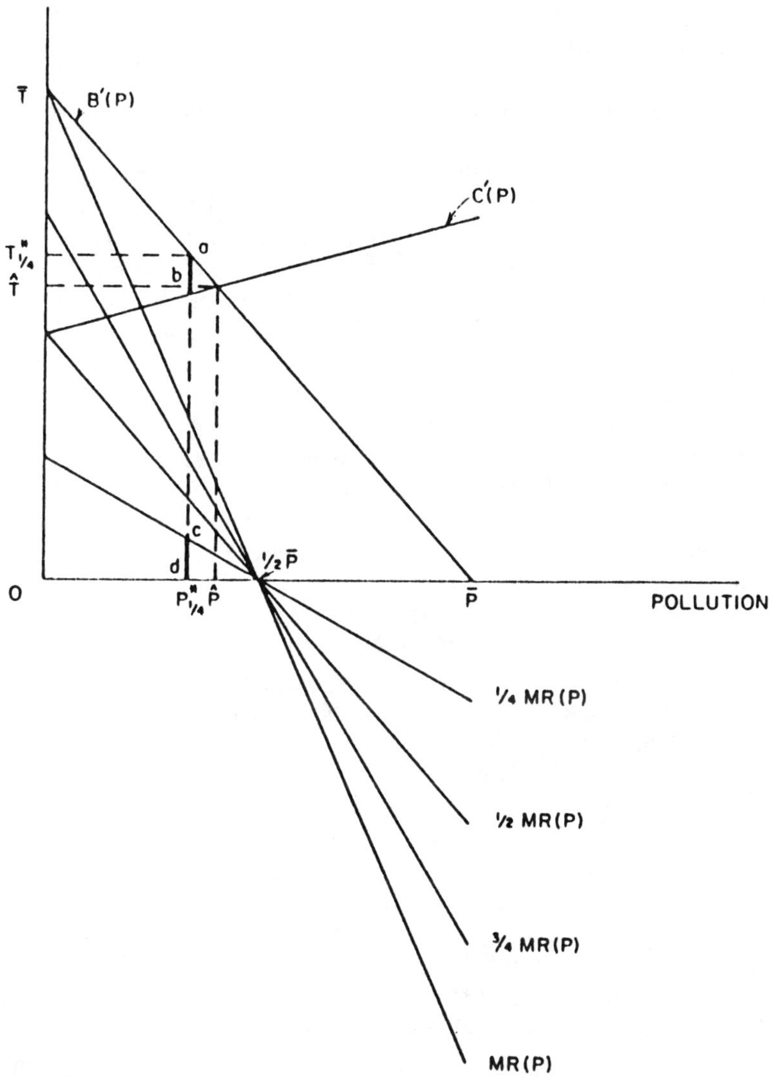

Figure 25–3

$\delta < 5/8$. This implies that $P = \bar{P}$ and $T = 0$ is a local minimum, rather than a local maximum, when $\delta = 3/4$. Notice that when the tax is increased above zero, and pollution is reduced below $\bar{P}$, we find $C'(P) - B'(P) > -3/4MR(P)(-3/4MR(P)$ declines more rapidly when P is reduced than does the distance between $C'(P)$ and $B'(P))$. This is easily seen to be the case at $1/2\bar{P}$, for example, where $C'(P) - B'(P) > 0$ and $-3/4MR(P) = 0$, and the marginal advantage remains with further tax increases. Below $1/2\bar{P}$, $-3/4MR(P)$ is negative, indicating that further increases in the pollution tax reduce rent-seeking costs. Below $\hat{p}$, $C'(P) - B'(P)$ becomes negative and there is a marginal loss from reducing pollution, but this loss is less than the marginal reduction in rent-seeking cost when the tax is increased. As shown in figure 25–3, this remains true until pollution has been reduced to zero. Any tax greater than or equal to $\bar{T}$, the tax that chokes off all pollution, is an efficient tax.

In this case, the solution $T^* \geq \bar{T}$ holds over the range of rent-seeking given by $1/2 \leq \delta \leq 1$. If $\delta = 1$, for example, it is seen from figure 25–3 that $C'(\bar{P}) < -MR(\bar{P})$ and reducing pollution by increasing the tax above zero will generate a marginal loss. As the tax continues to increase, the objective function (25.3) will continue to decline until some $P > 1/2\bar{P}$ is reached, at which point $C'(P) - B'(P) > -MR(P)$ (this follows from the fact that $C'(P) - B'(P) > - MR(P) = 0$ at $P = 1/2\bar{P}$). This is, of course, a local minimum and net marginal gains begin to be realized by continuing to increase the tax and reduce pollution. This remains the case until $T = \bar{T}$ and all pollution has been eliminated. We are left then with a comparison of two corner solutions for pollution, $P = 0$ and $P = \bar{P}$. It is clear from figure 25–3 that $B(\bar{P}) - C(\bar{P}) < 0$ and the solution $P = 0$ dominates, with $T^* \geq \bar{T}$. When $\delta = 1/2$ there is a monotone advantage in reducing pollution until $P = 0$, at which point $C'(0) - B'(0) = -1/2MR(0)$ and the global maximum to (25.3) has been reached with $T^* \geq \bar{T}$.

Only when $\delta < 1/2$ will the efficient pollution rate be positive, but it will remain less than $\hat{P}$ and the efficient tax will be greater than $\hat{T}$. For example, letting $\delta = 1/4$ and still referring to figure 25–3, it can be seen that $C'(P) - B'(P) > -1/4MR(P)$ until pollution has declined to $P^*_{1/4}$ in response to a tax $T^*_{1/4}$ (distances *ab* and *cd* are equal). At this point, the marginal benefit from reducing rent-seeking waste by increasing the tax is equal to the marginal loss resulting from lowering the pollution rate, and with $\delta < 5/8$ the sufficient condition is satisfied. As in case 1, the smaller is δ, the closer the efficient tax will be to that which is conventionally considered efficient. $\hat{T}$, and when $\delta = 0$ the conventional result holds. The difference between case 1 and the present case is that in the latter case the efficient tax declines, rather than increases, as δ becomes smaller.

Total Benefits vs. Total Costs

There is no limit, of course, to the number of different possibilities that could be examined within the above three cases. But the above examples are sufficient to establish that, once rent-seeking waste is recognized as a by-product of pollution taxation, the efficient tax can be either less than, equal to, or greater than the tax conventionally considered to be efficient. Furthermore, given that $B'(P)$ and $C'(P)$ are linear, case 1 and 3 illustrate the following general proposition:[9]

PROPOSITION 1. *The efficient pollution tax will be less (greater) than or equal to* $\hat{T}$ *when the intersection between* $B'(P)$ *and* $C'(P)$ *occurs where* $\epsilon_T < 1$ (> 1).

Given this proposition, and continuing to assume linearity of $B'(P)$ and $C'(P)$, it is possible to establish a relationship between $B(P) - C(P)$ at $\bar{P}$ (the point of unrestrained pollution), and the range within which the efficient pollution tax will lie. Consider the fact that over the relevant pollution range, $[0, \bar{P}]$, the horizontal axis establishes a lower limit on marginal pollution costs. Therefore, even if the intersection between $B'(P)$ and $C'(P)$ occurs where $\epsilon_T < 1$ it is possible that $B(P) - C(P) < 0$. Examples are easy to construct when $C'(P)$ has a positive horizontal intercept. Of course, it is obvious that $B(\bar{P}) - C(\bar{P})$ can also be positive when $\epsilon_T < 1$ at the point where $B'(P)$ and $C'(P)$ intersect (see figure 25–1 for example). On the other hand, it is impossible to construct a case in which $B(\bar{P}) = C'(\bar{P}) > 0$ when intersection between $B'(P)$ and $C'(P)$ occurs where $\epsilon_T > 1$. From this, and Proposition 1, we have

PROPOSITION 2. *If* $B(\bar{P}) > C(\bar{P})$, *then* $T^* < T$, *and* T^* *may be* $< T$ *when* $B(\bar{P}) < C(\bar{P})$. *On the other hand,* T^* *will be* $> \hat{T}$ *only if* $B(\bar{P}) < C(\bar{P})$.

On the basis of these results and some casual empiricism, an argument can be made that a pollution tax less than that conventionally considered efficient will be called for in most situations. The "empirical" basis for this argument is that for most pollutants, though certainly not all, the total benefits from unrestrained pollution exceeds the costs; i.e., if the choice is between no pollution and pollution out to $\bar{P}$, the advantage will be in the latter. The inframarginal benefits from the unrestrained generation of the pollution arising from automobile transportation and the production of electricity, for example, are certainly much larger, in total, than the inframarginal costs. This is, of course, completely consistent with the marginal benefits being low (in fact zero) and the marginal costs being quite high in comparison. The large difference in marginal costs and benefits will be more readily perceived than the even larger difference, in the opposite direction, between total benefits and costs. This means that a pollution situation can be perceived as a significant problem which, when viewed from a total benefit and total cost perspective, is not an important problem at all.

Of course, as every good economist will quickly point out at this point, it is the marginal, not the total, values that are important when assessing problems of this type. True, but care has to be taken that the margins being considered are the relevant ones. And as indicated by the analysis in this section, when the total benefits from unrestrained pollution exceed the total costs and rent-seeking costs are positive, the relevant marginal conditions call for a pollution tax that is less than $\hat{T}$. The larger are the total benefits from unrestrained polluting relative to the total costs, the greater will be the marginal rent-seeking costs of reducing pollution relative to the marginal benefits from doing so, and the lower will be the efficient tax. Indeed, it does not seem implausible that situations exist where, because the total benefits from pollution are large, the efficient pollution tax is zero despite significant marginal costs from the pollution.

It is clear that without the linearity assumptions the connection developed in this section between total benefits and costs and the position of the efficient tax relative to $\hat{T}$ is no longer guaranteed. As a useful example, consider the rather extreme case in which the tax elasticity of demand is everywhere unity. Such a marginal benefit from pollution curve, $B'(P)$, is shown in figure 25–4, with a horizontal truncation at $\bar{P}$.[10] Also shown is the marginal cost curve $C'(P)$, which is shown to be increasing at an increasing rate. Because of the unitary elasticity of $B'(P)$, the marginal tax revenue equals zero for all $P \epsilon (0, \bar{P})$. Therefore, no matter what the value of δ, once the pollution rate is being reduced in response to a tax, the marginal rent-seeking cost of reducing it further is zero. The necessary condition (25–4) is satisfied at the point where $B'(P)$ and $C'(P)$ intersect as in the conventional case, no matter what the relative magnitudes of $B(\bar{P})$ and $C(\bar{P})$.[11] This solution is shown as $T^* = \hat{T}$ and $P^* = \hat{P}$ in figure 25–4.

Yet, if total benefits are sufficiently large relative to total costs at $\bar{P}$, the global maximum will occur at $T^* = 0$ and $P^* = \bar{P}$. consider the marginal cost curve $c'(P)$ in figure 25–4. In this case the revenue raised by the tax $\hat{t}$ (area $\hat{t}b\hat{p}0$) is large relative to the net pollution costs eliminated by the tax (area abc). If δ happens to be greater than the ratio area abc/area $\hat{t}b\hat{p}0$, then the total rent-seeking costs generated by $T = \hat{t}$ will exceed the total benefits resulting from pollution reduction, and the global maximum of (3′) is realized at $T^* = 0$.[12]

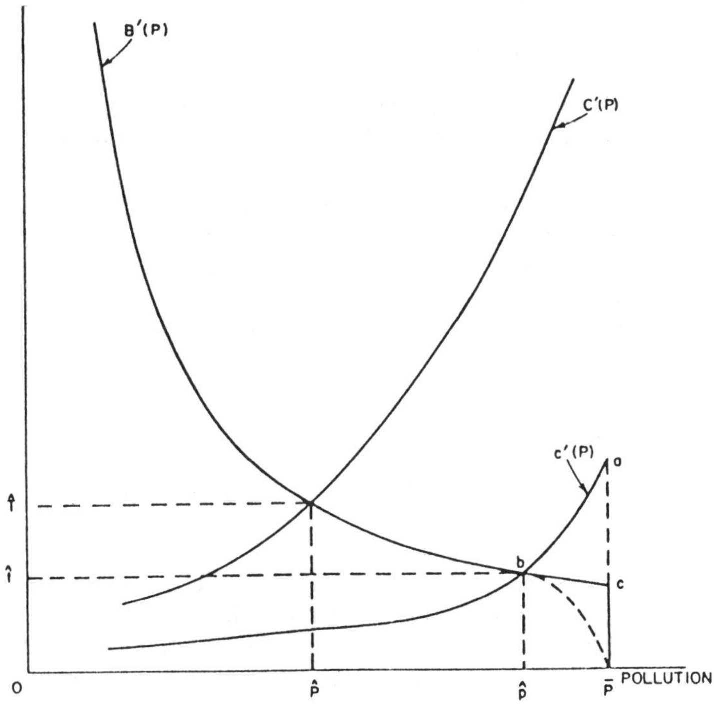

Figure 25–4

But once we cut ourselves loose from the linearity assumption on B′(P) and C′(P) many possibilities arise. For example, marginal tax revenue can be increasing in pollution and/or the efficient tax can be greater than $\hat{T}$ even though $B(\bar{P}) > C(\bar{P})$. These possibilities are no doubt of some interest, and deserve mention if not detailed elaboration. Typically, however, it seems reasonable to expect that, unless the total costs of pollution at $\bar{P}$ exceeds the total benefits, the efficient pollution tax will be less than $\hat{T}$. Furthermore, for a large number of pollutants over which concern is expressed, it is almost certainly true that $B(\bar{P}) > C(\bar{P})$. Even if this possibility is the prevalent one, however, important cases surely exist where $B(\bar{P}) < C(\bar{P})$. When this is the case our analysis provides some basis for considering the possibility that the efficient pollution tax will lie above that which is conventionally considered efficient. This is a possibility that seems not to have been recognized in previous analyses of pollution taxation.

Conclusion

Of necessity, all useful models of complex issues make simplifying assumptions and, in so doing, ignore certain aspects of the problem being considered. The rent-seeking model of pollution taxation developed in this paper is certainly no exception. The hope is that the usefulness of those insights gained by being able to simplify is not jeopardized by those considerations that have been neglected. In this regard, some of the simplifications that have been made in the above analysis have already been discussed, but not all.

For example, it has been assumed throughout the analysis that rent-seeking occurs only in response to the tax revenue raised. In our simple model, when the tax equals zero no revenue is raised and rent-seeking cost is zero. Similarly, when the tax is greater than or equal to $\bar{T}$ both revenue and rent-seeking costs are zero. This is obviously not true. If $T \geq \bar{T}$, for example, those who want to pollute will surely engage in rent-seeking activity designed to influence the political process in favor of a nonprohibitive tax. On the other hand, if $T = 0$ politically active coalitions would form in favor of a higher tax. So rent-seeking costs cannot be eliminated by going to either limit with respect to the pollution tax. Furthermore, there will be some rent-seeking over the magnitude of the pollution tax no matter what its value, with this rent-seeking being in addition to that motivated by the tax revenue raised.

But it is not clear how significantly this rent-seeking over the pollution tax level alters the conclusions of this paper. It may be argued that, because polluting activities provide private goods and pollution reduction generates a public good, rent-seeking to lower the tax if it is at $\bar{T}$ will be more costly than will rent-seeking to raise the tax if it is zero. If this is true, it may be that the total cost of rent-seeking over the tax level is minimized at a low tax level. This consideration could serve to reinforce the implications of our model when it calls for a low pollution tax, but indicate that the efficient tax is less than that established by our model when it calls for a high pollution tax. To the extent that the cost of rent-seeking over the tax level is independent of that level, the implications developed in this paper are unaltered.

Turning to another simplification, the discussion throughout this paper has proceeded as if the only way to reduce pollution is to increase a pollution tax. The government could create pollution rights and give them away. If this were done in such a way that the allocation of rights was completely independent of recipient behavior, then rent-seeking waste could be avoided. But there is not reason for believing the government will allocate valuable pollution rights in such a way that rent-seeking will be less than when government allocates revenue of equivalent value.[13] The market value of the rights issued will be the same as the tax revenue raised at each level of pollution, and the rent-seeking model developed in this paper applies fully to the pollution rights approach.

Despite the dominance of the pollution tax and rights approach in the economic literature on environmental management, it is direct regulations and controls that over-whelmingly characterize actual policy. The rent-seeking model developed in this paper, while not directly applicable to pollution regulation, does provide some new insight into the political appeal of the regulation approach. When pollution regulations are imposed individual polluters will engage in rent-seeking activities designed to secure exemptions. Having obtained an exemption from a pollution regulation, it is not possible to sell this exemption. A polluter with low abatement costs, for example, could not obtain a variance from a regulation and then sell it to a polluter with high abatement costs. This lack of marketability creates an opportunity for political operatives to realize advantages through "price" discrimination against rent-seeking polluters.[14]

The political advantage from pollution regulation can be increased by increasing the stringency of abatement requirements and thus creating a larger market for exemptions. This observation is certainly not inconsistent with the fact that pollution regulations typically create the threat for far more abatement than is actually realized. It should also be pointed out that, with sufficiently demanding regulations, the upper limit on the total value that polluters will be attempting to capture through rent-seeking will be given by the entire area under the demand curve for pollution. Thus the potential for rent-seeking waste will be greater with direct regulation than with either the pollution taxation or rights approach.

The model of pollution taxation presented in this paper is a simple one. But by incorporating rent-seeking into the analysis, it introduces a consideration that has important implications for the efficiency of pollution charges (and, more generally, political prices of any type), and which has been ignored in the previous literature on the economics of pollution control. The present model also suggests extensions that will allow comparisons to be made between pricing approaches and the direct control approach to pollution management that are more realistic than previous comparisons. Rent-seeking is a ubiquitous feature of political decision making. Policy analysis that ignores this feature will suffer from an innocence of the political realities that shape the outcomes of policy.

Appendix

The proof of Proposition I can be carried out in two stages, beginning with

PROPOSITION 1a. *When the intersection between* $B'(P)$ *and* $C'(P)$ (*both of which are assumed to be linear*) *occurs when the elasticity of demand for pollution,* ϵ_T, *is* < 1, *then* $T^* < \hat{T}$ *whenever* $\delta > 0$.

Proof: In this case $C'(\hat{P}) - B'(\hat{P}) = 0$ and $-\delta MR(\hat{P}) > 0$. Therefore, if the marginal conditions call for reducing the pollution level below $\bar{P}$ (i.e., $C'(\bar{P}) > -\delta MR(\bar{P})$), then the necessary condition is satisfied when $T^* < \hat{T}$ and $P^* > \hat{P}$. this is a local maximum, since by assumption $C'(\hat{P}) - B'(\hat{P}) < -\delta MR(\hat{P})$, and therefore the sufficient condition has to be satisfied. If the sufficient condition is satisfied, it is satisfied everywhere in the linear case (see (25.6')) and therefore this local maximum is a global maximum.

If $C'(\bar{P}) < -\delta MR(\bar{P})$, then there could be a local minimum at some $T < \hat{T}$ and $P < \hat{P}$, with it being necessary to compare $T = 0$ and $T \geq \bar{T}$. But in this case $C'(\bar{P}) < -MR(\bar{P})$ and this simplies, when the intersection between $B'(P)$ and $C'(P)$ occurs where $\epsilon_T < 1$, that $B(\bar{P}) - C(\bar{P}) > 0$. Therefore the comparison favors $T = 0$ and $P = \bar{P}$.

To complete the proof of Proposition 1, consider

PROPOSITION 1b. *When the intersection between* $B'(P)$ and $C'(P)$ (*still assumed linear*) *occurs where* $\epsilon_T > 1$, *then* $T^* > T$ *whenever* $\delta > 0$.

Proof: In this case $C'(\hat{P}) - B'(\hat{P}) = 0$ and $-\delta MR(\hat{P}) < 0$. If $C'(\hat{P}) > -\delta MR(\bar{P})$ then, if the necessary condition is satisfied, it is satisfied where $T > \hat{T}$ and $P < \hat{P}$. This will obviously be a local maximum and, by the argument in Proposition 1a, it has to be a global maximum. If $C'(P) - B'(P) \geq -\delta MR(P)$ for $P \epsilon [0, \bar{P}]$, then $T^* = P^* = 0$.

If $C'(\bar{P}) < -\delta MR(\bar{P})$, then the necessary condition will be satisfied when $T < \hat{T}$ and $P > \hat{P}$. But this is a local, and global, minimum. Further increases in the tax will find $C'(P) - B'(P) > -\delta MR(P)$. In this case, the efficient tax is determined by comparing $T = 0$ and $T \geq \bar{T}$. Since it is geometrically impossible for $B(\bar{P}) > C(\bar{P})$ when the intersection between a linear $B'(P)$ and $C'(P)$ occurs where $\epsilon_T > 1$, the comparison favors $T \geq \bar{T}$ and $P = 0$.

Notes

1. The literature on pollution taxation is far too vast to be representatively cited. See Kneese and Schutze (1975) and Ruff (1970) however, for clear and nontechnical statements of

the advantages economists see with imposing taxes on pollution.

2. In the words of Baumol and Oates (1975, 134), the objective is to realize "efficiency without optimality."

3. Choosing the tax that accomplishes this is not trivial and would surely require a costly series of iterations. With this problem in mind, some economists have recommended marketable pollution rights as the most efficient means of environmental management. See J.H. Dales (1968), chapter 17 of Baumol and Oates (1979) and Tietenberg (1980) for useful discussions of the pollution rights approach.

4. For an instructive article on this point, see Maloney and McCormick (1982).

5. The problem of sudden changes in the efficient pollution tax due to changes in environmental receptors is discussed in Chapter 20 of Baumol and Oates (1975). The problem of enforcing environmental management policies (standards as well as taxes) is discussed by Harford (1978), and Downing and Watson (1974).

6. For example, a recent Rand study by Palmer, et al. (1980) on the effect of controlling chlorofluorcarbon (CFC) emissions from nonaerosol sources estimated that using taxation to reduce these discharges 15 percent below the anticipated unregulated level would raise approximately 1.5 to 1.7 billion dollars in tax revenue over the decade 1980–90. Considering a more significant pollution problem, but with concern limited to a relatively small geographic area. Seskin, Anderson, and Reid (1983) have estimated that achieving a maximum level of 250 mg m^2 of nitrogen dioxide (NO_2) per hour, over the city of Chicago, with a uniform pollution tax would raise 414 million dollars annually.

7. This marginal rent-seeking waste is positive when the price (tax) elasticity of demand for pollution is less than one, and negative when this elasticity is greater than one.

8. Because B′(P) is linear, $\epsilon_T = 1$ when $P = 1/2\bar{P}$.

9. This proposition is established in the appendix. When the intersection between B′(P) and C′(P) occurs where $\epsilon_T = 1$, examples are easily constructed showing that the efficient tax can be any where betwen 0 and $\bar{T}$.

10. Without a truncation we would be making the absurd assumption that, unless somehow restrained, polluters will expand pollution beyond all limit.

11. In this case the sufficient condition is satisfied as long as $B''(P) - C''(P) < 0$.

12. When B′(P) is a rectangular hyperbola, as shown in figure 25–4, the truncation of B′(P) along the horizontal axis is necessary if the possibility $T^* = 0$ is to arise (assuming $C'(P) > B'(P)$ for finite P). But it is not necessary that this truncation occur sharply as shown by the segment $bc\,\bar{P}$. The B′(P) curve could drop off smoothly, as shown with the dashed line in figure 25–4, and it would still follow that $T^* = 0$ if $\delta >$ area $ab\bar{P}$/area $\hat{t}b\hat{p}0$. The only difference is that in this case the necessary condition will also hold at some P between $\hat{p}$ and $\bar{P}$, but it will be a local minimum.

13. The benefits from privatizing rights are vulnerable to the same type of rent-seeking activities here that the beneits from privatizing land are vulnerable to in Anderson and Hill (1983).

14. It is not the purpose of this paper to elaborate a positive theory explaining why environmental regulation takes the form it does. The suggestion here, however, is that the incentives of those in government supplying the regulations are important. Previous work or the positive theory of environmental regulations; e.g., Buchanan and Tullock (1967), and Maloney and McCormick (1982), has emphasized the important role of those to be regulated in demanding particular types of regulation.

References

Anderson, T. L., and Hill, P. J. "Privatizing the Commons: An Improvement?" *Southern Economic Journal*, (October, 1983): 438–50.

Baumol, W. J., and Oates, W. E. *The Theory of Environmental Policy: Externalities, Public Outlays, and the Quality of Life*. Englewood Cliffs, New Jersey: Prentice-Hall, Inc., 1975.

——. *Economics, Environmental Policy, and the Quality of Life*. Englewood Cliffs, New Jersey: Prentice-Hall Inc., 1979.

Buchanan, J. M.; Tollison, R. D.; and Tullock, G. (eds.) *Toward a Theory of the Rent-Seeking Society*. College Station: Texas A&M University Press, 1980.

—— and Tullock, G. "Polluters' Profit and Political Response: Direct Controls Versus Taxes." *American Economic Review* (March, 1975): 129–47.

Dales, J. H. *Pollution, Property, and Prices*. University of Toronto Press, 1968.

Downing, P. B., and Watson, W. D., Jr. "The Economics of Enforcing Air Pollution Controls." *Journal of Environmental Economics and Management* (November, 1974): 219–36.

Harford, J. D. "Firm Behavior Under Imperfectly Enforceable Air Pollution Controls." *Journal of Environmental Economics and Management* (March, 1978): 26–43.

Kneese, A. V., and Schultze, C. L. *Pollution, Prices, and Public Policy*. Washington D.C.: The Brookings Institution, 1975.

Krueger, A. O. "The Political Economy of the Rent-Seeking Society." *American Economic Review* (June, 1974): 291–303.

Maloney, M. T., and McCormick, R. E. "A Positive Theory of Environmental Theory Regulation." *The Journal of Law and Economics* (April, 1982): 99–123.

Palmer, A. R.; Mooz, W. E.; Quinn, T. H.; and Wolf, K. A. *Economic Implications of Regulating Chlorofluorocarbon Emissions from Non-aerosal Applications*. Santa Monica, California: Rand, 1980.

Ruff, L. E. "The Economic Common Sense of Pollution." *The Public Interest* (Spring, 1970): 69–85.

Seskin, E. P.; Anderson, R. J., Jr.; and Reid, R. O. "An Empirical Analysis of Economic Strategies for Controlling Air Pollution." *Journal of Environmental Economics and Management* (June, 1983): 112–24.

Tietenberg, T. H. "Transferable Discharge Permits and the Control of Stationary Source Air Pollution: A Survey and Synthesis." *Land Economics* (November, 1980): 391–416.

Tullock, G. "The Welfare Costs of Tariffs, Monopolies, and Theft." *Western Economic Journal* (June, 1967): 224–34.

26 PRIVATIZING THE COMMONS: AN IMPROVEMENT?*

Terry L. Anderson and Peter J. Hill

Introduction

Recent years have seen political economists turning to an institutional paradigm wherein the extent to which property rights are defined and enforced is an important determinant of human action. (Furubotn, 1972) The institutional or property rights approach has become an important component of explanations of both economic growth and economic inefficiency. The institutional environment now holds a prominent place in explanations of differential growth rates among political units and over time.[1] The property rights approach has also become commonplace in the analysis of the environmental crisis where the lack of well-defined property rights is seen as the cause of environmental problems and movement toward a more complete specification of those rights as the solution. Even bureaucratic inefficiencies have been analyzed in the context of property rights. (McKean, 1965).

* Helpful comments were received from Tom Borcherding, Jon Christianson, David Friedman, Ronald Johnson, and Steven Littlechild.

If one had to characterize all of the above literature in terms of one brief policy conclusion, it would be to "establish property rights." Such establishment would provide incentives for efficiency by internalizing social costs and benefits. In this way the market could promote economic growth, achieve optimal levels of pollution, and generally reduce inefficiency. Convincing evidence substantiating the important role of private property rights continues to be mustered, making it difficult to disagree with this policy conclusion.

The purpose of this paper is not to disagree with the importance of establishing property rights, but to point out and emphasize that the definition and enforcement process may preclude whatever gains might have been realized by the establishment of rights. We hypothesize that under certain institutional arrangements, the establishment of private rights to resources can leave a society no better off than when rights were held in common. In other words, the "tragedy of the commons" may be no worse than the rent dissipation that can result in the process of private property establishment. In what follows we will develop this theory more fully. The first applications are to the American frontier, which provides one of the best opportunities to compare alternative methods of defining and enforcing private rights. More current applications suggest that less centralization of definition and enforcement may improve efficiency.

The Economics of Property Rights Production

In 1972 Professors Alchian and Demsetz provided us with an innovative method for analyzing the firm which relied upon the nature of contractual obligations. (Alchian and Demsetz, 1972) In their framework the firm is viewed as a form of team production wherein multilateral contracts are replaced by a set of bilateral contracts between a residual claimant and the owners of inputs used in joint production. The result of their model is a series of testable implications suggesting that a set of bilateral contracts provides an efficient system for monitoring and rewarding inputs. The firm evolves as an efficient market which promotes competition in the form of "the *revelation and exchange* of knowledge or information. . ." When the benefits of this "revelation and exchange" can be captured by the owner in the form of a residual claim, the incentives for efficiency are obvious.

There are also institutional innovations that have efficiency advantages over alternative institutions when valuable resources are being used in the joint production of private property rights. We have pointed out elsewhere that "establishing and protecting property rights is very much a productive activity toward which resources can be devoted." The efficiency of this productive process will depend upon whether the gains (rents) from having private rights accrue to a residual claimant or to a common pool. Our hypothesis, which follows from the Alchian-Demsetz interpretation, is that when the methods of defining and enforcing private rights are devised through residual claimant action there is a greater incentive to conserve on resources used in the process than when that process is imposed exogenously by non-claimants. The definition of property rights generates rents to resources which would otherwise be dissipated under communal ownership. Considerable attention has been paid to the necessity of defining and enforcing rights in order to prevent this rent dissipation. However, there appear to be few efforts to apply this framework to property rights definition in order that we might predict how different definition processes impact on efficiency.[2]

As illustrated in figure 26–1 the first owner of labor will equate the wage rate with the value of his marginal product and therefore allocate L_1 units of labor to resource exploitation, in this case let us say farming. The area OVWU will represent the rent to the resource that is captured by the owner of the labor.

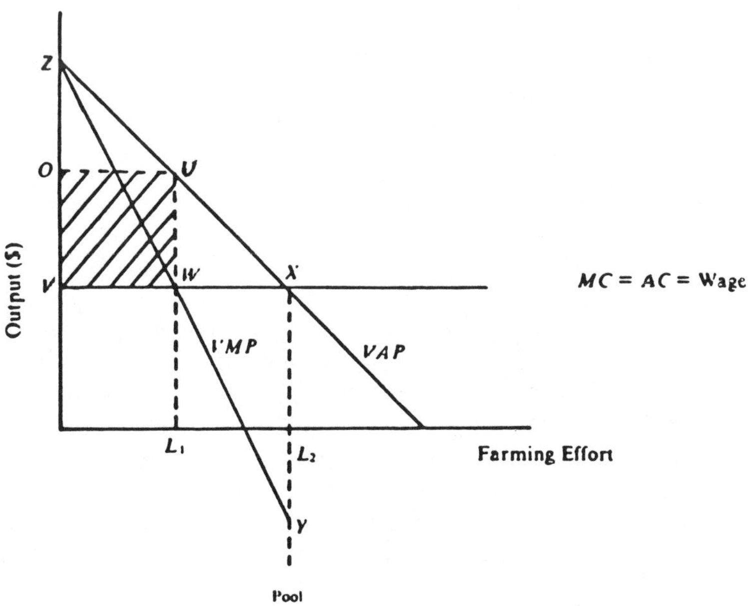

Figure 26–1

Since there are no exclusive rights to the resource and assuming no collusion among potential laborers, "rent becomes a residual, with every decision-making unit. . .maximizing the portion left behind by others." (Cheung, 1970, p. 59) Thus, as Cheung has shown, all of the rents to resources will be dissipated through increased effort when institutions governing the use of resources are not developed. In the limit, L_2 total units of labor will be committed to farming. This results in economic waste since the marginal product at L_2 is less than the opportunity costs from alternative occupations. It is even possible for the marginal product to be negative. The inefficiency generated by the over-commitment of effort to the fixed resource is shown by triangle WXY, the area where MC lies above VMP. This inefficiency is just equal to the rent which would have existed had L_1 units of effort been expended, i.e., triangle WXY equals triangle VZW equals rectangle OVWU.

Of course the situation represented in figure 26–1 is not a stable one because there are gains to be had through institutional innovation. Social output would rise by the amount of rents to natural resources if fewer units of labor were devoted to farming. The size of the efficiency loss can be reduced, and thereby rents increased if farming effort is reduced. Professor Cheung expressed it this way in his example of a fishery:

> . . . there exists incentives to fishermen to restrict the *number* of decision units who have access to the fishing right. That is, even if each decision unit is free to commit the amount of fishing effort, the "rent" captured by each will be larger the smaller the number of decision units. (Cheung, 1970, p. 63)

Potential rents to resources are valuable and, therefore, will attract efforts to claim them. When the method of claiming rents is through increased fishing effort, rent dissipation and inefficiency are the result.

Another method of claiming the rents is through the definition and enforcement of exclusive rights to use the resource without actually harvesting it. Establishing and protecting property rights can be as fruitful to the individual as increased fishing or farming effort. It follows then that as the potential rents from resources rise, as the value of the resource increases, more efforts will be devoted to definition and enforcement activity. The worth of perfectly defined and enforced rights is represented by the net present value of the rents and individuals would be willing to spend up to that amount to obtain these rights. If the rents can be obtained for less than this amount, net rents will be positive and society's output will be greater. The point which has been missed in the property rights literature is that even though inefficiency from too much farming effort may be reduced through the assignment of private rights, the gains from such assignment can be lost in the efforts to define and enforce private rights. This says that while private property rights are a necessary condition for efficient market allocation, they are not a sufficient condition. The definition and enforcement process can simply shift the inefficient allocation of resources from the resource commons to the property rights commons and on net, society may be no better off with private property rights.

Returning to figure 26–1 allows a comparison of the two types of inefficiencies. L_2 units of farming effort generate inefficiency of WXY = OVWU. The farming effort in excess of L_1 can be characterized as the rent dissipation effort. If property rights to land could be established, rents OVWU would go to the owner since farming effort would be reduced from L_2 to L_1. Our point is that the process of determining who gets rent OVWU can also attract resources. Individuals would be willing to expend up to the expected value of capturing the rents in the definition and enforcement of private rights, and under certain gaming conditions they might even expend more.[3] If the expenditure for well-defined and enforced rights is in the form of ownership claims to other assets, the transaction is merely an exchange of wealth. The exchange may be between the new "owner" and the collective (society) as in the case of a government auction of rights, or it may be between the new "owner" and a politician/bureaucrat as in the case of bribes.[4] On the other hand, if the expenditure is in the form of real resources for "lobbying," the transaction becomes net social waste and, in the limit, will equal the common pool inefficiency of WXY.[5]

Whether or not rents will be dissipated by definition and enforcement activity, therefore, depends upon the process whereby rights evolve. The Alchian-Demsetz framework of a residual claimant provides interesting insights into the efficiency of different processes. Consider two individuals faced with the problem of defining rights to an unclaimed acre of land. They have an incentive to establish ownership in the cheapest manner, since they bear the cost of the resources consumed in the property rights production. Of course, one person could capture all the rents if he were able to get to the land first, but since each has this opportunity, competition between them would tend to dissipate at least some of the rents. Squatter sovereignty will result in a race wherein each would be willing to expand up to the expected value of getting the land in attempting to win the race. If, however, they could agree to reduce expenditures on the race, the residual for each would increase.

As long as those bargaining for the property rights are free to choose their own definition process, there is an incentive to reduce definition costs since they are residual claimants. This is not to say that they will always resolve the issue and define property rights at the lowest cost. The

		Individual *B*	
		Walk	Run
Individual *A*	Walk	90,90	0,95
	Run	95,0	0,0

Figure 26–2

prisoners' dilemma problem, in fact, may result in full dissipation. Consider a piece of land with rent of $200 when property rights are well defined and enforced. Suppose that, if the two parties agree to walk to the parcel and to divide it equally, each will expend $10 worth of resources. The residual for each becomes $90 as shown in Cell 1 of figure 26–2. If on the way to the land, however, one potential claimant can get the jump on the other insuring an earlier arrival and ownership of the entire acre, he can spend up to $110 worth of resources in the race and still be better off. Potential claimant B, of course, faces the same possibility. The results of these two actions are shown in Cells II and III. If both decide to run, however, rent dissipation is the result and the pair find themselves in Cell IV. In this simplified two-person world, James Buchanan has noted that

> it is surely plausible to suggest that rationality precepts will direct each person to adhere to the initial contractual terms. Each person will recognize that unilateral defection cannot succeed and that any attempt to accomplish this would plunge the system back into a position that is less desirable for everyone than that which is attained from adherence to contract. (Buchanan, 1975, p. 65)

The "rationality" to which Buchanan refers is related to the fact that the two parties have a claim on the resources saved through adherence to the initial process and that the cost of detecting a rule-breaker is relatively low. As the number of participants in the game increases, the prisoner's dilemma problem becomes more acute because the share of the residual declines while the cost of detection rises.

In the limit the share of the residual is zero and the incentive for reducing the amount of resources consumed in the definition process will be the same. This is in fact exactly what happens when the person determining process is a governmental official who has no claim on the residual rent but whose only claim is on power within the bureaucracy. Returning to the example of land worth $200, suppose a third party chooses the process for deciding thc division. Allocating the property to whichever individual arrives at the location first might seem "fair," but many resources can be wasted in the process. This assumes that participants could not rig the race by agreeing beforehand that one person would walk to the property while the other waited at the starting line and that they would later split the property 50-50. In fact, without collusion each would be willing to spend up to the expected value of the rent to win the race. With probabilities of success accurately estimated, all of the potential rents would be dissipated. As the number of entrants to the race increases, the likelihood of collusion declines, and the potential for rent dissipation rises. In this case we ensure the worst solution to the prisoner's dilemma. However, this resource waste costs the third party nothing since he had no claim on the rents anyway.

Our prediction that rent dissipation results when the property rights definition process is designed by a non-residual claimant is likely to be even stronger given the nature of modern bureaucracies. Since decision makers legally cannot claim a share of rents derived from increased efficiency, they must seek alternative forms of payment. Corruption is one possibility, but this may simply be one way of collecting a portion of the rents. Another possibility is that the bureaucrat can gain power and command over political resources if the definition process necessitates an even larger bureaucracy. Thus the controlling authority may require activities that dissipate rents in order that it can be given command over some political resources. Competing claimants to common property resources may have to prove themselves "worthy" of having rights bestowed upon them, with, of course, the bureaucrat needing considerable allocation of funds in order to make judgements of "worthiness." Or the bureaucrats may find that they can require activities that produce positive utility for bureaucrats. Hence, rather than there being no incentive to reduce resources expended in the definition of property rights, there may actually be an incentive to increase such expenditures.

The ability of the bureaucracy to induce this type of rent-seeking activity will of course be constrained by the number of alternative "firms" which can establish rights without causing rent dissipation. Other agents can "organize opposition and attract supporters from among the constituents by offering a better division of the existing rents." Residual claimant types of organizations offer one possibility for a "better division" by eliminating rent dissipation activities.[6]

In summary, the major implications of our model are:

1. Rent dissipation can occur in the *process* of establishing private rights to a common property resource as well as in the use of a common property resource.
2. The rent dissipation from the process of establishing rights to a resource can be every bit as large as the rent dissipation from exploitation of the resource under common property rules.
3. When the process of establishing rights is determined by residual claimants (potential owners of the rents) there is a greater incentive to conserve on the resources used in that process than when the procedure is determined by non-claimants.

Alternative Processes in the American West

We not turn to the American West to examine cases of property rights definition and enforcement. Our theory predicts that early efforts at establishing rights to land, where those involved in the definition and enforcement procedure were clearly the residual claimants, would have been considerably different from definition and enforcement activity under the Homestead Acts, where the rules were established by those who had little or no claim to residual rents.

The American frontier has long been noted as a place where extralegal institutions for defining and enforcing property rights arose. Since the frontiersmen were aware of the rent dissipation which accompanies common ownership, these institutions represented their efforts to eliminate that dissipation by defining private rights.[7] These institutional innovations occurred in the absence of a formal government and took the form of land clubs or claims associations, cattlemen's associations, mining camps, and wagon trains. Rights were established to land, water, timber, minerals, livestock, and personal property. The actual methods used for establishing private rights varied from case to case, but, if the above theory is correct, we should make an effort in all cases to conserve upon the real resources consumed in the definition and enforcement process. Evidence from the land claims clubs, mining camps, and livestock associations suggests that this was the case.

Much of the land in the West was settled before it was formally opened by the federal government to legal ownership. In the absence of pre-established methods for determining ownership rights, claims associations sprang up. Their primary purpose was to register the settlers' claims to land

and to insure those claims would be honored when the federal rules were put into effect. Clubs could establish whatever rules they wanted; they adopted their own constitutions and bylaws, elected officers, and established rules for adjudicating disputes and procedures for the registration of claims.[8] If lands were surveyed, such registration was relatively simple and was carried out through the range, township, and quarter section of the claim. In the absence of a government survey, the claims clerk was provided a physical description of the claim, including landmarks and the names of surrounding claimants. The club provided coercive power, if necessary, to enforce the members' rights. The association also attempted to insure that the squatters could buy the land at the minimum price when it was put up for sale by the government.

In addition to providing private ownership for members, another alleged purpose was to protect the farmers from "speculators," and much of the historical research on the clubs has debated whether in fact they accomplished this task [4]. An alternative explanation of their efforts to limit land ownership to those actually on the scene is that they clearly understood that the larger the number of users of the common pool resource, the greater the likelihood of rent dissipation. Thus the purposes of claims clubs can be seen as twofold: first, to reduce the claimants on the resource, and secondly, to find low-cost methods of defining and enforcing rights to the resource. The evidence indicates that the associations had a reasonable amount of success in doing both.

As predicted by our theory, the definition process of land claims clubs followed a relatively low-cost method, and the available evidence on enforcement activity is also consistent with the hypothesis that residual claimant associations will discourage rent dissipation. Of the 25 to 100 claims associations in Iowa,[9] only three show any evidence of requiring rent-seeking activity. In his study, "The Iowa Claim Clubs: Symbol or Substance," Allan Bogue concludes that "regulations prescribing the degree to which the member must improve his claim appear in the manuscript records of Poweshiek, Johnson, and Webster county associations, but *not* in the selections of the club laws printed in the histories of other counties."[10] When resource investments were required, they did not approach the requirements of the Homestead Acts. For example, in Webster County claimants had to expend labor worth $10 for each month after the first month, while Poweshiek County required labor worth $30 during the first six months and $30 for each succeeding six months. In Johnson County resident members were not required to invest any resources into their land until they so desired. Nonresidents did have to expend $50 worth of labor for each six months the claim was held [4, 51]. It should be emphasized that these expenditures were specified in terms of labor, allowing the farmer a great deal of latitude with his investment. In this way the claimant could count effort that would have been expended regardless of the club rules. This is in sharp contrast to the Homestead Acts which specified the investments in terms of cabin size, irrigation ditches, and planted trees, most of which were unnecessary.

The rules in the gold mining camps of California provide similar evidence consistent with our hypothesis. John Umbeck [26] examined the contracts formed by miners for the purpose of defining and enforcing rights. His evidence shows that the contracts did require miners to work their claims for a certain number of days each week because their presence was an effective means of enforcing rights. At the same time, however, the contracts did not specify what constituted working a claim. In this way the miner organizations were able to minimize typical dissipation due to common property as well as dissipation in the definition and enforcement process.

Another example of residual claimant effort to define and enforce property rights is the cattlemen and livestock associations that existed throughout the West. These groups also acted in ways which conserved upon the resources devoted to definition and enforcement activity. Louis Pelzer summarizes, in his book *The Cattlemen's Frontier*, the role these groups played on the frontier:

> From successive frontiers of our American history have developed needed customs, laws, and organizations. The era of fur-trading produced its hunters, its barter, and the great fur companies; on the mining frontier cam the staked claims and the vigilance committees; the camp meeting and the circuit rider were heard on the religious outposts; on the margins of settlement the claim clubs protected the rights of the squatter farmers; on the ranchmen's frontier the millions of cattle, the vast ranges, the ranches, and the cattle companies produced pools and local, district, territorial, and national cattle associations [21, 87].

The problem of unrestricted entry was clearly understood by the settlers, and these associations were designed to restrict that entry. Granville Stuart, an early rancher said, "The business was a fascinating one and profitable so long as the ranges were not overstocked" [25, II, 185]. The lure of free grass sounded attractive, but those who came to use it soon discovered that others also came until all rents to the common resource were dissipated.[11]

The cattlemen's associations, members of which were residual claimants, devised two methods of restricting entry and establishing rights which discouraged rent dissipation. The first was squatter sovereignty or prior use which was as old as the frontier itself. Members of associations simply had to announce their squatter claims as shown by the following newspaper advertisement:

> I, the undersigned, do hereby notify the public that I claim the valley, branching off the Glendive Creek, four milcs cast of Allard, and extending to its source on the South side of the Northern Pacific Railroad as a stock range. Chas. S. Johnson. (Osgood, 1929, p. 183)

Such a definition process required almost no investment of resources, though enforcement was not without cost. Such a claim was not enforceable in any court of law, but had to be enforced through the local cattlemen's associations. Such groups also used the local newspapers to announce their intentions to enforce the "accustomed range."

> We, the undersigned, stock growers of the above described range, hereby give notice that we consider said range already overstocked; therefore we positively decline allowing any outside parties or any parties locating herds upon this range the use of our corrals, nor will they be permitted to join us in any roundup on said range from and after this date. (Dennen, 1976, p. 427)

The last portion of this advertisement points out the other way that cattlemen's associations were able to reduce wasteful rent dissipation. The normal operation of a cattle ranch on the frontier necessitated cooperation among neighbors, especially in the case of the twice yearly roundups. The ranchers in an area would work together in the late spring to brand the year's calf crop and again in the fall to gather cattle for marketing. Given the high costs of fencing and the redundancy of each rancher gathering cattle with independent roundups, cooperation provided a way of minimizing costs. The organization of this joint effort was through the cattlemen's associations which in turn could restrict entry by excluding entrants from the roundup. As a special agent of the U.S. General Land Office put it, "This mode of controlling the public lands is quite as effective as if the parties referred to had gone to the expense of fencing the entire tracts." (Dennen, 1976, p. 427) Since the roundup was already something which was necessary for production, using it as a means of defining and enforcing range rights required little or no additional resource expenditure.

As our theory suggests, attempts by the claims clubs, mining camps, and the cattlemen's associations to establish rights over scarce resources were through processes which conserved upon resources expended in the definition enforcement activity. Although there are a few cases when claims clubs required improvements upon the land to insure ownership, in the others the simple filing of a claim was sufficient. In establishing range rights some resources were expended to prevent rent dissipation through common ownership. However, the fact that the stockmen accepted newspaper claim advertisements and that they tied establishment efforts to other ranch activities, such as the roundup and the drive, suggests that as residual claimants of the rents they did attempt to conserve on definition and enforcement activity. There is no evidence that they required the construction of unnecessary buildings or the utilization of inappropriate ranching techniques in order to determine ownership. They were well aware that such requirements would have consumed valuable resources for which they had alternative uses.

Of course this is not to argue that property rights were "perfectly" enforced. Within the groups there were those who broke the rules, attempting to capture more of the rents. Furthermore, as more people migrated to the frontier, the existing residual claimant groups had to increase their expenditures on definition and enforcement.[12] In some cases this was accomplished through fencing, in others through range wars, and in others through government intervention.

In contrast, the definition and enforcement processes of the federal land distribution system following the Civil War suggest that non-residual claimants did encourage rent dissipation. The history of land policy in the United States is one which saw land either awarded to squatters, sold, granted to encourage production of certain goods or services, or given to those willing to make certain investments in the land. But these federal requirements for distribution of the public domain never seemed to suit the frontiersmen. From the Ordinance of 1785 to the Homestead Act of 1862, complaints ranged from prices which were too high to size limitations which were too low. The Easterner had a different frame of reference and different set of goals, but perhaps more important for our analysis, the lawmakers who had the authority to set the rules for definition and enforcement of property rights did not have the incentive to reduce wasteful rent dissipation.[13]

Were there any more efficient methods by which the public domain could have been converted to private ownership? One that is clearly superior to those used is an auction system. Although the highest bidder has to give up claims to resources in order to get ownership, the advantage lies in that these resources are merely transferred to another owner, in this case the government, rather than dissipated in the enforcement process. As Taylor Dennen expresses it:

> Under the auction system, settlers will exchange money, that is, a command over resources, for a land title. However, with the price of land set at zero, individuals will use up real resources to get to the land at the moment when its present value turns from negative to zero. . . . The problem is fully analogous to

> the dissipation of consumers' surplus under price controls or rationing by waiting. That is, where prices are inhibited in their role of allocating commodities, consumers will use up valuable resources such as capital equipment or labor time in order to obtain commodities. From the point of view of those interest in maximizing the value of output, such resource expenditure is pure waste. (Dennen, 1977, pp. 729–30)

Some of the early land laws approached this system in that they disposed of the land by auction with the provision that a minimum price be paid. As long as the actual present value of the land exceeded the minimum price, no resources were wasted. However, in many cases the minimum price did exceed the present value and thus encouraged squatting. To the extent that claims associations were successful in establishing private rights to the land without resource waste and to the extent that preemption rights were allowed, the disposal policy during the first half of the nineteenth century was relatively efficient. Moreover, the Graduation Act of 1854 provided for successive reductions in the minimum price at which unsold public lands would be offered. Though the Act was only in effect for eight years, it did approach the simple auction.

With the Homestead Act of 1862 there was a significant shift in the land disposition policy, one which encouraged much more waste of resources. This Act and those which have followed explicitly required expenditures of labor and capital in order to establish ownership. Under the Homestead Act of 1862, property rights could be established to 160 acres through five years of residence. However, under this first act, land could be preempted by the payment of a $1.25 fee per acre after six months of residence. The original act was revised and expanded in 1873 with the Timber and Culture Act, followed by the Timber and Stone Act in 1878, the Desert Land Act in 1877, the Enlarged Homestead Act in 1909, and finally the Stockraising Homestead Act in 1916.

In all of these rent dissipation occurred in two major ways. First, since the allowable size of holdings was far below that which was economically most efficient, too many people lived on the land. As with any common pool resource entrants were willing to continue homesteading as long as rents were available. Second, rent dissipation occurred because unnecessary resources had to be invested. Land was irrigated that otherwise would not have been, trees were planted when they would not have been, and, in much of the West, plowing was required on land that was more suited for grazing. Stories abound of resources employed in land rushes.

> For example, considerable time was spent simply waiting, or jockeying for an advantageous position at the starting line. On occasion special vehicles were

constructed which would presumably speed more quickly over the land to a claim site. Supposedly in one instance an individual who had a right to enter the unsettled territory spent considerable time training a pony to race to a particularly good claim.

The exact extent to which the government's means of public domain disposal wasted resources must a wait further research, but there is evidence that it did encourage substantial rent-seeking activity. When prices entered into the process, such activity was reduced. For example, the Timber and Stone Act and the Preemption Act provided that $2.50 and $1.25 per acre, respectively, be paid for land. In addition, however, other rent-seeking activities were encouraged and required. For the Timber and Stone Act and the Preemption Act, Professors Libecap and Johnson have estimated that "expenditures attributable to Federal restrictions and which involved real resources: agent payment, development costs, and miscellaneous expenditures," amounted to between 60 percent (Timber and Stone) and 80 percent (Preemption) of the total land value. (Libecap and Johnson, 1979, p. 137) When one considers that 27 percent of over one billion acres disposed of by the federal government passed through this type of disposal system and that of these, 285 million acres were taken up more than once, the potential for waste becomes staggering. As Dennen concludes, "There is no reason to believe that the impact of the federal land-disposition system on the national economy was insignificant." (Dennen, 1977, p. 736)

Modern Applications

Examples of residual claimant groups active in definition and enforcement are difficult to find outside the frontier setting. On the other hand, examples abound of rent dissipation in the process of privatizing rights. In the case of oil, problems associated with unitizing common pools have brought bureaucracies into the allocation process. Though one can conceive of a collective means for establishing rights to all pools, these means have not been adopted. As Robert Haveman points out, "public regulatory bodies have been established and elaborate rules have been designed to control the behavior of users of the resource. Rule setting, behavior monitoring, and rule enforcement is the standard pattern." (Haveman, 1973, p. 870) When rights to oil on public lands are defined the "work effort bidding" method is often used. In 1977 the House and Senate debated amendments to the Outer Continental Shelf Land Act that were designed to reduce the "unfair advantage" of cash bidding by forcing parts of the bid to be in the form of work effort. (U.S. House Reports No. 95-590 and 95-284, 1977) Just as the Homestead Act generated too many cabins on the American Frontier, exploration requirements on the outer continental shelf generate an excessive amount of drilling activity. This has been particularly true under the British and Norwegian rules for drilling in the North Sea. Kenneth Dam summarizes the impact of the British Ministry of Power's effort to establish rights there:

> More significant, however, was the Ministry's request for a statement of each company's work programme for the blocks for which it was still in the running. It came to be known that the Ministry expected much more active drilling programmes in areas which were widely sought after than in the least covered area. Indeed, by a process which is none too clear to the outsider looking in after the fact, a "going price" came to be known for each area. This going price was denominated in such things as holes drilled and exploration work undertaken. He who is unwilling to pay the going price could not expect to be awarded a licence. (Dam, 1965, p. 60)

Another familiar example illustrates simple rent dissipation through the assignment process. The methods used by the Federal Communication Commission to assign rights to radio and television frequencies forced applicants to prove their "worthiness." as Ronald Coase put it, "when rights, worth millions of dollars, are awarded to one businessman and denied to othes, it is no wonder some applicants become over anxious and attempt to use whatever influence they have (political or otherwise), particularly as they can never be sure what pressure the other applicants may be exerting." (Coase, 1959, p. 26) The fact that WFTV, Orlando, Florida, a television station estimated to be worth $40 million, has been in front of regulatory commissions and courts for 27 years trying to obtain its license suggests that rents are being dissipated through the licensing process. In the end someone will obtain control of the station, but in the meantime considerable rents will be dissipated through resource expenditure.

Conclusion

We have argued in this paper that the rules for defining and enforcing rights are much more likely to promote rent dissipation when the rule makers are not potential residual claimants. On the American frontier residual claimant organizations systematically reduced rent seeking in the definition and enforcement process; on the other hand, the Homestead

Act which followed these groups promoted dissipation. The bureaucratic struggle for power and budget builds in an incentive for rule makers to encourage rent seeking. This conclusion is extremely relevant today when privatization of public land and other resources is being considered. Selling public land at auction will generate revenue for the Treasury, itself a common pool (Baden and Fost, 1980), but if our theory is correct, we can predict efforts on the part of agencies to resist such an auction. The current process for assigning rights to public land ensures that agencies such as the Forest Service and the Bureau of Land Management retain power and budget. If those agencies could auction off land and retain the proceeds, they might have an incentive to do so. However, if the proceeds become a common pool, the bureaucratic incentive is to maintain rent dissipating policies. The important conclusion to remember is that removing the inefficiency of open access through privatization or other entry restrictions can simply shift rent dissipation to another arena.

Notes

1. See for example North and Thomas (1979).
2. Exceptions are Buchanan (1980), Dennen (1976), and Southey (1978).
3. This is true only if the VAP curve is linear. With nonlinearity it is possible to have OVWU either greater or less than WXY. If OVWU is greater than WXY, rent dissipation can be worse than common pool inefficiency.
4. For an elaboration on these differences see Buchanan (1980).
5. To conclude that this expenditure represents net social waste necessitates the standard assumption of the rent-seeking literature than "the costs incurred... have no socially valuable by-products" (Posner, 1975, p. 809).
6. There is the possibility that competition to become a member of the residual claimant organization will occur and that rent dissipation will occur at this level. In this case one can imagine an infinite regress such that *no* gains are *ever* possible from *any* establishment and or definition of property rights. All gains from the possession of such rights would be competed away at one level or another. However, if one allows for heterogeneous claimants, some will be among the first to perceive opportunities for rents to be created from establishing rights to common property resources. Thus these perceptive entrepreneurs, as the individuals with a comparative advantage in "rights production," will be the first to become involved and will likely see the advantages of contracting with other similar entrepreneurs to limit rent dissipation. Without the assumption that information is imperfect and that all potential claimants to resources are not homogenous in their abilities and perception, the property rights argument becomes an empty one. We should never concern ourselves with alternative property rights arrangements because all the gains from more efficient institutions will be dissipated at some margin.
7. For a discussion of some of these institutions see Anderson and Hill [2].
8. For an example of a constitution of a claims club see Shambaugh [23].
9. Shambaugh [23] says there were 100 associations in Iowa while Bogue [4] says there

were only 25.

10. [4, 51] emphasis added.

11. For a detailed discussion of the theory of common property as it applies to the open range problem in the West, see Dennen [10].

12. For a more detailed discussion see Libecap (1987, pp. 15–20).

13 See Dennen (1976) and Higgs (1971) for specific discussions of the Homestead Acts.

References

Alchian, A. A., and Demsetz, H. "Production, Information Costs, and Economic Organization." *American Economic Review* (December, 1972): 777–95.

Anderson, T. L. and Hill, P. J. "The Evolution of Property Rights: A Study of the American West." *The Journal of Law and Economics* (April, 1975): 163–79.

Baden, J., and Fort, R. D. "Natural Resources and Bureaucratic Predators." *Policy Review* (Winter, 1980): 69–81.

Bogue, A. G. "The Iowa Claim Clubs Symbol and Substance." In: V. Carstensen (ed.), *The Public Lands*. Madison: University of Wisconsin Press, 1963.

Buchanan, J. M. *The Limits of Liberty*. Chicago: University of Chicago Press, 1975.

—— "Rent Seeking Under External Diseconomies. "In J.M. Buchanan, R. Tollison, and G. Tullock (eds.), *Towards a Theory of a Rent-seeking Society*. College Station: Texas A&M Press, 1980.

Coase, R. H., "The Federal Communications Commissions." *The Journal of Law and Economics* (October, 1959): 1–40.

Cheung, S. N. S. "The Structure of a Contract and the Theory of a Non-Exclusive Resource." *The Journal of Law and Economics* (April, 1970): 49–70.

Dam, K. "Oil and Gas Licensing in the North Sea." *Journal of Law and Economics* (October, 1965): 51–75.

Dennen, R. T. "Cattlemen's Associations and Property Rights in the American West." *Explorations in Economic History* (October, 1976) 423–36.

——, "Some Efficiency Effects of Nineteenth-Century Federal Land Policy: A Dynamic Analysis." *Agricultural History* (October, 1977) 718–36.

Furubotn, E., and Pejovich, S.: "Property Rights and Economic Theory: A Survey of Recent Literature." *Journal of Economic Literature* (December, 1972): 1137–62.

Haveman, R. H. "Efficiency and Equity in Natural Resource and Environmental Policy." *American Journal of Agricultural Economics* (December, 1973): 868–78.

Higgs, R. *The Transformation of the American Economy, 1865–1914*. New York: John Wiley and Sons, Inc., 1971.

Libecap, G. D. *Locking Up The Range*. San Francisco: Pacific Institute for Policy Studies, 1981.

—— and Johnson, R.N. "Property Rights, Nineteenth-Century Federal Timber

Policy, and the Conservation Movement." *The Journal of Economic History* (March, 1979): 129–42.
McKean, R.N. "The Unseen Hand in Government." *American Economic Review*, June (1965): 496–505.
North, D.C. "A Framework for Analyzing the State in Economic History." *Explorations in Economic History* (July, 1979): 249–59.
—— and Thomas, R.P. *The Rise of the Western World*. London: Cambridge University Press, 1972.
Osgood, E.S. *The Day of the Cattleman*. Minneapolis: University of Minnesota Press, 1929.
Pelzer, L. *The Cattlemen's Frontier*. Glendale, Calif.: Arthur H. Clark Co., 1936.
Posner, R.A. "The Social Costs of Monopoly and Regulation." *Journal of Political Economy* (August, 1975): 807–27.
Shambaugh, B.F. "Frontier Land Clubs, or Claim Associations." *Annual Report of the American Historical Association*, Vol. 1 (1900): 67–84.
Southey, C. "The Staple Thesis, Common Property, and Homesteading." *Canadian Journal of Economics* (August, 1978): 547–559.
Stuart, G. *Forty Years on the Frontier*, 2 Vols. P.C. Philips (ed.) Cleveland: The Arthu H. Clark Company, 1925.
Umbeck, "The California Gold Rush: A Study of Emerging Property Rights." *Explorations in Economic History* (July, 1977): 197–226.
United States House Report No. 95–590, 1977.
United States Senate Report No. 95–284, 1977.

G *The Law and Legal Evolution*

27 CORPORATE CHARTERING: AN EXPLORATION IN THE ECONOMICS OF LEGAL CHANGE

William F. Shughart II and Robert D. Tollison*

Introduction

The corporate form of business organization, characterized principally by limited liability, share transferability, and perpetual life, existed far in advance of its official recognition by government. In the early nineteenth century and before the unincorporated joint stock company offered through private contracts many of the advantages typically thought to reside exclusively in the corporation.[1] Despite these deep historical roots, however, the legal framework surrounding the corporation as we know it today is a relatively recent phenomenon. Permission to incorporate was long granted sparingly by the state and, when granted, was accompanied by restrictions on the amount of authorized capital, on the scope of operations, and on the length of the corporate franchise; "permission to

---

* We wish to thank Claire Friedland for directing us to some useful data sources. We are also grateful to Henry Butler, Mark Crain, C. M. Lindsay, Henry Manne, Fred McChesney, Robert McCormick, and Clark Nardinelli for helpful comments; the comments of an anonymous referee on an earlier version were particularly valuable in improving the paper. The usual caveat applies.

incorporate for 'any lawful purpose' was not common until 1875..."[2] Thus, while corporateness flourished early, regulation delayed the beginning of the chartered corporation's rise to prominence until not much more than a century ago.

In the United States, legal limitations on the rights associated with incorporation vary from state to state because the federal government has not chosen to exercise the option of federal chartering. (Henn, 1970, p. 18) The spread of the contemporary corporation therefore came about through the gradual deregulation of the market for corporate charters as states competed for the revenue generated by corporate franchise taxes.[2] Although several "waves" of such deregulation have occurred, the earliest and one of the most important was the adoption by states of statutory or constitutional provisions necessitating incorporation under general laws. This deregulatory episode, which spanned the years 1837 through 1913, brought to an end the era of the special charter. (Evans, 1948, pp. 10–11) Incorporation for business purposes became more routine; the granting of individual charters by specific legislative act passed into history.

In this paper we examine the nineteenth-century spread of incorporation under general laws to discover whether its adoption by states displayed any regularities. In particular, we present evidence on an economic rationale for the pattern of adoption across states that focuses on the benefits and costs to firms of lobbying for "liberal" corporation codes. Although we do not attempt to explain the initial site of adoption, it is clear that once it had appeared in Connecticut, incorporation under general laws would inevitably spread to every state.

The paper is organized as follows. Section 2 provides a sketch of the law of corporations prior to the deregulatory period. The empirical analysis appears in section 3. Section 4 contains some concluding remarks.

Historical Background

Although today Delaware dominates as a charterer both of new corporations and of corporations changing their state of incorporation, it was slow to eliminate the special charter.[4] Delaware's eventual rise to preeminence did not occur at random, however, but rather came about "as corporations have sought charters in states with less restrictive codes" (Winter, 1977, p. 255). In this section we provide a brief sketch of the main developments in the spread of general incorporation laws.

In colonial times, nearly all of the American corporations were "churches, charities, cities, or boroughs." (Friedman, 1973, p. 166) The few organizations incorporated for business purposes were patterned after the English trading company and their charters typically conferred monopoly privilege for the term of the corporate contract. (Fletcher, 1974, p. 6) Grants of authority to incorporate were the exclusive province of the state: "As in the Eighteenth Century negotiations for these contracts were carried on with the crown, so in America they were carried on with the sovereign power of the various states as successors to the crown. In practice this meant the state legislature." (Berle and Means, 1968, p. 121) The era of the special charter was exemplified by the separate legislation into law of each incorporating contract (*Id.*).

Accordingly, few incorporating charters were issued, and those that were contained a great many restrictions on the rights given thereunder.[5] Principal among these restrictions were limitations on the scope of the corporation's activities, on the amount and structure of paid-in capital, and on the rights and authority of management. (Berle and Means, 1968, pp. 122–24) To illustrate, charters commonly limited the corporation to a single purpose (e.g. canal building), required a certain number of shares to be paid up before business could be commenced, set an upper limit on the amount of authorized capitalization, and restricted the life of the corporate franchise to at most 50 years (*Id.*) In consequence, most of the business of the colonial and early nineteenth century period was conducted by organizations that avoided the restrictions of the special charter by operating as unincorporated joint stock companies. (Fletcher, 1973, p. 166)

The major legal innovation of the nineteenth century was the adoption by states of statutes or constitutional provisions permitting incorporation under general laws.[6] The idea of general incoporation, which Posner (1977, p. 296) likens to provision of a set of standard contract terms, substituted the filing of documents with a state government official for the rather more arduous negotiation of individual corporate charters with the legislature.

The invention of incorporation under general laws was not a once-and-for-all change that was adopted everywhere. Occurring principally by constitutional amendment, the disappearance of the special charter, which began in 1837, was not complete until 1913.[7] Moreover, early general incorporation codes contained restrictions on scope and financing similar to those imposed in special charters.[8] Some states retained for a time dual chartering systems. (Friedman, 1973, p. 447) Only gradually were the various limitations relaxed.[9]

Competition among the states, facilitated by the commerce clause, is generally credited with the eventual universal acceptance of general incorporation codes.[10] The law itself erected no important barriers preventing corporations from switching the location of their charter: "A few early cases held that a corporation could not be chartered in one state, if it intended to do all of its business in another. But from an equally early date, precisely this was done, and successfully."[11] the deregulatory process was not completely smooth, however. "Charter-mongering" by states was condemned in some quarters, and reactionary legislation was passed by a few states.[12] Calls for reform continue to this day. (Winter, 1977) The diffusion of general incorporation was nonetheless inevitable.

Because special chartering represented a system for the buying and selling of monopoly privilege, deregulation was an unusual event. The granting of incorporation on a case-by-case basis gave full play to rent-seeking activities; the state legislatures would not have let such a system go voluntarily. However, as Anderson and Tollison (1983) and others have argued, the unincorporated joint stock company flourished during the late eighteenth and early nineteenth centuries, and it flourished precisely because the joint stock form of organization offered many of the benefits of corporateness while avoiding many of the costs of incorporation. Pressure for change therefore arose because the growth of the unincorporated joint stock company made the special charter increasingly ineffective for regulating business activity. Under this interpretation, general chartering came about as the next best method for states to take advantage of the emergence of business as a source of revenue.[13] It is to an empirical examination of this process that we now turn.

An Economic Model of Deregulation

Deregulation of the market for corporate charters occurred gradually throughout the last two-thirds of the nineteenth century as states replaced special chartering with statutory or constitutional provisions necessitating incorporation under general laws. Table 27–1 shows the chronology of this process for 47 states.[4] Of particular note is the wide geographic dispersion of the states where general incorporation codes first appeared. Although Connecticut was the innovator, the next state to eliminate the special charter was Louisiana, followed closely by Iowa, New York, Illinois, and so forth. General incorporation laws were not adopted by the majority of the states until the mid 1870s.

Whether or not one excludes states where deregulation coincided with statehood, the same general pattern is apparent: deregulation spread quite quickly until the early 1850s, at which time about a dozen states had eliminated the special charter. The deregulatory process then paused until

Table 27–1. Chronology of Adoption by States of Incorporation under General Laws

State	Year Adopted	State	Year Adopted
Connecticut	1837[a]	New Jersey	1875
Louisiana	1845	Maine	1875
Iowa	1846[b]	Texas	1876
New York	1846	Colorado	1876[b]
Illinois	1848	Georgia	1877
Wisconsin	1848[b]	North Dakota	1889[b]
California	1849[b]	South Dakota	1889[b]
Michigan	1850	Montana	1889[b]
Maryland	1851	Washington	1889[b]
Ohio	1851	Idaho	1889[b]
Indiana	1851	Wyoming	1889[b]
Massachusetts	1851[a]	Mississippi	1890
Minnesota	1857[b]	Kentucky	1891
Oregon	1857[b]	Utah	1895[b]
Kansas	1859[b]	South Carolina	1895
West Virginia	1862[b]	Delaware	1897
Nevada	1864[b]	Florida	1900
Missouri	1865	New Hampshire	1901[a]
Nebraska	1866[b]	Virginia	1902
Alabama	1867	Oklahoma	1907[b]
North Carolina	1868	New Mexico	1911[b]
Arkansas	1868	Arizona	1911[b]
Tennessee	1870	Vermont	1913
Pennsylvania	1873		

[a] Enacted by statute rather than by constitutional amendment.
[b] Coincided with statehood.
Source: Evans (1948, p. 11).

the end of the War Between the States, when there commenced a second round of adoptions that lasted through the mid 1870s. Finally, during the two decades surrounding the turn of the century, a third group of states replaced the special charter with general incorporation codes.[15] In this section, we offer an economic model of the deregulatory process which focuses on the differences across states in the benefits and costs faced by those lobbying for change.

The interstate rivalry that produced deregulation involved competition both for new incorporations and for reincorporations, i.e., firms switching the location of their charters. The latter "is usually achieved by establishing a subsidiary with the same name in the desired state. The parent is then merged into the subsidiary, and the subsidiary becomes the surviving corporation." (Dodd and Leftwich, 1980, p. 263) New firms can also choose to incorporate in states other than the one where they intend to conduct business.[16] The cost of so doing would involve expenses such as retaining an attorney to file chartering papers in the desired state and, perhaps, establishing a corporate office there. In any case, the choice of chartering location is an economic decision made by weighing the benefits of incorporating in another state—mainly the reduction in costs associated with obtaining a more "liberal" corporation code than that available in the state where business is to be conducted—against the costs of obtaining a foreign charter.

On the supply side, chartering of foreign corporations can be viewed as a tax exportation device.[17] That is, the advantage to states of encouraging incorporations by firms located elsewhere is in the opportunity for transferring a portion of the state's tax bill from domestic taxpayers to foreign corporations. In addition, the liberalization by states of their chartering provisions benefits domestic firms by lowering their costs (both start up and operating expenses) relative to those faced by corporations chartered in states having more restrictive codes.[18] Deregulation may also raise state wealth by reducing the possibility that local entrepreneurs will sell out to foreign companies or simply give up their ventures rather than comply with domestic chartering regulations.[19] Depending on the competitive structure of markets, such cost reductions also provide benefits for the out-of-state customers of domestic firms. The fact that the deregulating state may have to share some of the gains associated with its new corporation law with outsiders mitigates, but does not remove, the incentive to liberalize corporate chartering.

In short, "voting with the feet" by corporations and the wealth-transfer opportunities faced by state legislators both work toward encouraging deregulation of the corporate charter market. Moreover, there is evidence that states recognized the competitive disadvantages of maintaining restrictive corporation codes. For example, the governor of Michigan warned the state legislature that a stringent corporation act was useless because "all of our corporations will come back to us as foreign corporations." (Kaplan, 1968, p. 436)

As we stressed earlier, additional pressure to eliminate the special charter may have arisen from its ineffectiveness as a device for regulating business activity. Because of the availability of the unincorporated joint-stock alternative, American firms may have ignored special chartering as readily as British companies evaded the Bubble Act. (Anderson and Tollison, 1983) Under this interpretation, general chartering came into being as the next best method for states to take advantage of the corporation's emergence as a source of revenue. At a minimum, adoption of general incorporation codes allowed a state to collect charter fees and keep track of the activities of corporations located outside its borders.

The elimination of the special charter by Connecticut created an incentive for interest groups located elsewhere to lobby their state government for similar deregulation.[20] Such lobbying activities would be subject to the familiar benefit-cost calculus applied by Stigler (1971) to the political process. In broad outline, legislative outcomes are the rational result of groups using the political machinery of the state (cost) to seek wealth transfers (benefit). Of importance here is that because the size and composition of the legislative apparatus differs from state to state, the cost of obtaining a given legislative outcome varies across states. Moreover, it is apparent that the cost of obtaining legal change will depend upon the incentives of voters to monitor their representatives. On the benefit side, the amount of wealth at stake is an important determinant of the willingness and ability of interest groups to lobby for deregulation.

Specifically, to test the importance of such factors in explaining the order of adoption by states of incorporation under general laws, we estimated the following reduced-form regression equation.

$$\begin{aligned}\text{YEAR} = {} & b_0 + b_1\text{SIZE} + b_2\text{HSR} + b_3\text{POP} + b_4\text{MFGINC} + b_5\text{LARGE} \\ & + b_6\text{VADDED} + b_7(\text{K/L}) + b_8\text{SHDUM} + b_9\text{STDUM} + e,\end{aligned}$$

where

YEAR = year of adoption of general incorporation code,
SIZE = size of state legislature (house size plus senate size),
HSR = ratio of house size to senate size,
POP = state population (in thousands) during decennial census closest to year of adoption,
MFGINC = income from manufacturing in 1880 ($ millions),
LARGE = percentage of manufacturing establishments producing output in 1904 valued at $100,000 or more,
VADDED = 1899 value added in manufacturing ($ millions),
K/L = ratio of book value of capital to wage and salary expenses in manufacturing (1899),
SHDUM = dummy variable denoting states where adoption of general chartering coincided with statehood,
STDUM = dummy variable denoting states adopting by statute rather

than by constitutional amendment, and
e = regression error term.

Our model is in the spirit of that used by Stigler (1971) to explain the pattern of state occupational licensing requirements.

McCormick and Tollison (1981, pp. 29–45) have laid out a theory that suggests several reasons for believing that legislature size affects the cost to interest groups of influencing legislative outcomes. At the simplest level of analysis, a larger legislature makes it more difficult for legislators to reach agreement. This implies that states having relatively large legislatures would be predicted to eliminate the special charter later, *ceteris paribus*. On the other hand, a greater number of vote suppliers lowers the cost of votes through the resulting competition among lawmakers, suggesting that larger legislatures can be policed more easily by interest groups. Moroever, as the size of the legislature increases, each legislator will have a smaller influence on the law-making process. This implies a negative relationship between size of legislature and date of adoption of general incorporation codes. The overall effect of legislature size on the costs of lobbying and of supplying laws is thus indeterminant *a priori*.

For a given legislature size, increases in the disparity of house and senate membership raise the cost of lobbying. (McCormick and Tollison, 1981, pp. 44–5) Assuming that the cost of influencing votes increases at an increasing rate, the marginal cost of obtaining an additional vote in the larger house will exceed the saving from buying one less vote in the smaller house. Thus, the cost of obtaining a majority will be less the more equal the two chambers are in size. We therefore predict that in states where the ratio of house size to senate size is large, adoption of general incorporation laws occurred late, i.e., b_2 is expected to be positive.[21]

States with larger populations are expected to have deregulated later for two reasons. First, individual voter influence on legislators is inversely related to total population. That is, as population increases, individuals have a smaller incentive to become informed and to vote. Second, a larger population means that the cost of regulation is spread over a larger group. Thus, in states with larger populations, each individual's vote is worth less and he bears a smaller portion of the cost of regulation. This leads to a smaller incentive for voters to become involved in the political process and delays deregulation because voters do not monitor their legislators as closely as they are monitored in less populous states.[22]

On the benefit side, our model attempts to proxy the existence of a group with an effective demand for deregulation. That is, the size of the stake in deregulation is given by the value at the margin of obtaining an incorporation contract on more liberal terms. We employ four alternative benefit measures, each of which is expected to be negatively related to the year of adoption of general chartering—the higher the expected benefit, the earlier the expected date of deregulation. Two of these proxies for the willingness and ability to influence legislative outcomes, MFGINC and VADDED, account for the size of the manufacturing sector in each state. Although the corporate form was not equally important to all types of manufacturing activity, it is nevertheless true that such firms had more to gain from liberal incorporation laws than did firms in other sectors of the economy. States in which manufacturing was important—measured either in terms of income generated or value added—are therefore expected to have deregulated early, other things equal. Alternatively, if capital raising is a key motive for incorporation, large-scale manufacturing firms using capital-intensive production processes would receive larger benefits from deregulation of chartering than smaller, labor-intensive firms. Accordingly, we employ measures of firm size and capital intensity as explanatory variables. In particular, LARGE represents the proportion of manufacturing establishments in each state producing output in 1904 valued at \$100,000 or more, and K/L is the overall capital-labor ratio for each state calculated from census data. Specifically, K/L is the reported book value of capital owned by manufacturing establishments in 1899 divided by total manufacturing wage and salary expenses during that year. States in which firms tend to be large and to use relatively capital-intensive production are predicted to deregulate sooner, *ceteris paribus*.

Of the 47 states in our sample, 20 adopted general incorporation codes coincidently with statehood.[23] The cost of obtaining general incorporation codes may have been lower coincident with statehood in the sense that territorial legislatures merely copied from existing states what appeared to be the most efficient body of laws. In any case, SHDUM, which equals unity for new states and zero for existing states, controls for those jurisdictions that deregulated at the first opportunity.

STDUM is set equal to unity for states eliminating the special charter by statute, and equal to zero for states adopting general incorporation by constitutional amendment. The former are predicted to have adopted general incorporation codes early because statutory change is less costly than constitutional change. In particular, enactment of general chartering by statute would fall under the normal voting rules of the legislature, necessitating only a simple majority vote in both houses, with final approval requiring the governor's signature. By contrast, constitutional amendment usually falls under more restrictive rules, which perhaps involve ratification by super majorities in each legislative chamber, executive signature, and the subsequent passage in a referendum by the voters in the state.

We estimated various specifications of our model by ordinary least squares.[24] (Summary statistics for each of the independent variables are reported in table 27–2.) The regression results shown in table 27–3 strongly suggest that the characteristics of the legislative apparatus are important in explaining the pattern of deregulation. Other things equal, states with larger legislatures tended to deregulate early, and adoption of general chartering was delayed in states having more disparate house sizes.[25] All of the estimated coefficients on SIZE and HSR are significantly different from zero at the 5 percent level or lower. The negative sign on SIZE indicates that those lobbying for change in the law of incorporation found it easier to obtain deregulation in larger legislatures. This would be the case if the effect of competition between legislators on the price of influence more than offsets the tendency for transactions costs to rise as the number of lawmakers increases. On balance, deregulation occurred earlier in states having larger legislatures, perhaps because each representative was better able to specialize in narrower constituent concerns. Calculating the elasticity at the means using the smallest of the estimated coefficients, a 1 percent increase in legislature size advanced the elimination of special chartering by 17.75 years. Similarly, a 1 percent increase in the ratio of house size to senate size delayed deregulation by just over 16 years.

Table 27–2.

Variable	*Mean*	*Standard Deviation*	*Coefficient of Variation*	*Minimum*	*Maximum*
SIZE	126.85	75.98	0.60	22	353
HSR	3.69	4.05	1.10	1.44	28.42
POP	758.28	784.30	1.03	6.86	3,521.95
MFGINC	54.03	86.57	1.60	2.60	439.00
LARGE	9.45	3.46	0.37	3.10	19.60
VADDED	100.95	174.56	1.73	0.60	853.45
K/L	3.65	0.92	0.25	1.58	6.02
SHDUM	0.43	0.50	1.16	0	1
STDUM	0.04	0.20	5.00	0	1

Sources: The data on state legislatures are from *The World Almanac for 1875*. State population figures were obtained from U.S. Department of Commerce (1975). As mentioned in the text, the population numbers for each state relate to the decennial census closest to the year of adoption of general chartering. The manufacturing income data are from Easterlin (1960), and pertain to 1880. The remaining manufacturing data were obtained from U.S. Department of Commerce (1918) the observations on firm size are for 1904, and the data on value added in manufacturing, the value of capital, and labor expenditures are for 1899.

Table 27–3. Regression Results

	Dependent Variable: Year of Adoption of Incorporation under General Laws									
Intercept	1867.96	1907.78	1869.83	1892.61	1887.54	1890.13	1895.08	1886.10	1889.88	1894.66
SIZE	−0.1425	−0.1734	−0.1494	−0.1898	−0.1407	−0.1610	−0.1418	−0.1415	−0.1604	−0.1425
	(−2.60)**	(−2.96)***	(−2.68)**	(−3.09)***	(−2.75)***	(−3.22)***	(−2.77)***	(−2.72)***	(−3.15)***	(−2.74)***
HSR	4.8582	4.4344	4.7913	5.2029	4.4546	4.8441	4.5092	4.4071	4.7694	4.4620
	(3.63)***	(2.99)***	(3.50)***	(3.38)***	(3.37)***	(3.67)***	(3.41)***	(3.27)***	(3.56)***	(3.31)***
POP	0.0190	0.0050	0.0178	0.0056	0.0162	0.0159	0.1624	0.0159	0.0158	0.0160
	(3.48)***	(1.09)	(3.23)**	(1.16)	(3.62)***	(3.50)***	(3.62)***	(3.46)***	(3.40)***	(3.48)***
MFGINC	−0.1626				−0.1342	−0.1480	−0.1365			
	(−3.96)***				(−3.46)***	(−3.84)***	(−3.51)***			
LARGE		−2.6696			−1.5579		−1.2741	−1.5179		−1.2145
		(−2.63)**			(−1.87)*		(−1.45)	(−1.78)*		(1.35)
VADDED			−0.0757					−0.0638	−0.0718	−0.0655
			(−3.64)***					(−3.18)***	(−3.64)***	(−3.26)***
K/L				−4.0620		−3.9921	−2.7451		−4.0789	−2.8834
				(−1.34)		(−1.54)	(−1.02)		(−1.55)	(−1.05)
SHDUM	8.1573	−10.3564	5.7466	0.1332						
	(1.12)	(−1.24)	(0.79)	(0.02)						
STDUM	−50.5217	−35.9234	−49.5867	−57.2385	−39.8654	−52.7565	−42.9247	−39.1977	−51.6008	−42.3959
	(−2.16)**	(−1.36)	(−2.08)**	(−2.13)**	(−1.69)*	(−2.29)**	(−1.81)*	(−1.64)	(−2.21)**	(−1.76)*
R^2	0.478	0.381	0.455	0.305	0.505	492	0.518	0.487	0.478	0.501
F	6.11***	4.10***	5.57***	2.93**	6.81***	6.46***	5.99***	6.34***	6.10***	5.60***

Notes: t-values in parentheses; asterisks denote significance at the 1 percent (***), 5 percent (**), and 10 percent (*) levels.

Special charactering was eliminated later in states having larger populations, and earlier in jurisdictions where the benefits were greatest.[26] In particular, compared with less populous states, each 1 percent increase in population was associated with a delay of slightly more than 3.75 years in adoption of general chartering. Deregulation occurred earlier in states having larger manufacturing sectors. The estimated coefficients on MFGINC and LARGE are uniformly negative and significantly different from zero at the 1 percent level. This suggests that general chartering was adopted first in states where the stake in legal change was the greatest: each 1 percent increase in the size of the manufacturing sector moved the elimination of special chartering ahead on the order of six to seven years. The results also suggest that the timing of deregulation was advanced in states where more of the manufacturing output was produced by large, capital-intensive firms. Although the estimated coefficients on K/L are not different from zero at standard significance levels, the overall evidence is consistent with the hypothesis that deregulation happened sooner in states where the capital-raising advantages of incorporation were most important.

As predicted, adoption of general chartering by statute occurred prior to deregulation by constitutional amendment, but those jurisdictions deregulating at statehood tended to do so at about the same time as existing states. We take this latter result to mean that given their population, legislature size, and characteristics of manufacturing, the territories would not have adopted general chartering earlier even if they had had the opportunity to do so. However, we do not know how the territorial governments operated, including whether or not the legislatures could grant corporate charters.

Overall, our model explains about half of the variation across states in the timing of corporate chartering deregulation. The results are strongly consistent with the hypothesis that the order in which states adopted incorporation under general laws was determined in part by the relative benefits and costs of deregulation. That is, deregulation tended to occur first where the benefits were greatest, and where the costs were least.

Concluding Remarks

When applied to corporate chartering, the conventional wisdom among legal scholars would see innovations in law as being the result of public-spirited government in enlightened states taking the lead in adopting progressive corporation codes which only later would be emulated by less advanced jurisdictions. In contrast, our analysis suggests that the spread of deregulation followed a pattern explained by the comparative benefits and costs of using the political machinery of states to obtain a given legislative outcome. Legal change is like economic change: it tends to occur first where the cost of using the political process is least, and where the benefits are greatest.

Notes

1. On the history of the modern corporation, see Ekelund and Tollison (1980), and Anderson and Tollison (1983).

2. *Liggett Co. v. Lee*, 288 U.S. 517 (1933) (Justice Brandeis, dissenting in part, p. 555).

3. Dodd and Leftwich (1980, p. 260) note that "in 1971, corporate franchise taxes represented 25% of Delaware's tax collections."

4. Dodd and Leftwich (1980, pp. 261–62) calculate that in 1977 there was one company incorporated in Delaware for every 39 people in the state. Moreover, 40 percent of the corporations then listed on the New York Stock Exchange held Delaware charters. Romano (1984) recently has put forth several reasons for Delaware's success, including a comprehensive body of corporate case law, a large stock of corporate attorney human capital, and a dependency on franchise tax revenues as an income source that assures the state will remain responsive to corporate demands.

5. Friedman (1973, p. 166) states that "in all of the 18th century, charters were issued to only 335 businesses. Only seven of these were during the colonial period; 181 were issued between 1796 and 1800."

6. According to Henn (1970, p. 19), the innovation first appeared with the adoption by North Carolina in 1795 of a statute allowing general incorporation. The principle was limited to canal companies, however.

7. Notwithstanding the North Carolina statute of 1795, the first state to offer general incorporation for "any lawful purpose" was Connecticut in 1837 (Henn 1970, p. 19). Anderson and Tollison (1983) observe that England deregulated at about the same time that general chartering first appeared in the U.S.

8. Brandeis's dissenting opinion in *Liggett Co. v. Lee* contains a description of the early restrictions. See n. 2, especially pp. 550–9.

9. Hessen (1979, p. 43) notes that there was a gradual evolution of contractural forms from partnership to corporation.

10. *Liggett Co. v. Lee*, p. 557, Friedman (1973, pp. 456–7), and Winter (1977, p. 255) all make this point.

11. Friedman (1973, p. 457). In discussing the case law on corporations between 1800 and 1830, Dodd (1954, p. 56) observed:

> that lawyers as well as laymen generally took for granted that a corporation could engage in such business transactions in non-domiciliary states as were within the scope of its charter and not forbidden by the laws of the state in which it was acting

Dodd went on to note that when in 1838 an opinion by Justice M'Kinley for the Alabama Circuit Court held otherwise, the "decision 'frightened half the lawyers and all the corporations of the country out of their proprieties.'" M'Kinley's decision was overturned one year later by *Bank of Augusta v. Earle*, 13 Pet. 519 (U.S. 1839).

12. Henn (1970, p. 20) notes that "Governor Woodrow Wilson took New Jersey out of the competition by his antitrust measures known as the "Seven Sisters Acts' in 1913."

13. Butler (1985) offers a complementary interpretation of the demise of the special charter.

14. All but four states—Connecticut, Massachusetts, New Hampshire, and Rhode Island—initially adopted general incorporation codes by constitutional amendment. Of these, we were unable to determine the date Rhode Island enacted a general incorporation law. See Evans (1948, pp. 10–11).

Evans's data appear to be an internally consistent snapshot of the deregulation chronology. However, there are hints elsewhere in the literature that other chronologies are possible. For example, Ekelund (1978, p. 137) dates the movement toward general incorporation from a New York law passed in 1811, through the adoption of a similar statute in 1882 by Massachusetts. He suggests that "the main rush to general legislation by the states came during the years 1837 and 1838." In contrast, Mofsky (1978, p. 144) states that "the first general incorporation laws were enacted as early as 1809 in Massachusetts, and 1811 in New York. . . . It was not unitl 1875 that the first modern, 'liberal' general incorporation act was passed. That occurred in New Jersey." Butler (1985) observes that state legislatures moved gradually from special charactering to general chartering. In particular, so-called dual chartering systems, in which the adoption of general incorporation codes was not accompanied by elimination of special chartering, existed for a time in some states. And, early general chartering laws sometimes contained many of the restrictions on capitalization and other incorporating rights that had existed under special chartering.

The important point, however, is that adoption of the general chartering principle by a given state would have been the event on which various interest groups focused their lobbying efforts. Once a general chartering law had been adopted, proposals for further liberalization would have raised less momentous issues. (Compare adoption of the principle of deficit spending with proposals to increase the debt ceiling.) Thus, although there may be some debate as to when each state adopted a "modern" general incorporation code, such discussions put one in the position of asking. "How liberal is liberal?" We choose to not enter such a debate and to use Evans's chronology because his data date the most important event in the deregulation process.

15. When graphed against time, the cumulative number of states adopting incorporation under general laws displays the S-shaped pattern characteristic of the diffusion process for many technological innovations (see Griliches 1957, 1960, and Mansfield 1968, for example). In order to test whether or not deregulation of corporate chartering proceeded in such a fashion, we fit the 47-state adoption chronology to the logistic curve.

$$y_t = 1/[\ + a_0 \exp(-a_1 t)],$$

where y_t is the cumulative proportion of states with general incorporation laws in year t, and the a's are the parameters to be estimated.

The results were as follows:

$$y_t = 1/[1 + \underset{(12.47)^{\bullet\bullet\bullet}}{12.1058} \exp(\underset{(-33.92)^{\bullet\bullet\bullet}}{-0.0694t})]$$

$$R^2 = 0.994 \qquad F = 12{,}808.35^{\bullet\bullet\bullet}$$

As is apparent, the estimates provide strong support for the hypothesis that deregulation of the corporate charter market followed an S-shaped growth curve. This evidence tends to confirm the results obtained in other diffusion studies of legal change (Walker 1969, Gray

1973), and suggests that innovation is an economic not a technical phenomenon.

16. "The organizers of a corporation may obtain their charter in any state, without regard to the place it will conduct its activities or to the residence of the interested parties" (Kaplan 1968, p. 435).

17. See McLure (1967), and Maloney, McCormick, and Tollison (1984).

18. This is likely to entail differential effects for large and small firms Kaplan (1968, p. 435) asserts that relatively few small firms incorporate in states other than the one where they conduct business.

19. This argument is made by Mofsky and Tollison (1977, p. 370) in discussing state "blue-sky" securities regulation.

20. Baysinger (1979) suggests that competition among jurisdictions leads to a menu of efficient chartering laws in which each state offers corporate contract terms appealing to a specific set of firms and investors. The structure of franchise taxation across states would be one of the results of this competition. Deregulation thus took a variety of forms.

21. Crain (1979) offers additional arguments concerning the effect of house-senate disparity on the cost of legislative output.

22. Population density also affects the costs of organizing coalitions either to support or to oppose specific legislation. However, because density did not turn out to be empirically important in our estimates, we did not include it in our final model. A similar result was obtained by Stigler (1976).

23. Rhode Island, Alaska, and Hawaii are excluded from our sample.

24. We would be happy to supply our data set upon request.

25. In the process of searching for state legislature membership data contemporaneous with deregulation, we estimated various specifications of our model employing sequentially 1980–1981 and 1935 figures (Council of State Governments 1935, 1980), and 1910 data (North 1911, pp. 195–6). Similar coefficients and significance levels for SIZE and HSR were obtained throughout, with the 1875 and 1935 data yielding the most statistically alike results. We are thus able to offer independent confirmation of Stigler's (1976) finding that legislature size has been quite stable over time.

26. The results concerning the size and characteristics of the manufacturing sector raise an interesting causality question that unfortunately cannot be answered given the available data. That is, did these states have an incentive to adopt general chartering sooner than other jurisdictions, or did deregulation spur the growth of manufacturing in those states that eliminated special chartering early? However, there are not a sufficient number of observations on the nineteenth century manufacturing variables to perform such a test. We thank Mark Crain for bringing this point to out attention.

References

Anderson, Gary M., and Tollison, R. D. "The Myth of the Corporation as a Creation of the State." *International Review of Law and Economics* 3 (December, 1983): 107–20.

Baysinger, B. D., "A Theory of the Efficiency of Jurisdictional Choice: The Case of Corporate Federalism." Unpublished Ph.D. dissertation, Virginia Polytechnical Institute and State University, 1979.

Berle, A. A., and Means, G. C. *The Modern Corporation and Private Property*, rev. ed. New York: Harcourt, Brace & World, Inc., 1968.

Butler, H.N. "Nineteenth-Century Jurisdictional Competition in the Granting of Corporate Charters." *Journal of Legal Studies 14* (January, 1985): 129–66.

Council of State Governments. *The Book of the States*. Lexington, Ky: Council of State Governments, 1935 and 1980.

Crain, W.M. "Costs and Outputs in the Legislative Firm." *Journal of Legal Studies* 8 (June, 1979): 607–21.

Dodd, E.M. *American Business Corporations Until 1860*. Cambridge, Mass: Harward University Press, 1954.

Dodd, P., and Leftwich, R. "The Market for Corporate Charters: 'Unhealthy Competition' versus Federal Regulation." *Journal of Business* 53 (July, 1980): 259–83.

Easterlin, R.A. "Interregional Differences in Per Capita Income, Population, and Total Income, 1840–1950." In *Trends in the American Economy in the Nineteenth Century*. National Bureau of Economic Research. Princeton: Princeton University Press, 1960.

Ekelund, R.B. Jr. "Have State Regulations Led to Corporate Monopoly Power?" In *The Attack on Corporate America*. M.B. Johnson (ed.) New York: McGraw-Hill, 1978.

Ekelund, R.B. Jr., and Tollison, R.D., "Mercantilist Origins of the Corporation." *Bell Journal of Economics* 11 (Autumn, 1980): 715–20.

Evans, G.H. Jr. *Business Incorporations in the United States, 1800–1943*. New York: National Bureau of Economic Research, 1948.

Fletcher, William M. *Cyclopedia of the Law of Private Corporations*, Vol. 1. Rev. by Morton S. Wolfe. Chicago: Callaghan & Co, 1974.

Friedman, L.M., *A History of American Law*. New York: Simon and Schuster, 1973.

Gray, V. "Innovation in the States: A Diffusion Study." *American Political Science Review* 67 (December, 1973): 1174–85.

Griliches, Z. "Hybrid Corn: An Exploration in the Economics of Technological Change." *Econometrica* 25 (October, 1957): 501–22.

Griliches, Z. "Hybrid Corn and the Economics of Innovation." *Science* 132 (July, 1960): 275–80.

Henn, H.G. *Handbook of the Law of Corporations and Other Business Enterprises*, 2nd ed. St. Paul, Minn.: Est Publishing Co, 1970.

Hessen, R. *In Defense of the Corporation*. Stanford: Hoover Institution Press, 1979.

Kaplan, S.A. "Foreign Corporations and Local Corporate Policy." *Vanderbilt Law Review* 21 (May, 1968): 433–81.

Maloney, MT.; McCormick, R.E.; and Tollison, R.D. "Economic Regulation, Competitive Governments, and Specialized Resources." *Journal of Law and Economics* 27 (October, 1984): 329–38.

Mansfield, E. *The Economics of Technological Change*. New York: W.W. Norton & Co., 1968.

McLure, C. "The Interstate Exporting of State and Local Taxes." *National Tax Journal* 20 (March, 1967): 49–77.

McCormick, R.E., and Tollison, R.D. *Politicians, Legislation, and the Economy: An Inquiry into the Interest-Group Theory of Government.* Boston: Martinus Nijhoff, 1981.

Mofsky, J. "Have State Incorporation Laws Established Monopolies or Promoted Competition?" In: M.B. Johnson (ed.), *The Attack on Corporate America*. New York: McGraw-Hill, 1978.

Mofsky, J. and Tollison, R.D. "Demerit in Merit Regulation." *Marquette Law Review* 60 (Winter, 1977): 367–78.

North, S.N.D. (ed.) *1910 American Year Book*, New York: D. Appleton & Co., 1911.

Posner, R.A. *Economic Analysis of Law*, 2nd ed. Boston: Little, Brown & Co., 1977.

Romano, R. "Some Pieces of the Incorporation Puzzle." Working Paper no. 19. Stanford Law School (December, 1984).

Stigler, G.A. "The Sizes of Legislatures." *Journal of Legal Studies* 5 (January, 1976) 17–34.

Stigler, G.A., "The Theory of Economic Regulation." *Bell Journal of Economics* 2 (Spring, 1971): 3–21.

U.S. Department of Commerce Bureau of the Census. *Census of Manufactures 1914.* Washington, D.C. USGPO, 1918.

U.S. Department of Commerce Bureau of the Census. *Historical Statistics of the United States, Colonial Times to 1970*. Washington, D.C.: USGPO, 1975.

Walker, J.L. "The Diffusion of Innovations Among the American States." *American Political Science Review* 63 (September, 1969): 880–99.

Winter, R.K. "State Law, Shareholder Protection, and the Theory of the Corporation," *Journal of Legal Studies* 6 (June, 1977): 251–92.

The World Almanac for 1875. New York: The New York World, 1875.

28 WHY DID THE INDUSTRIAL REVOLUTION OCCUR IN ENGLAND?

Gordon Tullock

Like most economists, I am a great admirer of Adam Smith and feel, again like most economists, that the application of his ideas had much to do with the efflorescence of British civilization in the 19th century. The industrial revolution, however, got its basic start, and indeed according to some historians was completely accomplished, before *The Wealth of Nations* had significant influence on government policy. The Savery steam engine was built in England in 1698, the Newcomen in 1721, and by 1763 Watt had created the modern steam engine. Hargreaves' spinning jenny was invented in 1765 and Arkwright's water frame in 1769. Crompton introduced his "mule" in 1774. *The Wealth of Nations*, of course, was published in 1776, but it is hard to argue that the introduction of the power loom by Cartwright, in 1785, was the result of policies based on Adam Smith's work. In fact, Smith had little or no effect on English governmental policies before 1815.

Thus, the industrial revolution was well underway before Adam Smith wrote. Basically, it was in place before the Smithian Revolution in government policy even began. Indeed, England was widely regarded as the most technically advanced country in Europe as early as 1725 or thereabouts. In a way, the whole point of the French revolution was to transfer to France certain English institutions which people like Voltaire thought were the explanations of England's success. Voltaire visited England before Adam Smith's book was published.

What then was the reason for this great economic development in England before Adam Smith produced the theory and policies which led to its even greater prosperity in the latter 19th century? I propose to argue that it was an accidental by-product of certain political changes arising out of what I would like to call "the English revolution", i.e., the series of events in the 17th century beginning with Charles I's difficulties with Parliament.

In most the world, throughout most of history, rent-seeking has been a major activity for the more talented and aggressive members of society. This is one of the reasons, albeit not the only one, why progress in general has been slow. If a large number of the most talented people in society spend almost all their efforts in the attempt to obtain special privileges for themselves, they firstly generate no social surplus for others; secondly, they actually reduce the total output by at least sometimes obtaining their monopoly, special privilege, etc. England, like most of the rest of the world, was a society dominated by rent-seeking in 1600. By 1750 rent-seeking was relatively unimportant. A combination of the sharp reduction in the number of monopolies, restrictive practices, etc., together with the fact that the most talented and aggressive people in society turned from rent-seeking to more productive activities, jointly constitute, in my opinion, the principal cause of the industrial revolution. Of course there were, as I shall point out below, other major causes.

The problem obviously is why the industrial revolution occurred in England and not in France, Italy, or Germany. Firstly, it must be said that it would be very hard to argue that in 1600 or, for that matter, in 1750 science was more advanced in England than in those three other countries, or the Netherlands, Sweden, etc. Further, it is clear that the general state of civilization was at least as high in say, France, as in England. Indeed, most people in those days would have said it was higher. There were far more Englishmen studying in continental universities than there were continentals studying in English universities. Indeed, the state of the universities in England (well described by Adam Smith) was such that it is very dubious that anyone would have studied there for intellectual reasons. The Scotch universities were, of course, different, but even they did not deserve anything like the reputation of Paris, Heidelberg, or Leyden.

The general standard of civilization in England was no higher and probably somewhat lower than that on the continent. It should also be said that the general standard of public morals was probably worse in England. It is no great compliment to the French government of that date to say that on the whole it was a more honest government than that of England. The British government ran on corruption.[1] The king quite literally bought approval of laws in Parliament. Further, a very large number of the seats in the Lower House were owned in fee simply by someone, usually someone who personally sat in the House of Lords. The House of Pitt, for example, owned six seats in Commons.

This corruption of government, together with the fact that it depended on handing out special favors, surely was an atmosphere where one would anticipate large scale rent-seeking. Indeed, the government itself ran almost entirely by rent-seeking. Individuals would invest resources in obtaining appointment as collector of customs or promotion to captain in the Navy.[2]

But if this is the way the government operated internally, the rest of society was remarkably free of rent-seeking, granted the date and the world in which England lived. It could not be said that there was none. Occasionally, Parliament granted some group of businessmen special monopolies, but it was rare, and in most cases there was at least a colorable argument of public interest, as in the famous case of the Honorable East India Company's special privileges on the import of tea. It should be pointed out, of course, that the special privilege in this case was a low tax rather than tariff protection.[3]

There were, of course, a large number of regulations still on the books which had been enacted mainly before 1620 or so and which had originally given people various important and valuable privileges. Gradually, however, these regulations had become largely obsolete. They were, as Adam Smith pointed out, a burden on trade, albeit not too much of a burden because people had worked out ways of getting around them. The bulk of English manufacturing, for example, was located outside of incorporated towns and hence avoided the guild regulations. The competition of this extramural industry meant that the guilds in town had to recognize they faced competition and hence could not be as extortionate as they were in France, for example.[4]

This development can hardly be regarded as the result of conscious policy. Indeed, there is practically no evidence of anybody having consciously thought about these issues before Adam Smith. Those people who did think about them, normally felt that what was needed was improved regulations rather than letting the old regulations gradually disintegrate. Smith then inspired the intellectual revolution which later had great effect on British policy, but by 1776 England had already moved a very long way from the rent-seeking society.

Why did this happen? It is the thesis of this paper that the basic cause was the English revolution of the 17th century, and that it was essentially a by-product of decisions of a political nature taken for other reasons.

If we consider English history, the first thing we note is that England had in many ways the most disturbed political history of any European country that actually succeeded in achieving central government. Germany and Italy, of course, had more disturbed histories and ended up divided into small countries instead of single countries. Spain, France, the Netherlands, and Sweden, all, like England, achieved a central government and unification, but did so with much less in the way of civil wars and turnovers of dynasty than England. From the time of the Norman conquest to the time of the American revolution there were few examples of the throne of England passing peacefully from father to son to grandson. George III was in this way, as in many other ways, an exception to the general rule of the English history. Still, with the accession of Henry VII, who in fact had practically no claim to the throne of England beyond his victory at Bosworth field, things became at least temporarily stable. Henry, a cold-blooded, unscrupulous, and extremely clever man, felt that he must protect his dynasty first by killing anyone who had even any faint claim to the throne, and secondly by weakening the power of the great nobles. In achieving the latter objective, he turned to a number of expedients, one of which was strengthening of the power of Parliament. This was intended to and indeed did reduce the power of the great nobles, but it should be pointed out it was also intended to increase the power of the king, and did so as well.

If we move forward to Henry VII's granddaughter, Elizabeth,[5] we then see a government in which the Queen had more power than any English king had had for a long time. The greater nobility had pretty generally been brought to heel and the commons were in general obedient. There was, however, no professional army, which clearly meant that the Queen was not as powerful as the king of France or Spain. Elizabeth, like the two other children of Henry VIII who sat on the throne of England, had no children of her own, and the throne passed to a rather distant relative, the king of Scotland. James I, having been impressed by his current contemporaries in France and Spain, wished to improve the power of the throne even more, but he was one of the most tactless man who has ever sat on the throne of England, and it is likely that his reign actually weakened the crown.

Before discussing the events of the reign of his son, Charles I, however, it is sensible to pause briefly and explain the rent-seeking situation then in England. It was the policy of the Tudor kings in England to make use of royal monopolies for various private citizens to a considerable extent as a revenue-raising device for the king.[6]

Nevertheless, these monopolies were a product of rent-seeking activity, and there was much other rent-seeking activity in the economy as a whole. Tollison has suggested that the basic cause of the civil war was the desire of the House of Commons to take over the profits of this rent-seeking activity from the king.[7]

The monopolies, however, had to be enforced. At that time there were a number of courts in England. First, there were the Courts of Chancery, which will not be dealt with again here, because of their rather special jurisdiction. They in fact played little role in the events that followed. Secondly, there were the common law courts. These had developed into a system in which judges appointed for life administered jury trials, although the basic decisions as to guilt or innocence in any criminal charge was made by the jury. Lastly, there was the court which we now refer to as the "Court of the Star Chamber," which was simply an appointed commission set up by the king for the purpose of carrying out such laws as he wished. The latter was primarily used to enforce the various monopolies and the special privilege grants which the king made. The "Court of the Star Chamber" was used among other things to impose certain taxes on the English upper classes, particularly ship money, and as a general rule annoyed the non-royal part of the British society.

We now proceed to the unpleasantness between king and Parliament, which I think is normally badly described as a revolt against the king. As a matter of fact it was a revolt by the king against Parliament. The king found it necessary to leave London in order to raise his standard. The only professional part of the military apparatus, the Navy, remained loyal to Parliament. The Parliament, throughout the war, also had access to a more regular revenue than did the king, with the result that their army was characteristically larger, better equipped, and better paid. In the early part of the Civil War, nevertheless, the king won a number of battles. Eventually, however, the Parliamentary forces were brought under the control of Cromwell who was capable of winning if he had numerical superiority. In a way it was rather like the Army of the Potomac, which was regularly beaten by Lee in spite of numerical superiority until it came under the control of Grant, who was capable of winning if he had numerical superiority.

The war, of course, ended with the complete defeat of the royal forces and the execution of the king, but it also ended with Pride's purge and Parliament being brought completely under the control of Cromwell. The result in essence was merely another and stronger king. Indeed, Cromwell probably had more power than any king of England had ever had.

The incidents of the struggle, however, are of more interest to us than this specific outcome, particularly since Cromwell's government was swept away after his death.

Firstly, there was the statute of monopolies passed by Parliament. This prohibited royal monopolies except for patent monopolies. Note the accidental characteristic of this development. Parliament passed a bill prohibiting the king from establishing monopolies but made an exception. Gradually over the next century the issuing of monopolies for new inventions switched from being a matter of royal favor to being a bureaucratic step carried on at the lower level of government. This made it possible for people to invest sizeable resources in attempting to develop new devices, i.e., it opened up a new area of research. This certainly had much to do with the development of new inventions in England. I shall, however, argue below that although it was certainly important, there were other steps which were at least of equal or perhaps of greater importance.

It seems likely that, as Ekelund and Tollison pointed out,[8] Parliament's motive in passing the statute of monopolies was not to eliminate monopoly rents or rent-seeking, but simply to transfer these rents to their own hands. As it turned out, Parliament was unable to get very much profit from this rent for a number of reasons. One, a fairly obvious one, is that the transactions cost of fixing a large body of men like Parliament was much higher than that of dealing with the king. This would certainly have reduced the amount of rent-seeking activities. There are however other reasons.

The first problem encountered by Parliament in its desire for rents is that Charles I in the early part of his long dispute with Parliament dealt with Parliamentary opposition in a simple, straightforward way. He did not call Parliament into session for twenty years. This certainly eliminated any possibility of rent-seeking by Parliament during that period. Further, when Parliament finally did come into session, the developments very rapidly moved into Civil War, and Parliament in general had little time to devote to such matters. At the end of the war, Cromwell purged Parliament of everyone whom he thought could not be trusted to vote exactly as he thought was desirable, and hence there was another period of time in which Parliament was unable to capture any significant rents from the granting of monopolies. Functioning of Parliament was eventually reestablished in the second half of Cromwell's reign, but the people who had passed the statute of monopoly were long gone.

But that does not explain why the new Parliaments—and for that matter the kings—did not revive rent-seeking at this point. Charles II was certainly not the type of person to shy away from establishing monopolies for his friends. The explanation, I think, comes from another by-product of the disturbances. As I have said, the "Court of the Star Chamber" enforced the various rent-seeking activities, i.e., the monopolies and special grants privileges. It did not, of course, enforce the payment of government officials who had obtained their jobs by rent-seeking activity, and it is notable that rent-seeking in that form continued to be very active and important in England right up to the 19th century.

The "Court of the Star Chamber," however, had been used to collect taxes from the upper class in England, who to a large extent were responsible for the revolution and had therefore acquired a very negative image. As a part of the revolutionary development it was abolished. This left the judiciary of England almost entirely[9] in the hands of the common law courts, where decisions basically were made by juries. To put it briefly, juries cannot be depended upon to put people in jail for having violated the monopoly privilege of some rent seeker. Under the circumstances rent-seeking ceased to be very valuable because the rent could not be protected.

A little more discussion of the jury is called for at this point. Juries in general are rather erratic in their performance, as I suppose we would expect from a group of people drafted into a service for which they are not in any way specially trained and then manipulated by two specialists in such manipulation, one for each side. There are certain characteristics of their behavior which can be predicted, however. They are, for example, generally speaking, prejudiced against large corporations and, for that matter, the government. More particularly, however, they generally do not enforce laws that they disapprove of. A maximum price is the kind of thing that they are apt to approve of, but a minimum price is not.

Not very long ago the Interstate Commerce Commission, becoming upset at the violation of its rules, arranged for a round up of independent truckers in the vicinity of Chicago who were violating regulations by charging too low rates and breaking into the monopolies that had been granted to larger companies. As we will explain below, under modern circumstances enforcement of this kind of special privilege is dealt with not by a jury but by a judge sitting alone. Hence the truckers were in fact fined and ordered not to continue. Now imagine the situation if the only way of dealing with them had been to call them before a jury. No district attorney in his right mind would have brought a poor black truck owner[10] before a jury and accused him of having unfairly competed with a large trucking monopoly, offering as evidence the fact that he was charging lower prices than the monopoly. If the district attorney was so foolish to do this, he would be lucky not to have the jury find him guilty.

The same problem would occur in most other areas where monopoly rents can be obtained. The jury would tend to feel that the person who violated this rent was either a person to be congratulated or in any event somebody who had done nothing particularly awful. U.S. experience in the early 19th century, when private persons competed with the Federal Mail Service and efforts to convict them were almost totally nugatory because the juries refused to do so, would be repeated.

In 17th and 18th-century England the reluctance of juries to convict in rent cases was reinforced by the fact that the jury was not drawn from the citizenry at large, but almost exclusively from the gentry and minor gentry classes. The basic source of revenue of such people was land rent. Typically a person who was accused of violating, say, the monopoly on soap by producing soap, would be tried in the area where he had his establishment. Finding him guilty would, to some, very slight extent, lower land rents in that area. Hence there was a positive (if minor) material motive for not convicting.

Indeed, in general, the result of the Civil War was to put the government of England for a long period of time in the hands of the land-owning classes, whether these classes were the great nobles with the great estates or the local gentry with their smaller properties. These landholders, who were without access to tax money and any real prospect of obtaining monopoly rents (because on the whole it was not possible to establish a monopoly on farm products under the conditions of England at that time), were primarily interested in increasing the total land rent of England. Expanding commerce and industry in general would have moved in that direction, albeit very modestly. These members of the gentry and great Lords were very anxious to obtain what privileges they could out of a state and were frequently quite ingenious in achieving such privileges. They found themselves in a situation in which the presence of the jury trial as the only way of enforcing any government regulation meant that, outside of securing government jobs for their nephews, there was very little they could do. They did what they could, but it was not very much.

Of course, the use of the jury was not the only factor, although before the adoption of "liberal" policies in England in the early nineteenth century, it was probably the most important factor. After 1815, as a result of Smith and Ricardo's influence, there was actually conscious planning for growth. The switch to free trade, which has been so much and so correctly extolled by economists, not only improved efficiency in and of itself, but made rent-seeking particularly difficult. There was little or no advantage in being given special privileges for the manufacture of anything in England if foreigners could always import it. Further, the very restricted size of the total government during the 19th-century heyday of *laissez-faire* in England not only lowered the tax burden, but also reduced the possibility of rent-seeking in other areas. I have mentioned above that the English govenment in the 18th century was the most corrupt in Europe, with government jobs being the principal source of corruption. There just were not very many government jobs in 19th century England, and hence the development of a non-corrupt civil service involved very little sacrifice for anyone.

In the eighteenth century the requirement of juries was much more important. Still it should be said that although economists can claim credit for the 19th-century English reforms, the United States did as well without consciously adopting good economic policies, simply because of the internal free trade provision in the constitution. The combination of the federal system, internal free trade, and a very small and relatively inactive central government (which was characteristic of the United States, certainly up to the end of the 19th century) also made rent-seeking difficult. Once again there is no evidence that the American government personnel were opposed to rent-seeking, or did not actively engage in what rent-seeking they could. Indeed, the way the tariff was manipulated by the federal government, land grants in the West, and the introduction of the spoils system in the government's personnel policies all were good examples of rent-seeking activity. Further, if we look at the states we find that they almost continuously attempted to provide monopolies to special groups or bend their budgets in such ways as to benefit particular areas.

The states found this behavior generally non-paying because of free trade within the United States. The national government was just too small to have any great impact on anything except perhaps such specialized areas as the arms industry. Even here, however, the early development of a significant export market meant that the importance of rent-seeking was small. Thus, the general absence of rent-seeking in 19th-century England and the United States was not solely the product of the requirement that juries be used to put people in jail. Still, economists can claim credit for the 19th-century English Reforms, although the United States did as well without consciously adopting good policies.

Reestablishment of rent-seeking as a major activity both in England and in the United States in this century has depended on the removal of the jury in these areas. In England the jury has very sharply been downgraded in all areas and to all intents and purposes is not available in civil cases. Nevertheless, the enforcement of rents depends in England as it does in the United States on a specific technique of evading the normal requirements that people must be convicted by a jury before they are put in jail. I am not sure exactly what the history of the development was, but in any event during the latter part of the 19th century it occurred to a number of people that a law of this sort could be enforced, not by accusing people of violating it and giving them a trial, but by getting a judge to order the person to obey the law and then holding him in contempt if he violated this order. People accused of this kind of contempt have no right to a jury trial, and since the judge would decide whether they had committed contempt or not was the judge who had issued the order, it was unlikely that they could escape punishment. Under the circumstances the enforcement of the rules became technically possible because of the denial of the right of jury trial for violations of this kind of regulation. The development of extensive rent-seeking activity beginning with the Interstate Commerce Commission, was, I suppose, the inevitable outcome.

Those who have read my books on the law[11] know that I am opposed to the jury system. This is because it is erratic, inaccurate and cannot be depended upon to enforce the law. When we have a law that I prefer not to have enforced and which I can predict the jury will be biased against, I favor the jury. In a way what we now have from my standpoint is the worst of all possible worlds. People charged with murder, theft, rape, etc., are brought before this inaccurate, frequently biased, decision-making body while people charged with violating an ICC-granted monopoly on trucking and charging too low prices are dealt with by a judge. This is the exact opposite of the arrangement I would favor.

In sum, I have argued that the development of the industrial revolution in England was essentially the result of a series of changes in the British political order that occurred during the period of the English revolution. These changes were not implemented as part of a plan for the industrial revolution, but as a by-product of the political struggle. Disestablishing the "Star Chamber" was primarily motivated by the desire not to be subject to future impositions like ship money. That the abolition would to a large extent abolish rent-seeking activity was probably totally unanticipated by either its proponents or its opponents. It did in fact have that effect.

Notes

1. See almost any one of the books of Sir Phillip Namier on 18th century English politics.

2. Nelson was captain at 21. In his case, he no doubt deserved it. His rapid promotion, however, depended not on his merits but on the fact that he had a close relative in the Admiralty.

3. The Boston Tea Party is a particularly good example of a democracy getting hopelessly muddled. Although a number of New England merchants who had expensive smuggled tea in their warehouses were about to lose money, the average American would clearly benefit from the much lower prices on tea.

4. R.B. Ekelund, Jr., and Robert D. Tollison, "Economic Regulation in Mercantile England: Heckscher Revisited," *Economic Inquiry*, forthcoming, 1980 and "A Rent-Seeking Theory of French Mercantilism," unpublished manuscript, 1980.

5. Her killing of Mary, Queen of Scots, was a continuation of the policy founded by her grandfather of killing all the people that had any, even remote claim to the throne of England.

6. Ekelund and Tollison.

7. Ekelund and Tollison.

8. Op. cit.

9. Once again exempting Chancery.

10. Subject to a 95% mortage.

11. *The Logic of the Law*. New York: Basic Books, Inc., 1971 and *Trials on Trial: The Pure Theory of Legal Procedures*, New York: Columbia University Press, 1980.

IV *Toward Tomorrow*

29 AGENCY, ECONOMIC CALCULATION, AND CONSTITUTIONAL CONSTRUCTION

Richard E. Wagner

Introduction

This paper has both positive and normative foundations. The normative foundation is an affirmation of the broadly liberal heritage of the American experiment with constitutionally limited government. The presumption reflected in the Declaration of Independence, that government derives its just powers from the consent of the governed, is taken seriously, which, among other things, requires rejection of the tautological version of this presumption which is so common, in which the mere presence of what are called "democratic" institutions is taken to mean that those institutions necessarily reflect such consent. Legislative actions may reflect such consent and hence be legitimate, but also they may not and hence be illegitimate. The victim who yields her purse and her body to the knife-yielding intruder "consents" to do so in light of the alternative, just as citizens "consent" to be taxed, regulated, and otherwise governed in light of the alternative. But it is possible to move beyond a statement of tautology only by recognizing that contractarian principles are the only principles that are appropriate for a society of free people. Such a free or liberal society requires in turn a political, constitutional order that is consistent with its own promotion, and such consistency in constitutional construction is a positive and not a normative matter.

The positive foundation is an acceptance of the recent literature on public choice that finds a significant "failure of representative democracy", to use Peter Aranson and Peter Ordeshook's formulation.[1] This recent scholarship draws upon several perspectives to develop a portrait of what can reasonably be called "government failure" as a description of contemporary democratic outcomes. In so doing, this scholarship has reaffirmed, with contemporary modes of reasoning and analytical techniques, the essential veracity of the insights of a host of past scholars, of which the authors of the *Federalist Papers* stand relatively late in the line of succession. According to these insights, governmental "failures" are not so much the result of people who are ill-informed or mal-intentioned as they are the result of inappropriate institutions that nonetheless lend strong survival value to those outcomes. From this perspective, better public policy does not so much require better scholarship about the consequences of particular policies as it requiries political reformation.

The conjunction of these normative and positive foundations leads to a particular formulation of the task of constitutional construction. Any effort at constitutional construction must blend normative and positive elements. The normative principle that informs this paper is the liberal principle of government as compact, which is a principle that has always been central to American rhetoric if not practice. But it is a task for positive analysis to establish whether particular constitutional rules are consistent with or contradictory to maintenance of that principle. In approaching this task of constitutional construction, the theories of agency and economic calculation would seem to have great pertinence. Principles of agency are pivotal because the normative point of departure within a liberal democratic society is surely one in which the relationship between citizens and public officials is properly seen as one between principals and agents. Furthermore, the theory of agency has explored the main determinants of how such a relationship is likely to work, and so offers useful insight into the task of constitutional construction. The theory of economic calculation is pivotal because it is concerned with the conditions under which it will be possible for the structure of production in a society to reflect efficiently the wants of its members. A joining of the theories of agency and economic calculation, then, provides an approach to constitutional construction that is both normatively satisfactory for a liberal democratic society and positively consisters, through its network of incentives, with the maintenance of such a society.

In a regime that takes seriously the dictum that government should reflect the consent of the governed, the only possible norm would seem to be the contractarian one of consent. The liberal ideal of government is one in which people and their rights come first, and the task of government is to support people in their efforts in those cases where people can do better for themselves through common action than they can do through individual action. "Better," however, is determined by those individuals themselves, so the standard of evaluation for policy outcomes must ultimately be a standard of consent among the participants. In such a society, people have their various rights of person and property, and government must itself operate within the same general principles as all other participants in society; government's actions are to fall within the constraints offered by the previously existing rights of property and contract, and not to operate by usurping and abridging those rights in various ways. Indeed the ageless problem of self-government has always been one of how to maintain a kind of schizophrenia for government: in one capacity government is a participant in the economic life of a society, playing by the same rules as others; but in the other capacity government is an umpire, and through legislation becomes a maker of rules for others to play by. Consequently it has the potential to bias the game in particular directions by changing the rules to favor some at the expense of others.[2] The theories of agency and economic calculation would seem to offer valuable insight into the problem of constitutional construction for a liberal democratic regime, as I try to explain in this paper; at base, they provide a grammar for any such effort of constitutional construction.

Principals, Agents, and the Economic Order

Agent-principal relationships pervade economic affairs. The relations between physician and patient, attorney and client, and manager and stockholder are three common illustrations. In any such relationship, a principal who lacks the time or the talent to perform a task engages an agent to perform that task instead. Should this relationship operate ideally for the principal, the agent will act in the same manner as the principal would have acted, had only the principal possessed the appropriate talent and chosen to devote the required time to the task. However, this ideal operation is not a necessary outcome, but rather will result only as a consequence of a congruence of interests between agents and principals. The extent of that congruence will itself depend upon the institutional setting within which the agent-principal relationship operates. An agent might be able to advance his interest more fully by acting contrary to the principal's interest than by promoting it. A physician might treat a patient more expensively or less effectively than their relationship would ideally call for, e.g., by performing unnecessary tests or prescribing unneeded medications. An attorney might write a will or create a trust that requires his client to bear a tax liability that is higher than necessary. A corporate executive might manage corporate assets in a way that reduces the return that stockholders receive. An automobile mechanic might replace a customer's radiator, when all that is needed to prevent the overheating is to replace the thermostat, or perhaps just to flush out the radiator, or possibly even just to add water.

In recognition of such conceptual possibilities as these, the theory of agency has explored how various methods of bonding and monitoring might circumscribe the incentive that agents might have to act contrary to the interests of their principals. To date, the theory of agency has focused mainly on the relationship between corporate managers and stockholders. Starting with publication of the widely acclaimed work of Adolf Berle and Gardiner Means, it has often been claimed that the managers of corporations will be able to a considerable extent to pursue their interests at the expense of the interests of stockholders.[3] In consequence, some of what otherwise would have been stockholder wealth will be appropriated by managers. Despite its surface plausibility, this argument about the divergent interests of owners and managers has several problematical features, as the literature on agency has explained. An important determinant of the specific nature of the relationship between agents and principals is the extent to which it is in the interest of managers to advance the interest of stockholders; this relationship might be tighter or looser, depending upon a variety of institutional circumstances within which it operates.

There are several reasons why the position of stockholders is stronger than the surface appearance of a separation of ownership and control might make it seem. Moreover, most of these reasons arise because of the presence of a capital market through which corporations operate. Corporations cannot draft capital; they cannot compel people to make investments, but must convince people to volunteer their capital. And people will not supply their capital to one particular use if the return they anticipate receiving is lower than what they could anticipate receiving from some alternative use of that capital. Should managers of corporate enterprises come generally to preempt stockholder wealth for themselves, the rate of return on such investments will fall, and people will supply their capital elsewhere. The very presence of an incentive to invest in corporate enterprises implies that there is some limit to the exploitation of stockholders by managers. Indeed, the practice of auditing developed as a response by corporations to the monitoring and bonding costs that are inherent in agency relationships, and for which some solution was essential for the development of corporate enterprise, as Ross Watts and Jerold Zimmerman have shown.

Capital markets also operate in various other ways to unite rather than to separate the interest of managers and stockholders. For one thing, the compensation of managers is commonly based to a significant degree on the performance of the corporations they manage. Both the payment of bonuses tied to corporate performance and the use of stock options, which become more valuable as the corporation becomes more valuable, are examples. In this respect, Wilbur Llewellen estimated, with observations from the 1955–63 period, that managerial compensation that is tied in one way or another to the value of the corporation's stock is typically about five times larger than the compensation that managers receive directly as wages. Moreover, and relatedly, the market for corporate managers tends to work in such a way as to reward more highly those managers who are more successful at enhancing corporate performance, as Eugene Fama points out. The demand for the services of managers will tend to be stronger the better their performance. Hence, and conversely, a diminution in the present performance of a manager will tend to reduce the future earnings of that manager, and the present value of this series of subsequent reductions represents the manager's self-inflicted reduction in the value of his own human capital.

Capital markets also protect stockholders through a market for corporation control, as Henry Manne has noted. Should the managers of a particular corporation pursue their interests at the expense of owners, stockholders will receive a lesser return than they would receive if the corporation was managed fully efficiently in the interest of stockholders. But so long as ownership shares are marketable, this decline in return will depress the market value of those shares. This decline in the value of ownership offers both information that the corporation is not being managed as efficiently as it might be and an incentive for someone to gain control of those assets and manage them more efficiently, because of the potential capital gain.

In various ways, then, the presence of a capital market for corporate equity creates a network of knowledge and incentive that tends to harness the interests of managers to the service of the interests of stockholders. It is the existence of a capital market that makes it possible to devise systems for compensating managers who depend upon the profitability of the corporation. It is also the existence of a capital market that leads to a decline in the value of the ownership shares in a corporation as its managers convert increasing amounts of stockholder wealth to their own uses. Moreover, this resulting divergence between the actual and the potential capital value of the firm, which is made possible by the transferability of ownership rights in corporations, both generates knowledge about the size of the potential gain that could be captured by taking over control of the corporation and operating it more successfully, and also creates an incentive for someone to act on this knowledge by actually attempting, in one way or another, to gain control of the corporation and to operate it more efficiently, thereby capturing the profit opportunities that are present.

Agency and the Democratic Polity

The central, essential perspective or outlook of a democratic society is surely one in which the relationship between citizens and public officials is one of principals and agents, at least in an economically meaningful sense even if not in a legally recognized sense. A government, after all, is owned by its individual citizens, for they are residual claimants with respect to the conduct of government, while its operation resides with a relatively few public officials. And as with other agent-principal relationships, there is always a potential for agents to act contrary to the interest of principals. Public officials might manage public assets inefficiently in any of several ways. They might pay themselves more than is necessary to elicit the required supply of labor. They might be careless in managing the inputs they hire, which in turn means that taxes will be higher than is necessary to produce any particular amount of real output. Stated alternatively, this means that real public output will be less than what it potentially could be in light of the taxes that government collects. As with corporations, the real significance of this nominal separation of ownership and control would seem to depend on the extent to which various institutions in the public sector operate to produce some union between the interests of citizens and public officials.

Although capital markets generally do not operate directly in the case of governments, such other institutions as elections and housing markets might provide a similar function, as shall be noted below. Governments, as they are presently constituted, are nonprofit cooperatives in which ownership shares are inalienable. People cannot buy and sell shares of ownership in governments, so those ownership rights cannot acquire a capital value. Consequently, managerial compensation cannot be tied directly to the efficiency with which assets are managed, as this efficiency is assessed by individual owners and reflected in market evaluations. Moreover, there can be no divergence between actual and potential capital value to provide knowledge about profit opportunities and to generate incentive to act on that knowledge. The absence of a market for ownership shares in governments makes it impossible for people to specialize in ownership. People cannot acquire multiple shares of ownership; they acquire ownership by virtue of residency and must relinquish that ownership upon changing residency. As a result of these differences, the system of signals and incentives that shape the activities of governments may differ in important respects from those of corporations. Because the agent-principal relationship operates under different constraints with government than with corporations, there may in turn be important differences in the knowledge people possess and in the incentives they have to act upon that knowledge.

There is, it should be noted, no necessary reason for the absence of ownership and capital markets in government; governments could be genuine corporations, as indeed the term municipal corporation suggests. It is interesting and instructive to note that hotels, amusement parks, apartment complexes, and shopping centers all illustrate the organization of government-type activities through ownership and capital markets. The corridors and elevators of a hotel are equivalent to the streets and sidewalks of a city. Both are means by which people travel from one place to another. Just as numerous questions arise concerning the allocation of resources to streets and sidewalks, so do the same questions arise with respect to corridors and elevators. Both can be kept more or less clean, more or less brightly lit, and constructed of a lesser or higher quality, all of which are choices about the use of resources. Likewise, cities and hotels both provide for open spaces of varying types; in both cases a choice is made as to how many resources to devote to such objects of shared consumption as parks in the former case and lobbies in the latter. Hotels, apartment complexes, shopping centers, and the like are not essentially different from governments. All organize the provision of items of shared consumption. Hotels provide such communal services as police, fire protection, sanitation, recreation, and transportation, in conjunction with the provision of such private services as rooms, meals, and shops. There is no essential difference between a hotel and a city, save that hotels are commonly organized in corporate fashion and cities are not.

If cities were organized corporately, they would compete among themselves by providing housing and public services, and so would be essentially like hotels, apartment complexes, or shopping centers. Stockholders would provide equity capital, and the actual operation of cities, as that of hotels and shopping centers, would reside with a set of managers. In such a network of competitive, corporate communities, the problem of agency would be about the same as it is in any other market situaton, for cities themselves would be corporations organized within essentially the same institutional framework as other corporations. But when cities are organized democratically, important differences arise in the institutional framework within which the agent-principal relationship takes place. Residents now become owners by virtue of their residency, and that right of ownership is inalienable. Corporate ownership in the presence of a capital market tends to produce unanimity among the owners, as both Harry De Angelo and Louis Mankowski explain. But in the absence of a capital market for ownership, such unanimity is no longer likely. For in the absence of capital markets and transferable ownership, an opportunity arises for conflict among owners, because of efforts of winning coalitions of owners to appropriate wealth from other owners. Different owners-residents may have different preferences for various types of public output, and for public policies generally, because of the opportunities for wealth transfer that those public choices can entail.

One particular illustration, of this conflict of interest is the difference in interest between the owners of developed and undeveloped land. As Jon Sonstelie and Paul Portney note, owners of developed land will commonly want to restrict the development of undeveloped land, because doing so increases the value of the land that is already developed. In contrast, owners of undeveloped land will commonly want to allow development to take place so long as the increase in their property value due to development exceeds the cost they bear because of that development. As compared with an outcome that maximizes the aggregate value of land, owners of developed land will prefer a policy that retards development, because their own wealth is thereby larger, so long as the supply suitable land is not perfectly elastic. And owners of undeveloped land will prefer a policy of excessive development, because such a policy increases the value of their land. Hence, a competitive system of local government, democratically organized, will not generally operate identically with a competitive network of communities, corporately organized. Therefore, the unanimity among owners as to the ideal operation of the governmental enterprise dissolves under democratic organization, thereby confounding the agent-principal relationship from the start.[4]

In other words, the system of alienable ownership that characterizes corporations tends to produce unanimity among owners by restricting the scope for wealth transfers. But with the inalienable ownership that characterizes democratic governments, opportunities for wealth transfers expand. Hence the very question of the degree to which agents advance the interest of principals becomes problematic, because there is no longer commonality in interest among principals in the first place. With respect to local government, however, there is a substantial line of thought that suggests that this commonality of interest might be relatively strong, mainly because of the relatively narrow scope for wealth transfers among the residents of a single jurisdiction. Relatedly, the ability of agents to preempt the wealth of principals will be more restricted at lower levels of government than at higher levels.

Public managers, like corporate managers, can gain if they are able successfully to appropriate the wealth of owners/citizens. However, the extent to which they might actually be able to do so will depend on how tightly various institutional features regarding the conduct of government harness the interests of public officials to the service of the interests of citizens/owners. Public officials will surely face rising pressures for their eviction as the rents they capture increase, due to competition from aspiring sets of public officials. An election is a formalized process for allowing aspiring managers to submit take-over bids, although one that operates without either the knowledge created or the incentive provided by a capital market for shares of ownership, as well as without the consensus among owners provided by a regime of transferable ownership. By increasing the probability that public officials will succumb to a take-over bid in the next election, as well as possibly reducing their value to other employers, managerial rent-seeking will impose some cost on managers. The cost of managerial rent-seeking, then, is the reduction in the present value of future income plus the reduction in the present value of future rents that results from an increase in the probability of electoral defeat. Rent-seeking by public officials reduces the wealth of owners/citizens, which in turn should increase the likelihood that those citizens will support the take-over bid of an opposing set of aspiring managers. However, the extent to which this formalized process for the submission of take-over bids reduces the amount of rent-seeking depends, among other things, on the operation of the processes by which information concerning managerial performance is transmitted to citizens.

Consider, for instance, a competitive system of local government, in which initially all managers are earning only competitive wages. Starting from this initial position, assume managers in one locality begin to capture rents, thereby reducing the returns to citizen/owners. Consequently, the tax-price per unit of public output, and hence the price of residency in this government, will rise, thereby reducing the amount of residency demanded sufficiently to depress property values until the net rate of return on the ownership of housing-and-government becomes equal to the market rate of return, as provided by the ownership of housing-and-government in other jurisdictions. In a competitive system of government, managerial activities in any one government will not affect the return to the ownership of housing-and-government within the market area. Therefore, a reduction in the net income from the ownership of housing-and-government in one jurisdiction will mean that those ownership shares are now overvalued. Consequently, property values in the jurisdiction where public officials secure rents will fall until the net rate of return to investment in housing-and-government in that jurisdiction equals the net rate of return that can be achieved from similar investments in other jurisdictions.

Since a single government in a competitive system of government cannot affect the net rate of return to the ownership of housing-and-government, managerial inefficiency will become capitalized into the values of ownership shares. The change in property values that results from managerial rent-seeking provides a basis on which an opposing set of aspiring managers can submit a take-over bid. This take-over bid would offer a reduction in the tax-price of public output, which, if accepted by the citizens-owners, would increase the attractiveness of that government as a place of residence, thereby leading to increased property values. The divergence in property values resulting from the capture of rents by managers indicates the size of the capital gain that could accrue to citizens/owners of the government if managerial rents were eliminated. Therefore, the greater the degree of managerial rent-seeking, the greater the return to citizens-owners from accepting the take-over bid of an opposing set of aspiring managers. While the services of government are not priced directly and while ownership shares in government are nontransferable, the tie-in between housing and government along with the transferability of ownership in housing operates to a considerable extent to overcome this difficulty. The market system creates a price for the *combination* of housing and government, so price-like information is produced about different governments in a system of competitive governments. Likewise, the transferability of ownership in housing operates to create an incentive system for eradicating managerial rent-seeking. Should the services of government be priced directly and should ownership shares be transferable, governments would, as noted above, be just like corporations, and the tightness of the agent-principal relationship would be about the same as it is with respect to corporations.

But should units of government become larger, with the limiting case being the existence of only a single government, there would be no possibility of a Tiebout-type migration among governments.[5] An increase in rent-seeking would still increase the tax price of public output. However, this increase in tax price would no longer be capitalized into the price of residency, or would be done so less fully, because the reduction in return on so substantial a portion of the capital stock would also bring about some reduction in the rate of interest. Although managerial rent-seeking would no longer, or would be less fully, capitalized into property values, the divergence between the actual tax-price of public output and the minimum possible tax-price would still provide a basis for the submission of a take-over bid. In this case the take-over bid must be based on weaker information signals. Consequently, the market for control would tend to operate less effectively in curtailing managerial rent-seeking as governments become less competitive.

For a given rate of managerial rent-seeking, the potential gain to owners-residents of an elimination of rent-seeking weakens as governments become larger, because the reduced income flow is less fully, if at all, capitalized into property values. This is so even if there is a commonality of interest among principals. Even in a world of equals treated equally, the extent of managerial rent-seeking should expand as the elasticity of demand for residency in any particular jurisdiction lessens. Perhaps more significantly, the commonality among principals will weaken due to greater opportunities for wealth transfers as the demand for particular locations becomes less elastic.[6]

With the expansion in the opportunities for transfers of wealth among owners, the degree of consensus among owners concerning the evaluation of managerial performance will also decline. The greater the homogeneity of preferences and the more general (or nondiscriminatory) the impact of fiscal measures, the more competition for managerial positions will become "non-partisan" in nature, in that competition will take place with regard to different presumptions or hypotheses about ways of maximizing the value of the enterprise (ownership of housing-and-government). As governments expand in size, however, ownership becomes less fully alienable, so the scope for rent-seeking activities widens, and political competition comes increasingly to center on transfers of wealth among owners. As a result, the agent-principal relationship becomes even more problematic because of the erosion of consensus among owners. Yet the normative vision of liberal democracy, in which rights of person and property are prior to government and are not a grant from government, surely requires some such relationship of agency to characterize its constitutional order. To fulfill such a relationship requires an institutional framework that promotes consensus among owners/citizens/principals.

Market Economy, Democratic Polity, and Economic Calculation

The theory of economic calculation originated in the 1920s as a result of various socialist proposals to replace markets with planning as the means of resource allocation. However, Ludwig von Mises succeeded in showing that in such a socialist system it would be impossible for the structure of production to adapt efficiently to consumer wants, because the knowledge necessary for economic calculation could not be generated.[7] In response, the subsequent socialist literature retreated from the abolition of markets and proposed instead some variant of what came to be called market socialism.

As a result, the existence of a market process became widely recognized as an essential requisite for economic calculation. What was not so widely accepted was whether or not economic calculation could take place in a quasi-market order in which there existed collective ownership of capital goods. Within an analytical framework of static equilibrium, there seemed to be no essential difference between the abilities of capitalist and socialist economies to solve the problem of economic calculation. As Karen Vaughn explains, it is not surprising that the adoption of different perspectives toward the nature of the economic process resulted in different formulations of what was required for economic calculation. A model of static equilibrium made the task of economic calculation under socialism appear simple and straightforward, as embodied in suggestions that socialist managers be instructed to set price equal to marginal cost. Within such a model, it is presumed that knowledge can be described fully, like the cards dealt in a poker game, and the problem of economic calculation is simply one of getting consumers and producers to say truthfully just what cards are in their hands.

But an important part of knowledge is tacit and not explicit, as Michael Polanyi explains. External observers are not able accurately to determine whether someone is properly using knowledge, so emphasis can no longer be placed on methods predicated on explicit knowledge. An alternative approach to the use of knowledge must be taken when an important part of it is non-articulable or tacit. In this regard, the theory of economic calculation explains that any such process for using knowledge must contain the central institutional elements of property, contract, and residual claimancy. Prices, which arise through contract, are an important source of the knowledge necessary for effective economic conduct. They are also an important source of incentive, for in conjunction with residual claimancy they provide a means of rewarding effective action and penalizing ineffective action.

The theory of economic calculation explains why it is impossible to determine just what would constitute an efficient public policy or set of policies (or budgetary outcomes) independently of some form of competitive market process operating within a framework of property, contract, and liability. Consequently, there is no set of articulable administrative rules or legislative constraints that would be capable of assuring efficient outcomes. This is analogous to the point that it is impossible for any external observer to tell whether a particular public enterprise is adhering to a rule of setting price equal to marginal cost. Cost is the anticipated value of the option that is necessarily given up to secure the option in question. While people might come to form the same anticipation in a truly static economy, no such identity of anticipations is possible in the presence of continuous change. When people differ in their assessment of future possibilities, the marginal cost of any particular action will depend on individual judgments regarding the future, as James Buchanan explains in *Cost and Choice*. Therefore, an instruction to set price equal to marginal cost will give no clear guidance, which means, among other things, that there is no objective means of checking the compliance of managers with some rule of setting price equal to marginal cost, as Jack Wiseman has explained.

In a market economy, there is a tendency for the resources in a society to be used in their most highly valued form, for it this were not so, people would have incentives to make trades that would make it so. To say that the process of trading is one that shifts resources from less valuable to more valuable uses is not a statement that requires an assertion that one person's judgement about value is superior to another's. Rather, it is an implication or inference about the operation of an institutional framework grounded in property and contract. On what basis, for instance, can a judgement be reached as to whether a proposal to use resources for growing bananas in North Dakota or for turning Atlanta into a port for ocean-going vessels will or will not represent a shift of resources from less valuable to more valuable uses? One person might own land in North Dakota, another might own unassembled greenhouses, and a third might own young banana plants. An entrepreneur will assemble the resources necessary to grow bananas in North Dakota if he thinks the value of the resources when assembled in that form will exceed their value in the forms they could otherwise take. Since choices concerning the utilization of resources take place within the institutional framework of property and contract, an entrepreneur's success in assembling resources in a particular manner means that there is actually a consensus among the members of a society that the entrepreneur's proposal for resource utilization seems to represent a more highly valued use of those resources than some other use. The land in North Dakota could be used to grow wheat instead of bananas. But if the entrepreneur who wishes to grow bananas is able to outbid others who wish to grow wheat, the value of the bananas he anticipates the land to yield must exceed the value of the wheat the others anticipate that land to yield. The institutional framework of property and contract, then, operates to produce a consensus about which possible use of resources has the highest anticipated value.

If this consensus did not exist, further trades would take place to change the pattern of control over resources. Suppose one person thinks a plot of land will be worth $20,000 for growing bananas. If someone else thinks it will be worth $40,000 for growing wheat, he will be the higher bidder for the land, and the advocate of growing bananas will tacitly agree that growing wheat is a more valuable use of the land. This agreement will be revealed either by the banana advocate selling the land to the wheat advocate, or by the banana advocate's unwillingness to pay enough to buy the land from the wheat advocate. Regardless of the actual outcome, the institutions of property and contract, which create the rules within which choices concerning the use of resources are made, operate to create a consensus as to which of several possible uses of resources is most valuable. As a result of this consensus, it is possible to conclude that a market economy operates to shift resources from less valued to more valued uses, as those valuations are held by the individual members of the society and who interact within an institutional framework of property and contract.

Where, then, does this concern with economic calculation lead with respect to the relation between a market economy and a democratic polity? The main theme of the theory of economic calculation is that resources can flow to higher valued uses only within an institutional order in which people are able to choose among options offered by suppliers, and in which suppliers face the value consequences of their actions. That is, some form of property and contract is necessary, the function of which is both to provide knowledge and to generate incentive. In such an institutional setting, choices concerning the use of resources actually reflect a consensus, under the prevailing rules of law within which economic activity is ordered, as to the anticipated value consequences of alternative uses of resources.

There is a single principle—consensus—for resource utilization to reflect individual valuations. Bananas can be judged to be a better use of resources in North Dakota than growing wheat, either because it is selected by some non-liberal value system, or because there is a consensus—explicit or implicit—among participants that growing bananas is a better use of the land than growing wheat. A market economy ordered through property and contract operates to produce such an agreement in an economical fashion. The problem of contemporary policy, from this perspective of economic calculation, is that the state and market are presently organized according to different principles, and do not simply represent different reflections of the same principle, and with those different reflections appropriate to the different tasks that each face. The theories of agency and economic calculation set forth some general principles—a grammar—that must obtain, if the pattern of resource usage is to reflect the consent of the governed, although it should also be recognized that there are many different ways of applying any set of principles to any concrete situation.

Wicksell's Legacy, Economic Calculation, and Constitutional Government

Knut Wicksell published probably the most important work to date on the concete implementation of principles of constitutionally limited government under a rule of law. Wicksell took it for granted that government's choices should reflect the consent of the governed, and went on to show how this principle could be used to construct particular institutional rules for a concrete historical situation. Wicksell sought to describe institutions that would promote what might be called consensual or concordant, as against factional or majoritarian democracy, and to do so within the Swedish context of his time. In that context, Sweden was a constitutional monarchy, so the two main institutions with which Wicksell was concerned were the Crown and Parliament. The Crown, like any executive agency, Wicksell thought, would be generally interested in expanding its operations. but it could do so only by receiving larger appropriations from Parliament. Should Parliament act by majority rule, Wicksell recognized that government would become excessively large, as evaluated by the principle of consent of the governed, because of the ability of winning majorities to impose costs on losing minorities.

But Wicksell also saw Swedish society as essentially consisting of a relatively small number of relatively homogenous groups. This feature of Swedish society meant that it would be possible to organize the Parliament in such a way as to give proportional representation to those various groups. With different parties representing the different groups, a system of proportional representation would bring about a fairly complete representation of Swedish society in a Parliament that contained a comparatively small number of relatively homogenous parties. From here, the rest of Wicksell's approach follows straightforwardly. To implement a principle of consensual or concordant democracy and to prevent the violence of factional or majoritarian democracy, Wicksell proposed to allow each group in Parliament to withhold the tax payments that would otherwise be due from its constituency, if it did not think its supporters were getting adequate value in return for their taxes. It is this feature of Wicksell's proposal that is referred to as a rule of near-unanimity. Wicksell proposed that taxing-and-spending choices require substantial consensus, say on the order of 75 to 90 percent among the parliamentary representatives. This type of near-unanimity among the representatives of a comparatively small number of relatively homogenous groups within a Parliament selected by proportional representation is not, of course, anything like merely applying a rule of near-unanimity to the existing Congress in contemporary America.

Wicksell took a general principle that government should reflect the consent of the governed and developed some particular institutional implications of that principle as he thought these would apply to Sweden in 1896. What is of general and enduring value in Wicksell's contribution is his recognition that government can act as a value-enhancing participant in the division of labor in society only if the polity and the economy both operate within essentially the same, consensually-oriented institutional order, in which rights of ownership are well-defined and protected, and in which resources get shifted from one use to another through agreement among the owners of those resources, and not through one subset of owners using the state to abridge the rights of other owners. Wicksell's specific proposals represented an effort to show, in a particular historical setting, how to erase the incongruity in the modes of operation of what we now call the public and private sectors, by placing both on the same contractual or consensual footing.

Wicksell suggested one particular constitutional regime that was both consistent with a liberal framework of consensus and in general conformity to the Swedish institutions of his time. Starting from a general normative premise of liberalism, Wicksell recognized that the institutional or constitutional framework within which government governs can be either subversive or supportive of that normative premise. Wicksell recognized, as has modern scholarship in public choice and political economy, that a constitutional order grounded in parliamentary majorities was inconsistent with the liberal or consensual value premise. Wicksell further recognized that for consistency to result between norms and outcomes, it was necessary that the pattern of incentives that a particular constitutional regime presents to people be compatible with the consensual principle. The point of departure for this effort lies in recognition that people are essentially the same regardless of whether they are engaged in what is conventionally called economic or political action. In either case, people pursue their interests within the constraints presented by and the opportunities offered by different institutional settings. They are in both settings, as William Meckling notes, purposeful, resourceful, and evaluating people. The problem of political economy is consequently one of trying to find an institutional or constitutional regime that is consistent with the consent of the governed, recognizing all the while that the extent to which the subsequent actual operation of that regime produces outcomes that are supportive and not subversive of consensual norms will depend upon the incentives generated within that regime.

Toward Constitutional Construction

Wicksell advanced one particular suggestion for implementing the general principle of the rule of law. There are many particular ways in which such a principle might be implemented, all of which will be characterized by, in one way or another, rights of ownership , will rely upon agreement or contract as the method of coverting resources from one use to another, and will contain some status of profit-and-loss so that people bear some personal responsibility for the value consequences of their actions.[8]

In the context of Wicksell's Sweden, the starting point for particular constitutional development was the separate but equal status of Crown and Parliament. In contemporary democracies, as the United States, the legislature is supreme. The Executive branch is not comparable to the Crown under a monarchy, so Wicksell's particular recommendations can not be applied to the American context. The Crown owned property which it could use to support its desired activities. But the American executive branch has no property from which it can derive revenue and thus act independently of Congress. What Congress appropriates, it can take away. And there are other ways in which the Congress is ultimately superior to the executive branch. High level appointments in the executive branch are subject to Congressional approval, and all appointments could be if Congress so chose. Moreover, Congress can impeach the President, while all the President can do to Congress is to require it to operate under a two-thirds voting rule through the veto power. And what holds for the executive holds for the judiciary as well. Despite much talk about judicial imperialism, the judiciary can only hear cases brought to it. Its judgments will moreover typically be enforced by an agency of the executive branch, whose revenues come from the Congress. Although Congress cannot reduce the salaries of judges during their tenure in office, it can reduce all other categories of judicial budgets, and it can eliminate courts inferior to the Supreme court.

Within the central features of American republicanism, then, the control of faction must focus ultimately on the legislature. It is fine to talk about means of making bureaucrats more accountable through instituting some system of bonuses for good work and penalties for bad work, for reigning in an imperialist judiciary by restricting its jurisdiction, and the like. But in our system of government Congress is, as Madison noted in *Federalist* No. 51, more than just first among equals. Hence, we must look to changes in the legislature to control the effects of faction. Madison's initial hope was that with the Senate and the House based on different principles of selection, the interests represented by a majority in one chamber would not constitute a majority in the other chamber. To secure a concurrent majority in the two chambers, then, would require an expansion in the extent to which the interest of the population at large was represented. It would always be possible to pursue this line of thought by considering changes in the basis on which legislatures are selected, with the intent of such changes being to reduce the similarity between the two chambers. If one chamber were elected by geography, the other could be elected by, say, occupational categories. Even more diversity might result if one chamber were elected by geography and the other by first letters of surnames, and with yet more diversity resulting through random selection. The point of any such revision in the means of selecting the different legislative chambers would be to increase the diversity between the two chambers. The greater the diversity between the two chambers, the more nearly true it will be that the legislation that receives majority support in both chambers will be of broad, general value rather than of narrow, factional value.

Another possible means of changing the method of electing legislators has been advanced by F. A Hayek (1979), though this possibility is based more on a revision of the British model of government than the American model. Hayek proposed that there be a distinction between two legislative bodies: a Legislative Assembly and a Governmental Assembly. This suggestion represents not so much an effort to expand the diversity represented by a concurrence of majorities as an effort to have one chamber be the custodian of *jurisdictio* while the other oversees *gubernaculum*. The Legislative Assembly, which would be essentially a revision of the British House of Lords, would be selected from among people 45 years of age who would serve for 15 years, and this assembly would have the function of enacting general laws that would remain in force for a long period of time. These laws would include those relating to the distribution of tax burdens among people, but would not deal with the actual amount of taxation. The Governmental Assembly would be constituted the same as the British parliament presently is, with the intention being that its particular choices about such governmental matters as budgets will be made in conformity with the general rules chosen by the Legislative Assembly.

None of these suggestions that essentially in one way or another are reflective of Madison's search for diversity through the basis for selecting legislators operates on the financial situation of legislators. But such possibilities might also be worth exploring. For instance, in the Athenian constitution of the 5th and 4th centuries B.C., for every bill that was proposed in the legislature, a committee was assigned to oppose it. Such a provision for systematic opposition immediately clashes sharply with our legislative setting, in which there are no legislators with a direct interest in opposing legislation *per se*, as distinct from favoring different legislation. But this provision for direct opposition was only a first stage. If the bill subsequently passed, the sponsor was held personally accountable. An opponent could act as a plaintiff and bring an action against the sponsor/defendant. If the plaintiff could make a satisfactory demonstration of the mal-effects of the legislation, the sponsor could be fined. The orator Demosthenes was one such plaintiff, whom the legislator Tymocrates had the misfortune of encountering.[9] The Athenian constitution provided, in other words, what is called substantive, as distinguished from procedural, due process, with the twist that legislators were personally responsible for their legislative initiatives.[10] In this way, legislators were no different from ordinary citizens, all of whom are personally responsible for their choices.

An alternative approach in this same vein might involve a change in the method of paying legislators. The problem with faction is that legislation is enacted despite its diminution of the common wealth because the concentrated gains it offers to supporters dominates the diffused, though larger in the aggregate, losses elsewhere. To the extent government undertakes those protective and productive activities that promote the common welfare while refraining from undertaking those activities that retard it, the total wealth of the society increases. But under the prevailing regime of majoritarian democracy, legislators can gain by supporting programs that transfer wealth to particular interests, even though aggregate wealth, and personal liberty as well, is diminished in the process.

This negative outcome is facilitated because legislators have a direct stake not in the common or aggregate wealth of the members of the nation, but only in the particular wealth positions of the members of the various warring factions that contend for favors. Madison thought that concurrent majorities among bodies with differing interests would produce a result that promoted the general welfare. In a somewhat different application of the same principle that Madison sought to implement, legislators could be compensated through a balanced portfolio of stocks, bonds, real estate, and other assets. To the extent this could be done, the incentive for each legislator to promote the general welfare would surely be strengthened. A legislator with a significant number of unemployed youths in his district and who might support some job creation program despite its demonstrated ineffectiveness, because most of the cost would be placed elsewhere, and who recognized that a reformation of minimum wage and child labor legislation would actually be more effective overall, would be more inclined to support the latter type of legislation. The reason is that the legislator would share in all the gains *and* losses of legislation. To the extent such a balanced portfolio could be put into effect, legislators would tend to be rewarded in direct proportion to the general increase in national wealth, rather than in proportion to the particular favors conferred upon the beneficiaries of particular legislation.[11]

A well-working or well-ordered state is, within a liberal or contractarian perspective, one that supports the peaceful pursuits of its members. To the extent government conducts its productive and protective activities in a manner that is consistent with liberal norms, the aggregate wealth of the members of the nation will rise. In like manner, should government fail to conduct its protective and productive activities properly, as this is assessed by a principle of consensus, and with such failure resulting either from government doing what it should not do or failing to do what it should do, there will be a diminution in the aggregate wealth of the members of the state. In either case, some type of compensation that was geared to the value of some balanced portfolio of assets might be constructed to operate similarly to stock options and related incentive plans in corporations. In such a manner, as well as with Wicksell's particular approach, some direct relationship between performance and reward might in turn lead to a greater congruence between the norms or justifications for public policies and the actual consequences of those policies.[12]

Summary

My main point in this paper is not, I should perhaps note in closing, to argue in support of any particular scheme as the way of overcoming the failure of representative democracy. My point is rather that if the generally liberal outlook that informed the American constitutional effort, and which still informs its rhetoric if not its practice, is to be taken seriously, the theories or principles of agency and economic calculation are quite pertinent. They give some shape or direction to the problem of constitutional construction. Our talk of public and private sectors and most of our ensuing efforts at modeling related phenomena proceed as if there are different principles suitable for organizing the economic activities of individuals and governments respectively—property and contract being the basis for organization in the private sector and confiscation (or infringement) and compulsion being the basis for organization in the public sector. However, the theories of agency and economic calculation combine to explain why the normative vision of liberalism requires a single organizing principle applicable to all forms of economic activity, and to set forth as well as a grammar for informing any effort at constitutional construction.

Notes

1. For a thorough survey of the rent-seeking literature that expresses this "failure," see Robert Tollison. For a wide ranging examination of various ideas about fiscal limitations that have been advanced as means of overcoming such "failure," see Cay Folkers.

2. This refers, of course, to James Buchanan's (1975) distinction between the productive and the protective states.

3. For a symposium on contemporary issues and assessments pertaining to the work of Berle and Means, see the entire June issue of the *Journal of Law and Economics* (1983).

4. There is other related scholarship that supports this point. Dennis Epple and Allan Zelenitz have shown that competition among democratically organized government is insufficient to prevent such opportunity for conflict among owners-residents. Werner Pommerehne and Frederich Schneider have shown that expenditure patterns in Swiss cities more fully reflect citizen preferences in those cities that are direct democracies than in those that are representative democracies. They also found that, among representative democracies, citizen preferences are more fully reflected when citizens have recourse to referenda than when they do not.

5. For a recent compilation of papers on this topic, written from a variety of perspectives, see George Zodrow.

6. This is, of course, though in a different context, the basis for the common argument, in the literature on federalism, that wealth redistribution is more "efficiently" performed by the national government than by local governments. It is also the basis of the common assertion that public output, unlike private output, is hard to measure. There is, however, no differential problem of measurement, but there is a difference in the degree of consensus among principals due to such institutional differences as those described above.

7. See the essays collected in Friedrich Hayek (1935).

8. The essential identify of Wicksell's principle and Pareto's, with both being grounded in consensus, is explored by P. Hennipman. With respect to Pareto, the distinction between a general principle of consensus and various concrete ways in which that principle might be put into operation, is set forth by Juergen Backhaus, (1980)(1981).

9. See the discussion in Bruno Leoni, pp. 79–80.

10. Strong support for a return to substantive due process is marshalled by Bernard Siegan. Also with reference to judicial remedies, Peter Aranson, Ernest Gellhorn, and Glen Robinson have proposed a revival of the non-delegation doctrine. While such judicial remedies as these have much in their favor, their sustainability seems somewhat problematical without changes in congressional incentives, because of the ultimate superiority of Congress in our system of government.

11. In a quite different context, W.H. Hutt has proposed a system of *shared entrepreneurship* between workers and owners as a way of overcoming the faction that often characterizes present labor management relations.

12. To the extent they were broadly representative of business interests, cities before the reform era of so-called good government may have operated in similar fashion, thereby illustrating yet another particular implementation of Wicksell's general principle of consensus.

References

Aranson, P.H.; Gellhorn, E.T.; and Robinson, G.O. *The Legislative Creation of Legislators: The Delegation Doctrine in a Public Choice Perspective*, forthcoming.

Aranson, P.H., and Ordeshook, P.C. "A Prolegomenon to a Theory of the Failure of Representative Democracy." In *American Re-evolution: Papers and Proceedings*. Tucson: University of Arizona Press, 1977. Backhaus, J. "The Pareto Principle." *Analyse & Kritik*, no. 2 (1980): 146–71.

——, "The Pareto Principle and Policy Analysis." *Analyse & Kritik*, no. 2, 3 (1981): 237–46.

Berle, A.A., and Means, G.C. *The Modern Corporation and Private Property*. New York: Macmillan, 1933.

Buchanan, J.M. *Cost and Choice*. Chicago: Markham, 1969.

——, *The Limits of Liberty* Chicago: University of Chicago Press, 1975.

Epple, D., and Zelenitz, A. "The Implications of Competition among Jurisdictions: Does Tiebout Need Politics?" *Journal of Political Economy* 89 (December, 1981): 1197–217.

De Angelo, H. "Competition and Unanimity," *American Economic Review* 71 (March, 1981): 18–27.

Fama, E.F. "Agency Problems and the Theory of the Firm." *Journal of Political Economy* 88 (April, 1980): 288–307.

Folkers, C. *Begrenzungen von Steuern und Staatsausgaben in den USA*. Baden-Baden: Nomos Verlagsgesellschaft, 1983.

Hayek, F.A. "The Political Order of a Free People." *Law, Legislation, and Liberty*, Vol. 3. Chicago: University of Chicago Press, 1979.

——, (ed.) *Collectivist Economic Planning* London: Routledge and Kegan Paul, 1935.

Hennipman, P.; Wicksell, K.; and Pareto, W. "Their Relationship in the Theory of Public Finance." *History of Political Economy* 14 (Spring, 1982): 37–64.

Hutt, W.H. "Every Man a Capitalist." *Policy Review*, no. 22 (1982): 141–53.

Lewellen, W.G. "Management and Ownership in the Large Firms." *Journal of Finance* 24 (May, 1969): 299–322.
Mankowski, L. "Competition and Unanimity Revisited." *American Economic Review* 73 (June, 1983): 329–39.
Manne, H.G. "Mergers and the Market for Corporate Control." *Journal of Political Economy* 73 (April, 1965): 10–20.
Meckling, W.H. "Values and the Choice of the Model of the Individual in the Social Sciences." *Schweizerische Zeitschrift für Volkswirtschaft und Statistik* 112 (December, 1976): 545–60.
Polanyi, M. *Personal Knowledge*. London: Routledge and Kegan Paul, 1958.
Pommerehne, W.W., and Schneider, F. "Fiscal Illusion, Political Institutions, and Local Public Spending." *Kyklos* no. 3, 31 (1978): 38–308.
Siegan, B.H. *Economic Liberties and the Constitution*. Chicago: University of Chicago Press, 1980.
Sonstelie, J.C., and Portney, P.R. "Profit Maximizing Communities and the Theory of Local Public Expenditure." *Journal of Urban Economics* 5 (April, 1978): 263–77.
Tiebout, C.M. "A Pure Theory of Local Expenditures." *Journal of Political Economy* 64 (October, 1956): 416–24.
Tollison, R.D. "Rent-Seeking: A Survey," *Kyklos*, no. 4, 35 (1981): 575–602.
Vaughn, K.I. "Economic Calculation under Socialism: The Austrian Contribution." *Economic Inquiry* 18 (October, 1980): 535–54.
Watts, R.L., and Zimmerman, J.L. "Agency Problems, Auditing, and the Theory of the Firm." *Journal of Law and Economics* 26 (October, 1983): 613–33.
Wiseman, J. "Uncertainty, Costs, and Collectivist Economic Planning." *Economics* 20 (May, 1953): 118–28. Reprinted in: J.M. Buchanan and G.F. Thirlby (eds.), *L.S.E. Essays on Cost*. London: Weidenfeld and Nicholson, 1973.

30 RENT-SEEKING IN CONSTITUTIONAL PERSPECTIVE

Charles K. Rowley

Introduction

As the essays in this book clearly indicate, Tullock's 1967 insight was to generate an extensive literature in the political economy of rent-seeking. The debate on this important topic is still comparatively young. The dust has still to settle on a number of controversies that have arisen. Little, as yet, has been finally resolved in detail, as Tullock's "back to the bog" lament in 1985 would seem to indicate. Yet we now know much more than was the case in 1967. What we have learned, immensely important as it is, does not however give cause for optimism concerning the efficiency of non-market decision-making. It is to this issue that the present essay addresses itself.

To illustrate the quite dramatic change in informed opinion over a period of twenty-five years concerning the performance of government, a change in which the rent-seeking notion has exerted an important influence, this essay retraces the steps from Buchanan and Tullock's vision of *A Calculus of Consent* to Buchanan's 1980 despair in requesting a search for *Reform in the Rent-Seeking Society*. Was the 1962 vision mere illusion, or was the 1980 despair mere personal dystopia? Or did the institutional changes operative over that time period shift the democracies from a process of wealth enhancement to one of wealth destruction—a kind of reverse path for Pilgrim from Paradise to Hell?

If the latter view is accepted, as this essay suggests it should, are there any routes to reform in an economy drenched in rent-seeking and rent protection, or is such a society locked irreversibly in some dreadful, worsening "prisoners' dilemma"? This question is addressed via the techniques of game theory applied within the framework of constitutional economics. The essay ends on a note of hope to the effect that efficient rent-seeking may prove to be ultimately self-destructive, destroying the very institutional structure on which it is dependent.

The Calculus of Consent

The Calculus of Consent was written during the dying years of the second Eisenhower administration and published in 1962 at a time when Kennedy was president; indeed, was all but king. The world, more or less, was at peace, with Europe inevitably divided, with the war in Korea long forgotten, and with intervention in Vietnam little more than a gleam in Kennedy's eye. The relationship between the Executive and Congress was cordial, with the latter rigorously controlled by rigid rules concerning committee seniority. Budgets balanced, and the economics of Keynes had yet to penetrate the U.S. polity. Macmillan had moved Britain to some post-Suez consensus; De Gaulle had wrested power in France from the Fourth Republic; the European Common Market appeared to augur well for the integration of Western Europe. It was not difficult, in such circumstaces, to be inspired by a contractarian vision.

The Calculus of Consent, for all that, was an ambitious book, written from the perspective of methodological individualism at the peak of acceptance within economics of constructivist rationalism, and applying the concept of *homo oeconomicus* to areas of non-market decision-making that had not been exposed to such sunlight for over 100 years. The book analyzed the calculus of the rational individual when faced with questions of constitutional choice at a time when the U.S. Constitution more or less was taken for granted and treated as of background relevance only to the more immediate and exciting arenas of legislative politics and of executive authority. Not surprisingly, most economists simply could not understand its insight during the prevailing conventions of 1960s scholarship.

The essential constitutional perspective of *The Calculus of Consent* was presented in chapter six, titled: "A Generalized Economic Theory of

Constitutions". Here we find the famous trade-off diagram between the external cost of collective action and the bargaining costs associated with various vote-requirement rules, which was the instrument utilized to offer Wicksellian unanimity validity to vote rules employing less than unanimity requirements. The rational citizen, essentially evaluating constitutional design behind a veil of ignorance concerning own-interest in collective action, was seen to favor increasingly high supra-majority vote rules as a means of restricting potential external costs while favoring decreasingly high vote rules as a means of controlling the costs of bargaining. By minimizing the joint cost function, vertically added, the rational citizen was seen to choose a favored rule. With sufficient similarity in "behind the veil" preferences, a unique rule, unanimously endorsed, would serve the purposes of in-period politics.

Via this mechanism, a political system was conceived of as an enabling mechanism to achieve Pareto-optimality in an economy characterized by pervasive externalities yet populated by *homo oeconomicus*. The politics of conflict thus were seen to be dominated by the politics of "gains-from-trade" or catallactics, to use the term subsequently employed by Buchanan. Despite the temptations offered by majority vote rules at the legislative level for decisive voter sets to take advantage of minorities, the higher constitutional consensus endorsed the system as a whole as the best available in a world that was inevitably spaced some distance *East of Eden*.

This vision was not shared, of course, by all reviewers of the book. Indeed, it was almost certainly an exaggerated ideal with respect to any real world constitution. For constitutions are not forged behind veils of ignorance, nor are they ever universally endorsed. The Founding Fathers, for example, simply imposed the U.S. Constitution on the anti-federalists without even bothering to seek accommodation with those like George Mason who pressed at least for a Bill of Rights.

A text on the logical foundations of constitutional democracy is simply not intended, of course, to be a handbook on constitutional design. Meade, in particular, detected as too unrealistic the authors' assumption that the existence of gains-from-trade would induce unanimous constitutional agreement to effect such gains. With considerable prescience he noted that bargaining costs might obstruct such an outcome, especially where distributive transfers as well as efficiency gains were under political debate. Furthermore, where externalities took the form not of ongoing marginal adjustment, but of once-for-all, essentially irreversible structural change, Meade doubted that the two-tiered decision-making paradigm of *The Calculus of Consent* could reasonably be expected to apply.

Meade's criticisms, together with the expressed doubts of other reviewers such as Downs and Olson, sharpen in focus once the rent-seeking insight is absorbed into constitutional economics. Even at the purely logical level of analysis, as we shall see, they pose serious problems for the trade-off diagram, even on "behind-the-veil" assumptions. In combination with real-world institutional adjustments in post-1962 U.S. politics, they came to mount a serious threat to the capability for survival of constitutional democracy in any remotely contractual form.

Rent-Seeking and the Path to Constitutional Conflict

Although the rent-seeking insight occurred in 1967, its implications for constitutional economics were slow to be recognized. Indeed, it was not until 1980 that Buchanan offered the first major application of the rent-seeking concept to the constitutional level of collective decision-making. Even then, Buchanan's analysis was couched in the real-world situation of a prisoners' dilemma rather than in the theoretical framework posited by *The Calculus of Consent*. Wagner's 1987 contribution, important though it is, retains the real-world thrust initiated by Buchanan, in which parchment is viewed to be inherently vulnerable to guns in a system where governments make laws for others in response to rent-seeking pressures. Rowley's 1987 contribution hints at the logical problem posed for chapter six of *The Calculus of Consent* by the rent-seeking concept. This hint is here developed further, though without any real solution at this time. It builds on the early criticism by Meade of the nature of equilibrium in constitution formation.

In essence, the problem posed is whether there would be any possibility of unanimity, even behind a veil of ignorance, for a decision-making rule of less than unanimity, once rent-seeking is recognized to be a reality of the political market-place. *The Calculus of Consent* explains why a unanimity rule would never be accepted on decision-making cost criteria. The concept of the external cost function as developed in that book was essentially based on externality resolution without commitment to actual compensation. Gains-from-trade would result from collective action in the sense of the potential compensation test, but majorities still might allow minorities to bear net losses by denying actual compensation.

Suppose, however, that individuals "behind the veil" recognize that the lower level of political decision-making will be invaded by rent seekers using government to effect wealth transfers, and that such invasion will provoke defensive measures in the form of rent protection. The shape of the external cost function may shift in a manner non-trivial for constitutional consent. Evidently, many aspects of collective action, especially concerning the provision of public goods, will be viewed as potentially wealth enhancing. Other aspects, however, involving transfers, will be viewed as wealth destructive. The great difficulty of discriminating effectively between these actions will be perceived.

In such circumstances, the external cost function cannot be defined in the absence of some judgment on the scope of collective action. If transfers could be excluded, then the "chapter six" external cost function continues to dominate. If not, then who knows what judgment might be passed "behind the veil" on the wealth enhancement/wealth destruction balance? If Tullock's latest horror story on rent-seeking (chapter four of this volume) is perceived to be correct, and if the scope of collective action is seen to be unrestricted at the constitutional level, the implications for the external cost function may be adverse indeed.

Specifically, the external cost function then might become vertical at the vote rule of unanimity and fail to intersect at all with a decision-making cost function that becomes vertical somewhat short of the unanimity vote. In such circumstances, there is no logical foundation for constitutional democracy in the sense defined by *The Calculus of Consent.* Constitutions simply will not arise via a process of contractarian consent, even when negotiated "behind a veil of ignorance." Moreover, constitutional failure is then not the consequence of a prisoners' dilemma problem, as most of the "post-Calculus" literature has suggested is the case. Rather the failure reflects the non-existence of any political market equilibrium predicated upon universal consent, no matter at what level of decision-making. Put bluntly, *The Calculus of Consent* would require a major overhaul, without any high expectation of ultimate success.

In reality, of course, constitutions, explicit or implicit, do exist in the real world democracies, albeit always imposed by some individuals upon others. In some instances, no doubt, fear of the Hobbesian jungle encourages a measure of supra-majority support for constitutional enactments, as essentially was the case with post-Revolutionary America. In other cases, the constitution is imposed from within, via some form of autocracy, as was arguably the case in late medieval England, when the royal courts became increasingly dominant in the evolution of the common law. In yet other cases, constitutions are imposed from without by allies victorious in war, as was the case both of The Federal Government of Germany and of Japan following their respective defeats in the European and in the Pacific theaters of the Second World War.

Constitutions thus acquired indeed represent some kind of equilibrium, however temporary, and however constrained. They do not reflect, however, any application of the Wicksellian unanimity principle in the process of collective action. Given the high cost to most individuals of outward migration, they cannot easily be rationalized in terms of *ex post* endorsement by those who live beneath them. The parchment of real-world constitutions is qualitatively different from that posited in *The Calculus of Consent.* It is important, therefore, to review the relationship between real-world constitutions and rent-seeking, or, following Wagner, between parchment and guns. In contrast to Wagner, however, it is not assumed here that this relationship interacts within the context of any constitutional *contract.*

Wagner utilizes the distinction between constitutional and post-constitutional levels of collective choice, much along the lines of *The Calculus of Consent.* He develops the notion that constitutional contract is the escape from efficiency losses imposed otherwise in collective choice as an implication of the prisoners' dilemma problem. He recognizes explicitly, as *The Calculus of Consent* really failed to do, that constitutional contract is not assured of continued existence by the parchment on which it is written; that parchment itself does not eliminate the potential gains to individual or group acts of predation on rights, or rent-seeking in the sense of this book.

The essence of a constitutional contract, in Wagner's vision, is the prior establishment of individual rights, and the creation of government as a referee, the function of which is to protect such rights, and to subject its actions to periodic consensual review. The crucial problem with this model is that of ensuring that the sphere of *gubernaculum* (government) is kept subservient to the sphere of *jurisdictio* (law). Parchment itself does not eliminate the underlying prisoners' dilemma problem but, at best, contains excesses. Only if the potential gains to rent-seeking are eliminated will rent-seeking subside and, with it, the ongoing threat to the rights embedded in constitutional contract.

Within real-world constitutions, however, including our own, Wagner recognizes that government is a maker of rules for others, rather than an adherent to the same rules as others. In such an institutional environment, a market inevitably exists in the securing of favorable rules and of favorable interpretations of those rules as well as of pre-existing ones. *Jurisdictio* essentially becomes subservient to *gubernaculum*, and the institutions conducive to rent-seeking emerge and become consolidated.

The republican government form of the U.S., despite the checks and balances imposed by a written contitution, has proved vulnerable to this syndrome, as Madison had predicted in Federalist No. 51: "In republican government, the legislative authority necessarily predominates". The legislature, despite its bicameral structure, is highly invadable by rent seekers, even when forced onto two-third majority voting by presidential vetos. The Supreme Court has demonstrated no enduring ability to maintain the constitutional contract but, rather, has been manipulated in its membership and behavior, both by the U.S. Senate and by presidents, to ensure the durability of rent-seeking contracts between interest groups and the Congress (Landes and Posner, 1975).

Parchment, in the U.S. context, has failed to stop guns in the drive toward a rent-seeking society. Fundamentally, as Wagner stresses, guns will always defeat parchment, if that is their intent. Such is the logic of collective action in the sense of Olson. At any point in time, the pen is not mightier than the sword. Only if the guns are mounted in sufficient force in defense of parchment will constitutional contract endure. To this longer term objective the pen does have a somewhat influential role. The institutional reforms required, together with the educational program that might be set in motion to reverse the drift in favor of rent-seeking, are the issues that will concern this pen through the remainder of the present chapter. In "doing well by doing good" it is to be hoped that *publicness* characteristics do not excessively curtail this particular contribution.

From the Illusion of Camelot to the Disillusionment of Dystopia

The title of this section, due to Buchanan (1986), embraces the shift in ideas and the changes in institutions within the U.S. over the period 1962 to 1986 which have contributed to the growth of the rent-seeking society and to the increasing disenchantment of individuals with the U.S. model of constitutional democracy. The section itself draws upon an analysis of interest groups by Rowley, Shughart, and Tollison (1987) which explained the dynamics of rent-seeking within the U.S. in terms both of changing ideas and of U.S. institutional adjustment. The emphasis throughout is that of public choice, in which government itself is endogenous, and not that of DUP, in which governments continue to play an essentially exogenous role.

The interest-group approach to politics (McCormick and Tollison, 1981) models politicians as providing a brokering function in the political market for wealth transfers. Special interest groups capable of effective economic organization "demand" such transfers. Other, more general, groups incapable of effective organization as a consequence of the logic of collective action, "supply" such transfers. Politicians affect market equilibrium, balancing benefits against costs in terms of currencies variously weighted in terms of expected wealth and expected votes. Bureaucracy typically exerts its influence, as an interest group, on the demand side of this market. In the political market, bureaucracy is not a supply factor, as is frequently asserted in analyses of representative government (Breton, 1974).

The interest group model asserts not just that rectangles tend to dominate trapezoids in political markets, with evident losses to society of Harberger triangles; it further asserts that the rectangles self-mutilate in this process, destroying the very surpluses that they attempt to seize (Rowley and Tollison, this volume). It is important to understand how such a process occurs in a constitutional framework such as that of the U.S., designed to establish "government within rules". It is also important to understand why rent-seeking tended to intensify in the U.S. over the period 1962 to 1986. To this end, it is helpful to remind ourselves of an insight offered in *The Calculus of Consent*, namely the importance of the distinction between the range and the extent of collective action and their interaction under differing vote-trading rules.

The range of collective action defines the resource categories deemed to be subject to the political process. The extent of collective action defines the volume of resources allocated via political markets to each such category. Although these categories appear to be politically distinct, with the former the prior and the latter the conditional dimension, in reality they tend to be interdependent. Judgments on range are influenced inevitably by evaluations of the implication for the extent of collective action, with experience on extent feeding back to decisions concerning range. In this interaction, institutional constraints on vote trading exercise a significant role.

Any form of vote trading, from simple logrolling to the open buying and selling of votes, allows group preference intensitiès on political issues, measured in some relevant currency, to be more fully expressed than is feasible in a simple majority vote process. As opportunities for vote trading increase, ignoring for the moment the rent-seeking insight, the expected cost of collective action curve will shift downwards. This indicates an increased willingness on the part of individuals to engage in collective action under any pre-specified vote rule. In such circumstances, both the range and the extent of collective action predictably will increase, with constitutional constraints either removed or ignored as the dimensions of political markets are augmented. Of course, to the extent that the rent-seeking insight becomes incorporated into the individual's collective action calculus, such augmentation will be countered. In the limit, the external cost curve would remain vertical at the rule of unanimity, as individuals perceived net losses from potential collective action.

The rent-seeking insight itself is relatively new and is only now spreading beyond the confines of a minority of professional economists and political scientists. Only when periodic examples of gross rent-seeking behavior experience press exposure is the average voter more than vaguely aware of the wealth destructive characteristics of such activities. For the most part, rational ignorance has protected the political market place from voter revenge. Expanded opportunities for vote trading in the U.S. Congress between 1962 and 1986 therefore stimulated a step increase in the range and extent of collective action.

The U.S. Congress is hindered with respect to vote trading opportunities both by its bicameral structure and by the geographic representation basis of both its chambers. Under such constraints, the rules of the legislative process tend to be important as a determinant of the "efficiency" of pork-barrel politics. In one respect, these rules have always encouraged vote-trading in the U.S. to a greater degree than is the case with most European parliamentary democracies: party discipline is much looser and policy cross-overs by individual congressmen always much more frequent. However, this stimulus to interest group rent-seeking is a consistent feature of the U.S. polity, and not an especial development of the past quarter century.

To explain the dynamics of vote-trading in the U.S. over the period in question, it is necessary, therefore, to scrutinize developments in the complex structure of internal decision-making institutions to which Congress delegates substantial authority. Choices registered in these institutions constrain the influence of House or Senate majorities, preventing comparisons between certain collective choice alternatives, while facilitating others. Preeminent among these institutions is the committee/subcommittee system. Committees are endowed with considerable authority to initiate legislation within their defined jurisdictions. In some instances, amendments to their proposals are confined, by convention, to the particular subject matter of such proposals. Bills, as amended, are usually voted up or down, though amendments from the floor are not completely precluded. In the event of disagreement between the House and the Senate, the committees select the conference representatives, whose compromises are protected from amendment.

The committee process facilitates vote-trading, within specific areas of jurisdiction, by bundling programs into a combined legislative package. Vote-trading between committee extends the "efficiency" of this operation. However, the committee structure is not an exogenous component of the U.S. Congress; is not enshrined in the written Constitution. It is essentially an endogenous component of the political brokering mechanism. As such, it has responded to market pressures over the period 1962 to 1986 which have favored increasingly efficient vote-trading procedures.

In particular, the declining importance of seniority as a criterion for committee chairmanships, the rising vulnerability of existing chairmen to supercession by less senior colleagues, the increasing staff support provided to committee members, and the decentralization of committee activities into sub-committees have all served to increase the efficiency of vote-trading in political markets. As the political market has widened and deepened, lobbying pressures on Capitol Hill have intensified, as is evident from the growth in the number of political action committees, and the yet more marked growth in the total outlays of such committees on vote-buying within the Congress.

Inevitably, such developments have ended the authority of the leadership of the political parties. Congressmen who raise their campaign expenses and purchase votes by catering to special interests, whether or not such interests are constituency-related, rely less upon party support than in the past. Indeed, access to the party leadership itself becomes dependent in part upon the ability of those successful in raising excess campaign finances to pay off the financial debts of their less successful party colleagues. Increasingly, committee chairmanships are bought and sold on such a basis, and sub-committee chairmanships are traded in return for vote behavior loyal to the interests of influential committee members.

Coincident to this continuous improvement in the efficiency of vote-trading in the U.S. Congress came radical shifts in ideas concerning the role of government in a free enterprise economy and the relevance of the U.S. Constitution as a binding constraint on the range and extent of collective action. The principle of self-help, so carefully inculcated by the Victorians as a fulcrum for rapid economic development, was jarred by the Great Depression, further shaken by the Second World War, and deeply eroded by the growing reliance of U.S. citizens on social expenditure programs during the subsequent twenty years. By 1964, it had given way to collectivism, with widespread support for transfer programs, and without any insight into the public choice, rent-seeking implications of such a major shift in political economy.

Simultaneously, the moral resistance to debt creation, which had constrained governments from deficit financing since the early years of classical political economy, was overwhelmed by a rising hedonism driven in part by a recognizable threat of nuclear annihilation and in part by the teachings of J.M. Keynes and his disciples (Buchanan, Rowley, and Tollison, 1987). In the absence of significant inter-generational linkages, the loosening of this constraint was to provide a significant opportunity for current rent-seeking by interest groups which perceived the opportunity to place the relevant burden on non-voting future generations.

One consequence of the shift from individualist to collectivist ideology, given the difficulty of amending the U.S. Constitution, was a powerful and successful attack by rent-seeking interest groups on the strict constructionist approach to judicial review. Appointments to the Supreme Court over the period 1960 to 1980 strongly favored judges who adopted an activist, "living Constitution" approach to judicial review. An early victim of such penetration, as Epstein (1985) has indicated, was the "takings clause" of the Fifth Amendment, which denies the right of government to seize property without due compensation.

The transfer society must be aborted by the strict interpretation of that clause, and with it, most of the rent-seeking thrust. Inevitably, it was deserted by a Supreme Court anxious to broker political markets dependent upon coercive transfers (Landes and Posner, 1975). The role of the postwar Supreme Court as the fulcrum of the rent-seeking society is worthy of a detailed analysis, outside the scope of this paper.

In combination vote-trading adjustments in Congress and the shift in ideas concerning collectivism, supported by an acquiescent judiciary, have facilitated a major growth in rent-seeking in the U.S. economy. Concomitantly, however, the electorate has become increasingly alarmed by media attention to rent-seeking scandals and has reacted with growing dystopia concerning the role of government. In this dystopia lies an avenue for institutional reform which, in the view of Buchanan (1986), offers an opportunity for U.S. citizens to achieve a tempered Utopia.

Effective Routes to Institutional Reform

Buchanan (1986) criticized both the delusion that was Camelot and the dystopia of the mid-1980s as sharing a fatal flaw. Specifically, both images are widely intepreted, by their own proponents, to be complete descriptions of political reality, when in fact both are partial. In Buchanan's view, politicians and bureaucrats, as well as voters, act to some extent in pursuit of what they genuinely consider to be "the general interest". But also, to some extent, they act in pursuit of perceived pecuniary gain. It is the essence of constitutional inquiry to determine that the constraints, rules, and institutions influence the relative importance of these motivating factors; and, more important, that these structures reduce the importance of self-interested political behavior.

Although "Tullock's Law", to the effect that individuals are motivated by altruism five percent of the time, probably holds, attempts via constitutional inquiry, or otherwise, to shift individuals' utility functions further in that direction commit "the fallacy that individuals can be different" (Demsetz, 1968). It is to the constraints and the information sets rather than to the utility functions that such constitutional inquiry is more appropriately addressed.

Institutional Constraints on Rent-Seeking

Constitutional contracts may exist, or may be negotiable, in forms fully capable of obstructing rent-seeking, even in economies highly vulnerable to the logic of collective action, should a sufficiently well-informed electorate choose to defend itself. But this is not enough. As Tullock first emphasized in 1974, and as Wagner elaborated in 1987, the non-enforceability even of the best articulated of such contracts may imply the persistence of a rent-seeking social dilemma in the wake of constitutional contract. Parchment can always be torn up, following a sufficient display of force by special interests anxious to maintain rent-seeking privileges. In such a world, the contractarian vision dissolves into Tullock's second Law: "might is might".

Even where special interests would not obstruct enforcement, however, constitutional contracts may fail to materialize as a consequence of transaction cost constraints, perceived *ex ante*, on the *ex post* or execution side of the contract. Recent research by Williamson (1979) suggests that governance impediments to contract formation are especially apparent with respect to long-term contracts executed under uncertainty. Such is the nature of all constitutional contracts, whether or not they are negotiated "behind a veil of ignorance."

Long-term contracts of this kind do not fit comfortably into the classical contracting framework. Problems of several kinds arise. First, not all future contingencies, for which adaptations are required, can be anticipated at the outset. Second, appropriate adaptations may not be evident, for many contingencies, until the circumstances materialize. Third, where changes in states of the world are ambiguous, veridical disputes over state contingent claims may arise, either genuinely, or for opportunistic reasons. In such circumstances, contracts that might otherwise emerge from a calculus of consent will be aborted by fears of a principal-agent problem in the post-contract governance machinery.

The failure of the contract nexus, given bounded rationality, is quintessentially the consequence of opportunism or strategic behavior expectations in the post-contract environment. Absence of mutual trust in the

Table 30–1. Prisoners' Dilemma Problem With Asymmetric Matrix

		B (1)	B (2)
A	(1)	6, 6	−1, 8
A	(2)	8, −1	8, 0

preconstitutional situation propels individuals into a prisoners' dilemma outcome (Buchanan, 1980). As Buchanan noted, where the prisoners' dilemma problem takes the form of table 30–1, it is especially intractable:

The payoff for A, in table 30–1, is lower in cell 1, the highest total benefit outcome, than it is in cell 4, where the prisoners' dilemma has placed A and B. In such circumstances, gains-from-trade will not lead the actions to cell 1, though such a move is efficient, unless B offers a side-payment to A, outside the game, of at least 2 units of currency involved. Side payments of this kind are not easily organized in a complex economy like the U.S.A.

The rent-seeking prisoners' dilemma problem is yet more intractable, as is depicted in table 30–2:

In table 30–2, *ex ante*, the game matrix is symmetrical, offering some expectation of a resolution of the cell 4 prisoners' dilemma problem. However, *ex post*, the matrix becomes asymmetric, requiring a side-payment either from A to B or from B to A as part of any contractual move from cell 4 to cell 1. In this situation, not at all atypical of rent-seeking/rent protection games, *ex post*, there are winners and losers. Side payments from the loser to the winner, following an intense rent-seeking battle, are less likely than in the table 30–1 environment. In such circumstances, contractual resolution is much more likely in the *ex ante* than in the *ex post* situation, a small amount of protection being equivalent to a large amount of cure.

Table 30–2. Prisoners' Dilemma Problem With Asymmetric Matrix and Uncertainty

		B (1)	B (2)
A	(1)	6, 6	−1, 8
A	(2)	8, −1	8, 0 or 0, 8 (.5 Prob.) (.5 Prob.)

Buchanan (1980) generalized his pessimism concerning constitutional reform in the rent-seeking society when such reform is pursued on a piecemeal basis. Even in the absence of transaction cost barriers, moral constraints will prevent efficiency resolutions. However, as rent-seeking becomes more generalized, paradoxically, resolution may become easier rather than more difficult. Whereas no single set of winners will agree to uncompensated rent releases, many groups simultaneously may agree to eliminate all rent-seeking opportunities, in return for some share of the wealth enhancement that must result. Such an outcome is especially likely when there is an absence of consistent winners in the overall rent-seeking game. Rent-seeking reform, in this vision, must be a root-and-branch exercise, conducted at the highest level of constitutional decision-making.

Buchanan's instinct in favor of constitutional reform is predicated on the notion that rents remain, even in a rent-seeking society, as sirens beckoning interest groups into continuous wealth destruction. Rowley and Tollison (this volume) have suggested, however, that this may not prove to be the case. Suppose that rent-seeking transfers can be achieved only at a heavy cost in terms of rent dissipation, with the implication that rent margins swiftly drop to zero. The social cost per instance of monopoly thus is high; but few monopolies exist since the return on such activity is low. Suppose, alternatively, that rent-seeking transfers can be achieved at a minimal cost in terms of rent dissipation (the model of the "Divine Right" King). In such a system, monopoly abounds, but the social cost per instance is very low. In neither case is the importance of constitutional reform especially high.

Public choice theory predicts that majority vote systems of government are conducive to high social costs from monopoly. Although the level of Tullock costs per instance of monopoly may be controlled in the regulation market to ensure that congressmen receive transfers, dissipation then occurs at the secondary level as potential politicians, their advisers, and their bureaucrats rent-seek their ways into office. The problem of institutional reform at this level is essentially one of adjusting the information set of voters and, to the extent possible, of overcoming rational ignorance concerning issues of public choice.

Information Constraints on Rent-Seeking

If rent-seeking and rent protection totally dissipate all rents created via public choice, then presumably interest groups will abate political expenditures in recognition of the uneconomic nature of their outlays. In such circumstances, the prisoners' dilemma problem will simply disappear, though the new equilibrium will be unstable. For as wealth enhancement displaced wealth destruction, and as private market surpluses signaled entrepreneurial activity, so the political market once again would beckon interest group activity. At best, in such unconstrained circumstances, rent-seeking will follow a Markov process alternating between low and high rates of dissipation (Cooter and Kornhauser, 1980). As information grows concerning the cyclical nature of this process, some trend abatement may occur. But if the rent-seeking market itself is contestable, hit-and-run entry remains the dominant prediction.

Where the rent-seeking/rent protection game manifests itself as a prisoners' dilemma problem in symmetric matrix form, there is some prospect of spontaneous piecemeal reform. The gains available from trade and unencumbered by compensation problems, once recognized by the players, tempt them into contractual resolutions. Scholars specializing in public choice to the extent that they adhere to scholarship rather than to the pursuit of rents and/or to the extent that they can do well while doing good, will accelerate information flows favorable to efficient outcomes. Such is the intent of this paper.

The obstacle confronting the actors, in their mutual pursuit of efficiency gains, is the absence of mutual trust in the prisoners' dilemma situation. The pressure for the actors to defect is intense given the short-term gains to such activity. Yet, given relevant information, the actors rationally will abstain from such temptation. In an important entrepreneurial contribution, Axelrod (1984) has demonstrated that stable rules offering relatively costless gains from trade are available where game interactions are frequent and where no end-game is discernible.

Specifically, if actors operate with "a nice" strategy, namely "tit-for-tat", and apply this irrespective of rival responses, computer simulations indicate that they will maximize wealth. They will not always fare better than individual opponents. But such opponents will lose heavily elsewhere against equally "less nice" rivals. "Tit-for-tat" is a robust strategy, essentially proof against invadability by alternative strategies. Rent seekers and rent protectors would do well to adopt it as a rational, expected wealth maximizing strategy.

Unfortunately, "tit-for-tat" cannot be implemented in games characterized by an asymmetric matrix, which typify, at least *ex post*, so much of the rent-seeking/rent protection environment. In the absence of compensation, there are no mutual gains from trade. In such circumstances, a more general institutional reform predictably is the only realistic public choice route to wealth enhancement. In this respect, if the thrust of section 4 is accepted, reforms should take a route that will appear counter-intuitive to the mindsets of most economists.

Economists are trained to revere efficiency and to object to obstacles that are placed in its path. Yet efficiency in vote-trading is the fulcrum of the rent-seeking problem, destructive of the principle of majority vote and stimulative of a pluralist, interest group dominated political process. Reforms dedicated to the erosion of rent-seeking must be directed at those institutional characteristics of the U.S. legislature which encourage vote-trading efficiency. In essence, party discipline must be restored over the elected members of both Houses, and the venality of pluralist politics must be sharply curtailed if rent-seeking waste is to be significantly reduced.

To this end, candidates for political office would be prohibited from receiving campaign contributions and would be subjected to strict limitation on individual campaign expenditures. To run for office under a party label, they would require adoption by the relevant local party organization, which itself would raise campaign finances and outlay upon candidate promotion. Failure to vote the party line on issues subject to whip requirements would involve disciplinary action which, in the limit, would involve forfeiture of the party label and of associated support. Committee chairmanships would be allocated by and retained at the discretion of the relevant party leadership. The leadership itself would be elected by a secret ballot of their elected representatives, thereby ameliorating interest group invasion of this crucial body.

Such institutional reform would radically alter the nature of the U.S. Legislature, constraining the wealth motive as an objective of a political career, and centralizing policy formation along party lines. It brings with it major costs in the loss of individual representative discretion, in the accentuation of non-wealth motives, and in tightening entry barriers into politics. It reduces the efficiency of the legislature to reflect preference intensities in vote behavior. It raises the specter of government as a monopoly firm. All these characteristics are deplored in the analytics of private markets. Yet, if the thrust of this paper is correct, what would be shackled by such reforms is a discommodity, characterized by social waste. In such circumstances, reforms designed to render the process inefficient may well be deemed to be socially desirable.

Even if the solution here outlined is seen to be attractive by those who are distanced from the political market place, public choice obstacles to its adoption are manifold. Politicians whose wealth prospects or whose committee assignments rest on anticipated excess campaign contributions will be loathe to sacrifice on behalf of the common weal. Political action committees whose tenure on the Hill depends on a continuing market in votes also will be reluctant to lobby for their own annihilation. The entire contract nexus of the existing venal system will pit itself against the median vote. In the absence of presidential support, powerfully applied, such reform has little prospect of success. Yet wealth is at risk, and that familiar American dream, "accumulate, accumulate: that is Moses and all the prophets" surely will exert an influential thrust against the extreme rent dissipation of pluralist politics.

References

Axelrod, A. *The Evolution of Cooperation*. Basic Books, 1984.

Bernholz, P. *The International Game of Power*. Mouton, 1985.

Breton, A. *An Economic Theory of Representative Government*. Macmillan, 1974.

Buchanan, J.M. "Positive Economics, Welfare Economics, and Political Economy." *Journal of Law and Economics* II (October, 1959): 124–138.

Buchanan, J.M. *Reform in the Rent-Seeking Society*. In J.M. Buchanan, R.D. Tollison, and G. Tullock (eds.), *Toward a Theory of the Rent-Seeking Society*. College Station: Texas A and M University Press, 1980.

Buchanan, J.M. "Quest for a Tempered Utopia." *The Wall Street Journal*, November 14, 1986.

Buchanan, J.M., and Tullock, G. *The Calculus of Consent*. Ann Arbor, 1962.

Cooter, R., and Kornhauser, L. "Can Litigation Improve the Law Without the Help of Judges?" *Journal of Legal Studies* IX (January, 1980): 139–163.

Downs, A. *Inside Bureaucracy*. Rand, 1966.

Epstein, R.A. *Takings: Private Property and the Power of Eminent Domain*. Cambridge: Harvard University Press, 1985.

Landes, W.M., and Posner, R.A. "The Independent Judiciary in an Interest Group Perspective." *Journal of Law and Economics* XVII (December, 1975): 875–902.

McCormick, R.E., and Tollison, R.D. *Politicians, Legislation and the Economy*. Martinus Nijhoff, 1981.

Olson, M. *The Logic of Collective Action*. Cambridge: Harvard University Press, 1965.

Rowley, C.K. "The Calculus of Consent." In C.K. Rowley (ed.), *Democracy and Public Choice*. Basil Blackwell, 1987.

Rowley, C.K. "The Legacy of Keynes: From the General Theory to Generalized Budget Deficits." In J.M. Buchanan, C.K. Rowley, and R.D. Tollison (eds.), *Deficits*. Basil Blackwell, 1987.

Rowley, C.K., and Tollison, R.D. "Rent-Seeking and Trade Protection." *Swiss Journal of International Relations* (Fall, 1986): 141–166.

Rowley, C.K.; Shughart, W.F.; and Tollison, R.D. "Interest Groups and the Deficit." In J.M. Buchanan, C.K. Rowley, and R.D. Tollison (eds.), *Deficits*. Basil Blackwell, 1987.

Tullock, G. "The Welfare Costs of Tariffs, Monopolies, and Theft." *Western Economic Journal* 54 (June, 1967): 224–232.

Tullock G. "Rents and Rent Seeking" This volume, chapter 4.

Wagner, R.E. "Parchment, Guns, and the Maintenance of Constitutional Contract." In C.K. Rowley (ed.), *Democracy and Public Choice*, Basil Blackwell, 1987.

31 FUTURE DIRECTIONS FOR RENT-SEEKING RESEARCH

Gordon Tullock

In the existing literature there is not a single direct measure of rent-seeking cost. It is true that there are a great many indirect measures, but these involve both theoretical and practical problems. Direct measures would clearly be much more useful. The problem here is very much like the problem of measuring the black economy. Indeed, it can be argued that the rent-seeking industry is a very important part of the black economy. A large part of the total cost of rent-seeking activity is concealed by the people who bear it, partly because in many cases it is actually illegal (bribes, for example), and partly because publicity would be counter-productive. Nevertheless, it would be highly desirable that this screen be penetrated, and that we obtain direct measures. Theoretical reasons, which will be discussed below, indicate that these measures would almost certainly be partial, but still better than nothing.

Having said that direct measures are desirable, I should, I suppose, at least point in a direction for accumulating such measures. Unfortunately, this is an area where my own abilities are not very great. I can only suggest two areas where there are some data which could be used to at least make some kind of direct estimate of the cost of certain types of rent-seeking.

The first of these is the cost of legal proceedings. Legal proceedings sometimes are rent-seeking, e.g., a particular company attempting to enforce some kind of a restriction on its competition. More often they are simply fights about a given sum of money. Nevertheless, they are clear-cut cases of what we might call civil conflict; places where there is a strong incentive for both parties to invest resources in attempting acts of persuasion. In other words, they do to some extent resemble lobbying activities.[1]

Rent-seeking would no doubt be quite inexpensive if there were no conflicts of interest. The rent seeker is characteristically trying to get something which will injure other people. Those other people may fight back, either by hiring a contrary lobbyist or by their vote at the next election. Thus, the resemblance between rent-seeking and a lawsuit is somewhat closer than one might think at first glance. If the analogy is accepted it should perhaps be pointed out that under the present circumstances in this country, the total sum invested by the two parties in attempting to win lawsuits is characteristically about the same as the total value of the amount at issue. Thus what is now called the "Tullock Rectangle" is indeed totally consumed.

As another area where direct measurement is possible, in South America there are a number of places where the black economy is at worst light grey, i.e., it is very visible indeed. Forty percent of the land area of Lima is occupied by illegal entrants. Further, these people engage in a large number of activities which have not been properly licensed. Research has begun in Lima, and to a lesser extent in Caracas, on the actual behavior of this part of the economy. Measures of the size of the bribes that they have to pay would be fairly easy to obtain and fairly reliable.

Further, most of the entrepreneurs engaged in this kind of business would be quite willing to explain any inefficiency in the production process imposed upon them by the quasi-legal character of their business. We thus have possible direct measures of at least a very large part of the rent-seeking cost. I do not wish to argue that it would be easy. It would be necessary for somebody to spend quite a lot of time poking around in the less pleasant parts of Lima and Caracas. It could, however, be a very significant contribution to our knowledge of rent-seeking.

But these are direct efforts to obtain information which only bears indirectly on rent-seeking in the United States and indeed in Western Europe. Most actual efforts to measure the size of the rent-seeking cost have simply accepted the statement made in "The Welfare Effects of Monopolies, Tariffs and Theft", that the monopoly profit now sometimes referred to as the "Tullock Rectangle" would be completely exhausted by resources invested in attempting to get it. I can hardly criticize people for following my advice, but I now think that this is at best an approximation. My first reason will be obvious to anyone who has read the exchanges which make up chapters 7–12 of this volume.

My "Efficient Rent-Seeking"[2] raised a mathematical issue having to do with the lack of an intelligible equilibrium in many rent-seeking cases. The lack of equilibrium could lead to either overinvestment or underinvestment of resources in rent seeking, proper investment being taken as fully discounting the profit of the rent-seeking. Thus the "Tullock Rectangle" remains as only an approximate measure of the cost of rent-seeking.

We need a more rigorous specification. So far, this problem has turned out to be mathematically intractable. It should be pointed out, however, that it is just possible that empirical work could get rid of our mathematical difficulties. I do not say this because I think we should stop working on mathematics. Indeed, I think we should try and solve the problem mathematically as well as practically.

The basic reason for the problems raised in "Efficient Rent-Seeking" and further canvassed in this volume is the fact that rent-seeking apparently does not have a U-shaped cost curve. The general view of most economists is that almost any production activity has a U-shaped cost, i.e., the cost per unit falls as production is increased and then begins rising again after a period. Public utility economics is almost the only place we ever worry about continuously declining marginal cost. Even there no one believes that it continues declining forever, only in the relevant range.

Just as there is no solution with any degree of elegance for the natural monopoly, there is no solution for rent-seeking in the area of declining marginal cost. There is on the contrary the possibility of rising marginal costs. This also leads to absurd results, except in special cases.

If empirical work on rent-seeking led to the conclusion that we have a U-shaped cost curve, then the problem would vanish. Theoretically, there doesn't seem to be any reason why the cost curves should be U-shaped, but it is not obvious that theorists would have deduced that the market cost curves were normally U-shaped if we did not have a lot of empirical data. Thus, my conclusion is that we should both continue the mathematical work and simutaneously try and get measures of the productivity of investment in rent-seeking. If it turns out that the cost curve is U-shaped, the mathematical puzzle will cease to be anything more than an intellectual exercise. Until such data has been produced (and it is by no means obvious it ever will be) we must continue with the mathematical research.

In chapter 4 of this volume I raise another empirical problem. I argue that the total cost of rent-seeking in most cases is considerably larger even than the sum of the Harberger Triangle and the Tullock Rectangle. Specifically, the benefit to society from the alternative investment of the resources which are otherwise wasted in rent-seeking should also be taken into account.

If we knew the size of the resources invested in rent-seeking, this would be comparatively easy, because we already have some measures by Mansfield on the degree to which cost saving inventions are transmitted to the general populace rather than being retained by the inventing organization. Duplicating this research in other areas should be fairly easy. In fact, simply taking Mansfield's results, which imply that the innovator actually retains only about one-third of the social value of his innovation, would be a good first approximation. But for this purpose we again need a measure of the actual size of the rent-seeking activity.

All of this depends on some method of measuring direct costs of rent-seeking. This could be divided into two general categories: firstly, the direct expenditures on lobbying, etc., engaged in by individuals, corporations, and, for that matter, trade associations; secondly, dispersed resource investments, involved in such things as putting your factory in the constituency of a relevant congressman, or endowing a distinguished visiting chair at Baruch School,[3] etc.

I am by no means discouraged about obtaining accurate data on the first category. After all, corporations and trade associations all publish their accounts. It should be possible with some ingenuity to get inside the published accounts, to the actual detail of the accounts, in at least a sample of corporations. To say this can be done, however, is not to say that it would be easy or that the standard economic technique of looking at published statistics and putting them in a computer would be of much help. Hiring private detectives to penetrate the accounting system of General Electric would be a more highly paying approach to this particular kind of research. Still, to say that it is difficult is not to say it is impossible.

The second category, the indirect expenditures, is much more difficult. It is particularly difficult because a lot of these indirect expenditures take the form of people voting for politicians who on general grounds they detest because that politician is in favor of some expenditure by the government which will benefit the voter. To take an extreme example, in 1964, a wealthy man who was in his spare time the head of the finance committee of a small private college was an extreme conservative. His general political position was well to the right of Goldwater, but he strongly opposed Goldwater because the latter opposed large scale payments supporting higher education.

The total cost of this kind of activity and this kind of voting spread over society may be very great. Then again, it may not. We do not know how much of it is done, and it is very hard to decide what the social cost is, or indeed whether there is a social cost.

Here we have a problem rather analogical to that of advertising. It is clear that to some extent advertising increases the information of the purchaser, and hence makes the market work better. It is also clear that to some extent advertising simply is a competitive arrangement in which one firm's advertising cancels another's. We like the first kind of advertising and dislike the other, buut there doesn't seem to be any way of disentangling them in practice.

The Calculus of Consent had as one of its main themes the desirability of a sort of market in which people traded votes on "projects" which were of benefit to themselves. We emphasized that the desirable data here was that a market should exist and that is should not be too perfect. In other words we wanted a market of the right degree of inefficiency. This kind of cost of vote specialization raises somewhat the same issues. We do indeed want people to both vote for and especially press for things which are to their advantage, but only to a certain degree, and it is very hard to say exactly how much.

Since this chapter is devoted to suggesting future research, I do not have to solve the problem here. I simply suggest that other people work on it. Speaking truthfully, I have thought about it a good deal myself but do not have any solution. I will continue thinking about it. I hope someday to solve it, but I certainly would not be unhappy if one of the readers beat me to it.

There is still another problem which requires much research. As Rowley points out, the rent-seeking perspective raises difficulties for the whole analysis of *The Calculus of Consent*. Further research is most certainly called for to integrate rent-seeking and the theory of constitutions.

There is another problem which has been bothering me ever since I wrote "The Purchase of Politicians", a long time ago. This is that the total amount spent in lobbying, etc., in Washington, does not seem to be even close to the economic value of the favors dispensed by the government. Note that I say in Washington. I suspect that in Mexico City the two are in quite close agreement. One of the co-editors of this volume, Tollison, has done work on the mercantilist societies of the sixteenth and seventeenth century. He found royal governments, in essence, put this kind of favor up to auction. This presumably obtained the full economic value. Since they used the funds for various governmental purposes, this was a kind of taxation. We may regard building Versailles as a waste, but is it not the same kind of waste we normally associate with rent-seeking.

In any event, the amounts derived were much larger as a share of GNP or even of government activity than the apparent expenditure on rent-seeking in most modern democracies. There is a sort of canonical explanation for this, which is that much rent-seeking is a public good for the members of the special interest. One would anticipate that the individual people who are potential members of pressure groups would choose not to invest funds in attempting to get a favor for that entire pressure group. Hence the investment of funds would be less than "optimal".

The basic problem with this "solution" is that it assumes that only the present collection of special government favors is feasible. Its proponents normally offer no intrinsic reason why people should not seek out very special narrow government favors and then invest the full amount in them. If there were no restrictions on the kind of things that can be bought by rent-seeking, then these public-good type monopolistic restrictions, tax exemptions, etc., would not exist at all, because they would lose out on the competition from the better financed special gifts.

In other words, we might expect that the bulk of rent-seeking would be devoted to fairly narrow, specific gains to small groups, and that they would in general pay the full value. There would be little or nothing in the way of special gifts to large groups of people because of the public good problems of organizing such an interest group.

The first thing to be said is that it is conceivable that this is a correct albeit partial description of the way our government operates. It is possible, although I do not believe it is true, that all special privileges and advantages distributed by the government to large numbers of people are distributed to them entirely in return for their vote. Thus for example, farmers vote in terms of the farm program, and older people in terms of Social Security. It must be assumed that the people who are taxed for these expenditures are badly informed, or that they are themselves voting in terms of some other special interest.

What would then be added on by direct lobbying is the gigantic collection of minor clauses which make up the bulk of almost every one of the immensely long bills passed by Congress. Most of these special clauses would have been purchased at their fair prices by groups of people small enough so that the public good argument does not apply.

But having said that this is feasible as a description of our present system, I shall go on and say that I do not believe it is accurate. Nevertheless, this would be an area where I think that valuable research would be possible. It would be difficult and tedious, but not impossible.

This still leaves us with the puzzle of why the total expenditures on seeking special favors in Washington, immense though it is, is still rather small compared to the value of the favors. I have a theory which points in the direction of future research to either confirm or disprove it. But before turning to this theory it is necessary for me briefly to deal with a recent twist in what we may call the "Chicago" doctrine.

When I was in the University of Chicago, it was fashionable to point out that the farm program was hideously inefficient. It would have been far cheaper to simply pay farmers the real value of their special privileges rather than establishing the complicated set of quotas and subsidies which in fact were being used.

Recently Chicagoans, Becker in particular, have attacked this form orthodoxy. They point out that it would be quite difficult to produce a set of cash payments to farmers that would exactly duplicate the benefits that different farmers are now receiving. Indeed, the gradual development of agriculture under these government programs, with some farmers actually being driven out of existence by the program and many farm laborers suffering, the great expansion of the fertilizer industry, etc., would have been quite difficult to reproduce if the technique had been direct cash payments.

Clearly, these claims about the difficulty of reproducing the present pattern by cash payments are correct. It would be difficult or almost impossible. The problem with this line of reasoning as an explanation of why we do not use "efficient" means is that it assumes that the pattern of payments that was in fact made was the politically optimal pattern. The only evidence for this assumption is that it was the pattern which was adopted.

There is of course another explanation, one which was in fact believed by the people who presented the original or the older Chicago view. This is simply that for political reasons, direct cash payments were not possible, and hence the politicians were forced to turn to an inefficient method of rewarding some of the farmers. The present pattern could be explained by either of these two explanations, but it seems on the whole absurd that the people starting this program (actually under President Hoover) properly foresaw all of the developments which would occur. There is certainly no reason to believe that they consciously intended to help one group of farmers, injure another, injure farm laborers, etc. It is certainly more plausible that they were simply trying to get the votes of a large number of farmers and were compelled by the circumstances they faced to choose a relatively inefficient method.

Thus we have two possible explanations for the present farm mess. One of these is that it is an ideally efficient method chosen by the politicians to reward exactly the people who in fact were rewarded and penalize exactly the people who are penalized. The other is that the politicians were in general trying to increase the incomes of farmers, but were faced with political difficulties in making direct cash payment and so turned to inefficient methods. Both of these would explain the present distribution of income among farmers. They would also explain the evolution from the beginning of the program with President Hoover to the present day. But the modern Chicago theory requires really quite extraordinary foresight on the part of the politicians. Perfect information has never been carried this far before.

Moreover, the Becker-Chicago theory would require some explanation of why the politicians who put this particular program through didn't get a very large part of the return on it themselves. That is the problem which I was addressing when I found it necessary to digress and deal with this new Chicago position. I believe that the basic problems here are a combination of knowledge or ignorance on the part of most voters, most politicians (and indeed many other people), and a set of political beliefs which are very widely held.

Two European scholars say: "The first and decisive stage of decision making is determined by constraints and knowledge about the alternatives available to an individual."[4] We will begin with information, and then turn to my view about the views which most people have about politics, and then once again turn to the effect which all of this has on rent-seeking. Finally we will consider the effect that rent-seeking has on information.

That people are not very well informed about political matters is something that most of us know, although political scientists argue that they should be informed. I do not quarrel with the political scientists' view that people should be informed. I merely point out that they usually are not.

Almost any empirical examination of what the common man actual knows immediately indicates that it is not very much. He does not even think very much about his opinions. To take but one example, the November–December[5] issue of *Public Opinion* contains a lot of data on ethics. From it we discover that seventy-one percent of all people asked thought that congressmen "will tell lies if they felt the truth will hurt them politically" and forty-four percent thought they "have a high personal moral code".[6] It is obvious from these numbers that either at least 15% of the respondents to these polls must have thought that "telling lies if the truth will hurt" is consistent with "a high personal moral code", or, more likely, that a considerably larger number of the respondents literally did not think very much about what they were saying. This is but one example. We could easily get many more.

This of course is a statement about reality. Since Anthony Downs wrote *An Economic Analysis of Democracy*, most public choice scholars have realized that the individuals are behaving quite rationally in being ignorant. There is little or nothing to be gained from an individual looking into the details of government policy, unless he actually enjoys it. Since most of the readers of this article probably do follow politics to at least some extent, they are abnormal in this regard, but even they would turn out not to be very well informed if we asked them any significantly detailed questions.

There are nevertheless, in addition to this general lack of information, some fairly strong opinions held by most people. Firstly, they have a "general image" of what government should do. This general image includes most of the major duties of the government. For example, most people think that the government should repress crime. For a less pleasant example, most Aztecs thought their government should engage in large scale human sacrifice. For most modern societies, direct payments to well off people are not part of that public image.

In addition to this general image, most citizens would also like to get various special privileges from the government. But they realize that the government can be expected to do things in their personal interest only if it at least superficially fits the public image. This rather vague public image is, of course, not a well calculated view of the world.

What I am trying to say here is that the government's activities must almost always have at least a veneer fitting the public image or be so inconspicuous that most people don't notice them. Granted the poor information of the average voter, the latter possibility is quite significant. The collection of special provisions in the Internal Revenue Code, for example, miss the notice of most people. Indeed, the author of this chapter must concede that he knows almost none of them.

What we observe then is a government which is engaging in a number of rather traditional activities which are part of the public image. It is also engaging in a lot of activities which are in the special interest of reasonably organized groups, but which are camouflaged to fit the public image. The farm program discussed above was in its early years pushed very heavily on the grounds that having a strong group of "yeoman farmers" was important for the success of the United States as a nation. Indeed, the same argument has been used in Switzerland, where the farmers are generally even more prosperous than those in Iowa.[7]

Assume that the above remarks are correct, as I believe they are. Imagine a politician in the 1930s had proposed simply paying the farmers cash with the intent that a good many of them would stop farming and retire to Florida. It would have been cheaper than what we did, but it would have been very hard to camouflage it to fit the public image.

The form program is a conspicuous program which had to be camouflaged and hence could not be done efficiently. A great deal of other special interest legislation depends on being inconspicuous. Most Americans were not aware of the fact that aid program wheat had to be carried on American ships. If they had become aware of it, and some did, the shipowners could claim it fit the public image as providing reserve shipping for military use.

The latter kind of program is probably the commonest single output of rent-seeking in Washington, (i.e., something which escapes the notice of the bulk of the population, which is not strongly opposed by any special group, and for which there is at least a superficially plausible explanation which fits the public image. There are two other kinds of programs which can get through. Firstly, there are fairly direct applications of the public image, which will have large scale voter support. Details of the military budget do not fit that description, but the general structure of it does. The second type are things like old-age pensions or large scale medical aid to large parts of the citizenry which can be sold as respectable duties for the government, primarily because a very large part of the population will (sometimes mistakenly) think that they benefit by them.

In these cases (which we may refer to as public image or possibly widespread benefit types of action), the amount of lobbying and rent-seeking done in Washington can be quite significantly less than the actual cost of the project. Carolyn Weaver, in her study of the origin of the social security act, discusses at great length the activity of a group of people whom she refers to as "potential administrators". It is likely that they were in fact rent-seeking but the profits that they were anticipating were quite modest. Hence the resources they were willing to invest were also quite modest. The bill went through because with quite modest resources it was possible to convince the average voter and the average congressman that it was desirable.

If we turn to more definite private interest legislation, private interest has to be at least disguised. In some cases of course this disguise takes the form of simply hiding a minor provision in a long bill. In other cases, e.g., the farm program, efforts are made to confuse the average voter, while the principal political payment for the program is made by farmers actually voting for people who will support it.

So far I have not directly referred to log rolling. As the originator of the present analysis of log rolling, I assure you that this is not because I am unaware of its existence. Indeed, it is vital to all of these programs. Here, however, we are talking about another aspect of the matter. All of these special interest bills are put through by log rolling, but I am now saying that there are certain restrictions on what can be done because the public image, whether we think it is rational or not, restricts the alternatives which are available.

In a way, the public image has the function of keeping some expensive items off the budget. It should of course be kept in mind that it also leads to great inefficiency in some areas. The American foreign policy from its earliest days to the present has been severely damaged by the fact that the voters think that one of the government's duties is to spread the American ethical system to other countries. They don't think that much effort should be expended in this direction, but they are sufficiently interested in it, so that efforts to carry out this objective seriously handicap more genuinely important aspects of foreign policy.[8]

Since the public image changes from time to time, there is some possibility for special interest groups to influence its general structure. In general, however, that is too expensive. The public image does, however, often make returns from rent-seeking much lower than you would otherwise expect. If we think of the federal government budget as "all up for grabs," it is hard to explain the relatively small size of the rent-seeking community in Washington. If we assume, however, and I think this is correct, that anyone attempting to get hold of parts of the federal budget must, because of public image considerations, choose a very inefficient way of getting that money, then we have at least a partial explanation for the small size of the establishment.

Suppose for example that we have a nearly bankrupt company which makes aircraft engines. It can, through influence on Senator Kennedy who represents the area in which they are operating, get the federal government to buy a number of its not such wonderful engines. This will permit it to continue employing its workers at an imcome which to the workers is $100 million more than they would make if they were fired and had to seek other employment. The company will pay its stockholders and higher management another $50 million. The excess cost to the American government of buying these inferior engines is, shall we say, $500 million.

The economist traditionally would look at this and say: "Aha, the government should simply give the company $151 million and buy their engines elsewhere." The Beckerite Chicagoan would say that it was impossible to distribute the money to give exactly the same pattern of benefits as the purchase of the engines.

As the reader will guess, I do not accept either of these explanations. I would say that a straightforward payment of $151 million to the company would fail to fit the public image and hence is politically impossible. Purchasing these defective engines fits the image, particularly since the government can claim that the engines are really pretty good. The voters will have neither the motive nor the technical knowledge to test the claim.

The company would be willing to invest a maximum of $50 million. The workers would be willing to invest more, but they will use their votes rather than cash. For a billion and a half dollar contract, it looks like an awfully small payment. But the bulk of the "rent" is eaten up in inefficiency which is required to fit the public image.

Note here that I am not saying that the dominance of the public image leads to an inferior result. If it were possible to get cash directly in the economist's efficient way, manipulating the government would become the primary activity of the American people. We would be much poorer. I am also not saying the public image leads to optimal efficiency. It leads to a mixed system which can be supported only on the grounds that there are other systems that are worse. We have only to look across our southern border to see a system which I am sure all of us would agree is very much worse.[9]

But all of this functions only because the average voter is badly informed. We have mentioned that he is rational in being badly informed, but it should also be pointed out that the rent-seeking activity probably means that he is even worse informed than he otherwise would be.

Take a very traditional example, the protective tariff. Anyone who has taught elementary economics knows that it is hard, indeed very nearly impossible, the convince the students that protective tariffs are a bad idea. Students who get an A in your course and regurgitate the standard arguments against protective tariffs on your exams may not believe a word of it.

The explanation is fairly simple, i.e., that the arguments for a protective tariff are simple and superficially obvious, while the arguments against it are unfortunately complicated and indirect. Granted that the voter has no motive for becoming well informed, he or she will buy the simpler of the two explanations.

Under these circumstances, a rent seeker seeking protective tariffs does not actually have to engage in too much lobbying. The system is already bent in their direction. Suppose that some particular industry does not now have a protective tariff and would like it. They do not have to use their votes, their campaign contributions, and other kinds of influence to move the government from opposition of the protective tariffs to actively favoring it. What they have to do is move the political system from a sort of vague feeling that the American worker must be protected against unemployment[10] to actual application in this case. Suppose that a tariff will be worth $100 million; the cost might be as low as $10–$15 million[11] because the government is rather inclined that way anyhow. It is just being-pushed from a 90% chance of passing the tariff to 100%. This is only worth $10,000,000, although the apparent gain is $100,000,000.

Thus the direct cost might appear to be quite low. Unfortunately there may well be an indirect cost not borne by the special interest group, but by the population in general. This is what we might call the expansion of ignorance. The economics of information usually takes the form of discussing a situation in which different people produce different bits of information with the result that the recipient over time becomes better informed. This is unfortunately not particularly typical of the real world. In addition to information there are lies[12] and deliberate fraud.[13]

It should be emphasized that not all of this is done by deliberate villains. The student who did not understand the arguments against protective tariffs, and who is later hired as a lobbyist by the cotton textile industry, probably operates with a good conscience when he retails false economic arguments. It is true that if he is presented with correct arguments, and they at least temporarily convince him, he is likely to deliberately turn away from thinking further about the matter. If really pressed, he will in all probability deliberately lie or mislead, or engage in other "opportunistic behavior". Primarily, however, he simply remains ignorant in the area and spreads his ignorance.

The result may not only be that a particular tariff is adopted. Indeed, the lobbyst may fail to get his tariff. But in his lobbying activity he in a real sense lowers the information held by the politicians and the public by introducing falsehood. This would be true even if what he said was literally true, but led to people forgetting truthful arguments on the other side. Adam Smith's remarks about protecting strategically important industries, for example, are probably better known in Washington than any other part of his discussion of tariffs.

Suppose then that we have ten tariffs, each of which in net would increase the value of an industry by a $100 million. Some of them are regarded as reasonably likely bets for the next two years, and the stock market has discounted them by valuing the stock in these industries at about $90 million more than it would be worth if there were no prospect of a tariff. Each of these industries sends lobbyists to Washington to promote those tariffs, spending about $1 million on the task. One of them wins this time; the others very likely will later. The direct rent-seeking cost here is $10 million and the apparent gain to the industry affected is a net of $99 million. Actually, however, its stock only goes up $10 million, because the possibility of this gain had already been discounted. There is of course somewhere in the economy, probably in the United States, possibly entirely abroad, a place where stock goes down in value because this change in tariff policy had been thought likely but not certain, and hence there was the company whose stock was selling at less than its value would be if the tariff were known to be impossible. The cost then seems to be very much less than the apparent benefit to the rent seeker, but they were moving not from a zero possibility of tariff to certainty of tariff, but from a 90% probability to certainty.

Unfortunately, there is here another very major and very hard-to-measure cost. The reason that the tariff was a reasonable possibility is of course widespread public ignorance and misinformation. Further, it is not just a congressman. Politicians and bureaucrats very likely share this misinformation. The activity of the lobbyist has surely strengthened and reinforced this unfortunate public image. The general feeling that it is one of the duties of the American government to protect its industries against vicious competition from the "gang of four" has been reinforced.

It will be harder for future economists to push for lower tariffs after this lobbying campaign than it was before. There is no way of measuring this change in money terms, but it does seem to me it might be possible to measure it in terms of the change in attitude of citizens, politicians, and bureaucrats. In any event, I would be very much interested in seeing people attempting to measure this phenomenon or, for that matter, merely obtaining some empirical evidence proving or disproving the theoretical argument.

We note here that although lobbying activities will have this kind of unfavorable externality, there is no law of nature that says that they will win. Opinion is affected by things other than the professional lobbyist. Further, there actually are some professional lobbyists who are pushing for lower tariffs. Such organizations as Brookings, Cato, Heritage, etc., may not like to think of themselves as professional lobbyists, but as a matter of fact, they are. All of them of course do favor lower protective tariffs.

Another important group in the regard is the professors of economics in the United States. It is true that many professors of economics have left the real world for the abstractions of mathematics, but most of them do at least occasionally tell their students that protective tariffs will not achieve the goals for which they are normally urged.

There have been successes in reducing rent-seeking. The CAB is no longer with us, the ICC is much less dangerous than it was, and the banking industry is very largely deregulated. From about 1930 to about 1975, American tariffs and indeed tariffs all over the world were steadily lowered. Towards the end of that period, there was of course a rise of non-tariff barriers, but I believe that up to about 1975, the net effect was a freeing up of American trade. Unfortunately, since that time, that trend has reversed. All of this is evidence that ignorance will not necessarily prevail in public affairs. It is usually true however that rent-seeking activity which is directed at obtaining government favors will have as a by-product an increase of public ignorance in the area concerned.

If we look at history, the world in, say, 1600, was a place in which rent seeking was overwhelmingly the most common way of becoming wealthy. The "mercantilist" society was a society organized by rent-seeking. For a variety of reasons, this fell away, in England and to a lesser extent in Europe. It was still quite strong even in England in 1800. From 1800 to about 1870, England steadily dismantled the remaining mercantilist rent-seeking structure of its government.

As a result, we had the industrial revolution, and through the copying of the English system by other countries the spread of prosperity throughout most of Europe and, to a lesser extent, the world. There seems to be no explanation for this radical change in society, except intellectual conversion of a very large number of people, including of course Mr. Gladstone and Napoleon III, to the economics of Adam Smith and Ricardo. Unfortunately, beginning with the inventions of Bismark, this trend was reversed at the end of the 19th century.

I have ended this chapter on future directions of research in rent-seeking by this discussion of changes in information, not only because I think they are important areas of research, but also because I think it is a practical matter. We know from the study of history, that an elaborate rent-seeking state was dismantled once in the early 19th century. If it happened once, it can happen again. Economists today know much more than Ricardo and his friends did. It is to be hoped that their political and propaganda activities will also be more effective than those of their predecessors.

Notes

1. There is now quite a large body of data on the cost of legal proceedings collected by the Rand Corporation. Since the project is continuing to produce data, I see nothing much to be gained by giving specific citations. The interested student can write to the Rand Foundation and get a list of their publications.

2. Published in full in *Toward a Theory of the Rent Seeking Society*.

3. I will be occupying such a distinguished chair in the Spring of 1987.

4. Bruno S. Frey and Klaus Foppa, "Human Behavior: Possibilities Explain Action", *Journal of Economic Psychology* 7 (1986), 137–60, pp. 137.

5. 1986, the quotation is taken from page 26.

6. 56 of them also thought that the congressmen "make a lot of money by using public office improperly".

7. The Iowa farmers have recently undergone quite a financial crisis because a number of them had borrowed too much money on their land. The bulk of them however, did not have large mortgages and the crisis meant that their personal wealth fell from let us say three quarters of a million to half a million.

8. I am not saying it would not be nice to have foreign countries carry out our ethical system. The fact is, however, that we do not have enough power to achieve this goal. Hence efforts to do so normally have no effect on ethics and a considerable effect on our relations with the government which we are attempting to influence. When I was in Korea as an American diplomat, it was perfectly obvious that President Rhee thought of the United States as his principle foreign ally and his principle domestic enemy. This led to a series of difficulties on policy, which could have very easily been avoided if he had not suspected us (correctly) of attempting to overthrow him.

9. Two such systems; Cuba is somewhat different, but even more unpleasant.

10. Frequently the voter is sufficiently badly informed so that he believes both that the American voter must be protected against the Japanese competition which would unemploy him, and that free trade is a good thing.

11. Including the vote somehow as part of this value.

12. Oliver Williamson usually refers to this kind of thing as "impacted information".

13. Once again, Williamson usually refers to this as "opportunistic behavior".

Index